PARK'S
SUCCESS WITH SEEDS

PARK'S
SUCCESS
WITH
SEEDS

by

Ann Reilly

with

Photographs from the files of and by the staff
photographers of the Geo. W. Park Seed Co.

GEO. W. PARK SEED CO., INC.
GREENWOOD, SOUTH CAROLINA

Contents

FOREWORD

In 1868, a fifteen year old boy began collecting seeds, packaging them and selling them to his neighbors. This young boy was my father, George W. Park. From that day until the present one, Park Seed Company's primary goal has been to bring to you, our customers, the finest products available from the Plant Kingdom. Another principal aim has been to provide you with as much information as possible to assure success in your gardening ventures.

Our horticulturists search throughout the world for the newest and finest varieties of seeds. Many of these are unusual and little-known species for which there has been no readily available publication providing instructions for their germination and care. It was our concern over your need for this material that has prompted the publication of this new book, which is an easy-to-follow yet specific guide for success with the popular as well as the obscure plant that can be grown from seed.

In discussing this venture with my friend, Ann Reilly, an unusually talented garden writer and horticulturist, Ann was challenged with the possibility of this book and agreed to author it for us. I am personally pleased that she accepted this task, for she has a flair for writing, demands accuracy, and is a delightful person. She has fulfilled her commission with excellence.

Within these pages you will find the most complete selection of seedling photographs of garden subjects in the world. These, as well as virtually all the photos, are from our picture files and by the photographers on our staff. There is no doubt that many of our gardening friends need a good method of recognizing seedlings.

We feel confident that this book will be valuable to you, enabling you to be a more successful gardener, and it is our hope that you will enjoy using it.

William J. Park, President
Geo. W. Park Seed Co., Inc.

INTRODUCTION

I did my share of the things that children did when I was growing up in Brooklyn—bicycle riding, roller skating, jumping rope. But unlike other children, I passed many hours in our small back yard, planting Nasturtiums or Radishes or watching (and trying to help) my aunt with her garden. When I was in college, in the days before the house plant boom, I was the only person in the dormitory whose room was decorated in greenery. Once I owned my own garden, I grew everything I could beg, borrow or buy.

The world has caught up with me, for now most everyone has a garden, even if it is only on a windowsill. House plants have become a part of the decor, and vegetables are grown from terraces to empty lots to combat the rising cost of food. People, in their return to nature, are realizing the beauty of the world of flowers.

Sharing my experiences with the world of seeds and plants has always been in me, and I thank Bill Park for asking me to put it down on paper. It could never have been done alone, however, and credit must go to the staff of Park Seed, who have always been ready to help in any way they could. Jim Alston, Research Director, is not only a Ph. D. and very intelligent, he's also one of the nicest people I've ever met. Without him, the technical information within these pages would never have been. Carol Dalrymple, before she left to become a mother, and Earlene Freeman, both from the Seed Germination Laboratory, spent countless hours answering questions, growing seedlings and checking facts. The Advertising Department put it all together, ably led by Gene Kaufman and Al Scheider, with thanks to David Brownlee for his ability as a photographer.

Closer to home, my neighbor Ann Dooley deserves a vote of thanks for swift fingers that flew over the typewriter keys and helped me deliver my manuscript on time.

Please enjoy the book, and more important, enjoy your plants.

Massapequa Park, New York   Ann Reilly
1978

Fiber Seed Flat   *Plastic Seed Flat*

CHAPTER I

GETTING READY

Why Seeds?

Ask six different people why they grow plants from seeds, and you will probably get six different answers. Growing plants from seeds is more than a matter of economics (no one will dispute the money saving value of plant propagation from seeds); it is often the only way to obtain wanted, rare or unusual plants. The choice for your indoor or outdoor garden is unquestionably increased by growing plants from seeds, be it the type of plant you want or a specific variety. No garden center stocks the numbers of marigolds, zinnias, tomatoes or other bedding plants that are available from seed catalogs. Seeds may also be the only way to obtain and try new introductions.

Some annual and vegetable plants have such a long growing season that they must be started from seeds indoors weeks or months before planting outside. With others, sowing seeds early may just give a head start on harvesting or blooming time. And some vegetables, like radishes and beans, are so easy to grow from seeds that few people would even consider any other method.

Perhaps it is the thrill of being a "creator" that moves people to sow seeds. Watching a seed poke its first leaves through the medium, grow and finally bloom, can easily be thrilling and cause anyone proudly to say, "I did it myself"!

Containers

The first thing you'll need to sow and grow your seeds is, naturally, some sort of a container. The best containers for sowing seeds are the ones made especially for the purpose. Seed flats made of fiber vary in size from 5½″ x 7½″ to 10″ x 12″; all are approximately 2½″ deep. These and plastic flats which are available in about the same sizes are the answer for sowing a number of seeds. Seeds may also be sown in peat pots or strips (also good for transplants), or in compressed peat pellets (which are sowing, growing and transplanting units) after they have been expanded to seven or nine times their compact size by the addition of water. One type of peat pellet has netting around the medium; another does not.

Peat pots are made of light, compressed peat moss and are either round or square, ranging in size from 2½″ to 3″. Seeds, especially large ones or those of species which resent transplanting,

Jiffy Pots

Fertl Cubes

can be sown directly into medium placed in the peat pot or in a peat pellet and grown until it is time to place them in their final home. At that point, pot or pellet and all are planted, often with roots coming through the walls, making them very easy-to-use methods. Peat strips (which are peat pots joined together at the top) are used in the same manner; the pellets have the advantage of being pot and medium all in one. Plastic trays are available as an outside protective covering and support for the pots, strips or pellets.

Another handy device for germinating seeds is the "Fertl-cube", composed of peat moss, perlite, vermiculite and fertilizer in a 1" cube. There's a depression in the top of the cube where the seeds are placed to germinate and grow.

Of all the containers available, those made of compressed peat moss or fiber are most desirable. They are not only sterile, but are also porous and allow the container and medium to breathe, insuring proper aeration. One word of warning must be given, however; never re-use a peat pot or other peat container for sowing, as it may not be sterile and will in the long run be more trouble than it's worth with the fungus growth that may develop.

There are also many make-shift containers lying about that will do for seed sowing, such as cut down coffee cans, paper cups, aluminum baking trays, cottage cheese containers, shallow flower pots (bulb or azalea pans), shortened milk containers, plastic food storers, or wooden crates that you can obtain or make yourself. If you do use one of these containers, wash it well before use so it is as clean as it possibly can be, and then leave it out in the sun for a few days.

Another suitable seed sowing device is what is known as a Forsythe Pot. It consists of a 2½" clay pot with the drainage hole corked sitting in the middle of a 7" bulb pan. The space between the inside pot and the rim of the outside pot is filled with medium on which the seeds are sown. The inside pot is filled with water and the entire set-up slipped into a plastic bag to maintain high humidity during seed germination. As water in the inside pot diminishes, it is replaced.

Whatever you choose, there are certain requirements for any seed germinating container. It should be just the right depth (2¾ - 3½") so that the medium is 2½ - 3" deep. Any less medium than that will allow no room for root growth and will dry out too quickly. If the container is deeper than 3½", and less than 3" of medium is used, the seedlings will soon become lost in it, receiving poor air circulation and insufficient light, and they will be difficult to handle and transplant later on.

A second requirement for a germinating container is that it have a good drainage. If there are no drainage holes in the bottom, punch several small ones. If the container is made of such a material that holes cannot be punched in it, then place a layer of gravel in the bottom, covered with a layer of newspaper and then germinating medium. This situation is not ideal and should be avoided wherever possible.

Germinating Media

There is no one sowing and growing medium that is absolutely "perfect", but one or two come close, and some are better than others. Following is a brief description of the most common media and recommendations for use:

Sow & Grow   Milled Sphagnum

MIXTURES

The best media for germinating seeds are sterile soil-less mixtures of peat or sphagnum moss with perlite and/or vermiculite. You can make these yourself, using from 1/3 to ½ sphagnum or peat moss, with the remainder perlite or vermiculite or a combination of the two. Experiment and choose the one that works best for you.

The easiest way to obtain your germinating medium is to buy it, ready-made. One, Park's "Sow and Grow", is a soil-less, fine textured sowing medium that contains peat moss, perlite, vermiculite and just enough nutrients to get the seedlings off to a good start, plus it's perfect for transplants and house plants. It's light, sterile, firm but airy; it drains properly yet retains the right amount of moisture for plant development. "Sow and Grow" exhibits all the characteristics of the "perfect medium": 50% solid material, 25% air spaces in which roots grow and obtain necessary oxygen, and 25% moisture. It helps to eliminate "damping off", reduces the need for constant watching and expert judgement, promotes ideal growth and lets you grow the most difficult plants from seeds.

Seeds will germinate on moist paper towels, blotters or newspapers, but they won't grow into plants there. You'll need a good sowing and growing medium to do that, so choose yours carefully.

SPHAGNUM MOSS

Sphagnum moss is harvested green from bogs and then dried. It is relatively sterile, light in weight, and is able to absorb 10 to 20 times its weight in water. Sphagnum moss is generally milled (shredded) before use as a seed sowing medium. It is occasionally used in its natural state for potting mature plants or to line hanging baskets to hold the medium in the containers. Its fertilizer value is low, so weak fertilizer solutions must be used with it, after seedling emergence and is very acidic (pH 3.5). It does, however, have the ability to inhibit the "damping off" of seedlings growing in it.

For years milled sphagnum moss was enthusiastically recommended as the best germination medium. It does, unfortunately, have several drawbacks—it is very difficult to moisten evenly and it often cakes when drying out. It has now given way to more desirable mixtures which may contain sphagnum moss and are easier to use.

PEAT

Baled peat moss sold commerically in the United States is the result of decomposed aquatic plants, and its composition varies greatly. It can range from very acidic to almost neutral. Peat has a high water holding capacity and contains some nitrogen (about 1%), one of the elements necessary for plant growth. Baled peat is rarely used by itself for any type of propagating or growing, as water does not penetrate it easily, nor does it have good drainage or aeration qualities by itself. It is however, a widely used component in sowing and growing mixtures.

Vermiculite

Perlite

VERMICULITE

Vermiculite is expanded mica which has the capacity to hold tremendous amounts of water for long periods of time. Although not usually used alone for seed germination, it is an excellent addition to a mix because it is light, sterile, neutral in pH, holds nutrients, provides good aeration and contains a high percentage of magnesium and potassium, two more elements necessary for good root growth.

PERLITE

Grey-white perlite is a volcanic ash which does not absorb water but will hold water on its surface. It contains no essential elements and does not hold nutrients, but is valuable as a mixture component as it is light, sterile and causes good aeration. Like vermiculite, it is neutral.

Perlite stays cool and, therefore, is good in mixes used for germinating seeds that prefer lower temperatures. Its main disadvantage is that it will float to the top of the seed bed when it is watered.

SAND

Coarse builder's sand is often recommended for asexual propagating, but it is not a good choice for seed sowing. It is heavy, contains no essential elements, does not hold nutrients and is far from sterile. Stay away from it!

SOIL

Soil from the garden should not be used to germinate seeds if avoidable. It will not, in most instances, be of the right texture to give proper drainage and aeration, and as a result, the seedlings may drown in it.

If soil must be used, it should be sterilized to kill the large number of weed seeds, insects and fungus pathogens that may be present. Bake it in a shallow pan in the oven, holding a temperature of 180° F. for 30 minutes. (Use a meat thermometer to make sure the temperature's right). Be prepared! This process will smell up your house, and badly; one thing you can do to avoid this is to sterilize the soil outdoors on your barbecue (if your neighbors don't mind).

Soil can also be sterilized with steam, chlorpicrin (tear gas), methyl bromide or formaldehyde, but the procedures for using these are dangerous and should be left only to commercial growers.

Damping Off

Has this ever happened to you? Your seedlings are growing fine, look healthy, and then suddenly keel over and die for no apparent reason. What probably happened is known as "damping off".

"Damping off" is caused by soil borne fungi, usually *Rhizoctonia*, occasionally *Pythium* and less often *Botrytis* or *Phytophthora*. Using a sterile medium will help considerably to control it, and sphagnum moss will actually inhibit it, but unfortunately a sterile medium alone will not always completely prevent it. The fungus spores can also be on the seeds or in the water.

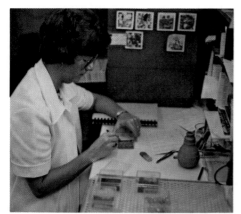

Park's Germination Laboratory

Problems with "damping off" can be virtually eliminated using the following precautions: allow proper spacing between seedlings and do not over crowd, do not over water, provide good air circulation, and use a sterile medium with perfect drainage. Before sowing seeds, drench the seed flat and medium with a solution of Benomyl fungicide made at the rate of one-half tablespoon per gallon of water. Benomyl is perfectly safe for any type of seed.

"Damping off" activity is highest between 68° and 86° F., and will cause few problems with those seeds that need a cool temperature (55° F.) to germinate.

Seeds

The most essential ingredient in sowing seeds is, naturally, the seed itself. Before you begin any work at all, look over seed catalogs or seeds racks and choose those seeds which will best fill your needs. The encyclopedia sections of this book give a complete description of almost every plant that is available and can be grown from seed, so study it well so the plants you pick will be the right size, bloom at the right time with the right color, or bear the vegetables you and your family want. If you're a beginner, start with those seeds marked "Easy". Also, check the Appendix for listings of plants that grow under special conditions, such as in shade, moist soils or at limiting temperatures.

Always buy the best quality seeds from reliable seedsmen. Their seeds will be true to species or variety, free of other crops, weeds or inert material and as free from disease as possible. They will also be fresh and have a capacity for high germination.

The Federal Seed Act controls those seeds that are sold in interstate commerce; regulations set minimum standards of quality, germination percentage and freedom from weeds. At the Park Seed Co. Germination Laboratory, seeds are tested when new and retested at regular intervals during storage to insure gardening success as well as to meet the regulations. Seeds are sown on blotters and placed in germinators where light, moisture and temperature are controlled.

It is possible for you to collect your own seeds from wooded areas, roadsides or your flower gardens, but be advised that your results probably won't be as good as with purchased seeds. Your seeds probably will not produce plants identical to the parental plants.

Commercially grown seeds are carefully rogued to keep quality high, harvested at maturity, collected properly, and cleaned, processed and stored in the most modern ways so that they are the best possible seeds you can buy.

Getting Botanical

A brief explanation of the hows and whys of seed formation and germination will help you to understand what you are doing and why certain requirements are necessary.

Plant propagation by seeds and spores falls under the category of sexual propagation, as opposed to asexual propagation which is propagation by cuttings, division, layering, specialized plant parts or grafting.

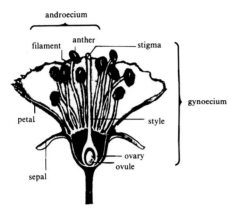

Flower Cross Section

Seeds are produced by flowers and are the result of the fusion of male and female gametes. Gametes are the vehicles by which hereditary genetic material is passed from parent to offspring. The male gamete is called the sperm and the female gamete the ovule. Pollen contains the male within the anther from pollen mother cells. The anthers and their stalks, known as filaments, constitute the male part of the flower called the androecium or stamen. The ovules are formed within the ovary. The ovary, style, and stigma make up the female part of the flower, which is called the gynoecium or pistil.

Pollination and the subsequent fusion of gametes occurs after pollen is transferred from the anther to the stigma by wind, insects or hand. Once on the stigma, the pollen grain germinates, producing a pollen tube that grows through the style to the ovary. The male gamete or sperm travels through the pollen tube and enters the ovule through a small opening called the micropyle. At this point fertilization takes place, fusing the genetic material of the parents. The fertilized ovule matures into the seed.

Self-pollination occurs when male and female gametes of the same individual plant are fused, either in the same flower or different flowers. Cross-pollination would then be the fusion of gametes from different individuals.

Varieties are naturally occurring selections within a species, while cultivars are selections resulting from man's endeavors. Hybrids in the strictest sense are the product of cross-pollinated genetically unlike parents. Hybrids of the seed trade are crosses between highly selected individual strains and are completely repeatable year after year by using the same parental strains.

Hybrids retained in the trade are improvements over their parents and are of increasing importance in flower and vegetable gardens because of the high degree of uniformity of plant habit, leaf and flower color, flower form, productivity and other desirable characteristics. Hybrid seeds are more expensive because of the extensive breeding efforts that go into their production. Seeds from hybrid plants should not be saved for general garden use because the offspring will segregate, yielding many less desirable types. Since hybrids are superior, they are worth the added cost.

The primary parts of a typical seed are a seed coat, endosperm, and embryo. The seed coat encloses the other parts and gives protection. The endosperm is stored energy, usually in the form of carbohydrates, and can be either developed or undeveloped. The embryo is the small dormant plant. The lower part of the embryo develops into the roots and is referred to as the radicle or hypocotyl. Towards the middle of the embryo are one (monocotyledon) or two (dicotyledon) cotyledons. The cotyledons or cotyledonary leaves are the first to appear after germination in many plants with two cotyledons. At the top of the axis above the attachment point of the one or two cotyledons, the shoot growing point appears, known as the plumule or epicotyl. Sometimes a small shoot is already present at seed maturity.

At the end or along the side of the seed is a scar, the hilum, which marks the point of attachment of the seed to the ovary wall. On seeds of some species the micropyle may be seen by the hilum.

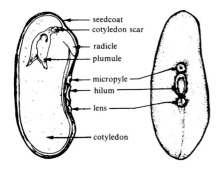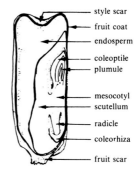

Cross Section Dicot Seed   *Cross Section Monocot Seed*

For germination to take place, the seed must be viable, the internal conditions of the seed must be right, and there must be proper balance of the environmental conditions of moisture, temperature, light, and air. When these environmental requirements are met, enzymes are activated. These enzymes convert the stored carbohydrates (mostly starch) into sugars usable by the embryo. As the embryo grows, the seed coat bursts and then the radicle emerges and anchors in the ground. Following that, the growing tip emerges.

Special Treatments

No special treatment is needed to obtain germination of most annuals, vegetables and some perennials and woody plants, if the conditions above are provided. However, in other plants, germination can be delayed by one of several factors. The seed may have a hard, moisture impermeable seed coat; it may have dormant embryo; it may contain a chemical inhibitor; it may need either total light or total darkness to germinate. There are special treatments that can be applied to these seeds which will cause them to germinate and grow. If a special treatment is needed on a particular seed, it is so stated in the encyclopedia sections; the Appendix also lists seeds that need special treatment.

SCARIFICATION

The seed coats of some seeds are so hard that they cannot absorb moisture and may need to be broken, scratched or mechanically altered so they are permeable to water. This is called scarification, and it may be done with a knife, sandpaper or a file. Be very careful when you nick or file seeds that you do not injure them, for they either may not germinate or pathogens may enter through the wound.

Hard-coated seeds have one advantage—they usually have a longer storage life. In general, you can expect some seeds of the Leguminosae, Malvaceae, Cannaceae, Geraniaceae, Convolvulaceae, Solanaceae, Chenopodiacae and Palmae families to have hard seed coats.

Some seeds (*Pelargonium,* for example) are shipped from the producer already mechanically scarified. (These, unfortunately, do not have as long a storage life.) Others have been treated with sulfuric acid, another method of scarification, but since sulfuric acid is very corrosive, it is not recommended for the home gardener and should be left for the commercial seedsman.

Some seeds are too small to be handled and mechanically scarified, and these should be soaked to soften the hard seed coat.

SOAKING

Soaking of seeds has a dual purpose—it can soften a hard seed coat, and it can leach out chemical inhibitors that prevent germination. With some slow to germinate seeds, soaking will shorten the time necessary for germination.

Soaking for 24 hours is usually sufficient. If soaking for more than 24 hours is recommended on a particular plant, change the water once per day to achieve necessary aeration and eliminate the buildup of microorganisms.

Place seeds to be soaked in a container and add 5-6 times their volume of hot (190° F) water. Never boil seeds in water, as this can injure them and make them inviable. Plant the seeds immediately after soaking and do not allow them to dry out before sowing.

STRATIFICATION

Stratification is the process of subjecting seeds to moist-cold treatment before sowing. This method is necessary with seeds that have an immature or dormant embryo when harvested, which include perennials and woody plants for the most part. Some plants, like lettuce and delphinium, become dormant if they are subjected to temperatures over 75° F. for an extended period and must be chilled to induce germination.

Seeds to be stratified must be sown or mixed with moistened medium and kept at 32° (freezer) - 40° F. (refrigerator) for a certain period of time. If seeds are sown first, simply slip the seed flat into a plastic bag and place it in the refrigerator or freezer for the time specified in the encyclopedia section. An alternative is to mix seeds in 2 to 3 times their volume of moistened medium, place them in a plastic bag tied tight and place the bag in the freezer or refrigerator. When the chilling period is over, do not separate the seeds from the medium, but sow them together.

The encyclopedia section and the Appendix outline which seeds need cold treatment and for how long. For stratification purposes, do not refrigerate or freeze the seed while in the packet, or cold treat seeds in water; seeds must be in contact with moisture and with air for the chilling to be effective. If they are not in contact with both moisture and air when chilled, they may go into a second dormancy or be severely injured.

SIMPLE AND DOUBLE DORMANCY

Dormancy in seeds does not have the same connotation as dormancy in woody plants, perennial or bulbs, which is a resting period. Dormancy in seeds refers to the various conditions that prevent the seed from germinating as previously outlined.

When only one special treatment is needed (stratification in most instances) to break the condition, the seed is said to have a simple dormancy. When two treatments are necessary, which could be two stratifications or stratification combined with one of the other special treatments, the seed has a double dormancy. For example, some *Ilex, Taxus, Viburnum,* some lilies and tree peonies need a warm period (68-86° F.) of three months in which the root develops, followed by stratification for one to three months which triggers stem development before emergence of the growing tip will occur. *Trillium* needs a three month period of chilling, followed by a three.month high (68-86° F.) temperature period, plus a second three-month cold period before it will germinate.

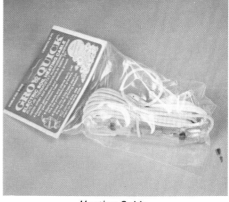

Heating Tray   Heating Cable

OUTDOOR TREATMENT

An alternative to placing seeds in the refrigerator or freezer is to place them outside for their chilling period, provided you live in an area which is cold enough in winter for a long enough period of time. Seeds may be sown in beds or in flats in late fall or early winter and wintered outdoors. Germination will occur as weather warms in spring. If using flats, place them on the north side of the house away from drying winds and sun, sink them into the ground to just below their top or place them in a coldframe.

WET SHIPMENT

Seeds of some tropical and woody plants are shipped fresh in moistened sphagnum moss immediately after they are harvested and must be sown immediately. If the seed coat is allowed to dry out, nothing in the world will cause these seeds to germinate. These seeds include *Anthurium, Philodendron, Ginkgo, Clivia* and *Corynocarpus.*

STORING SEEDS

The question is often asked, "How long can I store seeds and still have them be viable?" Seeds of most annuals and vegetables may be safely stored for 2-3 years, provided they are kept in a cool place and not subjected to moisture. There are stories of evening primrose seeds lasting 50 years and lotus germinating after 1,000 years, but these are the exception and not the rule. If seeds are kept in an unopened, moisture resistant foil package such as the "Parkspak" and not subjected to abnormal temperatures, most will keep perfectly for several years. Some vegetables, such as beets, cucumbers and radishes, will keep for as long as ten years. Store the seeds as cool as possible, for reduced temperatures will lengthen storage life.

If the foil package has been opened, store seeds in a dry, airtight container in a cool place. Seeds of woody plants should be stored in the refrigerator for best results.

There are some seeds that are short-lived and should not be stored for any length of time as they will not be viable no matter how you handle them. These include *Asparagus* species, *Chrysanthemum coccineum,* perennial delphinium, *Dimorphotheca, Franklinia, Geranium, Gerbera, Kochia,* some lilies, *Magnolia, Passiflora, Potentilla, Salvia splendens* and *Sophora.* A listing of seeds that should not be stored also appears in the Appendix. Other seeds that should not be stored are those shipped wet and fresh (see previous section on "WET SHIPMENT").

Germination Temperature

As previously explained, correct temperature is one of the environmental conditions critical for seed germination. Throughout the encyclopedia sections a specific germination temperature is given for each type of seed. Pay attention to it, for it is important, and in some instances you will have to assemble some special equipment to achieve it. Also, be aware that the temperature

Coldframe

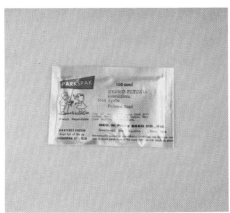

Foil Packet

given is the temperature within the medium and *not* the air temperature. Evaporation at the surface of the germinating medium causes the temperature within the medium to be cooler than the air by about 5-10° F.

It makes sense that different seeds require different temperatures to germinate. Tropical plants will naturally require a higher temperature than, for instance, an alpine which in its natural habitat germinates at a lower temperature than a tropical does. Few plants germinate at sustained temperatures below 40° F. or above 104° F., although a short exposure to these temperatures will not harm them.

Although the temperature within the room of a house may be 70° F., the medium in the germinating flat will be lower, as we have stated. To keep the medium at 70° or above when necessary, gentle bottom heat is recommended. This heat may be obtained from a warm spot in the house, such as the top of the refrigerator, or from a heating cable or heating tray. Heating cables and trays may be spread out wherever seeds are germinated, whether it be on a windowsill, countertop or under fluorescent lights, and the flats or trays of pots placed on the top of them. They will heat flats to 70-75° depending on their use (when the flat gets warm enough, simply pull the plug); some have a built-in thermostat which automatically controls temperature. Waterproof soil heating cables may also be used outdoors in beds and in cold frames.

For several types of seeds, it is recommended that the temperature within the medium be 68-86° F. These seeds respond better when the temperature alternates between 68° for 6-8 hours per day and 86° for 16-18 hours per day. To achieve this, use a heating cable for the required time, or germinate seeds under lights for 16-18 hours per day which will give off warmth and effect the higher temperature, turning the lights off at night and allowing the temperature to drop. Seed flats may also be placed in a sunny window which will heat up during the day and cool off at night.

When house plant or perennial seeds are germinated indoors in the midst of the heat of summer, room temperatures will probably go high enough that heating cables and heating trays will not be necessary (unless the house is air conditioned).

When 55° F. is specified, germinate the seeds indoors in an unheated garage, attic, basement or porch which must, of course, have a source of natural or artificial light. Outdoors, this temperature is achieved in early spring. Sow directly into seed beds; or set flats outside in a spot protected from sun and wind, or in a cold frame.

22

| *Flat covered with Plastic Bag* | *Flat covered with Glass* |

Temperatures given throughout the book are in Fahrenheit; for Celsius (Centigrade) followers, here is a conversion of the most commonly used readings:

°F.	°C.
32	0
40	4.5
55	13
68	20
75	24
86	30
104	40
190	88
212	100

Temperatures that are missing can easily be figured from a metric convertor or the age-old formula: $C° = 5/9 (F°-32)$

Moisture and Humidity

Moisture and humidity are also critical to seed germination. The germinating medium must be kept evenly moist, but never sopping wet. Too little moisture and germination will not occur; too much and rot will. If a good medium such as "Sow and Grow" is used, watered thoroughly and allowed to drain for several hours before sowing, the moisture level should be "perfect".

Outdoors, seed beds will have to be checked frequently to make sure they don't dry out during germination and early growth. Indoors, it is best to slip your seed flats into plastic bags or cover them with glass until the seeds germinate. Another excellent route is the miniature greenhouse, which is small and compact enough to sit on a table top or windowsill. Any of these methods will keep the level of moisture and humidity just right, so the seed flats will not have to be watered often, if at all, before germination. This will eliminate overwatering, forgetfulness, or accidentally dislodging tiny seeds before they germinate.

Light

The final environmental factor, but one equally as important as the others, is light. Some seeds require light to germinate, some need a complete absence of light to sprout, and others will germinate under either condition. If light is needed to germinate, the answer is simple—do not cover the seeds. If darkness is necessary, cover the seeds completely with medium unless they are too fine to be covered. In that instance, place the seed flats in total darkness or cover them with a material like newspaper or black plastic which will block out the light until germination occurs.

Once germinated, all seedlings need ample light to develop into strong, healthy plants; in fact, they have the highest light intensity requirements of all plants. Use of fluorescent lights or growing in a greenhouse is best, but if you do not have these available, an unshaded south window will do well.

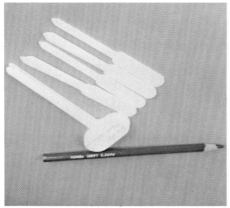

Labels

Bulb Sprayer

Light is necessary to enable the plants to convert water and carbon dioxide into sugar (its food),in a process known as photosynthesis. If light intensity is too low, which often happens during the short days of winter or prolonged cloudy periods, the plants will be unhealthy, tall and spindly.

For more information on growing seedlings under fluorescent lights, refer to the section "Growing Under Lights" in Chapter IV.

Other Needs

There are one or two more things needed to make the act complete. Labels are a must, for no matter how good your memory is, you can't possibly remember which seed is in what flat, or when it was sown. Heavy white plastic markers are widely used, for they are durable and reusable. Whatever you write on them in pencil will stay there until you erase or scrub it off. Let them stay with your plants even after they're moved outdoors in case a friend asks about a certain plant or variety—the information will be at your fingertips.

Young seedlings will have to be watered carefully so they don't become damaged. Water from the bottom or with a bulb hand sprinkler that sprays gently with a fine mist.

One more thing is a good "extra"—a record book. If you keep records this year, you'll appreciate being able to double check next year on what you planted, how long it took to germinate, whether you started it too early or too late, or whether you grew too few or too many.

Now that you have everything together, it's time to sow. Read on!

CHAPTER II

SOWING AND GERMINATING

By Definition

The type of plant, whether annual, biennial, perennial or pot plant, that you are going to grow determines when the seeds should be sown and how they should be handled. Annuals are plants that grow, flower, set seed and complete their life cycle the same year the seeds are sown. Biennials have a two-year life cycle; seeds sown this year will flower next year, and then set their seeds and die. Most herbaceous perennials die to the ground each winter and come back each spring, living for varying numbers of years depending on the genus and/or species. The plants designated in the encyclopedia section as pot plants are those suitable for container growing, particularly for house plants and patio plants; most are perennials.

In general horticultural use and in this text the word annual denotes a plant that blooms the first year from seed and is treated as an annual even though it may live and bloom for many years. Geographic location can also play a role in how certain plants are treated. For example, *Salvia splendens* is grown as an annual because it is not hardy, but the plant is perennial in its native habitat of Brazil.

Annuals are started indoors or in seed beds outdoors, depending on the type of plant. Most are frost tender, and should not be set in place outside until all danger of frost has past (this date may be determined from your local County Agent). Some annuals are hardy, which means they may be sown in early spring as soon as the soil may be worked and they are not killed by frost. A complete listing of hardy annuals is in the Appendix, and the instruction to "sow outdoors in early spring" is given wherever appropriate in the encyclopedia.

Biennials and perennials are started in spring or summer up to two months before frost so the plants will be of sufficient maturity to be transplanted into their permanent location before cold fall weather sets in. Hardy perennials and those requiring stratification are often sown outdoors in late fall or early winter for spring germination.

Seeds of house plants may, in almost every case, be sown indoors at any time of year.

Sowing Seeds Indoors

Why start seeds indoors? As Chapter I has already told us, seeds are started indoors for a number of reasons. Many annuals and vegetables have such a long growing season that they

Flat with Growing Medium   *Drenching with Benomyl*

won't flower or fruit if they don't get a head start on the season indoors. Others may not need to be started indoors, but will flower or be productive for a much longer time with early seed-starting indoors. Almost every house plant needs the environmental protection of indoor sowing and growing, as do fine seeded outdoor plants which would in all likelihood be washed away if planted in outdoor beds.

Many annuals may be started indoors before being transplanted outside, and throughout the encyclopedia section they are so indicated. Those that <u>must</u> be started indoors are listed here, for these will otherwise never perform or will bloom too late to be of much good to the garden (warmest parts of the country excepted): ageratum, begonia, coleus, geranium (*Pelargonium*), impatiens, lobelia, African marigold, petunia, salpiglossis, salvia, snapdragon, verbena.

While many vegetables are sown directly into the garden bed, others must be started indoors as the growing season in all but the warmest parts of the country is not long enough for them to produce. They include: broccoli, Brussel sprouts, cabbage, eggplant, okra, peppers, tomatoes.

Lettuce, onion and melons often join the above in the indoor seed flat. Double check in the encyclopedia section for specific recommendations.

CONTAINERS AND MEDIA

Start your seed sowing process by assembling your containers and getting them ready. If the container has drainage holes, fine; if it doesn't, punch a few. Whenever possible, use a container with good drainage provisions.

If the container is made of fiber or peat, it must be watered throughly before medium is placed in it or it will act as a wick and pull moisture out of the medium later on. Fill the flat or pot with water and allow it to soak up what it needs and drain off the rest, or place the flat or pot in a larger container of water until it has absorbed all it can. When the flat is thoroughly moistened, place a layer of stones, gravel, old panty hose or newspaper in the bottom.

To judge how many seed flats to prepare, use this rule of thumb: A 5½″ x 7½″ flat will hold 100 seedlings from large seeds, 200 seedlings from medium seeds and 300 seedlings from fine seeds. Always sow about twice as many seeds as the number of plants you want since all of the seeds won't germinate, and some seedlings will be lost in the thinning and transplanting processes.

The container should be filled with pre-moistened sowing medium to within a ¼″ of the top. One of two methods may be used to moisten the medium—wet it down in a plastic bag or a pot before placing it into the container (four cups of medium and one ½ cups of water should be enough for one 5½″ x 7½″ flat), or put it in the container dry and let it draw up water from the bottom only, and slowly, or it will separate. Dry medium is very difficult to evenly moisten with top watering. Once the medium is moist, make sure it is patted down firmly, especially in the corners, and level it out with a flat tool like a label.

At this point, drench the sowing medium with a solution of Benomyl fungicide (½ tablespoon per gallon of water) to prevent "damping off". The medium should be moist but not wet for sowing; if the medium is allowed to drain for approximately two hours after moistening and drenching before the seeds are sown, it should be "just right".

26

Making Row with Pencil   *Tapping Seed from Packet*

Fiber and peat containers and sowing medium should never be reused for seed sowing, for their sterility cannot be guaranteed. There's no need to worry about waste, for they can be used for transplants and given other odd jobs about the garden.

If compressed peat pellets are to be used, soak them in water and watch them grow before your eyes into their full size—it takes only minutes. These peat pellets or small peat pots should be used to sow and grow seeds that don't like to be transplanted later on (check the encyclopedia and Appendix for a listing of which ones they are).

SOWING

Gather together your seeds and double check in the encyclopedia and/or Appendix if they need any special treatment before sowing, such as soaking, scarification or stratification. Also, watch the calendar carefully so that seeding can be done at the proper time. If a seed is supposed to be started 6-8 weeks before final frost, don't start it four weeks or ten weeks before. Immature seedlings started too late will not be large or strong enough to move outside when it's time, and those started too early will be too tall, lanky or progressed to transplant well. Seedlings are best transplanted all-green and not in bud or flower.

Many growers do not place all their eggs in one basket and do not sow all of the seeds in a packet just in case something goes awry and they have to start all over again.

If you're sowing two types of seed in the same flat, be sure you pick ones that have the same temperature requirements and germinate in approximately the same length of time.

It is best to sow seeds in rows, as it makes transplanting easier, so make depressions the thickness of the seed in the top of the medium with a label or pencil. Very slight depressions are needed for fine seeds and those that need light to germinate as they must not be covered by the medium.

Write the name of the plant and the date of sowing on a label—you may think you have a good memory but chances are you won't remember what's what after weeks have gone by.

Cut the seed packet open across the top. Sow the seeds carefully and evenly as you can. You can hold the seed packet in one hand, squeeze it together slightly, and tap it gently with your finger or a pencil. A few seeds should fall out with each tap; if too many come out at one time, they may be separated with a pencil.

As an alternative, crease a piece of paper and transfer the seeds to it. Let the seeds roll out or tap the paper with a pencil as above. Plastic seed sowers may also be used; these are clear plastic tubes with a hole at one end. Larger seeds may be individually placed by hand; large flat ones should be sown vertically in the flat or their chance of rot increases.

The seed coats of some seeds, such as *Anemone* and *Gomphrena*, are covered with hairy protrusions which give the seeds a cottony appearance. These seeds are handled and shipped in this condition because no method exists at the present to economically clean them. Plant them in the condition you receive them, "cotton" and all. Others like *Calceolaria* and *Begonia* are very fine and dusty, and extreme care must be taken that they are evenly spread over the sowing medium. This is the one case where broadcasting rather than sowing in rows might be necessary and more practical.

27

Sowing Pelleted Seed   *Using Seed Tape*

Be careful when sowing that seeds aren't planted too close together. Seeds should not be sown too thickly, for seedlings need room for growth, which provides proper water, light and air circulation. In addition, transplanting later on of properly spaced seedlings will be easier and done with less damage.

Very fine seeds, such as snapdragons, petunias, ageratum and begonias should not be covered with medium after sowing, but merely pressed into the surface of the sowing medium with a pencil, label or a very fine mist from a rubber bulb sprinkler. The seeds must be in contact with moistened medium, not air, to germinate. All other seeds, except those that need light to germinate, should be covered once to twice their thickness with dry, sowing medium, and then watered carefully with a fine mist of room temperature water. Rubber bulb sprinklers are recommended because they deliver a fine spray that will not dislodge the seeds or the medium.

Those seeds that need light to germinate should not be covered with medium but merely pressed into contact with medium as is done with fine seeds. Those seeds which need darkness, as long as they are not fine, should be completely covered with sowing medium. Tiny seeds which need darkness to germinate are treated in one of two ways: place the flat in a dark spot until germination occurs, or cover the flat with black plastic, newspaper or some other material that will block the light until the seeds have sprouted.

The seed flat is now ready to await germination. Place the entire flat into a plastic bag and tie tightly, cover the flat with a piece of glass or place the flat into an indoor miniature greenhouse. Any of these methods will keep the humidity high enough so that the seed flat should not need to be watered before germination, thereby reducing the chance of drowning or dislodging the seeds. If the plastic bag route is taken, be sure the bag does not rest on top of the medium. An extra label or two set at the corners of the flat will keep the bag high enough and off the medium.

PELLETED SEED
Some very fine seeds, such as petunias, coleus, pinks and snapdragons, are pelleted to make them easier to handle and space properly, and may be used in place of untreated seeds. They are coated to increase their size, protect the seed and furnish plant food and a disease barrier; they germinate reliably and quickly. Do not cover the pellets when sowing, but merely press them gently into the surface.

SEED TAPES
Seed tapes for both indoor and outdoor germination are available and a big asset to proper spacing and less waste. Merely lay the tape down as instructed on the label, and cut to desired length. The tape will dissolve, exposing the seeds encased in it to the medium or soil.

SOWING CACTI AND SUCCULENTS
Cacti and succulents are sown and germinated in much the same way as other plants, but since they thrive in dry conditions, they have to be treated a little differently. Sowing medium should

be only ¼ peat or sphagnum moss. If you mix your own, make it ¾ gravel or perlite; if you use Park's "Sow and Grow", add an equal volume of gravel or perlite (the gravel sold for bird cages will do just fine). Some seeds may be slow to germinate, and seedlings usually are slow to grow so you may not be able to transplant for many months.

FERNS FROM SPORES

Ferns are germinated from spores, not from seeds, and because the life cycle of ferns is different from that of other plants, the germination procedure must also be different.

Sterility is of utmost importance with the container, the medium and even the water which should be boiled and cooled before use. Dust the spores on the surface of the medium, not covering them. Cover the container with a piece of glass or plastic and set it on a saucer of water so the medium will be constantly moist. Temperature should be maintained at 60-70°.

Within a few days to several weeks, a green moss-like growth will appear on the surface of the medium. Don't be alarmed, this is the prothallia starting to form, the first step in the life cycle of a fern. The prothallia will become flat, thin, heart-shaped structures within another one to three months. At this point the female egg cells in the prothallia are fertilized by the male spermatozoids and the new fern starts to develop.

Transplant the young ferns into a flat and place them one inch apart. When the fronds start to touch, move each fern into its own 2″ or 3″ pot. This whole process may take 8-12 months, so be patient. Prevent the young ferns from drying out by keeping them in a covered container or terrarium.

GERMINATING

Once your seed flat is ready, place it in a location where it will receive the proper temperature for seed germination (Refer to Chapter I). It also wouldn't hurt if you had a spare room, attic or basement where your seed garden would be out of sight and where a water spill or other accident wouldn't cause a problem. If the windowsill is the site choice, it's wise to protect it from moisture with a tray or a strip of aluminum foil.

With very few exceptions, seed flats should be placed in good light but not in direct sun while germination is taking place. Those that require very high temperatures (80-85° F.) to germinate may be safely placed in a sunny windowsill. If you're germinating seeds under lights, refer to "Growing Under Lights" in Chapter IV.

Soil thermometers are on the market and it would be beneficial to use one to make sure your germinating temperature is right.

The germination times given in the encyclopedia section are average ones and may vary by 25% in either direction, depending on environmental factors. Don't give up too early and think your seeds aren't making progress towards becoming plants.

Even though the plastic bag, glass or indoor greenhouse used with the seed flat should keep the need for watering to a minimum, check the medium once in a while where seeds that take a long time to germinate were planted to make sure it hasn't dried out.

Condensation on the plastic, glass or indoor greenhouse does not mean the flat has been overwatered; a variation in temperature may cause moisture to form. Feel the medium to be sure. If it is too wet, leave the glass or plastic off or remove the flat from the greenhouse for several hours to dry a little, and try again. Don't, however, let the medium dry out completely at any time.

Once the seeds have poked their heads through the medium, remove the plastic or glass from the seed flats or take them from the indoor greenhouse. Gradually move them into full sun or strong light; don't do it all at once or the tender seedlings will be injured.

OF GROWING CONCERN

The next few weeks or months will tell the tale of the success of your new plants.

Watering of course, is critical. The root systems of the new seedlings are not yet well developed, so the medium must always be kept moist, but never completely wet or the seedlings will drown from poor aeration. The sowing medium is dark brown when moist, changing to light brown as it dries out. When watering is needed (check every day), bottom watering is best until the seedlings reach a fairly good size. Spraying young plants can dislodge them and possibly bring on a fungus attack. If spraying must be done, trickle the water on lightly and slowly between the rows.

Most plants will grow successfully at normal room temperatures of 60-70° F. Those that need cooler growing temperatures are so noted in the encyclopedia section; many tropicals will be happy with temperatures as high as 75° F.

If seedlings are grown on the windowsill or at the edge of the light garden, they should be turned regularly to insure that they will grow straight and evenly.

Once the first true leaves have developed (cotyledonary leaves, which are food storage tissues, appear on many seedlings before the true leaves), it is time to start fertilizing. No food is needed prior to this point since the seedling is using food that was stored in the seed. Use a soluble plant food such as Hyponex, Miracle Gro or Peters at ¼ the label strength when seedlings are small, increasing to ½ label strength as the plant matures.

It is best to fertilize with this weak solution once a week rather than to feed with full strength solution once a month, as growth will be more even and burning of young plants will be avoided. When bottom watering young seedlings, mix the fertilizer into the water; later on, the seedlings can be fertilized from above.

TRANSPLANTING

It is possible to plant seedlings directly from the seed flat into the garden, but it is not a good idea. The seedlings should be transplanted or at least thinned so they will not be crowded, leggy, weak or susceptible to damage. One transplant is usually enough, and it will guarantee good, strong root development and easier adjustment of the plant to its final home. Seedlings started in individual pots, naturally, do not need to be transplanted.

Transplanting with Spoon   *Transplant in Peat Pot*

After the seedlings have developed four true leaves, it is time to transplant or thin. If thinning, leave at least one inch between seedlings in the flat, and more for larger plants. These seedlings may be left to grow as-is until it is time to move them to their permanent home.

There's one interesting fact to be aware of when thinning or transplanting seedlings: the weakest seedlings in annual mixtures such as snapdragons and phlox often include colors and types not present in the stronger seedlings. For a good balance of colors and types, transplant all seedlings, large and small.

When transplanting, first water the seedlings thoroughly until they are soaking wet. If the seedlings are being transplanted into peat pots or flats, wet them down also, and don't forget to moisten the medium to be used for transplanting. Indoor plants are best transplanted into clay or plastic pots, while peat pots or pellets are best for outdoor plants. Seedlings for outdoor use can also be transplanted into flats; those with dividers or compartments lead to more compact root development and easier, unshocked transplanting.

You may use the same medium you used for sowing for transplanting, or use leftover medium from previous seed sowings. It is not critical that medium for transplants be sterile, as it is for sowing and germinating.

Using a label, spoon handle, fork or similar tool, gently lift the seedlings from the flat. Separate them carefully so as not to break any more roots than necessary. A small amount of medium should cling to the seedlings' roots. Always handle a seedlings by its leaves and NEVER by its stem; if damage is accidentally done, the seedling will grow a new leaf, but it will never grow a new stem.

Fill the seedling's new home with pre-moistened medium level with the top of the container. With a label or pencil, open a hole in the center of the medium deep and wide enough to fit the seedling's roots. Lower the seedling into the hole slightly deeper than it was growing in the seed flat, and gently press the medium around the roots.

Don't forget to put a label in the container!

Transplants will often droop or wilt because they have lost some of their roots. They will recover quickly if properly protected for a few days as follows:

Keep the transplants in good light but not full sun for several days, increasing light intensity gradually. If you've transplanted during cloudy weather, the containers can go right onto the windowsill; if you grow under lights, the transplants can go under the fluorescents right away. If the plants become tall and spindly later on, they're not getting enough light.

Water when necessary, never allowing the transplants to wilt and keeping the medium evenly moist but not soaking wet at any time.

Once a week when watering, add soluble fertilizer at ½ the recommended label strength.

Peat pots are light brown and hard when dry, but dark brown and soft when wet, when they require special handling. They will need some type of protection and support, such as a tray or an empty seed flat. There is a device available called the "Easy Does It Tray" which will not only support peat and other pots but will give you freedom from constant care. A reservoir in the bottom provides a continuous supply of moisture for about a week in the right amount for the

Peat Pots

Peat Pots with Plants

young plants—neither too much nor too little. Spread fine vermiculite on the tray and place the pots on it to insure perfect and continuous moisture supply to the transplants.

Several types of plants benefit from pinching while in the transplant stage. Single stemmed plants such as snapdragons, dahlias, and chrysanthemums will be more bushy and colorful if pinched. Those that are getting too tall before the weather is right for outdoor planting should also be pinched. Simply reach into the center of the plant and nip out the growing tip.

Once roots show through the container walls, the plants are ready for their permanent homes. If it's too early for outdoor planting, they may be held in the container for up to four weeks until the weather is right. Indoor plants may be planted, pot and all, into larger pots, baskets or containers when ready.

HARDENING OFF

One week before indoor grown annuals, vegetables or perennials are shifted outdoors to the growing beds, start to harden them off. This process acclimates the soft and tender plants that have been protected from wind, cool temperatures and strong sun and gradually gets them used to their new environment.

Move the trays or flats of potted plants outside into a sheltered, shady area such as a porch, cold frame or under a tree or shrub. If it gets chilly at night, move them back inside. After two or three days, give them a half a day of sun, then a full day, always increasing the exposure gradually. Make sure the transplants are well watered during this "hardening off" period. If at all possible, don't place transplants on the ground if slugs are a problem in your area.

For planting into the garden and growing instructions, turn to Chapter III.

Outdoor Sowing

There are many seeds that germinate quickly and may successfully be sown outdoors where they are to grow. These include, among many others, sweet alyssum, chrysanthemum, marigold, nasturtium, flowering tobacco and zinnias, plus most vegetables. Double check in the encyclopedia section for instructions for the specific plants you are growing.

SOIL PREPARATION

The first step in outdoor seed sowing is soil preparation; the soil must be open, rich and fertile for most plants to grow properly. Turn the soil over to a depth of at least 6-8 inches and, better yet, 12-18 inches, with a spade or fork, breaking up large clumps and removing stones and debris. Alternately, use a roto-tiller to make the job less back-breaking.

To make sure soil is workable in spring, take a handful of it and squeeze it into a ball. Drop it onto the ground, and if it doesn't break up, the soil's still too wet and not friable enough. Wait a few days and try again. If you work soil that is not ready, the texture will be ruined.

Spread a one inch layer of peat moss, compost, leaf mold or other organic material over the bed and rake it into the top two inches of soil as level as possible. None of these have fertilizer

Sowing a Row   *Covering Seed in Row*

value but do improve the soil, condition it and make necessary bacteria available. The soil pH factor is very important; most plants and vegetables in particular, need a soil pH near 6.5 (slightly acid). Soil pH should be checked annually either by the local County Agent or by using a soil test kit. If the soil pH is too low or too high, use lime to raise it or sulphur to lower it. If you use hydrated lime, which is quick acting, apply it a couple of weeks prior to planting and water it well. This will avoid any likelihood of burning (plasmolysis). Crushed limestone is much slower acting and longer lasting in its effect, requires a heavier application, but can be used in already planted areas without danger. Dolomitic limestone is particularly good, as it contains the trace element magnesium. Heavy clay soils can be broken up and improved in texture by incorporating organic matter, gypsum, vermiculite, or coarse builder's sand, thus promoting drainage.

The last step to soil preparation is the spreading and mixing in of dry fertilizer such as 5-10-5. In general, a good rule of thumb is to apply 2 pounds of 5-10-5 per 100 square feet; once again, a soil test should be performed to be sure. Rake the soil level.

SOWING

First, look at the date. Some seeds (sweet peas, bugloss, California poppy, beets, carrots and radishes, for example) can be sown as soon as soil is workable in spring, while others have to wait until after frost for planting (zinnias, marigolds, squash and beans fit into this category). Check the encyclopedia sections to be sure.

Planning is the next important step. Vegetables and flowers for a cutting garden should be sown in rows, while others may be planted in a free form. For other than free form, mark straight rows first, checking the seed packet for suitable distance between the rows. Use of stakes and twine will help you to keep your rows straight. Rows in the vegetable garden should run from north to south to make the most out of the sun and prevent shading. See Chapter IV for ideas on plans and layouts.

First, water the soil well. Then, using a yardstick or similar straight edge, make shallow furrows in the prepared soil, about the thickness of the seed to be planted. Sow the seeds thinly and evenly by tapping the seed packet with a pencil. Large seeds can be placed by hand. After sowing, pinch the row together with your fingers and firm the soil. Seeds need close contact with the soil and moisture in order to germinate properly.

There's a tool available called the Precision Garden Seeder which makes outdoor vegetable seed sowing almost foolproof. It opens the soil to the proper depth, spaces the seeds, plants and covers them, and packs the soil. It comes with different seed plates which are changed, depending on what you're sowing.

Proper sowing depth is critical to good germination and emergence. If the seeds are planted too shallow, they might dry out and not germinate. If they are planted too deep, they may not germinate or emerge for a number of possible reasons: the soil could be too cold, there could be insufficient oxygen for the seed, the seed may have exhausted its food supply and died before it

Labeling

Watering

reached the surface, or the seed may not have been strong enough to push through the soil. Fine seeds are best planted indoors, but if sown outdoors should not be covered and should be cared for very carefully.

Put a label in the bed, marking (with water-proof ink) the name of the plant and the date, and you're ready to wait for seeds to sprout.

GERMINATING

After sowing is completed, water the seed bed with a very fine spray, every day if necessary, so the soil never dries out. After the seeds germinate, gradually reduce watering frequency as the plants mature. This will actually encourage better and stronger root growth as the roots will reach out into the soil looking for moisture.

If sowing is done in the hot summer, some sort of shading device is needed to slow evaporation and protect the seedlings from sunburn.

Keep the area well weeded, as weeds will compete with the seedlings for food and water and will cut down good air circulation, inviting disease. Consult the seedling pictures in the encyclopedia sections so the good seedlings can be distinguished from the weed seedlings. Remove the weeds carefully so you don't disturb the seedlings' roots, and water after weeding just in case the roots have been disturbed.

Although this book does not deal with insect and disease problems (your local County Agent is the best person to contact for help in this area), a word must be said about slugs, which munch on young seedlings while we sleep. They may be controlled with bait, stale beer, grapefruit halves—call your County Agent for local recommendations. Don't use non-approved bait on vegetable seedlings!

After the seedlings have reached about 2"-3" in height, it's time for thinning. Do this according to packet or encyclopedia directions, leaving seedlings the proper distance apart. Thinning is best done after a rain or watering, and don't throw the thinnings away. Give them to neighbors or friends, or use vegetable thinnings as flavoring for soup.

At this point, the seedlings will be well along and growing into strong, healthy plants. For cultural directions from this point onward, look ahead to Chapter III.

ANNUALS FOR FALL SOWING

Hardy annuals (See the Appendix for a complete listing) can be fall sown to produce sturdier plants, earlier bloom and longer stems.

The purpose of fall planting in the north is not to get the seed to germinate in autumn, but to get the seed in place, ready to grow with the first favorable sign of spring. Plant the seeds slightly deeper than you would in spring, protecting the beds with boards or other siding material to prevent the seeds from washing away. Ideal planting time is just before the ground freezes, after which a protective mulch should be applied.

From Philadelphia southward, larkspur may be sown in September so the seeds germinate in

Properly spaced Seedlings   *Properly spaced Seedlings*

fall. With a protective mulch after the ground freezes, they will live over winter and give extra-early long stemmed flowers. From Washington, D.C. southward, sweet peas may be handled the same way. From southern Virginia southward, add to these snapdragon, pinks, annual phlox, annual poppy, pot marigold, sweet alyssum, candytuft, California poppy, baby blue eyes, stock, baby's breath, love-in-a-mist, and bachelor's buttons.

SUCCESSION PLANTING

Some annuals, like love-in-a-mist, have a short blooming season, while some vegetables, like carrots and radishes, are harvested once and gone. To have a continual supply of color or food, plant seeds of these in succession, one to two weeks apart, from early spring to early summer.

SOWING PERENNIALS AND BIENNIALS

Perennials are sown the same way as other seeds, the only difference being the timing and the weather.

In the north, most perennials are sown outdoors from spring through summer, up to two months before frost which allows time for the plants to mature before the rigors of winter set in. Others are sown in early spring or late fall because they need cool or freezing temperatures. Whatever the case, it is so stated throughout the encyclopedia section.

Handled this way, most perennials will bloom the second year from seed. Some, like shasta daisy, chrysanthemum and gloriosa daisy, will bloom the first year from seed if started early enough.

Summer sown perennials may be started in beds or may be germinated in flats indoors or outdoors. Using flats outdoors instead of open beds does give you more control of growing conditions. Simply rest the flats on tables, benches or other racks, but try to avoid the ground, which may invite insects and slugs.

Seeds sown in hot summer require heavy shading, otherwise it will be impossible to keep them constantly moist. Benches, tables or whatever is used for the flats should be in the shade of a tree or under some sort of roof. If a coldframe is used, cover the sash with burlap or other shading material. Or build a simple frame of wood which can support shading material such as boards, burlap, heavy cloth or the like. Remove the shade gradually as the seeds germinate.

Biennials are treated in much the same way as perennials. Plant the seeds spring or summer and place them in their permanent position in fall for bloom the following spring or summer.

Planting   *Tapping out of Pot*

CHAPTER III

GROWING

By this time, your seeds have germinated and the seedlings are growing strong and healthy, and so it's time to plant them into their permanent home.

Planting Into The Garden

Consult the calendar before doing anything. Most annuals and vegetables must wait until frost is past to be placed outside. Some can go out earlier; others, like tomatoes and peppers, should wait a little longer until the ground has completely warmed up. Check the encyclopedia sections to be sure.

Next, look to the sun. If a particular plant need lots of light, don't put it in the shade, and vice-versa.

The soil must be well prepared in advance to get the most from your flowers or vegetables. For the sake of not being repetitive, look back at Chapter II for soil preparation directions.

The day before you are going to move your plants into their final home, water both the ground outside and the transplants to cut down on any possible shock. If it's at all possible, do your transplanting on a cloudy day so the heat of the sun won't cause any excess wilting. If you've used individual peat pots or peat pellets, transplanting shock and wilting will be held to a minimum.

Dig a hole (about twice the size of the root ball that will be going into it) with a garden trowel. Set the transplant into the hole so the root ball will be covered by ¼ inch of soil, and press soil firmly about its roots so there is good contact between the soil and the roots.

If you've used peat pellets, the job is simple—just plant. Peat pots have been known to confine a transplant's roots, so peel whatever you can off the pot before planting. Be sure the peat pot is completely covered and not visible because the pot may act as a wick allowing moisture to escape and the pot becomes hard and dry, making root penetration impossible. If your transplants have been growing in flats that are not compartmentalized, very carefully cut out a root ball with a knife or a trowel. If the transplants have been growing in individual plastic pots or flat compartments, turn them upside down and tap them on the bottom, and they will come out easily.

Pay attention to spacing directions on the seed packet or in the encyclopedia sections. The newly set out plants may look a little sparse at first, but they will grow and fill in quickly, and you don't want them to be overcrowded. Adequate spacing also cuts down on disease.

Soak the plants with water immediately after transplanting and every day for about a week until they're well established and growing. Some transplants may wilt at first, but misting them every day or shading them with something like a lawn chair will help them to quickly revive.

Outdoor Growing Care

From here on in the job is a simple one—a little maintenance, and a lot of enjoyment.

WATERING

Water deeply (unless encyclopedia directions say otherwise) about once a week if the skies do not cooperate. Shallow watering only encourages poor root systems that stay near the surface of the soil, causing the plants to dry out too quickly. If it's extremely hot or your soil is very sandy, you may need to water every five days, but however often you need to do it, never apply less than one inch of water at a time. To check this, place a coffee can half way between the sprinkler and the furthest plant it reaches. When one inch of water accumulates in the can, you'll know how long to run your sprinkler, assuming water pressure remains constant.

If disease is a potential problem, water only in the morning so the foliage does not have to go through the night wet. Otherwise, water any time, even in the heat of mid-day. It makes sense that your plants like a cooling drink of water when it's hot, just as much as you do.

FERTILIZING

Except where noted differently in the encyclopedia sections, your plants will benefit from a monthly feeding, either of a dry 5-10-5 or a solution of soluble fertilizer. The three numbers that are always on a fertilizer label signify the percentage of nitrogen, phosphorus and potash present. Nitrogen is necessary for foliage and stem growth and dark green color, phosphorus for root development and flower production, and potash (potassium) for plant metabolism and food manufacturing. For most flowering and vegetable plants, the percentage of phosphorus should be double or at the very least equal to the percentage of nitrogen. In other words, don't use your lawn fertilizer on your flowers or vegetables (or you'll have no or few flowers or vegetables).

A great boon to fertilizing ease is the relatively new slow release fertilizer. You fertilize only once, at the start of the growing season, and the food is released throughout the summer as it is needed. When the soil cools down in fall, the tiny fertilizer pellets stop releasing food. No other fertilizer should be used when using a slow release fertilizer such as Mag-Amp or Osmocote.

WEEDING AND MULCHING

Always keep the garden free of weeds. It not only shows off your good housekeeping, your flowers and vegetables also won't be robbed of food, water or light nor will disease problems that are the result of poor air circulation be invited in.

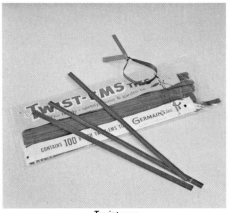

Twistems   *Bamboo Stakes*

Weeds may be pulled by hand, but be careful when doing so that you don't disrupt your plants. There are herbicides on the market you can use—some are spot killers, others prevent weed seeds from germinating. With either, handle with care and read the label very carefully.

The best weed preventative is a good mulch, which not only keeps weeds down but also keeps the ground cool, conserves moisture and is a neat finishing touch. Black plastic is becoming a very popular mulch, especially for vegetables, followed closely by a number of organic mulches which have the advantage of adding enrichment to the soil as they decompose. Buckwheat hulls, chopped leaves, hay, straw, dried grass clippings, cocoa bean hulls, bark, sawdust and wood chips make up the list for the latter.

When using mulch, always apply it after the ground has warmed up, or it will do more harm than good by keeping the soil too cool.

WINTER PROTECTION

Hardy perennials can endure sub-freezing temperatures well. However, continued thawing and freezing of the ground causes it to heave plants from the soil, sometimes resulting in the loss of the plants. After the ground has frozen, cut off all dead leaves and stems and cover the plants to a depth of six inches. Oak leaves, pine needles, salt hay, straw or any other coarse light materials are fine. A lasting snow cover is the best winter mulch nature can provide.

Newly planted perennials and biennials must be mulched over the winter as soon as the first hard freeze hits the garden.

INSECTS AND DISEASE

This book will not go into detail on how to relieve the garden of insect and disease problems. There are several reasons for this: these problems vary from state to state and climate to climate, and so do the chemicals that are available for sale. New products come on the market as others become restricted.

The best thing for you to do is to contact your Cooperative Extension County Agent to diagnose your problem and get specific recommendations for your area.

The best way to fight disease problems is to prevent them. Work clean. Keep the garden weeded, don't work in the garden when the leaves are wet, and disinfect tools from time to time. If diseased plants crop up in the garden, isolate them before they infect others.

STAKING AND TRELLISING

There are some plants, like snapdragons, delphinium and hollyhock, which grow tall or have weak stems and will therefore need some sort of support to keep them upright. The simplest way to take care of these is to place a metal or bamboo stake in the ground next to the plant and secure the stem to it with twine or "twistems" as the plant grows. Annual vines like morning glories will also need a support to grow on, which could be a wooden or metal trellis or a netting secured between two posts. It's best to avoid growing vines on wires as the wires get hot in the sun and can burn new growth and delicate tendrils.

Tomatoes (except the dwarf varieties) will need help in standing up straight. Stakes placed around the plants in three or four places and strung with twine will work nicely, but easier to use are metal tomato pens or cages.

Peas, beans, cucumbers and other plants that grow as a vine will also need something to grow on. They can be trained against trellises or netting, but there are metal fences and towers made especially for the purpose, some strung with nylon monofilament, which are easy to use, more attractive and store away compactly in the winter.

COLDFRAMES AND HOTBEDS

The coldframe should be placed high on the list of primary gardening necessities. It will hasten spring, forestall winter, protect tender plants, act as a refrigerator for bulbs and serve the gardener in all seasons to assure more successful results in many growing activities.

There are basically three types of "frames". All are bottomless boxes covered with a sash to permit maximum light to enter.

The COLDFRAME is heated externally, by sunlight.

The HEATED FRAME is one in which the AIR temperature in the plant area is artifically maintained. A greenhouse could be considered a large heated frame.

The HOTBED is one where the SOIL in which the plants grow is artificially heated.

All three of these units have common basic functions, but each has its limitations and advantages. The costs of each, both from an installation and operating standpoint, vary considerably. The home gardener's choice will be determined by the economics and the prime use intended for the "frame".

COLDFRAMES

The first consideration in the construction of a frame is to determine the size of the sash you plan to use. Perhaps you have a discarded storm door or large window sash which will dictate the size of the frame required. If not, your garden center or lumber and millwork supplier will have coldframe sash in stock, glazed or unglazed. They are available in 3 sizes: 2 x 4 ft., 3 x 3 ft., 3 x 6 ft. (standard).

It is most economical of course, to build a frame that will accommodate 2 or more sashes, particularly if the smaller sashes are used. Frame construction is the same as with a single sash except for a supporting member running from front to back of the frame where 2 butting sashes meet. The single 3 x 6 ft. frames provide greater flexibility. Redwood, cypress and cedar are most desirable, and their durability warrants their premium costs. The useful life of all these woods will be enhanced by the application of one of the copper naphthenate solutions such as Cuprinol.

Although your local lumber mill can supply you with a completely assembled or a knocked-down frame, let us assume you are a venturesome soul and prefer to build your own. Two inch planks of redwood, cedar or cypress are long lived, but the lighter weight 1 inch boards are preferable.

Decide where the frame is to be located. Set it where natural drainage prevails or you will have to provide artificial drainage under the frame. Place it, sloped back to front, facing south, protected from the winter and spring winds.

The frame should be set 6 inches into the ground and be pitched a minimum of 3 inches from rear to front to provide fast sash drainage. Most frames provide 12 inches of growing space at the rear and 9 inches at the front. Accordingly, then the rear panel must be 3 feet wide and 18 inches deep, the front panel 3 feet wide and 15 inches deep and the sides 6 feet long, 18 inches deep and tapered to 15 inches on the front end. Use 3″ x 3″ corner posts, starting flush with the top of the frame, pointed and extending 1 foot below the bottom of frame. Secure the sides to the posts using galvanized through-bolts, nuts and washers or 3″ long brass wood screws spaced 6″ apart. To keep sash from shifting use a hook and screw eye (on the sash) at each corner of the frame.

It is much easier to completely assemble the entire frame in the garage or cellar than try to assemble the parts independently on location. Be sure you can get it through the cellar door. Remember to apply a good coat of a copper preservative.

Now that the mission is accomplished, what returns might you anticipate in reward of your expense and labor? This "tool", like any other, is only productive to the extent it is used. Even part-time use will pay handsome dividends but a year-round efficiently managed coldframe will provide unlimited gardening opportunities and experiences.

In early spring, flower and vegetable seeds can be started several weeks earlier than they can be sown in the open garden. The quick growing vegetables, onion sets, radishes, turnips and early varieties of lettuce can be grown to provide an advance showing of the early spring taste delights. Seedlings of many of the hardy vegetables such as cabbage, broccoli and lettuce as well as perennials and some of the hardy annuals such as snapdragons, stocks and pansies which have been started indoors can be assigned to the coldframe for 10 days to 2 weeks for hardening off prior to out-of-doors planting.

In early summer, start perennial and biennial seeds to refurbish your flower beds next spring. Start plants of those delightful fall harvest vegetables, cauliflower, Brussels sprouts, etc. so they may be transplanted to the open garden on schedule.

In the fall you can again plant for early winter eating those same greens you enjoyed last spring. Dig up those clumps of favorite varieties of doubtfully hardy chrysanthemums, tritoma, gerbera and others and set them tight, shoulder to shoulder, well firmed in their usual depth to protect them from those few nights of deep cold temperatures beyond their endurance. Pot up your favorite bulbs, be they tulips, hyacinth, narcissus or others, and assign them to the coldframe for 6 to 8 weeks to provide spectacular living bouquets for the house during January and February. Those seeds that need stratification can also be started in the coldframe in late fall.

THE HEATED FRAME

The heated frame, economically situated between the coldframe and hotbed, will permit earlier starting than in a coldframe and assures protection against sudden freakish temperature plunges that necessitate emergency treatment under coldframe conditions.

Research and development in this field discloses that 200 watts per 3 x 6 foot frame not only provide protective temperature control but the light output, as a night supplement to daylight, induces growth. To afford uniform distribution of light and heat the wattage is distributed by using eight 25 watt, inside frosted, incandescent lamps in porcelain sockets mounted in a line on a board at the center of each 3 x 6 foot frame directly under the sash. Bulbs should be located not less than 12 inches above the soil for utmost efficiency and their operation thermostatically controlled by a sensing element within the frame to maintain air temperature, day or night, at 60 to 65 degrees. Covering the frames at night with mats, quilts or blankets and uncovering during sunlight hours will considerably reduce maintenance costs of operation.

HOTBEDS

Before the advent of rural electrification and mechanized farm equipment, the farmers resorted to the materials at hand to procure fresh produce as early in spring as possible to whet their jaded appetites after a long winter of the "keeper" crops.

The heat energy for their hotbeds resulted from the decomposition of the waste from their living tractors—horses!

Very few people, suburban or rural, have access today to stable manure nor would they, if it were available, use it to provide the heat for the hotbed. Present day hotbeds, with temperatures scientifically controlled, are a far cry from the manure heated beds of yesteryear. Once the basic installation is made, the annual work chore of rejuvenating the growing medium is a pleasure compared to the annual replacement of all materials in grandfather's hotbed.

Dig out the soil in the area within the frame about 2 feet deep. Place a 12 inch bed of cinders, firmly tamped to provide insulation and drainage. Install bronzefly screening over the gravel on top of which is placed heating cable in a continuous loop with cable loops 6 inches apart and 3 inches from frame ends and sides. Bury cable in a 1 inch layer of coarse sand. Cover sand with a protective layer of ½ inch mesh galvanized hardware cloth to safeguard the cable from mechanical damage by digging tools. If the frame is to receive plants in flats to continue growing, set them on a 3 inch bed of sand. If plants are to grow in soil, install a 6 inch layer of enriched soil directly on the 1 inch sand bed. The heating cable is activated by a sensing element placed IN THE SOIL to maintain the soil temperature at 65 degrees.

Unless you are electrically knowledgeable, it is advisable with either a heated frame or a hotbed installation to consult your Public Utility representative or a local electrical contractor to determine if you have adequate service capacity for the added use. He will also advise you of the cost of the installation and the cost of operation.

You can also buy redwood coldframes with plastic tops which automatically open at 72°F. and close at 68°F., with no electricity needed, just like magic!

Variations on this theme are outdoor plastic greenhouses approximately 9 inches high which are put in place over tender plants and seedlings in early spring to keep them warm and protected from wind and rain. Individual plastic protectors are perfect for tomatoes and peppers which normally should not be planted outside until the weather is evenly and reliably warm. These guards not only protect the plants from frost, they also seal in moisture and humidity which helps in plant growth.

CONTAINER GROWING

Container gardening allows today's mobile society to change its taste in plants and color as quickly as it can change its mind. Portable planters are becoming very popular, dotting patios, paths, entryways, decks, porches—almost anywhere. Container gardening also makes it possible to garden without a garden on terraces and rooftops high above city streets.

The basic principles of gardening apply to containers, with a few exceptions. The mix in the container is best to be a light soil-less one, a half and half by volume mixture of peat moss with perlite and/or vermiculite. If soil must be used, it should be no more than 1/3 of the total volume. Medium in containers will dry out faster than the ground will, so watering will be necessary more often, and since fertilizers don't have a deep ground to leach out into, keep your eye open for salt build-up and don't overfertilize.

STORING BULBS, RHIZOMES AND TUBERS

There are many plants, dahlias and cannas included, that are not hardy in the north but can be dug and stored indoors over the winter and replanted in spring. Instructions for when to dig these bulbs, rhizomes and tubers are given throughout the encyclopedia sections.

After digging, hose away most of the clinging soil, and place the bulbs, rhizomes or tubers in a warm spot for a week to dry. Bulbs, rhizomes and tubers should be stored in cool (45°-60° F.) but not in areas subject to freezing as unheated garages and sheds may be. An ideal way to keep them is in a sealed plastic bag that contains dry peat moss. A light dusting with a garden fungicide before storing will help keep rot away, but check the bags from time to time to make sure they are all right. Dividing, if needed, should be done before planting in the spring.

DIVIDING PERENNIALS

After growing for two or three years (sometimes more), most perennials will need to be divided. You can tell when the time is right if the clumps become too large or crowded or if flower quantity and production starts going downhill. Dig the clumps in early spring or early fall, wash the soil from the roots, and divide the clumps by hand or with a trowel or spade. Discard worn out parts of the plant, and replant the new divisions (or give them away to friends and neighbors).

Window Garden   *Window Planter*

Indoor Growing Care

There are a few simple basics to guide you into helping your house plant seedlings grow into beautiful, mature specimens.

LIGHT

Follow directions in the encyclopedia sections to a "T" regarding the amount of light to provide. Shade loving plants will burn to death in the sun, while those that need bright light will be spindly and will not bloom or even grow well if the light is not strong enough.

If the cultural directions say "full sun", place your plants in an unobstructed south window. A sheer curtain will not hurt and actually help as it allows sun to pass through while blocking out excess heat. For indirect light, a west window is best, or set the plants away from a sunny window in a brightly lit room. Low light plants like a north window or a bright room away from the sun, but don't think you can grow most of them in a dark corner. You can't. If you're a fluorescent light grower, turn to the next chapter.

HEAT

For every plant in the encyclopedia section that can be grown indoors, a temperature is given. This is the temperature the plant room should be at during the night. During sunlight hours, the temperature should be 10°F. or at the most 15°F. higher than the night time hours.

Where night temperatures should be 60-65°F., this will cause no problem in most homes since this is where the heat is primarily set at night. Those plants that need a night temperature of 50-55°F. will need to be grown in a cool solarium, sunporch, basement, attic, scantly heated room or cool greenhouse.

The steady stream of hot, dry air that comes from radiators will do serious damage to most plants growing above them, so try to avoid a window ledge with a heat source under it for your indoor garden. If you can't do that, perhaps you could shut off the heat in the radiator if there is another one in the room.

The glass in a window on a winter night is cold and can damage plants that touch it, so keep them away. Also, be on the lookout for cold drafts.

HUMIDITY

Most house plants like a humidity in the range of 30-55%. Heated homes in winter are drier than this, so you will have to take special measures to keep the moisture up. Keep your plants in saucers or trays of pebbles filled with water to just below the bottom of the pot, mist the plants with a fine spray on mornings of sunny days, grow the plants in a terrarium or indoor greenhouse or put a humidifier in the room. Plant leaves naturally transpire a lot of water vapor, so clustering plants together will help them to help themselves. Don't, however, let the plants touch each other to the extent it cuts down on air circulation, for this could be the start of disease. Plants that require 60% or more humidity should be greenhouse grown; if low humidity becomes a problem there, hose down the floor.

Humidifier

Pot Assortment

AIR CIRCULATION

Good air circulation brings carbon dioxide that the plants need for photosynthesis during the day and fresh oxygen which they need to breath day and night. Moving air also cuts down on the incidence of fungus disease. What you want is mild air movement. Cold drafts are murder and cause acute leaf drop, so be careful in winter if you open windows.

How do you provide good air circulation? If you use a humidifier, the fan will keep the air moving, or install a small fan near the garden. Try not to let the pots or plants touch each other. Fresh air from outside is beneficial and will help to keep the humidity where it belongs, especially in winter, but if it's cold outside open a window in another room and let the air temper first. In the greenhouse, open the vents on warm days to improve air circulation. The same principle that applies to cold drafts from windows, applies to air conditioners—keep your plants away from them.

POTS AND POTTING

Much controversy exists over clay vs. plastic pots, and each has advantages and dis-advantages. Clay pots do breathe, so the soil within them is cooler due to evaporation, which is great for low temperature plants. They do, however, need to be watered more often and can become unsightly with algae growth on the outside. Plastic pots are lighter, have better drainage, keep the medium within them moister for longer periods of time and are more attractive and decorative.

Whichever you choose, start with a 2½″ or so pot for a young seedling and gradually transplant it into larger pots as it grows to keep shock to a minimum.

If you use a fancy ceramic or metal container that has no drainage holes, use it as an outside container only and place your plant, pot and all, into it (double potting). Be sure to drain any excess water from the outside pot after watering.

Unless otherwise specified in the encyclopedia section, the same medium you used for sowing should be used for growing. Add additional sphagnum or peat moss if the medium needs to be richer, or more sand or perlite if it likes to be drier. Once again, try to avoid soil from the garden, for it may have insects or disease in it or will not be well drained.

WATERING

There are probably more plants killed from overwatering than from any other reason. Follow directions carefully. If they say "evenly moist", water well until water drains from the bottom of the pot, and then don't water again until the top ½ inch of medium is dry to the touch. If a plant likes to be dry between waterings, believe what it says, and let almost the entire pot dry out before watering (don't ever let it go bone dry).

How often to water is not an easy question to answer. It depends on the size of the pot, what's growing in it, the temperature, the humidity. Water when the plant needs it—you'll have to experiment for yourself to know when.

Salt Deposit on Pot   *Hyponex Plant Food*

You don't need to sing or talk to your plants, but it does do them good to be picked up and given attention from time to time. Plants are lighter when the need to be watered; they will need to be turned every so often so they will grow evenly; you can spot potential problems before they become serious.

FERTILIZING

Except where otherwise noted in the encyclopedia sections, feeding should be done once a month with a soluble fertilizer such as Hyponex, Miracle Gro, Rapid Gro, Peters or fish emulsion as long as the plant is in growth or flower.

Follow label directions exactly. To avoid uneven cycles of strong and short growth, feed at ½ of the label recommendation twice as often, or at ¼ strength four times as often.

Excessive growth and an obvious build up of salt around the rim of the pots are signs of overfertilizing. If this happens to you, flush the soil out with water for at least one-half hour or, better yet, discard the soil in the pot and start over.

CHAPTER IV

ENJOYING YOUR GARDEN

The sweet smell of success is an exhilarating one, but to double your enjoyment of the garden, expand your frontiers, or gain a deeper understanding of what's happening in the growing world, a deeper knowledge will prove rewarding. The following pages will plant the seeds of a few ideas in your mind.

Cut Flowers

There's nothing more delightful than bringing the color and the beauty of the garden indoors. Throughout the encyclopedia, many flowers are designated as "cut flowers" because they have long stems and a lasting quality in a vase.

The flowers should be picked just as buds are opening, either early in the morning or late in the afternoon or evening when moisture and sugar content are high. Cut the stems at an angle with a sharp knife or scissors and place them immediately into warm water. Bring the flowers into the house and re-cut the stems under water to bring maximum moisture to the petals. Remove any foliage that will be under water and "harden" the blooms by storing them in a cool, dark place or refrigerator for at least two hours and preferably overnight.

Now it's time to be creative—place your cut flowers in a vase or make an exotic arrangement.

Drying Flowers

During the dreariest winter days, your home may be made brighter and more cheerful with the use of colorful dried everlasting flowers. Everlastings are flowers that retain their shape, substance and other characteristics after being dried.

The trick for good dried flowers is to know when to pick them and how to dry them:

Achillea - (YARROW) - Cut before fully open; air dry or dessicant dry in a horizontal position.

Allium - (FLOWERING ONION) - Cut when partially open; air dry or dessicant dry, wiring first. Spray with gold or silver paint for decoration and preservation.'

Ammobium - (WINGED EVERLASTING) - Cut flowers before they mature; air dry.

Anaphalis - (PEARLY EVERLASTING) - Pick while foliage is still white and air dry.

Catananche - (CUPID'S DART) - Cut just as the flowers open, air or dessicant dry.

Celosia - (COCK'S COMB) - Cut when seeds begin to form in the lower flowers and air dry.

Circium - (THISTLE) - Cut as heads start to open and air dry.

Daucus carota - (QUEEN ANNE'S LACE) - Cut when flower heads are 2/3 open; dessicant dry.

Echinops - (GLOBE THISTLE) - Pick as heads just begin to open; air dry. Spray for added protection.

Emilia - (PAINT BRUSH) - Cut as seeds start to form and air dry.

Eryngium - (SEA HOLLY) - Cut when well developed but not overmature and air dry.

Gomphrena - (GLOBE AMARANTH) - Cut blooms when mature (late summer) and air dry.

Gypsophila - (BABY'S BREATH) - Cut when flowers are well formed and fully open; air dry.

Helichrysum - (STRAWFLOWER) - Cut just before center petals open; air or dessicant dry, wiring before drying.

Helipterum - (EVERLASTING) - Cut as soon as the buds show color, for the flowers open as they air dry. Wire before drying.

Limonium - (STATICE) - Cut blooms when at their best, fully open, and air dry.

Lunaria - (MONEY PLANT) - Gather plants as they start to brown and rub off the outer petals to expose the central translucent discs. Air dry.

Merremia - (WOODROSE) - Gather carefully just before seed pods mature; air dry.

Molucella - (BELLS OF IRELAND) - Cut when flower spikes are mature and open and remove leaves and spines. Air dry.

Nigella - (LOVE-IN-A-MIST) - To dry seed pods, cut stems when pods are mature and air dry or dessicant dry.

Physalis - (CHINESE LANTERN) - Pick when lower seed pods turn red. No further treatment is necessary—just slip into a vase or arrangement.

Xeranthemum - (IMMORTELLE) - Cut when flowers are fully open and air dry.

Ornamental Grasses - Cut spikes while in full head, air dry.

AIR DRYING

Cut the flowers in the stage of development indicated to achieve maximum color and lasting qualities, and never when they are wet from dew or rain. Strip leaves and tie the flowers in small bunches. Then, hang them upside down in a dark, ventilated attic, basement or out of the way place and let them dry for two or three weeks. Some types of flowers should have a wire twisted around the stem or pushed through the center of the flower before drying, for support later on.

DESSICANT DRYING

The flowers mentioned here, plus so many of your garden favorites (zinnias, marigolds, dahlias, mums, snapdragons, roses and many, many more), are perfect for dessicant drying, whether it be silica gel, sand or borax. Pick blooms that are as perfect as possible and in the stage you want to dry them for your preservation efforts.

Place 2″ of silica gel in a cookie container, cake tin or other sealable can and lay the flowers on it face up. Be careful not to let the flowers touch each other. Then sprinkle silica gel over the flowers until they are completely covered. Cover tightly and seal shut with tape for two to six days. When the flowers are ready, they will feel crisp or papery to the touch.

When finished, pour the mixture off slowly and gently lift out the flowers, blowing away any particles that stick to the petals. Store the flowers in a dark place in a sealed, air-tight container which contains several tablespoons of silica gel. For use in arrangements, use dried flowers only in the winter when the house is dry from the heat, as humidity ruins them.

Silica gel may be reused if reactivated in a 250°F. oven for one hour. Silica gel sold for flower drying has blue crystals in it which lose their color when the silica gel needs rejuvenation.

Flowers may also be dried in borax or fine sand. The method is similar with two exceptions - the flowers should be placed face down and the lid should be left off the container while drying is going on. It takes twice as long to dry flowers with borax or sand than with silica gel, and the color is not retained as vividly.

Growing Under Lights

Is your indoor growing hampered by short days, limited light, small windowsills? The solution is simple and will lead you to enjoy your indoor gardening to its fullest extent— fluorescent light gardening.

Growing under lights allows you to fool Mother Nature. Light intensity, light duration, temperature, water, humidity and air movement are in your hands. That's better than Mother Nature can do. Besides, fluorescent light gardening is easy, fun and an excellent way to pass the time, relax, learn or relieve tensions.

Fluorescent light gardens can be put any place—under shelves, on bookcases, on kitchen counters. Put them in full view in one of the living areas, or hide them away in attics, basements, closets or spare rooms.

ABOUT LIGHTS

Looking back to high school Physics, remember that all visible light is made up of wavelengths within the red, orange, yellow, green, blue, indigo and violet regions of the spectrum. White lights that we read by are strong in the center blue, green and yellow wavelength regions which do little or nothing for a plant's growth. A plant uses blue to violet light to produce foliage and regulate respiration, and orange and red light for growth, maturity and flowering.

Knowing these facts will help you to choose the correct lights for your purposes. Many of the early growth lights were low in the far red wavelength region of the spectrum needed for flowering, and so they were combined with incandescent lamps which are strong in far red. Incandescent lamps are, unfortunately, inefficient and become very hot. Household cool white (strong in blue and green) and warm white (high in red and orange) are combined successfully for use with low to medium light requirement plants. After many years of research, new high intensity plant lights are on the market which resemble full sun very closely and contain the proper amount of blue, red and far red for plant life.

How much light do you give your plants and what types of lamps should you use? This is the meaning of intensity, and it depends on what you are growing. Those plants that grow in shade or indirect light are low light intensity plants; those that need full sun are high light intensity plants. Among the more common are:

LOW LIGHT PLANTS (Use warm-white and cool-white combined or Gro-Lux lights)

Abutilon, African Violet, Begonia, Croton, Cyclamen, Episcia, Impatiens, Pentas, Primrose, Sinningia—In addition, all green foliage plants fit in this category.

HIGH LIGHT PLANTS (Use Gro-Lux Wide Spectrum, Agro-Lite or Vita-Lite)

Cacti and other Succulents, Calceolaria, Calla, Cineraria, Exacum, Fuchsia, Geranium, Kalanchoe, Lantana, Orchids, Passiflora, Roses (Miniature), Schizanthus, Streptocarpus. Plus these, grow all annuals, herbs, perennials and vegetables under high intensity light until they are moved into the garden.

HOW CLOSE?

The next question always is "How close should my plants be to the lights?" That is a hard question to answer since it depends on many variables, such as the number of tubes, how close

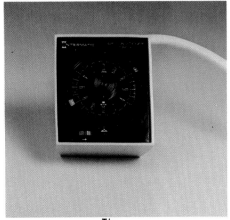
Timer

Plants in Gro-light

together they are, how long they are and if reflectors are used. All of these factors influence intensity to some degree. The best answer is trial and error. If the plants are very compact, and the leaves turning downward or looking sunburned, they are getting too much light. Move the plants or the lights further away. If the leaves and stems stretch upward and plants do not flower as they should, more light is needed.

The following distances from the top of the plant to the light are good starting ones, and then experiment from there:

African Violets—4-8"
Annuals, Herbs, Perennials, Vegetables—3-6"
Begonias—6-8"
Cactus and other Succulents—3-6"
Episcia—6-10"
Foliage Plants—4-10"
Geraniums—4-6"
Orchids—4-6"
Roses, Miniature—4-6"
Sinningia—4-6"
Streptocarpus—3-6"

HOW LONG?

The final question always is "How long should the lights burn?" This is important, for lights must burn a certain number of hours per day and, if possible, at the same time every day. Use an automatic timer to turn your lights on and off for you lest you forget.

Lights should be on 24 hours a day on seed flats of annuals, vegetables, herbs and perennials until germination occurs, after which the light duration should be cut down to 12 - 14 hours. Most flowering house plants like 14 - 16 hours of light, while foliage plants do well under 12 - 14 hours of light.

Be aware that some plants are affected by photoperiodism; that is, they will bloom only when their requirements of dark duration are met. And when it is dark, it must be totally dark; no stray lights should hit the plants at all.

Plants that like short "nights," or 14 - 18 hours of light during the "day," include tuberous begonias and some annuals. There are many more "long night" plants that need only 10 hours of light per "day" to flower, and these include cineraria, mums, cyclamen, kalanchoe and gardenias.

Other than light control, care of fluorescent garden plants is the same as that outlined for house plants in Chapter III.

Landscape View

Landscape View

Using Plants In The Garden

Using plants correctly and harmoniously in the garden will enable you to enjoy it more as it will be more attractive and/or productive.

Before you do any planting in your flower or vegetable garden ... plan! Use ruled or graph paper and set everything out to scale well in advance. This way, you'll know what you need and how many plants of each to grow. If there is a fence or screen in the back of the garden—marvelous. Put tall plants against it and work down gradually to the lower ones in front so they will be seen to their fullest and will not shade each other.

The garden plans outlined on pages 353-355 are a general guide to attractive and efficient use of Mother Earth. If they are too large or too small, scale them down or up to fit your needs. Garden designs are a personal thing and only *you* know what best expresses your personality.

Straight-edged garden beds are stiff and rigid and generally more formal than curved ones. Exercise a little restraint when you design the bed to keep it from being gaudy or overpowering. Make the most of natural or existing plants or features like a wishing well or pond. Also, the garden should be in keeping with the style of the house and blend and merge with it in some way. Find a unifying theme; shrubbery makes a good transition, as does complementary color.

Also consider the view from the house or patio when designing the garden. A pretty vista while you're relaxing makes life much more enjoyable.

Start small. Think of upkeep, and don't plant any more than you (or your spouse) can care for. If you managed nicely this year with what you planted, then you can expand the garden and the enjoyment next year. Keep the garden simple—it's not, or shouldn't be, a botanical garden. Your plants will be much more effective if massed in groups of at least three of a variety rather than having the garden contain one of everything you can grow.

Remember to leave paths through the garden so it can be easily worked and enjoyed from all angles. Paths should be at least two feet wide so lawnmowers, wheelbarrows and visitors can easily pass through.

Color and color harmony are the magic words in creating the drama of the garden. Bold and warm reds, yellows and oranges convey excitement; cooler tones of blue and violet are more relaxing. Borders can be all of one color and shades of that color, but more interesting is a garden with contrasting colors. Just be careful that colors don't clash. Use white as a buffer between two strongly colored plants, or substitute something with showy foliage.

If you're designing a perennial garden, think not only of height and color but also of blooming time, and plan it so there is a succession of flowers throughout the season. Everblooming roses and annuals can be used to tie the blooming period into a unified knot.

Throughout the encyclopedia pages, best uses are given for each plant. Those for edgings and borders are low growing, neat and tidy. A border plant does well in a group of three or five mixed with other flowers. A bedding plant is relatively low growing and floriferous, perfect for mass plantings. Hedges can be any height, but the plants recommended for them are dense and compact. Low growing, somewhat spreading or clinging plants are perfect as ground covers or in rock gardens. If it grows tall or as a trained vine, expect to use it as a screen or background. If it's suitable for container growing, the designation says "planters"; if it's so magnificent it can stand alone, it's a specimen.

Look for All-America Selections winners when you choose annual and vegetable seeds. These are plants that were put through rigorous tests in gardens all over the country and came out as the best new plants of the year.

Plant Families

To get botanical for a moment, a plant family is a grouping of genera that closely or uniformly resemble each other in general appearance or technical characteristics. Some families have only one genus; others have hundreds of genera. Many clues about a plant can be obtained from knowing its family—type of plant, flower form, general cultural requirements and often seed characteristics and germination requirements. Although there are many hundreds of plant families, only those that encompass plants commonly grown from seed are listed here. At the end of the description are listed the best known plants within the family.

ACANTHACEAE - (Acanthus Family)
Tropical, high humidity and sun loving plants are tender perennials or house plants and have five lobed flowers in racemes.
Acanthus, Crossandra, Hypoestes, Justicia, Thunbergia.

AGARICACEAE - (Mushroom Family)
These fungi produce an umbrella shaped cap on a stalk and grow in dark, moist, extremely rich conditions.
Agaricus.

AGAVACEAE - (Agave Family)
Plants like warm conditions and dry soil and grow in rosettes or branched tree-like plants with spikes of flowers.
Yucca.

AIZOACEAE - (Carpetweed Family)
Subtropical succulents love sun and well drained, gravelly soil and are heat tolerant. Fleshy-leaved plants have showy daisy-like flowers.
Lithops, Mesembryanthemum.

ALSTROEMERIACEAE - (Alstroemeria Family)
Parallel veined plants like tropical or warm conditions, have lily-like flowers.
Alstroemeria.

AMARANTHACEAE - (Amaranth Family)
Many weeds are in this family, but there are a few ornamental annuals and perennials which have no petals but, instead, highly colored scales that grow into plumes. Seeds germinate easily.
Amaranthus, Celosia, Gomphrena.

AMARYLLIDACEAE - (Amaryllis Family)
Mostly bulbous plants have strap-shaped leaves and lily-like flowers. They like tropical and warm temperatures and are semi-succulent, so do not overwater.
Agapanthus, Allium, Clivia, Hippeastrum.

ANACARDIACEAE - (Cashew Family)
This family contains trees and shrubs, mostly tropical, but a few from temperate climates. Some are toxic, others edible.
Harpephyllum.

APOCYNACEAE - (Dogbane Family)
Tender perennials, including many vines, have milky juice, distinctive seed pods and 5-parted phlox-like flowers.
Catharanthus.

AQUIFOLIACEAE - (Holly Family)
Hardy trees and shrubs, deciduous or evergeen, have single flowers, usually toothed leaves and berries on the female plant.
Ilex.

ARACEAE - (Arum Family)
Tropical, heat loving plants, for the most part, good candidates for the home. They often have attractively lobed leaves, and the flower is a spathe and spadix, many times highly colored. Plant them in rich, fertile soil and sow the seeds of most genera immediately as they are not long lived.
Anthurium, Monstera, Philodendron, Zantedeschia.

ARALIACEAE - (Aralia or Ginseng Family)
Herbs, trees and shrubs of temperate and tropical climates make excellent house plants. Leaves are large and compound and the flowers, which rarely appear in the house, have 5 to 10 petals.
Brassaia, Dizygotheca, Meryta, Schefflera.

ASCLEPIADACEAE - (Milkweed Family)
Semi-succulent vines and perennials withstand conditions from cold to tropical depending on the genus, but all have milky juice, hourglass flowers and are drought resistant.
Asclepias, Hoya, Oxypetalum, Stephanotis.

BALSAMINACEAE - (Balsam Family)
Warm climate succulent herbs with watery stems are excellent annuals and house plants. The flowers are showy, pastel, single and spurred; the pods explode easily so the plants self-seed readily.
Impatiens.

BASELLACEAE - (Basella Family)
Sub-tropical vines have small flowers in racemes or spikes.
Anredera.

BEGONIACEAE - (Begonia Family)
Tender tropical or sub-tropical plants are good for the home or as annuals. They are semi-succulent with showy single flowers and often times decorative foliage.
Begonia.

BIGNONIACEAE - (Bignonia Family)
Mostly tropical trees and vines have large, showy flowers.
Campsis, Jacaranda.

BORAGINACEAE - (Borage Family)
Annual and perennial plants are rough and hairy, easy to grow and have tubular flowers (usually blue) in sprays that resemble a question mark. Seeds germinate easily.
Anchusa, Cynoglossum, Echium, Myosotis.

BYTTNERIACEAE - (Byttneria Family)
Tropical trees and shrubs have balls of single flowers and are often found in greenhouses in the north.
Dombeya.

CACTACEAE - (Cactus Family)
Bizarre succulents, mostly tropical, have no leaves but thick fleshy stems and are usually spined. Flowers are showy; seeds are fine. These plants tolerate heat and lack of water.
Many genera.

CAMPANULACEAE - (Bellflower Family)
Herbaceous plants from the temperate region have 5-lobed, bell shaped flowers that are mostly blue. Flowers bloom in spikes from the bottom up.
Campanula, Jasione, Platycodon.

CANNABACEAE - (Hemp Family)
Aromatic vines have deeply lobed leaves and are grown for economic value.
Humulus.

CANNACEAE - (Canna Family)
This is a one-genus family of tall, large leaved plants with showy flowers that grow from rhizomes. Seeds need scarification before sowing.
Canna.

CAPPARACEAE - (Caper Family)
Herbs, shrubs, trees and annuals have 4-petaled blooms in clusters.
Capparis, Cleome.

CAPRIFOLIACEAE - (Honeysuckle Family)
Shrubs and sometimes vines are hardy with brightly colored tubular flowers that are usually fragrant. Seeds need stratification to break dormancy.
Viburnum.

CARYOPHYLLACEAE - (Pink Family)
Short lived annuals and perennials like full sun and a well drained alkaline soil. Flowers are notched and fragrant on plants with narrow leaves and swollen joints.
Arenaria, Cerastium, Dianthus, Gypsophila, Herniaria, Lychnis, Sagina, Saponaria.

CHENOPODIACEAE — (Goosefoot Family)
Some members of this family will tolerate marshes and high salt, alkaline soil. The family includes several vegetables—beets, Swiss chard, spinach.
Beta, Kochia.

CISTACEAE - (Rock Rose Family)
Small shrubs and bushy herbs are perennials and annuals with sepals that hang on longer than the petals.
Helianthemum.

COMMELINACEAE - (Spiderwort Family)
This family of watery-stemmed annuals, perennials and houseplants loves moisture and rich soil. There are three petals and three sepals per flower.
Tradescantia.

COMPOSITAE - (Composite Family)
The largest and most widely distributed family is this group of sun loving annuals and perennials that are the daisies of the garden. The thin seeds are easily germinated and grown. The family even contains a few vegetables like globe artichoke, endive and lettuce.
Achillea, Ageratum, Anthemis, Aster, Calendula, Chrysanthemum, Cosmos, Dahlia, Doronicum, Gaillardia, Gerbera, Helianthus, Rudbeckia, Senecio, Tagetes, Zinnia.

CONVOLVULACEAE - (Morning Glory Family)
Twisting annual vines with weak stems have large, brightly colored, funnel shaped flowers. Seeds need to be nicked or soaked prior to germination.
Dichondra, Ipomoea, Merremia, Mina.

CORNACEAE- (Dogwood Family)
Temperate climate trees and shrubs have four showy petal-like bracts surrounding inconspicuous flowers, followed by decorative fruits.
Cornus.

CORYNOCARPACEAE - (Corynocarpus Family)
Evergreen trees make good indoor plants in temperate regions. Flowers are single.
Corynocarpus.

CRASSULACEAE - (Orpine Family)
Temperate and tropical succulent plants with fleshy foliage, often in rosettes. Flowers appear in showy clusters. Give this family full sun and dry soil.
Echeveria, Kalanchoe, Sedum, Sempervivum.

CRUCIFERAE - (Mustard Family)
Annuals, perennials and hot or sharp tasting vegetables and herbs have clusters of 4-petaled flowers that are arranged in a cross. Seeds germinate easily.
Alyssum, Aurinia, Brassica, Hesperis, Iberis, Matthiola, Nasturtium.

CUCURBITACEAE - (Gourd Family)
This is an important economic family, containing pumpkins, melons, cucumbers and squash. Large and often odd shaped fruits follow trumpet shaped flowers on easy and quick growing vines.
Cucurbita, Lagenaria, Luffa.

CUPRESSACEAE - (Cypress Family)
Evergreen, coniferous trees and shrubs have flat, scale-like leaves and woody or berry- like cones.
Cupressus.

CYPERACEAE - (Sedge Family)
Leaves are grass-like and clustered at the top of long, slender triangular stems. The plants grow in swampy and other wet areas.
Cyperus.

DIPSACACEAE - (Teasel Family)
Annuals and perennials often have prickly stems and water is held at the base of the leaf.
Scabiosa.

ELAEAGNACEAE - (Oleaster Family)
Hardy trees and shrubs have leaves which are covered with silvery or golden scales, usually on the undersides.
Elaeagnus.

ERICACEAE - (Heath Family)
Cool climate small trees and shrubs are either broad-leaved evergreens or deciduous and prefer part shade and acid soil.
Agapetes, Calluna, Kalmia, Rhododendron.

EUPHORBIACEAE - (Spurge Family)
Tropical plants are frequently cactus-like; the sap is milky and sometimes toxic. Many members of the family have showy, colored bracts.
Codiaeum, Euphorbia, Ricinus.

FUMARIACEAE - (Fumitory Family)
Annual or perennial plants have heart shaped flowers. The ferny foliage gives off nitrous fumes when pulled. They like part shade.
Corydalis, Dicentra.

GENTIANACEAE - (Gentian Family)

Cool climate annuals and perennials have tubular flowers mostly of rich blue.
Exacum, Gentiana.

GERANIACEAE - (Geranium Family)

Semi-woody annuals and perennials have leaves that are often scented and 5-petaled flowers in showy umbels. Some seeds in this family need scarification before sowing.
Geranium, Pelargonium.

GESNERIACEAE - (Gesneria Family)

Plants from hot moist jungles have thick, hairy leaves that dislike having water on them. Flowers are tube shaped and showy. The members of this family prefer part shade; the seeds are very fine.
Achimenes, Aeschynanthus, Episcia, Gloxinia, Saintpaulia, Sinningia, Streptocarpus.

GINKGOACEAE - (Ginkgo Family)

There's only one plant in this family, the ginkgo, which has fan shaped leaves. Seeds must be stratified to break dormancy.
Ginkgo.

GLOBULARIACEAE - (Globularia Family)

This is a small family of small growing shrubs or perennials that have tiny flowers and like full sun.
Globularia.

GRAMINEAE - (Grass Family)

Annuals and perennials have linear leaves and flowers in spikelets. Some perennial forms spread by underground stolons or rhizomes. The family has ornamental and economic value.
Agrostis, Avena, Briza, Coix, Cortaderia, Hordeum, Lagurus, Pennisetum, Setaria, Stipa, Zea.

HYDROPHYLLACEAE - (Waterleaf Family)

These plants like damp, shady spots and have splotches on their leaves that look like water marks. Flowers appear in curved spikes.
Nemophila.

HYPERICACEAE - (Hypericum Family)

Temperate and tropical perennials and shrubs have coarse leaves and 5-petaled yellow flowers.
Hypericum.

IRIDACEAE - (Iris Family)
Members of this family have narrow, sword shaped leaves and flower parts mostly in 3's, and are available in a wide range of colors. This family encompasses hardy perennials, summer bulbs and greenhouse plants.
Belamcanda, Freesia, Gladiolus, Iris.

LABIATAE - (Mint Family)
This family of herbs, shrubs and perennials contains plants with square stems and 2-lipped flowers (often blue or purple) in clusters or spikes. Many have aromatic leaves. Many of the members can become invasive.
Coleus, Lavandula, Mentha, Molucella, Monarda, Nepeta, Physostegia, Salvia, Thymus.

LEGUMINOSAE - (Pea Family)
A family of ornamentals and food has compound leaves and pea-like flowers. These plants have the ability to live in mutual cooperation with certain nitrogen fixing bacteria (*Rhizobium* species) which collect nitrogen from the air and fix it in the soil. Seeds form in pods and most must be scarified before sowing.
Albizia, Baptisia, Caesalpina, Cassia, Cercis, Cytisus, Laburnum, Lathrus, Lupinus, Mimosa, Phaseolus, Sophora, Wisteria.

LILIACEAE - (Lily Family)
These plants produce narrow, grass-like leaves and flower parts mostly in 3's. Most members of the family are herbaceous; some members of the family have scaly bulbs.
Aloe, Asparagus, Gloriosa, Hemerocallis, Kniphofia, Lilium, Liriope, Trillium.

LINACEAE - (Flax Family)
Hardy perennials and annuals like cool weather and have 5-petaled blue flowers in spikes or racemes. They self sow readily.
Linum.

LOASACEAE - (Loasa Family)
Hardy perennials, shrubs or vines are rough and hairy and have single flowers.
Eucnide, Mentzelia.

LOBELLIACEAE - (Lobelia Family)
Annuals and perennials have flowers that are 5-lobed and 2-lipped.
Lobelia.

LOGANIACEAE - (Logania Family)
Sub-tropical and temperate climate shrubs have slender, funnel shaped flowers in spikes. *Buddleia.*

LYTHRACEAE - (Loosestrife Family)
Annuals, perennials and shrubs have long, highly colored, tubular flowers. *Cuphea, Lagerstroemia, Lythrum.*

MAGNOLIACEAE - (Magnolia Family)
Tropical and temperate shrubs and trees have large showy flowers and cone shaped fruits. *Magnolia.*

MALVACEAE - (Mallow Family)
Temperate and tropical perennials, annuals, trees and shrubs with large, showy, hoop skirt blossoms and a club-like pistil that protrudes from the center of the flower. Seeds are easy to germinate. *Abutilon, Alcea, Gossypium, Hibiscus, Malva.*

MARTYNIACEAE - (Martynia Family)
Tropical and subtropical plants are sticky and hairy, with 5-lobed flowers and curious fruit. *Proboscidea.*

MORACEAE - (Mulberry Family)
Trees, vines and shrubs have small flowers usually in spikes or heads followed by fruits, some of which are edible. *Ficus.*

MUSACEAE - (Banana Family)
Large tropical plants and trees have huge, stiff leaves and unique, showy flowers. *Ensete.*

MYRTACEAE - (Myrtle Family)
Tropical and sub-tropical trees and shrubs have dots on their leaves and are valued for their aromatic, volatile oils. *Eucalyptus.*

NEPENTHACEAE - (Nepenthes Family)
Tropical insectivorous plants require very rich and moist growing conditions. These more or less climbing plants have simple leathery leaves with pitchers on the elongated midribs. The flowers are small and greenish. *Nepenthes.*

NYCTAGINACEAE - (Four-O'Clock Family)
Night flowering tender perennials and annuals have flowers which open in the late afternoon and often have showy bracts instead of petals.
Bougainvillaea, Mirabilis.

NYMPHAEACEAE - (Water Lily Family)
This family of aquatic plants has large floating leaves and showy flowers rising from submerged rootstocks.
Nymphaea.

OLEACEAE - (Olive Family)
Tropical and temperate trees and shrubs have star shaped, tubular, frequently fragrant flowers.
Jasminum.

ONAGRACEAE - (Evening Primrose Family)
Annuals and both tender and hardy perennials have showy, scented flowers with parts in multiples of 4's, and large seed pods.
Clarkia, Fuchsia, Oenothera,

PAEONIA - (Peony Family)
Coarse perennials have compound leaves and showy, double or single flowers.
Paeonia.

PALMAE - (Palm Family)
Tropical, tree-like woody plants have trunks topped with clusters of huge compound leaves. Indoors, they like part shade, moist soil and high humidity. Seeds have a hard coat and often take a long time to germinate.
Chamaedorea, Livistona, Washingtonia.

PAPAVERACEAE - (Poppy Family)
Showy flowers have four petals; foliage is deeply cut; the stems carry milky or colored sap. Annuals and hardy perennials prefer cool weather.
Eschscholzia, Hunnemannia, Meconopsis, Papaver.

PASSIFLORACEAE - (Passionflower Family)
Herbaceous and climbing tropical plants with highly colored bizarre flowers with fringed centers.
Passiflora.

PEDALIACEAE - (Pedalium Family)
Annual and perennial herbs are native to the tropics and sub-tropics and have oily leaves and 5-lobed tubular flowers.
Sesamum.

PINACEAE - (Pine Family)
Coniferous trees and shrubs are evergreen, hardy, and have linear leaves.
Picea, Pinus.

PIPERACEAE - (Pepper Family)
Tropical plants have ornamental foliage and are semi-succulent, so do not overwater.
Peperomia.

PITTOSPORACEAE - (Pittosporum Family)
Evergreen, tender trees and shrubs have leathery leaves and small but showy flowers.
Pittosporum.

PLUMBAGINACEAE - (Plumbago Family)
Perennials and small shrubs with tiny, tubular flowers on spikes. All members of the family tolerate salt spray and alkaline soils.
Armeria, Limonium, Plumbago.

POLEMONIACEAE - (Phlox Family)
Annuals and perennials have showy, bright colored flowers in loose clusters. The flower parts are in multiples of 5's.
Cobaea, Ipomopsis, Phlox, Polemonium.

POLYGONACEAE - (Buckwheat Family)
Trees, shrubs, hardy perennials and vines have tiny flowers in sprays and stems with swollen joints. Seeds are 3-edged.
Cobaea, Ipomopsis, Phlox, Polemonium.

POLYPODIACEAE- (Polypody Family)
Most of the more common ferns belong to this family whose habitats range from the tropics to moist temperate woods. Sexual propagation of **Polypodiaceae** members is by spores rather than seeds. Many have ornamental pinnately compound leaves or fronds.
Adiantum, Asplenium, Nephrolepsis, Pteris.

PORTULACACEAE- (Purslane Family)
These spreading succulent annuals and herbs have 5-petaled flowers and prefer sunny locations and dry soil.
Lewisia, Portulaca, Talinum.

PRIMULACEAE - (Primrose Family)
Cool climate, moisture and shade loving plants are tender or hardy perennials with 5-petaled flowers in clusters or borne singly.
Cyclamen, Dodecatheon, Primula.

PROTEACEAE - (Protea Family)
Unusual but beautiful flowers bloom on sub-tropical plants from the arid regions of the southern hemisphere. The plants love heat and drought.
Grevillea.

PUNICACEA - (Pomegranate Family)
Bushy sub-tropical shrubs have large red or yellow flowers and red, edible fruit.
Punica.

RANUNCULACEAE - (Buttercup Family)
Annuals and perennials of the mild and colder zones have cut-leaf foliage and primarily single flowers. They thrive in moist soils; many go dormant after flowering. Seeds of many genera need stratification to break dormancy.
Aconitum, Anemone, Aquilegia, Clematis, Delphinium, Eranthis, Helleborus, Nigella, Ranunculus, Trollius.

RESEDACEAE - (Mignonette Family)
Annuals or perennials prefer cool climates and have very fragrant flowers in spikes or racemes.
Reseda.

ROSACEAE - (Rose Family)
Hardy perennials, trees and shrubs have compound leaves and single flowers.
Dryas, Fragaria, Geum, Potentilla, Rosa.

RUBIACEAE - (Madder Family)
Tropical plants grow very large and have tube or funnel shaped flowers.
Coffea, Gardenia, Pentas.

RUTACEAE - (Rue Family)
Mostly tropical and sub-tropical plants with a few herbaceous perennials are woody, aromatic and bear fragrant flowers. Some have edible fruits.
Dictamnus.

SARRACENIACEAE - (Pitcher Plant Family)
Temperate and tropical insectivorous plants like warm, moist and acid conditions. They have hollow, tubular leaves.
Darlingtonia.

SAXIFRAGIACEAE - (Saxifrage Family)
Basal rosettes of decorative leaves surround naked flower stems topped with spikes or clusters of single flowers. Members of the family prefer part shade and moist soil.
Astilbe, Bergenia, Heuchera, Saxifraga.

SCROPHULARIACEAE - (Figwort Family)
Annuals and perennials prefer cool temperatures and have flowers which are typically irregular, some with curious mouths.
Antirrhinum, Asarina, Calceolaria, Digitalis, Erínus, Linaria, Mimulus, Penstemon, Tetranema, Veronica.

SOLANACEAE - (Nightshade Family)
This family of ornamentals and vegetables contains both annuals and perennials that have star-shaped flowers and are strongly scented. They are all easy to grow from seed.
Browallia, Capsicum, Cyphomandra, Lycopersicon, Nicotiana, Nierembergia, Petunia, Physalis, Salpiglossis, Schizanthus, Solanum.

STRELITZIACEAE - (Strelitzia Family)
Large tropical and sub-tropical plants have large showy leaves and highly unusual flowers.
Strelitzia.

TAXACEAE - (Yew Family)
Slow growing sub-tropical and temperate evergreen trees and shrubs have dark, glossy green, needle-like leaves.
Taxus.

THEACEAE - (Tea Family)
Evergreen trees and shrubs need warm regions. Leaves are leathery, flowers single and showy. Seeds need stratification before sowing.
Camellia, Franklinia.

THYMELAEACEAE - (Mezereum Family)

Trees and shrubs of tropical and temperate regions having clusters of tiny 5-lobed flowers. *Daphne.*

TROPAEOLACEAE - (Nasturtium Family)

Quick growing vining annuals having succulent stems, showy flowers and edible seeds, leaves, flower buds and young fruits. *Tropaeolum.*

UMBELLIFERAE - (Carrot Family)

Most members of this family are used for food and flavoring. Members have cut, strongly scented foliage and flowers in flat terminal clusters. Most are easily grown from seed. *Angelica, Carum, Coriandrum, Daucus, Eryngium.*

URTICACEAE - (Nettle Family)

Creeping plants, mostly tropical, having hairy leaves and inconspicuous flowers. *Pilea.*

VERBENACEAE - (Vervain Family)

Mostly tropical plants, grown as house plants and annuals, have rough, notched leaves and dense flower heads. *Lantana, Verbena.*

VIOLACEAE - (Violet Family)

Temperate and topical plants like moist, rich growing conditions. Flowers have five petals and look like faces. *Viola.*

ZINGIBERACEAE - (Ginger Family)

Aromatic tropical plants commonly grown under glass have cane-like stems and showy flowers. *Hedychium.*

Native Habitat

Maybe you can't tell a book by its cover, but you can tell a lot about a plant and its culture by knowing its native habitat. If it comes from the tropics, it will need a greenhouse, be a house plant, or grow as an annual. If its home is a mountainous area, it will favor cool climates. If from a desert, keep it in the sun and a dry, gravelly soil. If a plant is distributed over a large area, it will withstand a variety of conditions. This book can't teach you geography, but the more of it you know, the better you'll understand what to do for your plants.

Hardiness

Enjoyment of your garden comes with success. One last thing to look at is hardiness. Don't try to grow plants that will not withstand the temperatures of your area. The map on page 356 will give you a good idea of the hardiness zone in which you live and the average minimum temperature you can expect in winter.

Be aware, however, that lines between zones are not strict ones, and that the zones can vary slightly in either direction depending on local conditions. Microclimates can also influence the minimum temperatures in your area and the plants you can grow. Cold air runs down and collects at the bottom of a hill, so if you garden there, you may need to choose hardier plants than your neighbors. Fences and dense plant barriers can block winds and trap heat and often allow you to grow plants of a higher zone.

CHAPTER V

GROWING ORNAMENTALS

FROM SEED

On the following pages are hundreds of ornamental annuals, perennials, biennials, trees, shrubs and pot plants that may be raised from seed. The encyclopedia is easy to read; follow along with the explanation of *Abutilon hybridum.*

l) **Abutilon hybridum** - Botanical name. The plants listed in the encyclopedia are alphabetically arranged by botanical name; if you know only the common name, the botanical name can be found in the Cross Reference Index in the Appendix.

If more than one botanical name is listed, it is because two or more genera or species are grouped together due to similar habit, germination and culture. When there are a number of species treated in one listing, they are each explained under HABIT and the heading reads, for example, **Asparagus** species.

If, on the other hand, a second botanical name is listed and is in parentheses, the second name is one that was formerly accepted or is currently and incorrectly used.

All botanical names conform with **Hortus Third.**

2) FLOWERING MAPLE - Common name. If more than one common name is in use, it is also listed.

3) POT PLANT - Category of the plant, be it ANNUAL, BIENNIAL, PERENNIAL OR POT PLANT. See Chapter II for a complete definition of these terms.

4) *Malvaceae* - Plant family. See Chapter IV for a brief general description of the various plant families.

5) Native to South America - Native Habitat.

6) Zone 10 - Hardiness zone. See page 356 for the hardiness map.

7) **USES** - How best to use the particular plant. See Chapter IV for a full report.

8) **HABIT** - A description of the plant, including size, foliage characteristics, flower shape and color, etc.

9) **GERMINATION:** How and when to sow and germinate the seeds. Refer to Chapter I and II for complete directions on sowing and special treatments. Remember that germination time given may vary by 25% in either direction.

10) **CULTURE** - The basic requirements for successful growing after the seeds have germinated. See Chapter III for more details.

11) **EASY** - Plants that are easy to germinate and grow. If you're a beginner, start here.

Abutilon   *Acanthus*

Abutilon hybridum   FLOWERING MAPLE   POT PLANT
Malvaceae, native of South America.   Zone 10.

USES: House plant, hanging basket, greenhouse plant, tubs.

HABIT: Vigorous, free flowering plant to 3' with 3" drooping, bell shaped crepe paper-like flowers of orange, red, pink or white which are ever-blooming outdoors and winter blooming indoors. Maple-like pubescent foliage may be green or variegated.

GERMINATION: Sow seeds at any time of year, covering lightly and maintaining a temperature of 75° within the medium. Germination takes 14-21 days. Spring sown seed will flower the following winter. For outdoor use, sow in early spring.

CULTURE: Keep plants in a well lit area with at least four hours of direct sun a day. Flowering maple can withstand partial shade during the summer. The medium should be rich and kept moist at all times, and the humidity kept high. For best growth, maintain night temperatures of 50-60° and day temperatures of 70-75°; for maximum flowering, keep potbound and feed lightly. Prune occasionally to produce a bushy plant.

EASY

Acanthus mollis   BEAR'S BREECH   POT PLANT
Acanthaceae, native to southern Europe.   Zone 8.

USES: House plant, cut flower, border in warmer climates.

HABIT: Perennial with ornamental dark green glossy leaves with pale veining which are up to one foot wide and two feet long. Flowers are white and rose, appearing in summer on 1½" spikes. Although the flowers are beautiful, *Acanthus* is generally grown for its foliage.

GERMINATION: Sow seeds outdoors in early spring while soil is cool, or anytime indoors, maintaining a temperature in the medium of 50-55° until germination has taken place in 21-25 days.

CULTURE: Outdoors, set 3' apart in full sun; indoors *Acanthus* needs bright light. Medium must be kept evenly moist during growth, but give less water after flowering when the plant will go dormant. *Acanthus* resents being transplanted and establishes slowly.

EASY

Achillea   Achimenes

Achillea species   MILFOIL, YARROW   PERENNIAL
Compositae, native to Europe and the Orient.   Zone 2.

USES: Border, rock garden, cut flower, dried flower.

HABIT *Achillea* is a drought resistant perennial with fern-like dull foliage. Stems 6″ to 4′ tall carry flat 2-6″ clusters of tiny flowers in white, golden yellow and red-violet which bloom in June and again in September if cut back after blooming. Species include *A. millefolium, A. ptarmica* (sneezewort) and *A. tomentosa.*

GERMINATION: Sow outdoors in spring or summer up to two months before first frost, or sow indoors, maintaining a temperature in the medium of 70°. The seed is very fine and should not be covered as it needs light to germinate, which will occur in 10 days.

CULTURE: Plant in full sun in average to poor soil, 1-2 feet apart.

EASY

Achimenes hybrids   MAGIC FLOWER   POT PLANT
              NUT ORCHID   WIDOW'S TEARS
Gesneriaceae, native to tropical America.   Zone 10.

USES: Hanging baskets, planters, house plant, borders in warmer climates.

HABIT: Slender stemmed plants clothed with round, crisp, bright to dark green hairy leaves and ½ to 2½″ waxy tubular flowers of pink, blue, lavender, red, orange, yellow or white which bloom spring through fall. *Achimenes* grows 8-12″ tall and spreads.

GERMINATION: Sow at any time of year, but do not cover the very fine seed. Germination will take 14-21 days at a temperature in the medium of 75-80°. Seedlings will bloom in 4-5 months.

CULTURE: Grow outdoors in part or full shade; indoors, in moderate light, or under 12-16 hours of fluorescent light. *Achimenes* require a night temperature of 65-70° and daytime temperature of 75° or higher. Water and feed heavily while in active growth. After flowering, allow the plant to go dormant, and store the scaly rhizomes in a dry, cool place until spring when they may be repotted ½ inch deep in a rich, well drained medium. They are often slow to start, so be patient.

Aconitum *Adiantum*

Aconitum Carmichaelii and hybrids MONKSHOOD PERENNIAL
Ranunculaceae, native to China. Zone 2.

USES: Borders, rock gardens, cut flower.

HABIT: Showy 3-5′ plant with helmet-shaped blue, purple, yellow or white flowers in late summer and early fall on stalks clothed with glossy dark green, deeply cut leaves. It is reported to be toxic when ingested.

GERMINATION: Sow outdoors in late fall or early winter for germination the following spring. Indoors, place seeds in water or moistened medium and place in the freezer for three weeks, and then germinate at 55-60°, which will take 30 days.

CULTURE: Set plants 12-18″ apart in full sun to partial shade in a cool, rich, moist soil. Avoid dividing or transplanting as roots do not like to be disturbed.

Adiantum species MAIDENHAIR FERN POT PLANT
Polypodiaceae, native to the tropics. Zone 10, 3.

USES: Houseplant, terrariums, greenhouse plant, shady wild garden.

HABIT: Dainty, delicate fern with compound lacy fronds on thin 12-36″ wiry stems with individual leaves forming a flat fan-shaped pattern.

GERMINATION: Moisten sterile medium being careful to use a sterile container. Firm medium and sow the dust-like spores on the surface, not covering them. Cover the container with a piece of glass or plastic and set in a saucer of water, maintaining a temperature in the medium of 60-70°. Germination is long and varied. For complete instructions see the section on "Ferns From Spores".

CULTURE: Grow in a rich, loose, well drained medium, keeping moist at all times, with a high humidity. Maidenhair ferns prefer part shade outdoors and diffused light inside, with a night temperature of 55°. In the winter the amount of water given should be reduced. There is a species, *Adiantum pedatum,* which is hardy to Zone 3 and does well outside but does not make a good house plant.

71

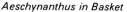
Aeschynanthus in Basket   Aeschynanthus

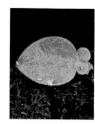

Aeschynanthus radicans LIPSTICK PLANT   POT PLANT
(lobbianus)   ROYAL RED BUGLER
   Gesneriaceae, native to Java.   Zone 10.

USES: Hanging basket, houseplant, greenhouse plant.

HABIT: Trailing fibrous rooted plants with 2-3′ stems and glossy leaves topped with 2-4″ velvety, scarlet tubular flowers blooming in summer.

GERMINATION: Sow indoors at any time, barely covering the very fine seed and maintaining a temperature in the medium of 75°. Germination requires 10-12 days.

CULTURE: Pot in a very rich mixture and keep moist at all times. Plants prefer bright indirect light, night temperatures of 65-70° and day temperatures of 75-85°. Mist daily as humidity requirements are high, and cut back stems to 6″ after flowering to induce new growth and give the plant a rest. Lipstick plant is a challenge to bring into bloom as it takes one year.

Agapanthus

AFRICAN VIOLET, see **Saintpaulia**

Agapanthus africanus 'Peter Pan'   POT PLANT
LILY OF THE NILE
Amaryllidaceae, native to northeast Africa.   Zone 9.

USES: House plant, cut flower, tubs, beds in warmer climates.

HABIT: Tender lily relatives grow from fleshy tuberous roots and send up mounds of strap-like ornamental leaves surrounding leafless 18-36″ flower stalks bearing clusters of 1-4″ bright blue, pink or white bell shaped fragrant flowers throughout the summer.

GERMINATION: Sow seed any time indoors, covering lightly and maintaining a temperature in the medium of 75°. Germination will take 21-35 days; plants flower 3-5 years from sowing.

CULTURE: Outdoors, set out 24″ apart in a rich humusy soil in full sun or very light shade; indoors, provide bright light. Water and fertilize heavily during the growing season, reducing both the balance of the year. The plant can go dormant in winter and should be stored in a dry location at 40-50°. Blooming occurs when the roots are crowded, and avoid transplanting as the roots do not like to be disturbed.

Ageratum   Agrostis

Ageratum Houstonianum FLOSS FLOWER   ANNUAL
Compositae, native to Mexico.

USES: Borders, bedding plant, window box, pot plant, cut flower, rock garden.

HABIT:*Ageratum* has heart shaped leaves and clusters of tiny, fluffy, powder-puff ¼-½″ blue, pink or white flowers from early summer to frost. Varieties vary from 4-24″ in height.

GERMINATION: Seed may be sown outdoors where plants are to bloom after all danger of frost has past, but for best results, sow indoors 6-8 weeks before planting time outside. Do not cover seeds as they are very fine and need light to germinate. Maintain temperature in the medium of 70-75° during germination which takes 5-10 days.

CULTURE: Set plants 9-12″ apart in a warm location in sun or light shade. Keep well watered to prevent wilting and fertilize monthly. The development of *Ageratum* hybrids has produced new varieties that are compact in growth and covered with bloom.

EASY

Agrostis nebulosa CLOUD GRASS   ANNUAL
Gramineae, native to Spain.

USES: Ornamental grass, dried bouquets.

HABIT: This decorative addition to the garden is 12-18″ tall with delicate cloud-like, graceful panicles that give a fluffy appearance.

GERMINATION: Sow seeds outdoors in early spring where plants are to bloom, or sow indoors maintaining a temperature in the medium of 50-55°. Do not cover seeds as they need light to germinate, which takes 20-25 days.

CULTURE: Plant 8″ apart in average soil in full sun or light shade. Cloud grass may be grown indoors if given full sun or placed under lights.

EASY

Albizia   *Alcea*

Albizia distachya   PLUME ALBIZIA   PERENNIAL
(Acacia lophantha)   PLUME ACACIA   POT PLANT
Leguminosae, native to Australia.   Zone 9.

USES: Houseplant, greenhouse plant, bedding plant in warmer climates.

HABIT:*Albizia* is a small tree with pinnate ferny leaves and 2" tassel-like spikes of brilliant yellow flowers in spring and summer.

GERMINATION: Sow seeds at any time of year indoors after they have been soaked in warm water for 24 hours or clipped on their long side. The use of a nitrogen innoculant for legumes may aid in germination. Maintain a temperature in the medium of 75° during germination which will take 15 days or more.

CULTURE: Indoors, grow in a sunny window or greenhouse which will be between 45-60° from October to May, and slightly higher the rest of the year. Outdoors, grow in a sunny location. Water heavily while in growth and flower, and prune back after flowers have faded.

EASY

Alcea rosea   HOLLYHOCK   ANNUAL, PERENNIAL
(Althea rosea)
Malvaceae, native to China.   Zone 2.

USES: Background, screen, borders.

HABIT: Traditional 4-6' and new dwarf 2' hollyhocks have stiff stems, maple-like leaves and spikes of single or double soft, powder puff-like flowers 3-6" across in a wide range of colors except blue. This old-fashioned plant blooms in summer.

GERMINATION: Sow perennial types outdoors anytime in spring or summer, up to two months before frost, or sow indoors maintaining a temperature in the medium of 70°. Annual types should be sown indoors in early spring, barely cover seeds as they need light for germination which takes 10-14 days.

CULTURE: Plant 18" to 3' apart in a rich soil in full sun. Staking may be needed on taller varieties. Water and feed heavily during the growing season. Older plants lose their vitality easily, and for this reason, hollyhocks are better treated as biennials. They self sow, but may produce plants with different colored flowers.

EASY

Allium   *Aloe*

Allium species   FLOWERING ONION   PERENNIAL
Amaryllidaceae, native to Asia, Europe.   Zone 4.

USES: Borders, edgings, rock gardens, cut flowers, dried arrangements, pots.

HABIT: These ornamental plants have green, grass-like leaves and balls of star shaped flowers in pink, violet, blue, yellow or white which bloom in summer. Some are fragrant. Depending on the species, flowers are in compact or loose round clusters, 1-12″ across, at the end of leafless stems, 4-36″ in height.

GERMINATION: Sow seeds outdoors in the fall for germination the following spring, or place seeds in moistened medium and refrigerate for 4 weeks, followed by sowing and maintaining of a temperature in the medium of 65-70°. Germination occurs in 14-21 days.

CULTURE: Set out plants in full sun in average, well drained garden soil. For potted plants indoors, give full sun, sandy soil, ample water and cool temperatures.

EASY

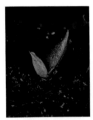

Aloe variegata   TIGER ALOE   POT PLANT
Liliaceae, native to South Africa.   Zone 9.

USES: House plants, beds in warmer climates.

HABIT: Handsome rosettes to 12″ with succulent stems bearing leaves that are thick, stiff, spiny toothed, and variegated green and white in bands. They rarely bloom indoors but outdoors give a spectacular display of red flowers.

GERMINATION: Sow indoors any time maintaining a temperature in the medium of 70-80° during germination which takes 25-30 days.

CULTURE: Pot in a rich, sandy, well drained soil and grow in full sun with a night temperature of 60° and daytime temperature of 70-75°. Allow to dry out between watering. Outdoors, plant in full sun and water sparingly. Other species of *Aloe* may be grown from seed but these are not readily available.

EASY

Alstroemeria

Alyssum

Alstroemeria aurantiaca hybrids   PERUVIAN LILY   PERENNIAL
  Alstroemeriaceae, native to South America.   Zone 7.

USES: Border, greenhouse plant, cut flower.

HABIT: Tender fibrous rooted plants bearing massive clusters of 1½-2″ lily-like orange, gold, apricot, yellow, lilac, pink or red flowers atop 1-4′ stems. The fragrant flowers, many of which are streaked or spotted with brown or green, bloom in summer.

GERMINATION: Sow outdoors in early spring while soil is cool, or sow indoors and maintain a temperature in the medium of 55° during germination which takes 15-20 days.

CULTURE: Plant outdoors in full sun, 15-18″ apart, and keep well watered. In zones where plants are to be left in the ground over winter, mulch well. Roots may be lifted and stored over winter in sand in a cool, damp place and replanted in spring. Indoors, grow in full sun in a cool location keeping evenly moist and cutting down on water during the winter dormant period.

EASY

Alyssum montanum   BASKET OF GOLD   PERENNIAL
Aurinia saxatilis (Alyssum saxatile)
  Cruciferae, native to the Mediterranean.   Zone 3.

HABIT: Showy, low growing mounded plants which are covered with masses of tiny pale yellow to gold flowers over grey-green foliage. Height varies from 6-12″. *Alyssum montanum* blooms spring and summer and is fragrant; *Aurinia saxatilis* blooms April and May.

GERMINATION: Sow outdoors where plants are to bloom in early spring, or sow indoors, spring or summer, maintaining a temperature within the medium of 55-75° during germination which takes 7-14 days. Do not cover seed which needs light to germinate.

CULTURE: Plant in full sun in a sandy, well drained soil, 6-8″ apart. Shear after blooming to encourage new growth.

EASY

Amaranthus

Ammobium

ALYSSUM, SWEET see **Lobularia maritima**

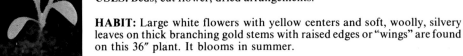

Amaranthus tricolor ANNUAL

SUMMER POINSETTIA, JOSEPH'S COAT, LOVE-LIES-BLEEDING

Amaranthus caudatus

Amaranthaceae, native to the Tropics.
USES: Beds, borders, house plant, cut flower. *A. tricolor* is eaten as Tampala.
HABIT: Brilliant plants 2-4' tall. Leaves of *A. caudatus* are red; those of *A. tricolor* are red or a combination of red, green and yellow. Flowers may be erect or drooping in tassel-like spikes of red, blooming from mid-summer to frost.

GERMINATION: Sow outdoors where plants are to bloom after all danger of frost is past or, for best results, sow indoors 3-4 weeks before planting time outside with a temperature in the medium of 70-75° until germination takes place in 10-15 days.

CULTURE: Plant 12-24" apart in full sun and any garden soil. Indoors, grow warm, with 65° nights and temperatures up to 80-85° during the day, in full sun with medium kept evenly moist.

EASY

AMARYLLIS see **Hippeastrum** species

Ammobium alatum 'grandiflora' BIENNIAL

WINGED EVERLASTING

Compositae, native to Australia. Zone 7.

USES: Beds, cut flower, dried arrangements.

HABIT: Large white flowers with yellow centers and soft, woolly, silvery leaves on thick branching gold stems with raised edges or "wings" are found on this 36" plant. It blooms in summer.

GERMINATION: Sow outdoors anytime, spring or summer, up to two months before frost or sow indoors maintaining a temperature in the medium of 68-75°. *Ammobium* may be treated as an annual and in that case should be sown indoors 6-8 weeks before planting time outside.

CULTURE: Set out 15" apart in full sun and rich, sandy soil, and keep well watered.

EASY

Anaphalis   Anchusa

Anaphalis margaritacea PEARLY EVERLASTING PERENNIAL
Compositae, native to the north temperate zone. Zone 3.

USES: Beds, dried arrangements.

HABIT: A 3′ stiffly erect perennial with narrow, woolly leaves and clusters of small white button-like flowers with yellow centers blooming July and August.

GERMINATION: Sow outdoors in late fall or early spring, or sow indoors with a temperature in the medium of 55-65° during germination which takes 10-14 days.

CULTURE: Plant 12-15″ apart in a well drained, light soil and full sun. *Anaphalis* will tolerate a cool dry soil.

Anchusa azurea 'Dropmore' ALKANET, BUGLOSS PERENNIAL
Anchusa capensis SUMMER FORGET-ME-NOT ANNUAL
Brunnera macrophylla (Anchusa myosotidiflora) PERENNIAL
    Boraginaceae.

USES: Borders, rock gardens, background, cut flowers.

HABIT: Showy spreading plants with brilliant small blue forget-me-not flowers in clusters. *A. azurea* 'Dropmore' is a perennial hardy to Zone 3, native to southern Europe, and blooming June and July on 3-5′ stems; *A. capensis* is an annual native to South Africa with ultramarine flowers from June to frost on a 8-10″ plant; *Brunnera macrophylla* is a perennial from Siberia, hardy to Zone 3, growing 1½-2′ and blooming May and June.

GERMINATION: Sow annual *Anchusa* directly into the ground after frost is past or indoors 6-8 weeks before planting time outside at a temperature in the medium of 68-86°. Perennial forms may be sown outside any time in spring or summer up to two months before frost or indoors the way as the annual *Anchusa*. Germination takes 14-21 days. Perennials will bloom the first year if started in early spring.

CULTURE: Plant *A. capensis* 10-12″ apart, others 1½-2½′ apart, in average light soil. All like full sun, and the perennials tolerate light shade. Feed little if any as this plant prefers poor soil. Cut back after flowering to encourage fall bloom.

Anemone

Anredera

Anemone species   WINDFLOWER   PERENNIAL

Ranunculaceae, native to the North Temperate region.   Zone 5, 8.

USES: Borders, rock garden, wildflower, cut flower.

HABIT: Anemones are gay and attractive perennials with deeply lobed or finely cut foliage in mounds. *A. coronaria* (POPPY ANEMONE) is 18″ tall with 2½″ flowers in shades of pink, red, white and blue, both singles and doubles. It is commonly known as "Lily of the Field"; the most popular cultivars are 'St. Bridget' and 'De Caen'. *A.* X *hybrida (A. hupehensis var. japonica)* is known as the JAPANESE ANEMONE and is 2½′ tall with 3″ flowers in August through frost. *A. Pulsatilla,* the PASQUE FLOWER, is a 6-12″ plant with bell shaped blue, red or purple flowers 2″ across in April and May followed by feathery seed pods. *A. coronaria* is hardy to Zone 8, the others to Zone 5.

GERMINATION: Sow seeds indoors in early spring, maintaining a temperature within the medium of 70-75° during germination which takes 21-28 days. Seeds of *A.* X *hybrida* and A. *Pulsatilla* may be sown outdoors in late fall or early spring for germination the following spring.

CULTURE: Plant in full sun or part shade in a rich, sandy soil, 6-15″ apart, in spring. Water well during hot, dry periods. They do not like windy or unprotected sites. Below Zone 8, lift tubers of *A. coronaria* after foliage dies down and store in a cool, dry spot until frost has past the following spring. *A. coronaria* may be grown indoors in a greenhouse using a 40-50° night until growth begins, then increased to 60-70° and fed and watered heavily.

Anredera cordifolia   MADIERA VINE   PERENNIAL
(Boussingaultia baselloides)   MIGNONETTE VINE

Basellaceae, native to South America.   Zone 9.

USES: Vine, screen, trellis.

HABIT: A vigorous, rapid growing tuberous rooted vine to 20′ or more with slender branches and glossy, fleshy evergreen heart-shaped leaves. The white, fragrant flowers appear in drooping 12″ racemes during late summer and fall.

GERMINATION: Sow outdoors any time spring or summer up to two months before frost where plants are to bloom, or indoors maintaining a temperature in the medium of 70° until germination in 25-30 days. This plant may be treated as an annual and if so, should be started indoors in early spring.

CULTURE: Set out in a rich, well drained sandy soil and keep moist during the growing season. Grow in full sun or light shade. In cold climates, tubers may be lifted and stored indoors during winter in a cool, dry place and planted out in the spring.

Anthemis   *Anthurium*

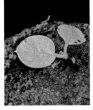

Anthemis tinctoria 'Kelwayi'   PERENNIAL
GOLDEN MARGUERITE
Compositae, native to Asia and Europe.   Zone 3.

USES: Border, rock garden, cut flower.

HABIT: Perennial plant bearing 1½-2″ daisy-like flowers of yellow, growing 2-3′ tall. Leaves are deeply cut, frilly, fern-like and pungent when crushed.

GERMINATION: Sow outdoors in spring or summer up to two months before frost, or indoors maintaining a temperature in the medium of 70° during germination which takes 8-14 days.

CULTURE: Plant 15-18 ″apart in full sun in a light well drained soil. *Anthemis* will tolerate hot, dry spots and poor soil. It self-sows readily. For white marguerite, see *Chrysanthemum frutescens.*

EASY

Anthurium Andraeanum   FLAMINGO FLOWER   POT PLANT
Anthurium Scherzerianum
    Araceae, native to South and Central American jungles.

USES: Greenhouse plant, terrariums, cut flowers.

HABIT: Upright plants with shiny deep green heart shaped or lance shaped leaves and upper bracts of orange, red, pink or white which are as shiny as patent leather. Tail-like structures (spadix) protrude from the bract and contain the plant's tiny flowers. Plants vary from 1-3′, bloom almost continuously with bracts lasting up to a month.

GERMINATION: Seeds are shipped wet and fresh and should be sown immediately. Sow in 4″ pots and cover with a bell jar, maintaining high humidity and a constant temperature withn the medium of 80°. Germination will take 20-30 days.

CULTURE: Potting medium should be rough and fibrous, and kept constantly moist. Night temperatures should be 65° and daytime temperatures 75-80°. Keep plants in indirect or diffused light, feed heavily, and maintain a high humidity (80%).

Antigonon   *Antirrhinum*

Antigonon leptopus CORALVINE   PERENNIAL
 Polygonaceae, native to Mexico.   Zone 9.

USES: Vine, screen, trellis, cut flower, greenhouse plant.

HABIT: Heat loving, tuberous rooted showy vine to 30' with heart-shaped, crinkled leaves, producing myriads of rose-pink flowers in long trailing sprays all over the plant's surface from late spring to early fall.

GERMINATION: Sow indoors at any time with a temperature in the medium of 75° until germination (14-21 days).

CULTURE: Plant in full sun in a light, well drained, poor soil, and do not feed. Keep well watered in spring and summer and taper off in fall. Cut back hard in fall. In a greenhouse, grow warm in full sun, keeping evenly moist during the growing season.

Antirrhinum majas and cultivars SNAPDRAGON ANNUAL
 Scrophulariaceae, native to the Mediterranean.

USES: Beds, borders, cut flowers, greenhouse plants.

HABIT: Summer to frost. Heat tolerant plants are available in dwarf, medium or tall varieties, 6"-3', with dark green, strap-like foliage and stiff erect spikes of showy, curiously sac-shaped, two-lipped flowers in all colors looking like dragon's jaws.

GERMINATION: Seed may be sown where plants are to bloom after soil has warmed up, but for best results, sow 6-8 weeks before planting outside, indoors, with a temperature in the medium of 70°. Germination takes 10-14 days. Do not cover the very fine seed as light is necessary for germination.

CULTURE: After danger of frost is past, set out 6-8" apart, in full sun and a light, sandy, rich, well drained soil. Pinch young plants to induce branching and produce more flowers. Water moderately and feed monthly. For greenhouse forcing, grow cool, in full sun, and allow to dry out between waterings.

EASY

Aphanostephus   Aquilegia

Aphanostephus skirrobasis   ANNUAL
LAZY DAISY,   PRAIRIE DAISY
Compositae, native to the United States.

USES: Borders, cut flowers.

HABIT: Plant with narrow, often toothed, hairy, grey-green leaves and 1″ daisy shaped white flowers that are suffused pink on the underside, with overlapping petals branching outwards from tiny yellow centers. It blooms summer through frost on 18″ stems.

GERMINATION: Seeds may be sown outdoors where they are to bloom after all danger of frost is past, or for earliest flowering, sow indoors 6-8 weeks before planting outside maintaining temperature in the medium of 70-75°. Germination takes 7-10 days.

CULTURE: Plant 8-12″ apart in light, dry, sandy soil and full sun. *Aphanostephus* tolerates winds and droughts.

EASY

Aquilegia species and hybrids   COLUMBINE   PERENNIAL
Ranunculaceae, native to temperate climates.   Zone 3.

USES: Borders, rock gardens, cut flowers.

HABIT: Clumps of deeply lobed green or blue-green airy and graceful foliage bear 1½-4″ spurred blossoms in red, pink, yellow, blue, lavender or white atop wiry stems in May and June. Height is 1-3′.

GERMINATION: Sow seeds outdoors any time from early spring through summer, up to two months before frost, although early spring is best. Indoors, sow and place in the refrigerator for 3 weeks and then germinate at 70-75° which will take 21-25 days. Do not cover the seeds as germination is improved by light. Seeds sown in early spring will produce flowering plants by that fall.

CULTURE: Columbines do best in moist, rich, well drained soil in light shade but will tolerate full sun except in hot and dry areas. Plant 1-2′ apart, feed monthly and keep well watered.

EASY

Arabis   Arctotis

Arabis caucasica (A. albida)   PERENNIAL
ROCK CRESS, WALL CRESS
Arabis blepharophylla
   Cruciferae, native to the Mediterranean.   Zone 3, 6.

USES: Rock gardens, edgings, wall, ground cover, border, bedding.

HABIT: Clouds of small white, pink or lavender flowers, often fragrant, cover the 6-12″ loose perennial plants in spring. The soft, mounded, grey-green foliage is attractive throughout the season and is evergreen in warm climates. *A. blepharophylla* is rare and hardy only to Zone 6.

GERMINATION: Sow outdoors from early spring through summer, up to two months before frost. Indoors, sow at a temperature in the medium of 70° and do not cover seeds which need light for germination. Indoor sowing will give better results. Germination takes 20-25 days.

CULTURE: Plant in spring or fall in full sun and a sandy well drained soil, 10-12″ apart. *Arabis* will tolerate a poor soil. Keep well watered and shear plants after blooming.
A. alpina is not common in cultivation and not a good ornamental. Those sold as *A. alpina* are usually the closely related *A. caucasica.*

EASY

Arctotis stoechadifolia var. **grandis** and hybrids   ANNUAL
AFRICAN DAISY
   Compositae, native to South Africa.

USES: Border, beds, cut flowers, greenhouse plants.

HABIT: African daisy hybrids are 10-12″ tall with 3″ flowers in brilliant shades of white, yellow, pink, brown, bronze, red and orange. *Arctotis stoechadifolia* vaɪ. *grandis* grows to 2½′ with spreading, almost woody stems and 3″ ray flowers of creamy white with red undersides and a black center. Flowers appear summer through frost and close at night.

GERMINATION: Sow seeds outdoors in early spring, or for best results, sow indoors 6-8 weeks before frost is past, maintaining a temperature in the medium 60-70°. Germination takes 21-35 days.

CULTURE: Set out in full sun 12″ apart in a light sandy loam. African daisy will tolerate drought and does best where summer nights are cool. In the greenhouse grow in full sun with 55° night temperature and allow to dry out between waterings.

EASY

84

Arenaria   *Armeria*

Arenaria montana   MOUNTAIN SANDWORT   PERENNIAL
Caryophyllaceae, native to southwest Europe.   Zone 4.

USES: Ground cover, rock garden, paths, walls.

HABIT: Moss-like, mat forming grey-green plants 2-4″ tall have grassy leaves and tiny white star shaped flowers in June.

GERMINATION: Sow outdoors in early spring, or for best results, sow indoors, not covering the fine seed, and maintaining a temperature within the medium of 55-65° during germination which takes 15-20 days.

CULTURE: Plant 6″ apart in full sun or light shade (especially in hot areas) in a rich, moist, slightly acid, well drained soil. Keep well watered.

Armeria maritima   THRIFT, SEA PINK   PERENNIAL
Plumbaginaceae, native to Greenland, Iceland, north Europe. Zone 3.

USES: Border, beds, edging, rock gardens, cut flowers.

HABIT: Low (6-12″), cushion-like evergreen plants with grass-like foliage and globular clusters of pink, red or white bell shaped flowers blooming late spring and early summer.

GERMINATION: Soak seeds in warm water for 6-8 hours before sowing. Sow outdoors any time spring through summer, up to two months before frost, or, for best results, sow indoors in spring maintaining a temperature in the medium of 60-70°. Germination occurs in 14-21 days.

CULTURE: Plant 6-12″ apart in full sun and a dry, light, sandy soil with excellent drainage. Water light to moderately. *Armeria* does very well by the seashore.

EASY

85

Arnica

Asarina

Arnica montana   MOUNTAIN ARNICA   PERENNIAL
   Compositae, native to Europe.   Zone 6.

USES: Borders, edgings, rock garden, cut flower, medicinal.

HABIT: Small tufted green leaved plants send up 24″ stems bearing clusters of large yellow fragrant daisy-like flowers in May and June.

GERMINATION: Sow seeds outdoors in early spring or indoors with a temperature in the medium of 55° during germination which takes 25-30 days.

CULTURE: Plant in spring 12-15″ apart in full sun and a moist, acid, sandy soil with excellent drainage.

EASY

Asarina antirrhinifolia   MAURANDIA   POT PLANT
   Scrophulariaceae, native to southern U.S. and Mexico.

USES: Hanging basket, house plant, greenhouse plant.

HABIT: Fast growing vine with soft hairy leaves and beautiful sky blue trumpet shaped flowers with a white throat, 1″ across in summer.

GERMINATION: Sow any time for indoor use; for outdoors use in summer, sow indoors 12 weeks before planting outside. Maintain a temperature in the medium of 70-75° during germination which takes 10-15 days.

CULTURE: Outdoors, grow in full sun in a rich, well drained soil that is well watered. Indoors, *Asarina* is free flowering, and should be grown at 55° nights in filtered light, planted in a medium rich in humus kept evenly moist. It requires high humidity.

EASY

Asclepias fruticosa   Asclepias tuberosa

Asclepias fruticosa   ANNUAL
(Gomphocarpus fruticosas)
  Asclepiadoceae, native to Africa.

USES: Background, cut branches, dried arrangements.

HABIT: Leaves are lance shaped and 5″ long; bronze, green or yellow bristly fruits appear in late summer and fall on 3′ stems.

GERMINATION: Sow outdoors where plants are to grow after danger of frost has past, or, for best results and earlier fruiting, sow indoors in February or March, maintaining a temperature in the medium of 70-75° during germination which takes 14-20 days.

CULTURE: Grow in full sun in average well drained soil, 18″ apart.

EASY

Asclepias tuberosa   BUTTERFLY WEED   PERENNIAL
  Asclepiadaceae, native to U.S. and Canada.

USES: Border, wildflower garden, cut flower.   Zone 3.

HABIT: 2-3′ plant with stems containing a milky juice and lined with slender 2-4″ hairy leaves, topped by flat clusters of small, fragrant, vivid orange blossoms in July and August.

GERMINATION: Seeds may be sown outdoors in spring or summer, up to two months before frost, but for best results, sow indoors at a temperature within the medium of 68-75° which will germinate in 21-28 days.

CULTURE: Plant 8-12″ apart in full sun and a well drained sandy soil. *Asclepias* has a long tap root and therefore withstands drought and does not like to be transplanted.

EASY

Asparagus asparagoides   Asparagus species

Asparagus asparagoides SMILAX   POT PLANT
  Liliaceae, native to South Africa.

USES: Hanging basket, houseplant, greenhouse plant, bouquets.

HABIT: Vining plant with many branches and handsome glossy 1″ oval, sharp pointed leaves and small fragrant white flowers followed by ¼″ blue-purple berries.

GERMINATION: Sow indoors at any season, maintaining a temperature in the medium of 75°. Cover seed well as it needs darkness for germination, which takes 25-30 days.

CULTURE: Grow in indirect or diffused light where nights are cool. Use average potting soil kept evenly moist.

Asparagus species   ASPARAGUS FERNS   POT PLANT
  Liliaceae, native to Africa and Asia.

USES: Hanging baskets, house plant, greenhouse, arrangements.

HABIT: Asparagus ferns are not true ferns, although they give a fern-like appearance. *A. densiflorus* 'Myers' features stiff, upright plumes of 2-3′ densely covered with needle like green leaves; *A. densiflorus* 'Sprengeri' has 3-6 arching, airy branches of needle-like light green foliage; *A. racemosus* is rich green with a climbing habit; *A. Macowanii (A. densiflorus 'myriocladus')* is an erect plant with dark green thread-like leaves on graceful sprays; *A. setaceus* 'Nanus' *(A. plumosus)* is a low growing, lacy fern, rich green with horizontal branching; *A. verticillatus* is a vining type and slightly more hardy than the others. All have flowers and berries which often do not appear when grown as a house plant; asparagus ferns are grown for their foliage.

GERMINATION: Sow any time of year indoors, but early spring is best, maintaining a temperature in the medium of 70-80° until germination occurs in 4 weeks. Soaking seed for 24 hours before sowing improves germination. Seeds are not long lived and should not be stored.

CULTURE: Plant in a light, fertile, rich medium and grow at 55-65° nights. Soil should be slightly acid. Plants need partial shade or diffused light. Water and feed heavily during summer, cutting down on water and feed October to March.

Asparagus Meyeri
(see p. 88)

Asplenium

Asphodeline lutea   KING'S SPEAR, JACOB'S ROD   PERENNIAL
Liliaceae, native to the Mediterranean.   Zone 6.

USES: Borders, beds.

HABIT: Fragrant yellow flowers in giant racemes appear in May, June and July on 3-4' plants.

GERMINATION: Sow outdoors where plants are to bloom any time from spring through summer, up to two months before frost. Indoors, sow at a temperature in the medium of 70-75°. Germination will take 30 days.

CULTURE: Plant 15-18" apart in full sun or part shade in average, well drained garden soil.

EASY

Asplenium nidus   BIRD'S NEST FERN   POT PLANT
Polypodiaceae, native to tropical Asia.   Zone 10.

USES: House plants, greenhouse, terrariums, shady gardens in warm climates.

HABIT: Upright rosette of simple and entire leathery, spreading, shiny green fronds 1-3' long. It has a leathery texture with prominent dark midribs and wavy margins. The crown from which the fronds arise is densely clothed with black scales.

GERMINATION: Moisten sterile medium being sure to use a sterile container. Firm the medium and sow the dust-like spores on the surface, not covering them. Cover the container with a piece of glass or plastic and set in a saucer of water, maintaining a temperature in the medium of 60-70°. Germination is long and varied. For complete instructions and description of germination see the section on "Ferns From Spores".

CULTURE: Grow outdoors in a loose, woodsy, slightly limey soil in a shady spot. Indoors, pot in a rich, loose, well drained medium, keeping moist at all times except winter when it should be kept barely moist. Grow in bright indirect light or in a north window with night temperatures of 60° and day temperatures of 70-75°. Bird's nest fern requires high humidity.

Aster   *Astilbe*

ASTER (ANNUAL) see **Callistephus chinensis**

Aster hybrids   MICHAELMAS DAISY   PERENNIAL
Compositae, native to temperate zones.   Zone 4.

USES: Borders, beds, rock gardens, cut flowers.

HABIT: Asters have daisy-like semi-double or double flowers, usually with yellow centers. *Aster alpinus,* the ALPINE ASTER, grows 9-12″ high and has flowers of soft blue, white, lavender or pink over basal leaves in May and June. It is a native of the mountains of Europe and Asia. *Aster novae-angliae* (NEW ENGLAND ASTER) grows 3-6′ tall, is bushy, comes from the eastern United States and has 1″ rosy-red flowers in August and September. *Aster novi-belgii* (NEW YORK ASTER) grows 4′ high and has 1″ flowers of violet, blue, pink or white in September and October. It is a native of the eastern United States coast. *Aster tongolensis,* native to West China, forms a 6-12″ tufted mound and has 2″ blue flowers in early summer.

GERMINATION: Sow seeds outdoors any time from spring through summer up to two months before frost. For best results, sow indoors, maintaining a temperature within the medium of 70-75° during germination which takes 15-20 days.

CULTURE: Plant in full sun or very light shade in good, well drained garden soil, 12-15″ apart. Pinch in late spring to induce branching and stimulate flowering.

Astilbe X Arendsii   FALSE SPIREA   PERENNIAL
Saxifragiaceae, native to the Orient.   Zone 6.

USES: Shady borders, cut flowers.

HABIT: Attractive plant with 6-36″ fluffy spikes of white, pink or red flowers in June. Fern-like leaves of green to bronze are formed in 12″ mounds.

GERMINATION: Sow outdoors in early spring, or for best results, sow indoors with a temperature in the medium of 60-70° during germination which takes 21-28 days.

CULTURE: *Astilbe* prefers a rich, very moist, well drained soil and a spot in part shade. Plant 15-24″ apart in spring or fall.

Aubrieta   Avena

Aubrieta deltoidea   PERENNIAL
FALSE ROCK CRESS,   PURPLE ROCK CRESS
Cruciferae, native to Greece.   Zone 4.

USES: Rock gardens, ground cover, edging, walls.

HABIT: Spreading, compact plant, 4-6″ tall, is free blooming from April to June with flowers of lilac, purple or red.

GERMINATION: Outdoors, sow spring or summer up to two months before frost. For best results, sow indoors, not covering the fine seed, and maintaining a temperature within the medium of 55-65° during germination which takes 8-15 days.

CULTURE: Plant 6″ apart in full sun or part shade (especially in hot areas) in a rich, well drained soil. Shear plants after flowering. It does best where summers are cool.

AZALEA, see **Rhododendron**

Avena sterilis   ANIMATED OATS   ANNUAL
Gramineae, native to the Mediterranean.

USES: Ornamental grass, dried arangements.

HABIT: Unique 3′ plants with long grass-like foliage and seeds borne on 1′ panicles. The florets move or twist suddenly when exposed to moisture.

GERMINATION: Sow outdoors where plants are to bloom after all danger of frost is past, or sow indoors in early spring maintaining a temperature in the medium of 60-70° during germination which takes 5-10 days.

CULTURE: Set out in average garden soil with good drainage, in full sun, 15″ apart.

EASY

91

Baptisia

BALSAM see **Impatiens Balsamina**

Baptisia australis   PERENNIAL
BLUE WILD INDIGO,   FALSE INDIGO
Leguminosae, native to eastern North America.

USES: Border, hedges, cut flower. Zone 3.

HABIT: Plants 2-4' with compound clover-like blue green leaves bear spikes
of pea-like rich indigo-blue flowers during May and June.

GERMINATION: Outdoors, sow in late fall or early spring for spring germination. Indoors,
nick or file the hard seed coats for fastest germination, and maintain a temperature within the
medium of 70-75° until germination in 5-10 days.

CULTURE: Plant 18" apart in full sun or part shade in average, well drained garden soil. Keep
well watered, and support taller varieties with stakes.

EASY.

A Spring Garden

Begonia   *Begonia*

Begonia species and hybrids   BEGONIA   ANNUAL
Begoniaceae, native to the tropics and subtropics.

USES: Bedding, border, hanging baskets, house plant, greenhouse plant.

HABIT: Begonias are divided into three groups: fibrous rooted, rhizomatous rooted and tuberous rooted. Best known of the fibrous rooted are the wax begonias, *B.* X *semperflorens-cultorum,* which form 6-12" mounds of green, bronze or mahogany leaves with single or double flowers in clusters in shades of pink, red or white. Their bloom is almost continuous. There are also many other species that have distinctive foliage and pretty flowers for year round interest to indoor gardens. *B. foliosa* has cascading sprays of glossy green fern-like foliage, and although it blooms, is primarily a foliage plant. Rex begonias are the best known of the rhizomatous group, noted for magnificent ornamental foliage with rich colors and varied leaf designs. Tuberous rooted begonias form hanging clusters of flowers up to 8" in white, yellow, orange, red or pink, solids or bicolors, and are spectacular in baskets. Most begonias are hardy to Zone 9 or 10, but the hardy begonia, *B. grandis,* is hardy to Zone 7, 18" tall with pink flowers.

GERMINATION: For indoor use, sow at any time. For outdoor use, sow wax begonias 12 weeks before planting outside and tuberous begonias 12-16 weeks before that date. Seeds are very dusty and should not be covered as they need light to germinate. Maintain a temperature within the medium of 70-75° except for tuberous begonias which will germinate at 65-75°. Germination will occur in 15-20 days.

CULTURE: Plant wax begonias 8-10" apart in partial shade; hybrids will do very well in full sun if the temperature does not regularly go over 90°. Soil should be rich and well drained, and allowed to dry out between waterings. Frequent fertilizing is beneficial. Tuberous begonias should be grown in partial shade in a rich, light, fertile soil with perfect drainage kept constantly moist. They prefer cool temperatures and high humidity. After the first light frost, lift the tubers, wash them clean, and store in a cool, dark and dry area until spring. Any begonia grown indoors will respond to a summer vacation outdoors in a partially shaded spot. Simply sink the pot into the ground and bring inside again in late summer.

Indoors, grow begonias at 65° nights and 70-80° days. Most prefer to dry out between waterings. Fertilize when in growth or flower. A good rule of thumb is to grow them in an east window in summer and a south window in winter, although Rex begonias prefer less light (west window) and may go dormant in winter, when they should be kept almost dry and not fed. Fibrous rooted begonias grow well in normal indoor humidity; Rex and tuberous begonias prefer a higher humidity.

Belamcanda　　　　　　　　　　　　　*Bellis*

Belamcanda chinensis,　BLACKBERRY LILY　　　PERENNIAL
Belancanda flabellata
　Iridaceae, native to China and Japan.　　　　　　Zone 5.

USES: Borders, wildflower gardens, dried arrangements.

HABIT: Above iris-like foliage, 12-24″ flower stalks bear clusters of 2″ flat, lily-like flowers in late summer followed by seed pods resembling blackberries. *B. chinensis* has flowers of orange with red spots; *B. flabellata* is pure yellow.

GERMINATION: Sow outdoors in spring or summer, up to two months before frost, or sow indoors, maintaining a temperature within the medium of 68-86° during germination which takes 15-20 days.

CULTURE: Plant 6″ apart in full sun or light shade in a rich, sandy soil with excellent drainage. Keep moderately moist during the growing period.

EASY

Bellis perennis　ENGLISH DAISY　　　　　　BIENNIAL
　Compositae, native to Europe.　　　　　　　　Zone 3.

USES: Bedding, border, rock gardens.

HABIT: Plant with 4-6″ stems carrying white, pink, red or purple single or double daisy-like flowers 2″ across in April, May and June above a rosette of basal leaves. Treat as an annual in Zones 8-10.

GERMINATION: In mild areas, sow outdoors in late summer; in ther areas, sow outdoors in early spring. Seeds may also be sown indoors at a temperature in the medium of 70° until germination is complete in 10-15 days.

CULTURE: Plant 6″ apart in full sun or light shade in a light, rich and moist soil. Keep well watered and fertilize monthly. Plants do best in cool climates.

EASY

Bergenia   *Bougainvillea*

BELLS OF IRELAND, see **Moluccella laevis**

Bergenia cordifolia HEART LEAF BERGENIA   PERENNIAL
Saxifragaceae, native to Siberia.   Zone 2.

USES: Borders, ground cover.

HABIT: Semi-evergreen plant with thick, 6-8″, heart shaped, fleshy, shiny leaves that look like cabbage and 18-24″ spikes of rose, purple or white flowers somewhat hidden by the foliage in late spring and early summer.

GERMINATION: Sow outdoors in late fall or early spring for spring germination. Seeds may also be sown indoors maintaining a temperature within the medium of 55° until germination takes place in 15-20 days.

CULTURE: Plant 12-16″ apart in a rich soil kept very moist in a shaded location. It is ideal by pools or streams.

Bougainvillea hybrids   PAPER FLOWER   POT PLANT
Nyctaginaceae, native to tropical South America. Zone 10.

USES: House plant, greenhouse plant, tubs, vine, ground cover in warm climate.

HABIT: Vining plant 2-20′ with cascading clusters of papery 1″ petal-like bracts in colors of bright purple, red, pink, copper, yellow or white from early spring to late summer.

GERMINATION: Sow seeds indoors at any time, germinating at a temperature within the medium of 70-75°. Germination takes 30 days or more.

CULTURE: Pot in a rich, well drained soil and grow in full sun, indoors or out. Give constant water in summer and fertilize frequently, holding off on water and fertilizer during the winter resting period. Temperatures should be 65° at night and 70-80° during the day. *Bougainvillea* may be grown on a trellis or pruned to keep bushy.

EASY

Brachycome

Brassica

Brachycome iberidifolia SWAN RIVER DAISY   ANNUAL
Compositae, native to Australia.

USES: Borders, planters, edging, cut flower, greenhouse plant.

HABIT: Masses of fragrant 1½″ daisy-like flowers in shades of blue, rose, white or violet with dark centers cover the 12-18″ plant in summer. Foliage is feather-like.

GERMINATION: Sow outdoors in spring, after all danger of frost has past or start indoors 4-6 weeks before last spring frost, maintaining a temperature within the medium of 70° during germination which takes 10-18 days.

CULTURE: Set out in full sun in a rich, warm soil, 6″ apart. It is not a long blooming plant so successive plantings 3 weeks apart insure continual bloom. *Brachycome* prefers cool temperature. Seeds sown in fall will bloom in spring in the greenhouse.

EASY

Brassica oleracea, Acerphala Group   ANNUAL
   FLOWERING CABBAGE,   FLOWERING KALE
Cruciferae, native to Europe.

USES: Bedding, borders, pot plant.

HABIT: Unusual decorative plant with thick leaves of green in rosettes 12″ across with centers of white, rose or purple in fall and winter.

GERMINATION: Sow indoors in June or July for fall and winter use outdoors. Flowering cabbage should be sown and placed in the refrigerator for 3 days followed by germination at a temperature within the medium of 65-70°. Do not cover seeds as light is beneficial to germination which takes 10-14 days. Flowering kale is sown at a temperature within the medium of 65-70° which also takes 10-14 days and is not aided by light.

CULTURE: Plant in a rich, fertile soil kept evenly moist. Temperatures must be cool, but either must be grown in full sun. Flowering kale may be eaten, but flowering cabbage is not edible.

EASY

Briza   *Browallia*

Briza maxima QUAKING GRASS   ANNUAL
  Gramineae, native to the Mediterranean.

USES: Ornamental grass, dried bouquets.

HABIT: Ornamental annual grass to 24″ which bears graceful, nodding, bronze colored fruit clusters in the shape of arrow heads. The spikes quiver and quake in the breeze.

GERMINATION: Sow outdoors in early spring where the plants are to bloom, or sow indoors maintaining a temperature within the medium of 55° during germination which takes 10-14 days.

CULTURE: Plant 12″ apart in a sandy soil with excellent drainage, in full sun.

EASY

Browallia speciosa BROWALLIA   ANNUAL
  Solanaceae, native to South America.

USES: Bedding, planters, hanging baskets, borders, house plant, greenhouse.

HABIT: Compact plants with 12-18″ stems bearing floriferous clusters of blue and white 2″ bell shaped velvety blooms during summer outdoors and everblooming indoors.

GERMINATION: For indoor use, sow at any time of year. For outdoor use, sow indoors 6-8 weeks before planting outside. Do not cover seeds, which need light to germinate, and maintain a temperature within the medium of 75° during germination which takes 14-21 days.

CULTURE: Grow 8-10″ apart in sun or part shade in a rich soil with good drainage; indoors, grow in diffused sunlight in a rich soil kept evenly moist. Temperature should be 55° at night and 70° during the day.

Buddleia   *Cactus*

Buddleia Davidii   PERENNIAL
        BUTTERFLY BUSH,   SUMMER LILAC
Loganiaceae, native to China.   Zone 5.

USES: Border, background, cut flower.

HABIT: Fragrant blue, purple, pink, white, orange, or red small flowers bloom in pyramidal spikes in late summer on woody stems 8-15′ tall. Leaves are long and coarse in texture.

GERMINATION: Sow indoors in early spring for fall flowering, or sow outdoors any time in late spring or summer up to two months before frost. Maintain a temperature within the medium of 70-75° during germination which takes 20-25 days.

CULTURE: Plant in sun or light shade in average garden soil. Cut down to the ground every spring.

EASY

CABBAGE, FLOWERING, see **Brassica oleraceae** Acephala

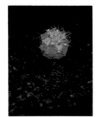

Cacti   CACTUS   POT PLANT
   Cactaceae, native to the Americas.   Zones 9 & 3.

USES: House plant, greenhouse plant, rock garden.

HABIT: Cacti are a large group of many genera and species with bizarre and curious shapes, from the size of a button to large trees. Exotic flowers from ¼″ to 1′ are waxy and in a full range of colors. Plants may be globular, columnar, flat, creeping or climbing. Stems are fleshy or flat, and most cacti are leafless and have spines or bristles. Most are hardy to Zone 9; the major exception is *Opuntia* which is hardy to Zone 3.

GERMINATION: Sow indoors at any time of year maintaining a temperature within the medium of 70-80°. Do not cover the seeds. Germination is erratic and will takes from 5 days to several months.

CULTURE: Cacti are divided into two groups, desert cacti and jungle cacti; those grown from seed are generally desert cacti. They require a porous, sandy soil, direct sun and low humidity. In the winter they should be watered only to keep them from shriveling and fertilized; water slightly more but still sparingly in spring, summer and fall, and fertilize once a month. Cool nights (50-55°) are generally necessary to induce blooming.

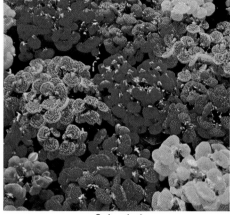

Caesalpinia   *Calceolaria*

Caesalpinia Gilliesii   POINCIANA   ANNUAL
(Poinciana Gilliesii)
Leguminosae, native to Mexico, Central and South America.

USES: Borders, pot plant, house plant.

HABIT: Tropical looking plants have acacia-like foliage and single, showy, yellow flowers with bright red stamens in summer followed by long, flat seed pods.

GERMINATION: Soak seeds in warm water for 48 hours before sowing. Maintain a temperature within the medium of 70-75° during germination which takes 7-15 days. For outdoor use, sow in early spring; for indoor use, sow anytime.

CULTURE: Outdoors, plant in full sun in a rich, well drained soil. Indoors, give full sun, night temperatures of 65°, day temperatures of 75° or higher, and an evenly moist soil.

Calceolaria crenatiflora   POCKETBOOK PLANT   POT PLANT
Scrophulariaceae, native to Chile.

USES: House plant, greenhouse plant.

HABIT: Masses of unique pocket-like flowers in red, yellow, orange or brown, solid or spotted, bloom on this 6-15″ plant excellent for winter blooming indoors.

GERMINATION: The best time to sow seeds is in fall for winter and spring bloom. Do not cover the very fine seeds which need light to germinate. Seeds will germinate at 55-70°, but best germination is achieved when the temperature within the medium is 70-75°, which will cause germination in 5-10 days.

CULTURE: Keep young plants sheltered from direct sun and the temperature 50-55° at night. Seedlings should be kept barely moist but never allowed to dry out; plants in bud and bloom should be watered heavily. Plants in bloom may be grown at warm temperatures but cool ones are preferred.

Calendula   Callistephus

Calendula officianalis POT MARIGOLD   ANNUAL
Compositae, native to southern Europe.

USES: Bedding, cut flower, greenhouse forcing.

HABIT: Single or double daisy-like or chrysanthemum-like flowers 3-5″ across in white, cream, gold, orange and apricot bloom from early summer to frost, and adorn the 6-24″ stems clothed with long, narrow and slightly sticky foliage. It is almost everblooming in the greenhouse.

GERMINATION: Sow outdoors in spring, or indoors in spring for summer use and in summer for fall and winter use outdoors in warm climates or indoors in the greenhouse. Maintain a temperature within the medium of 70° during germination which takes 10-14 days. Cover seeds completely as darkness is needed for germination.

CULTURE: *Calendula* performs best in cool weather. Plant 12-15″ apart in full sun in a rich, fertile soil, kept well watered. In the greenhouse, grow with cool (50-55°) nights in full sun, and keep moist.
EASY

CALLA, see **Zantedeschia** species

CALLIOPSIS, see **Coreopsis tinctoria**

Callistephus chinensis ASTER, CHINA ASTER   ANNUAL
Compositae, native to Asia.

USES: Beds, borders, planters, cut flower, greenhouse forcing.

HABIT: Single or double flowering annuals 6-36″ in height with blooms of blue, white, lavender, purple, yellow, pink or red on long cutting stems over basal foliage. Flowers appear from mid-summer to frost.

GERMINATION: Sow outdoors where plants are to bloom after all danger of frost is past, or sow indoors 6-8 weeks before planting outside. Sow indoors in fall and winter for greenhouse flowers in late winter and spring. Maintain a temperature within the medium of 70° during germination which takes 10-14 days.

CULTURE: Plant outdoors 6-15″ apart in full sun in a fertile, well drained, sandy soil kept well watered. For more continuous bloom, plant in succession at two week intervals, as asters stop blooming after they are cut. In the greenhouse, grow at cool (50-55°) nights in full sun with a rich porous soil kept evenly moist. Many new varieties have been introduced which are resistant to wilt and make growing asters worthwhile.

Calluna

Camellia Sasanqua

Calluna vulgaris HEATHER PERENNIAL
Ericaceae, native to northern Europe. Zone 4.

USES: Border, edging, rock garden, ground cover.

HABIT: Scale-like, overlapping evergreen leaves appear on this plant that grows 12-18″ high. Flowers are purple or pink and appear in late summer in 10″ spikes.

GERMINATION: Sow seeds outdoors in late fall or early spring for late spring germination, or sow indoors. Fresh seeds will germinate in 30-35 days if a temperature within the medium of 65-70° is maintained. Other seeds will benefit from being placed in moistened medium in the refrigerator for 4 weeks, followed by germination as above.

CULTURE: Plant in full sun in an acid, infertile, highly organic soil that is kept evenly moist. Shear in early spring. Heather will tolerate wind and heat.

Camellia Sasanqua SASANQUA CAMELLIA SHRUB
Theaceae, native to China and Japan. Zone 7.

USES: Foundation plantings, pot plant, cut flowers, greenhouse.

HABIT: Broad leaved evergreen shrub with an open habit growing to 20′ with pink or white single or semi-double fragrant flowers in fall.

GERMINATION: Soak seeds in warm water for 24 hours before sowing. Sow with a temperature within the medium of 70-75° during the germination period which will take 1-2 months.

CULTURE: Plant in light shade protected from winter sun in a well drained, rich, acid soil kept evenly moist. Mulch 2″ deep. In the greenhouse, grow with cool (55°) nights, keep evenly moist and provide 3-4 hours of sun a day.

101

Camellia sinensis

Campanula

Camellia sinensis TEA PLANT

Theaceae, native to Asia.

POT PLANT
Zone 9.

USES: House plant, shrub in warm climates, tea, greenhouse.

HABIT: Tender evergreen shrub to 30′ outdoors and smaller when grown indoors. Leaves are leathery and toothed; flowers are fragrant, white or pink, camellia-like in clusters of 2-5.

GERMINATION: Soak seeds for 48 hours, then place in moist medium and place in the freezer for 3 weeks. Germinate with a temperature within the medium of 70-75° which will take 2 months or more. Tea plant may also be sown outdoors in late fall for germination the following spring.

CULTURE: Plant outdoors in warm climates in light shade and a rich, acid, well drained sandy soil. Keep evenly moist and mulch 2″ deep. Indoors, grow with cool (55°) nights, keep soil evenly moist, and give 3-4 hours of sun a day.

Campanula species

ANNUAL, BIENNIAL, PERENNIAL BELLFLOWER

Campanulaceae, native to Europe and Asia.

Zone below.

USES: Borders, rock garden, ground cover, baskets, cut flower.

HABIT: Bell shaped flowers characterize this group of plants. *C. Medium* (Canterbury Bells) is 2-3′, biennial, but there is an annual form. White, blue, lavender and pink 2″ flowers bloom in racemes in June and July. *C. Medium* 'Calycanthema' (Cup and Saucer) is named for the flower shape. *C. carpatica* is 8-12″ tall, hardy to Zone 3, with 1½-2″ flowers of violet-blue or white from June to August. *C. Elatines* var. *garganica* is hardy to Zone 6, 6-8″ high on trailing stems, with ½″ blue flowers; *C. glomerata* 'Superba' is showy, with 1″ deep violet flowers in dense clusters on a 2′ plant, hardy to Zone 2; both bloom in June and July. *C. persicifoilia* (Peach Leaved Campanula) has 1½″ blue or white flowers in 2′ open racemes in June and July and is hardy to Zone 3. *C. rotundifolia* (Blue Bells-of-Scotland) is the daintiest of the *Campanulas*, with 1″ bright blue flowers on 1½′ wiry stems, hardy to Zone 2.

GERMINATION: Sow annual Bellflower indoors 6-8 weeks before planting outdoors with a temperature within the medium of 68-86° during germination which takes 10-14 days. Do not cover the fine seed. Sow perennial or biennial forms outdoors in late spring or early summer for bloom the following year, or sow indoors the same way as for annual forms. Germination will take 14-21 days, and light is beneficial for several of the species.

CULTURE: Set plants 4-18″ apart depending on the species in a rich, moist, well drained soil kept well watered. Most do best in full sun, but *C. Elatines* var. *garanica, C. persicifoilia* and *C. rotundifolia* will perform well in part shade.

EASY

102

Campsis   Canna

Campsis radicans   TRUMPET VINE   PERENNIAL
(Bignonia radicans)   TRUMPET CREEPER
Bignoniaceae, native to northeast North America.   Zone 4.

USES: Screen, vine, trellis.

HABIT: Fast growing deciduous vine to 30′ with dark green compound leaves and 3″ trumpet shaped orange and scarlet flowers borne in terminal clusters of 6-12 during summer.

GERMINATION: Place seeds in moistened medium in the refrigerator for two months, followed by germination maintaining a temperature within the medium of 70°. Germination will take place in 15-20 days. Trumpet vine may be sown outdoors in early spring.

CULTURE: Plant in sun or light shade in a rich, moist, well drained, sandy soil. Keep well watered and fertilize during the growing season. Pinch back frequently to promote bushiness. A trellis or some other support must be provided.

CANDYTUFT, see **Iberis**

Canna X generalis   CANNA   PERENNIAL
Cannaceae, native to South and Central America.   Zone 8.

USES: Borders, backgrounds, planters, cut flower.

HABIT: Striking broad-leaved 1½-4′ plants bear flower spikes of 4-5″ gladiolus like flowers of white, cream, yellow, pink, orange or red from July to frost. Foliage is in shades of green or bronze, bold and beautiful.

GERMINATION: Sow outdoors after all danger of frost is past where plants are to grow, or for best results, sow indoors, maintaining a temperature within the medium of 70-75° during germination. If the seed coats are nicked or filed and the seeds soaked in warm water for 48 hours, the seeds will germinate in 7-14 days. Plant the large seeds vertically.

CULTURE: Plant in full sun in a rich soil with good drainage, 9-24″ apart. In areas colder than Zone 8, dig rhizomes after tops have been blackened by frost and store in a cool, dry place. *Canna* needs to be heavily fed and watered during the growing season. New dwarf hybrids with compact growth habit have made *Canna* a popular plant once again.

103

Capsicum   *Cassia*

CANTERBURY BELLS, see **Campanula**

Capsicum annuum   ORNAMENTAL PEPPER   ANNUAL
Solanaceae, native to the Tropics.

USES: Beds, borders, pot plant, house plant.

HABIT: Plant 9-12″ tall with insignificant spring flowers, but showy fruit
½-2″ long from July to frost. Fruits are round or pointed, and change in
color from yellow to orange to red.

GERMINATION: Sow indoors 6-8 weeks before planting outside for summer use, maintaining
a temperature within the medium of 70-75° during germination which takes 21-25 days. Do not
cover seeds which will need light to germinate. Sow May 1 for fruiting plants for Christmas.

CULTURE: Outdoors, plant in full sun or part shade, 9-12″ apart. Indoors, grow at 65° nights
and daytime temperatures as high as 80-85°, in full sun and with soil kept evenly moist. For best
fruits at Christmas, summer the plants outdoors and bring inside before frost.

CARNATION, see **Dianthus**

Cassia alata   CANDLE BUSH   POT PLANT
Leguminosae, native to the tropics.   Zone 8.

USES: Houseplant, greenhouse, border and tubs in warm climates.

HABIT: Evergreen shrub, 3-8′, with dark green, glossy leaves and candle-
like spikes of large yellow pea-like fragrant flowers.

GERMINATION: Seeds are often shipped already nicked; if not, nick or file a small hole in the
seed coat. Maintain a temperature within the medium of 70-75° during germination which takes
5-10 days.

CULTURE: Outdoors, grow 2-6′ apart in full sun and a rich, sandy, well drained soil. Keep well
watered. Indoors, grow in full sun in a cool environment, and keep soil evenly moist.

Catananche   *Catharanthus*

CASTOR BEAN, see **Ricinus communis**

Catananche caerulea CUPID'S DART   PERENNIAL
Compositae, native to the Mediterranean.   Zone 4.

USES: Border, dried flower, cut flower.

HABIT: Perennial plant 2′ in height bears lavender-blue flowers with dark blue centers in June and July on thin wiry stems over narrow, woolly, grey-green foliage.

GERMINATION: Sow outdoors in early spring, or start indoors 6-8 weeks before planting time outdoors for bloom the first year. Maintain a temperature within the medium of 65-75° during germination which takes 21-25 days.

CULTURE: Plant 10-12″ apart in full sun and light to average soil. Grow on the dry side.

EASY

Catharanthus roseus PERIWINKLE   ANNUAL
(Vinca rosea)
   Apocynaceae, native to Africa and southwest Asia.

USES: Ground cover, hanging basket, bedding, borders, planters.

HABIT: Prostrate, or upright plant 4-10″ high, has shiny, dark green leaves and blooms from May to frost with 1-2″ phlox-like, waxy flowers of lavender, pink or white.

GERMINATION: Sow seeds indoors 12 weeks before last frost, maintaining a temperature within the medium of 70-75° during germination which takes 15-20 days. Cover the seeds completely as darkness is needed for germination.

CULTURE: Plant 12″ apart in full sun to partial shade in any well drained garden soil. It prefers to be kept moist but will tolerate drought and heat. It self-sows readily. It is perennial in Zones 9 and 10, and does not do well in cool soil. Indoors give 55° nights, full sun and a soil kept evenly moist.

EASY

Celosia   Celsia

Celosia cristata cultivars   COCKSCOMB   ANNUAL
Amaranthaceae, native to the tropics.

USES: Bedding, borders, cut flower, dried flower, greenhouse.

HABIT: Annual plants are noted for striking, long lasting flower heads
which are 2-10″ wide; the crested type resembles the combs of roosters, while
the plumosa type has ostrich plume sprays. Both come in shades of yellow,
orange, red and purple, grow 6-36″ high and flower summer to frost.

GERMINATION: Sow seeds outdoors where plants are to bloom after all danger of frost is
past, or sow indoors 4 weeks prior to planting outside, barely covering the seed, and maintaining
a temperature within the medium of 70-75°. Germination takes 10-15 days. Sowing too early or
planting outside too early spoils the performance of this plant.

CULTURE: Plant in full sun 6-18″ apart in a rich, well drained, sandy soil. In the greenhouse,
grow warm (65° nights and 80-85° days), in full sun with a soil rich in humus kept evenly moist.

EASY

Celsia Arcturus   CRETAN BEAR'S TAIL   PERENNIAL
Scrophulariaceae, native to Crete.   Zone 9.

USES: Borders, pot plant, greenhouse.

HABIT: ½-1″, sweetly scented bright yellow flowers with purple stamens in
long racemes adorn 12-18″ slender, hairy stalks during July and August.
Celsia Arcturus is everblooming when grown as an indoor plant.

GERMINATION: Sow outdoors after all danger of frost has past, or indoors at any time,
maintaining a temperature within the medium of 70-75°. Germination occurs in 10-15 days.

CULTURE: Outdoors, grow in full sun, preferably in a cool area and dry soil. Indoors, grow in
full sun with cool (50-55°) nights. Allow soil to dry out between waterings.

Centaurea   *Centratherum*

Centaurea Cyanus   ANNUAL
BACHELOR'S BUTTON   CORNFLOWER
Compositae, native to the Mediterranean.

USES: Beds, borders, edging, cut flower.

HABIT: Annual plant 12-36″ with frilly, ruffled tufted flowers of mainly blue but also shades of purple, yellow, white, pink or red which bloom above silvery foliage in summer.

GERMINATION: Sow outdoors where plants are to bloom in early spring, or sow indoors 4 weeks before planting outside maintaining a temperature within the medium of 60-70°. Cover the seeds completely as darkness is needed for germination which takes 7-14 days.

CULTURE: Plant 6-12″ apart in full sun and a light, rich soil. Water moderately; this plant will tolerate drought conditions. It is not a long blooming plant, so successive sowings and planting will give a more continuous bloom.

EASY

Centratherum intermedium   MANAOS BEAUTY   ANNUAL
Compositae, native to Brazil.

USES: Border, edging, rock gardens, bedding, house plant.

HABIT: Blue-green, crinkled and serrated leaved plants, 18-24″ tall, bear long lasting blue-lavender fluffy button flowers from summer to frost. The plant is everblooming indoors. It is a very uniform plant, giving the appearance of a clipped hedge.

GERMINATION: Seeds may be sown outdoors where they are to grow after all danger of frost is past, but for best results, sow indoors 4-6 weeks before planting outdoors, maintaining a temperature within the medium of 70-75° during germination which takes 10-14 days. For indoor use, sow at any season.

CULTURE: Plant 12-15″ apart in full sun or light shade in a light, sandy, rich, well drained soil. It tolerates heat and drought. Indoors, grow in full sun in average potting soil kept evenly moist.

Cerastium   *Cercis*

Cerastium tomentosum SNOW-IN-SUMMER   PERENNIAL
Caryophyllaceae, native to Europe.   Zone 3.

USES: Rock garden, ground cover, edging, border.

HABIT: Perennial 6-12″ high with small silvery-white leaves and small white shaped flowers blooming in May and June.

GERMINATION: Sow outdoors in spring or summer, up to two months before frost, or sow indoors, maintaining a temperature within the medium of 70-75° during germination which .takes 5-10 days.

CULTURE: Plant in full sun 12″ apart in average, well drained soil. Snow-In-Summer does very well in hot, dry spots and poor soils. Shear after flowering to induce bushiness.

EASY

Cercis canadensis REDBUD, JUDAS TREE   TREE
Leguminosae, native to the United States.   Zone 4.

USES: Ornamental, landscape accent.

HABIT: Deciduous tree to 40′ with light green rounded heart-shaped leaves preceded in mid-May by small but profuse magenta colored pea-like flowers.

GERMINATION: Sow seed outdoors in fall for germination the following spring or summer. Indoors, soak seeds in hot water for 24 hours, followed by placing in moistened medium and putting in the refrigerator for 2-3 months. Sow in a medium with extra coarse sand added and maintain a temperature within the medium of 70-75° during germination which takes up to several months. Germination may be aided by an innoculant for legumes.

CULTURE: Plant in full sun or light shade in a rich soil with excellent drainage. Plants are slow to become established and do not transplant well.

Chamaedorea   *Chamaemelum*

Chamaedorea elegans 'Bella'   PARLOR PALM   POT PLANT
(Neanthe Bella)
Palmae, native to Mexico and Central America.

USES: House plant, greenhouse, dish garden, terrarium.

HABIT: A dwarf palm, generally 12-30″ indoors, with shiny green pinnate leaves which gracefully curve and droop.

GERMINATION: Sow seeds at any season after soaking for 24-48 hours, maintaining a temperature within the medium of 70-80° during germination which will take one to several months.

CULTURE: Grow in indirect light or a north window with a night temperature of 60-70° and daytime temperature of 75-85°. Keep the soil evenly moist and take provisions to keep humidity high. Feed in spring and summer only.

Chamaemelum nobile   CHAMOMILE   PERENNIAL
(Anthemis nobilis)
Compositae, native to Europe.   Zone 4.

USES: Ground cover, lawn substitute, rock gardens, borders, medicinal.

HABIT: Creeping plant 3-8″ high with finely cut fragrant foliage and 1″ yellow or white flowers from August through the fall.

GERMINATION: Sow outdoors in spring or summer where plants are to bloom, or sow indoors maintaining a temperature within the medium of 70-75° during germination which takes 7-10 days.

CULTURE: Set plants 3-4″ apart in full sun. Chamomile must be mowed and flowers should not be allowed to form.

Cheiranthus   Chiastophyllum

Cheiranthus Cheiri WALLFLOWER   PERENNIAL
Erysimum hieraciifolium SIBERIAN WALLFLOWER
(Cheiranthus Allionii)
   Cruciferae, native to Europe   Zone 3

USES: Rock gardens, walls, bedding, border, cut flower.

HABIT: A multi-branched bushy plant with narrow bright green leaves, 12-30" tall, bears erect spikes of showy and unusually fragrant 1" flowers of yellow, orange, apricot, red, purple, copper or brown in spring. It is winter blooming indoors. Wallflower is often treated as a biennial or annual.

GERMINATION: Sow outdoors in early spring for annual or perennial use; spring through summer up to two months before frost for perennial use; or in late summer for biennial use; or sow indoors, maintaining a temperature within the medium of 55-65° during germination which takes 5-7 days.

CULTURE: Plant 12-15" apart in full sun or light shade in an average, well drained soil. It does best in coastal and mountainous areas where summer temperatures are cool and the air damp.

Chiastophyllum oppositifolium SILVER CROWN PERENNIAL
(Cotyledon simplicifolia) SILVER RUFFLES
   Crassulaceae, native to Caucasus.   Zone 7.

USES: Ground cover, rock garden, house plant.

HABIT: Creeping and rooting branches carry succulent, sedum-like leaf rosettes and ¼" yellow bell-shaped flowers in drooping racemes in late spring.

GERMINATION: Sow outdoors in late fall or early spring for late spring germination. Indoors, maintain a temperature within the medium of 55° during germination which takes 30 days. Do not cover the fine seeds.

CULTURE: Outdoors, plant in full sun in a light, dry, well drained soil. Indoors, grow at 55° nights and 70° days in a light soil that is allowed to dry out between waterings. Place in filtered or diffused sunlight.

Chrysanthemum carinatum   *Chrysanthemum coccineum*

CHRISTMAS CHERRY, see **Solanum pseudocapsicum**

Chrysanthemum carinatum   ANNUAL
        TRICOLOR CHRYSANTHEMUM
Chrysanthemum coronarium
        CROWN DAISY, GARLAND CHRYSANTHEMUM
Compositae, native to the Mediterranean.

USES: Beds, borders, cut flower.

HABIT:*C. carinatun* is 2-3′tall, with deeply cut fleshy foliage and flowers of white, yellow, red or purple, often banded, with purple centers. *C. coronarium* is a neat 1½-2′dome shaped plant with fern-like foliage and 1-1½″ button-type double flowers of golden or light yellow.

GERMINATION: Sow outdoors where plants are to bloom after all danger of frost has past, or sow indoors 8-10 weeks before planting outside, maintaining a temperature within the medium of 68-70° during germination which takes 10-18 days.

CULTURE: Plant 12-18″apart in a well drained average soil. Annual chrysanthemums prefer a mild, moist climate and do not do well in areas where summers are hot and dry.

EASY

Chrysanthemum coccineum   PERENNIAL
        PYRETHRUM,   PAINTED DAISY
Compositae, native to S.W. Asia.   Zone 2.

USES: Beds, borders, cut flowers.

HABIT: Perennial 24″ tall with mounded, dark green, fern-like foliage bearing single or double 3″ daisy-like flowers on long stems in red, pink, or white with yellow centers blooming in May and June.

GERMINATION: Sow outdoors in spring or summer up to two months before frost, or sow indoors in early spring maintaining a temperature within the medium of 70° during germination which takes 20-25 days.

CULTURE: Plant 12″apart in full sun or light shade in a light, rich, well drained soil. Cut stems to the ground after flowering to possibly produce a fall bloom.

EASY

Chrysanthemum frutescens   *Chrysanthemum X morifolium*

Chrysanthemum frutescens   PERENNIAL
(Anthemis frutescens)   WHITE MARGUERITE
Compositae, native to the Canary Islands.   Zone 10.

USES: Borders, beds, cut flowers.

HABIT: Bushy 3′ plant with lacy divided grey-green leaves and 2″ flowers of white or pale yellow with yellow centers.

GERMINATION: Sow outdoors in spring or summer up to two months before frost, or sow indoors maintaining a temperature within the medium of 70° during germination which takes 8-14 days. For use as an annual, sow 6-8 weeks before planting outside.

CULTURE: Plant 15-18″ apart in full sun in a light, well drained soil.

EASY

Chrysanthemum X morifolium CHRYSANTHEMUM PERENNIAL
Compositae, probably native to China.   Zone 5.

USES: Borders, bedding, pot plant, greenhouse, cut flower.

HABIT: Flowers from ½-12″ in shades of bronze, yellow, gold, orange, white, pink, red and lavender bloom outdoors from late August through November; indoors they can be forced to bloom any time. Many flower forms are available: cactus, incurve, spider, daisy, anemone, pompom, spoon, quill. Height varies from dwarf and cushion varieties of 6″ to exhibition types of up to 4′.

GERMINATION: Sow outdoors in spring or summer up to two months before frost. Sowing indoors in early spring will result in flowers the first year; maintain a temperature within the medium of 70° during germination which takes 7-10 days.

CULTURE: In spring after frost has past, plant mums 6-24″ apart, in full sun in a rich, well drained soil. Keep well watered. Indoors, grow in a cool greenhouse, in full sun, with soil kept moist. Mums initiate bloom on long nights and have to be shaded to bloom in late spring and summer.

EASY

Chrysanthemum Parthenium   *Chrysanthemum ptarmiciflorum*

Chrysanthemum Parthenium   PERENNIAL
MATRICARIA   FEVERFEW
Compositae, native to Europe and Asia.   Zone 4.

USES: Beds, borders, pot plant, cut flower, medicinal.

HABIT: Bushy 6″-2′ plant with strong scented foliage and many white petaled single or double daisy or anemone flowers which bloom in July and August.

GERMINATION: Sow outdoors in early spring where plants are to bloom, or sow indoors in early spring, maintaining a temperature within the medium of 70° during germination which takes 10-15 days. Do not cover seed as light is beneficial to germination.

CULTURE: Plant 6-12″ apart in full sun or light shade in a sandy, well drained soil. It is recommended that this plant be grown as an annual as it can get weedy.

EASY

Chrysanthemum ptarmiciflorum   PERENNIAL
DUSTY MILLER,   SILVER LACE
Compositae, native to the Canary Islands.   Zone 3.

USES: Borders, edging, arrangements.

HABIT: Shrubby perennial, 2-3′ high, with white, fuzzy, deeply cut leaves and 1¼″ white flowers with yellow centers. The texture is very fine.

GERMINATION: Sow outdoors in spring or summer up to two months before frost, or sow indoors, maintaining a temperature within the medium of 70° during germination which takes 20-25 days.

CULTURE: Plant 12-18″ apart in full sun and a well drained, sandy soil, which may be dry between waterings.

EASY

113

Chrysanthemum X superbum   Cirsium

Chrysanthemum X superbum   SHASTA DAISY   PERENNIAL
(Chrysanthemum maximum)

Compositae, native to the Pyrenees.   Zone 4.

USES: Beds, borders, cut flowers.

HABIT: Plants 1-4' in height flower in June, July or August with flower types such as single, double, daisy and anemone. The white flowers are up to 7″ across and are borne on stiff stems over mounds of tufted foliage.

GERMINATION: Sow outdoors from early spring through summer up to two months before frost, or sow indoors, maintaining a temperature within the medium of 70-75° during germination which takes 10-14 days. Do not cover seeds as they need light to germinate.

CULTURE: Plant in full sun in a rich, moist, well drained garden soil. All will tolerate partial shade and double flowers often prefer it in humid areas. Plant 12-24″ apart and keep well watered.

EASY

CINERARIA, see **Senecio X hybridus**

Cirsium japonicum   THISTLE   PERENNIAL
Compositae, native to Japan.   Zone 3.

USES: Border, cut flower, dried flower.

HABIT: Rose-red flowers 1½″ across in late summer and fall on this 2-2½' plant with lobed and spiny toothed leaves.

GERMINATION: Sow outdoors where the plants are to grow after all danger of frost is past, or sow indoors, maintaining a temperature within the medium of 70-75° during germination which takes 15-18 days.

CULTURE: Plant 12″ apart in full sun and a dry soil. *Cirsium* tolerates a poor soil and can become weedy.

EASY

114

Cladanthus   Clarkia

Cladanthus arabicus   PALM SPRINGS DAISY   ANNUAL
(Anthemis arabica)
Compositae, native to Spain and Morocco.

USES: Borders, pots, edging, greenhouse.

HABIT: Pure yellow daisy-like 2″ flowers in summer are borne on 2-3′ mounds of extremely lacy and finely divided pungent foliage.

GERMINATION: Sow outdoors where plants are to bloom after all danger of frost has past, or sow indoors 6-8 weeks before planting outside maintaining a temperature within the medium of 70-75° during germination which takes 30-35 days. For winter greenhouse use, sow in late summer.

CULTURE: Plant 12″ apart in full sun and average garden soil with good drainage. In the greenhouse, grow cool (50-55°) in full sun, and allow plants to dry out between waterings.

Clarkia hybrids   ROCKY MOUNTAIN GARLAND   ANNUAL
Onagraceae, native to California.

USES: Bedding, pot plant, cut flower, greenhouse.

HABIT: Delicate 1″ showy single or double flowers in spikes and colors of salmon, pink, lavender, purple, red or white flower from summer to frost on 18-24″ stems.

GERMINATION: Sow seeds outdoors where plants are to grow after all danger of frost has past. In frost-free areas, sow in fall for bloom the following spring. Do not start seeds indoors. Barely cover the seeds as they are very fine; germination takes 5-10 days.

CULTURE: Plant 8-10″ apart in full sun or light shade in a light, sandy soil that has excellent drainage and low fertility. Plants do well only where nights are cool, and especially on the Pacific coast. In the greenhouse, grow cool (50-55°) in full sun and allow to dry out between waterings.

EASY

115

Clematis   Cleome

Clematis species   VIRGIN'S BOWER   PERENNIAL
Ranunculaceae, native to temperate regions of the world.   Zone 5.

HABIT: Vine, 10-20', with compound leaves and 2" flowers in pink, white, purple, lilac, rose, blue, and crimson appearing in clusters and blooming in summer. Plumy seed pods 1-1½" long appear in fall. Those sown from seeds are not as showy as hybrids propagated from cuttings. Included are *C. Flammula, C. Vitalba, and C. Viticella.*

GERMINATION: Sow outside in late fall for germination in spring, or, indoors, place in moistened medium in the freezer for 3 weeks followed by germination at a temperature within the medium of 80-85°. Germination is slow and may not occur for several months.

CULTURE: Plant in a location where roots can be kept cool and shaded and the tops kept in full sun. Soil should be rich, limey, and have excellent drainage. Water heavily.

Cleome Hasslerana   SPIDER FLOWER   ANNUAL
Capparaceae, native to the Caribbean.

USES: Background, borders, cut flowers.

HABIT: Strong scented annual 3-6' tall with 6-7" heads of airy orchid-like blooms of rose, pink, white or lavender flowering in summer until frost, followed by spidery seed pods. The long stamens are characteristic.

GERMINATION: Sow where plants are to bloom after all danger of frost has past, or sow indoors 4-6 weeks before planting outside, maintaining a temperature within the medium of 70-75° during germination which takes 10-14 days.

CULTURE: Plant outside 2-3' apart in full sun and a warm dry location. *Cleome* withstands heat and drought.

EASY

Clitoria　　　　　　　　　　　　　　　*Clivia*

Clitoria Ternata　　BUTTERFLY PEA　　　　　PERENNIAL
Leguminosae, native to the Tropics.　　　　　　　Zone 10.

USES: Vine, screening, greenhouse.

HABIT: Slender stemmed vine to 15' bears single or double 1½-2" azure blue flowers with light markings and a white center, pea-like in clusters in summer. It is winter blooming indoors.

GERMINATION: Clip or file seeds and soak for 24 hours before sowing. Sow outdoors where plants are to grow, or sow indoors maintaining a temperature within the medium of 70-75° during germination which takes 15-20 days. Sow in early spring for outdoor use and daytime for greenhouse use.

CULTURE: Plant 3' apart in full sun in a rich, light, sandy soil. Indoors, grow at 55° in full sun, water well, and pinch frequently to promote bushiness. *Clitoria* can be grown as an annual in most parts of the country.

Clivia miniata　　KAFFIR LILY　　　　　POT PLANT
Amaryllidaceae, native to South Africa.

USES: House plant, greenhouse plant.

HABIT: Broad, straplike, waxy evergreen leaves grow from thick bulbous roots and clusters of 10-18 giant trumpet shaped flowers in orange and scarlet with yellow centers bloom in March through June at the end of 12-18" stems.

GERMINATION: Seeds are shipped ripe and fresh and must be sown immediately upon receipt. Maintain a temperature within the medium of 75° during germination which takes 30 days or more.

CULTURE: Grow indoors in light shade, cool (50-55°) nights in winter, and a rich, well drained soil. The resting period is October through January, when the plant should be watered sparingly and not fed. When growth starts, increase night temperature to 65°, water well, allowing to dry slightly between waterings, and increase humidity. *Clivia* blooms best when pot bound.

117

Cobaea   Codiaeum

Cobaea scandens CUP AND SAUCER VINE   PERENNIAL
CATHEDRAL BELLS
Polemoniaceae, native to South America and Mexico.   Zone 9.

USES: Vine, trellis, screen, greenhouse.

HABIT: Rampant, quick growing vine to 20′ per year, best treated as an annual. It has dark green leaves and bell-like flowers of blue or white resting on a broad saucer-like calyx from June through October. The flowers open a pale green and darken to purple as they mature.

GERMINATION: Sow outdoors where plants are to bloom after the soil has warmed up in spring, or sow indoors, maintaining a temperature within the medium of 70-75° during germination which takes 15-20 days. Stick the seed vertically into the medium.

CULTURE: Grow outdoors in full sun or light shade in a rich, moist, well drained soil. Indoors, grow cool (50-55°), in full sun, and keep the soil evenly moist.

EASY

Codiaeum variegatum var. **pictum**   CROTON   POT PLANT
Euphorbiaceae, native to the South Pacific.

USES: House plant, planters in warm climates, greenhouse plant.

HABIT: Striking multi-colored foliage plants to 3′ or more. The thick, smooth, glossy, leathery foliage is in colors of yellow, pink, orange, red, copper, brown, bronze and green. Some leaves are broad and smooth, others scalloped, others narrow.

GERMINATION: Sow seeds indoors at any season providing a temperature within the medium of 75-80° during germination which requires 30 days.

CULTURE: Plant in a very rich, moist soil. Night temperatures should be 65° and daytime temperatures 70-80° with no drafts. Grow in full sun; they will tolerate indirect light but will lose much of their coloring. Keep soil evenly moist and provide a constant high (70%) humidity.

EASY

Coffea   *Coix*

Coffea arabica   ARABIAN COFFEE PLANT   POT PLANT
Rubiaceae, native to tropical Africa.

USES: House plant, greenhouse.

HABIT: These plants are attractive foliage plants with shiny, dark green, oval leaves, white fragrant flowers and bright red berries. In the house, it will grow to about 3'.

GERMINATION: Soak seeds for 48 hours before sowing. Sow indoors at any season, maintaining a temperature within the medium of 75° during germination which takes 6-8 weeks or more. Do not cover seeds as light is beneficial to germination.

CULTURE: Grow in a rich, well drained soil kept evenly moist. This plant likes full sun, 30-50% humidity, and warm conditions (65° nights and 75° days).

Coix Lacryma-Jobi JOB'S TEAR'S   PERENNIAL
Gramineae, native to India.   Zone 9.

USES: Ornamental grass, edging, rock garden, jewelry.

HABIT: Three foot tufted grassy plant with narrow light green leaves from which arise stalks bearing spikes of small interesting "beads", ¼" wide, white, grey or brown, hard and shiny with a soft core.

GERMINATION: Sow where plants are to grow after all danger of frost is past, or for best results, soak seeds for 24 hours and sow indoors, maintaining a temperature within the medium of 68-86° during germination which takes 20-25 days.

CULTURE: Plant 18-24" apart in full sun or light shade in a sandy, rich, well drained soil. Grow as an annual in cooler climates.

119

Coleus   *Coreopsis*

Coleus X hybridus   COLEUS   ANNUAL
Labiatae, native to Java.

USES: Borders, bedding, planters, house plant, greenhouse plant.

HABIT: Very popular, curiously variegated, square stemmed, multi-colored foliage plants in combinations of chartreuse, white, bronze, gold, copper, yellow, pink, red, purple and green. Leaves may be smooth edged, fringed, toothed, wrinkled, splashy. Insignificant flower spikes appear in shades of blue or lavender in late summer. Plants vary from 6-36".

GERMINATION: For best results sow indoors 6-8 weeks before planting outside, not covering the seed which needs light to germinate. Germination takes 10-15 days at a temperature within the medium of 70-75°. Sow at any season for indoor use.

CULTURE: Plant 10-18" apart in full sun or shade in a good garden soil. Keep moist during the growing season, and pinch off flowers as they form. Indoors, keep warm (65° nights and up to 80° during the day), well watered, and give plenty of bright light. Pinch to induce bushiness.

EASY

Coreopsis grandiflora   TICKSEED, POT OF GOLD   PERENNIAL
Compositae, native to midwest and south United States.   Zone 6.

USES: Borders, rock garden, cut flower.

HABIT: Showy 2-3" yellow daisy-like flowers on 16-36" stems that are slender and wiry appear during summer and fall above narrow, lobed, dark green leaves.

GERMINATION: Sow outdoors any time from early spring through summer up to two months before frost, or in late fall for germination the following spring. Seeds may also be sown indoors, maintaining a temperature within the medium of 55-70° during germination which takes 20-25 days. Do not cover the seeds as light aids germination.

CULTURE: Plant 12" apart in full sun and a light, sandy, well drained soil. Keep moderately moist and remove faded blooms to extend flowering period.

EASY

Coreopsis   *Cornus*

Coreopsis tinctoria CALLIOPSIS   ANNUAL
Compositae, native to the United States and Canada.

USES: Bedding, edging, borders, cut flowers.

HABIT: Daisy-like, 1¼″ flowers in bright red, yellow, pink or purple, either solid or banded, appear from summer to frost on 8-36″ slender, wiry stems.

GERMINATION: Sow outdoors where plants are to grow after all danger of frost has past, or sow indoors 6-8 weeks before planting outside, maintaining a temperature within the medium of 70-75° during germination which takes 5-10 days.

CULTURE: Plant 8-12″ apart in full sun and light, sandy soil with excellent drainage. Calliopsis will tolerate poor soils.

Cornus species   DOGWOOD   TREE
Cornaceae, native to the temperate regions.   Zone 4.

USES: Ornamental tree.

HABIT: *Cornus florida* (Flowering Dogwood) is an outstanding ornamental tree to 30′ with white or pink petal-like bracts in May, bright red berries in fall, and brilliant scarlet fall color. Branches have a horizontal outline. *Cornus mas* (Cornellian Cherry) grows to 25′ and has numerous yellow flowers in umbels before the leaves in April. The berries are scarlet and resemble cherries and the lustrous green leaves turn red in fall.

GERMINATION: *C. florida* should be sown outdoors in fall for germination in spring, or placed in the freezer in moist medium for 3 months followed by sowing in a sandy medium with a temperature within that medium of 70-75°. Germination may take several months or the seeds may lie dormant for a year. *C. mas* needs a double dormancy period; keep at room temperature for 4 months, then freeze as above for 4 months, followed by sowing. As with *C. florida,* germination may be very slow.

CULTURE: Plant in sun or light shade in a rich, moist, well drained soil. Water well as they do not tolerate drought.

Coronilla   *Cortaderia*

Coronilla varia   CROWN VETCH   PERENNIAL
Leguminosae, native to Europe.   Zone 3.

USES: Ground cover.

HABIT: Crown vetch is a spreading plant with rich green leaves and pink crown shaped flowers produced in profusion from June until frost. Height is 15-24″. It is particularly useful for covering banks and slopes.

GERMINATION: Direct seed large areas in early spring at the rate of 1 lb. per 1000 sq. ft. with an equal amount of annual ryegrass which holds the soil until the crown vetch becomes established. Seed may also be sown indoors, maintaining a temperature within the medium of 70-75° during germination which takes 30 days. Germination can be hastened by nicking the hard seed coat or soaking in water before sowing, which will cut the time in half.

CULTURE: Thin or plant 6″ apart on almost any type of soil, which should be slightly alkaline. Crown vetch does best in full sun or light shade, but will tolerate shade. It withstands drought and can be mowed to a desired height. Although somewhat slow to start, it increases rapidly once established. For best results, mulch with hay or straw after planting.

Cortaderia Selloana   PAMPAS GRASS   PERENNIAL
Gramineae, native to Argentina.   Zone 7.

USES: Ornamental grass, dried bouquets.

HABIT: Fine and showy 8-10′ clumps have arching, silky, 1-3′ plumes of silvery white or tinged pink in late summer.

GERMINATION: Sow outdoors where plants are to bloom after the soil is warm in spring, or sow indoors 6-8 weeks before planting outside, maintaining a temperature within the medium of 65-75° during germination which takes 20-25 days. Do not cover the fine seeds, which need light to germinate.

CULTURE: Plant 4-5′ apart in full sun and a well drained, fertile soil. In areas colder than Zone 7, dig up the roots in fall and store in a cool, dry place, never allowing to dry out completely.

Corynocarpus

Corynocarpus laevigata NEW ZEALAND LAUREL POT PLANT
Corynocarpaceae, native to New Zealand.

USES: House plant, greenhouse plant.

HABIT: Evergreen plant with showy orange plum-like fruits and thick, 8″, leathery, oblong, dark green leaves on a symmetrical and well branched form.

GERMINATION: Seeds are shipped ripe and fresh and must be sown immediately upon receipt. Maintain a temperature within the medium of 70-75° during germination which takes 15-20 days.

CULTURE: Grow in a warm spot (65° nights and up to 80° days), in full or lightly filtered sun. Soil should be rich and well drained and kept evenly moist, and humidity should be high. A summer vacation outdoors is appreciated by these plants.

EASY

A Window Garden

Cosmos

Crepis

Cosmos bipinnatus COSMOS, MEXICAN ASTER ANNUAL
Cosmos sulphureus
   Compositae, native to Mexico.

USES: Beds, borders, background, cut flower.

HABIT: Bushy 1½-5′ annual with 2-6″ single or double daisy-like flowers with wide and serrated petals in white, gold, yellow, orange, pink or crimson with yellow centers. It flowers in July until frost on tall slender stems, clothed with finely divided thready foliage.

GERMINATION: Sow outdoors where plants are to grow after all danger of frost has past, or sow indoors 5-7 weeks before planting outside, maintaining a temperature within the medium of 68-86° during germination which takes 5-10 days.

CULTURE: Plant 9-24″ apart in full sun and in dry and infertile soil with excellent drainage. Stake tall plants.

EASY

COTTON, ORNAMENTAL, see **Gossypium hirsutum**

Crepis rubra HAWK'S BEARD ANNUAL
   Compositae, native to north temperate areas.

USES: Borders, edging, rock garden.

HABIT: Rose-pink dandelion-like flowers 1″ across bloom in summer and fall on 6-12″ stems above clumps of slender leaves.

GERMINATION: Sow outdoors after all danger of frost has past where plants are to grow, or sow indoors, 6-8 weeks before planting outside, maintaining a temperature within the medium of 68-86° during germination which takes 5-7 days.

CULTURE: Plant 4-6″ apart in full sun and a light, well drained soil which is poor and dry.

EASY

Crossandra

Cucurbita

Crossandra infundibuliformis   CROSSANDRA   POT PLANT
(Crossandra undulifolia)
   Acanthaceae, native to India and Malaya.

USES: House plant, greenhouse plant.

HABIT: Indoor plant, 12-30″ high, with 2-3″ waxy leaves and funnel shaped bright salmon flowers which bloom off and on the year 'round.

GERMINATION: Sow seeds indoors at any season, not covering them as they need light to germinate. Maintain a temperature within the medium of 75-80° during germination which takes 25-30 days.

CULTURE: Place pots in at least four hours of direct sun a day except during the hottest part of the year. Grow in a night temperature of 60-65° for ideal results. Potting soil should be rich and well drained and kept moist at all times.

Cucurbita Pepo var. **ovifera**   ANNUAL
                YELLOW FLOWERED GOURDS
   Cucurbitaceae, native to Texas.

USES: Screen, dried fruits.

HABIT: These vines produce yellow flowers and hard shelled fruits known as gourds in various shapes, sizes and colors of green, yellow and orange. The gourds are long lasting, colorful, decorative, and smaller than the white flowering gourds *(Lagenaria).*

GERMINATION: Seeds may be sown where plants are to grow outdoors, but for best results, germinate indoors at a temperature within the medium of 70°. Seeds sprout in 8-14 days and germination may be hastened by soaking seeds in warm water for 24 hours before sowing.

CULTURE: Plant in full sun in a soil suitable for vegetable growing. Gourds need a long, hot growing season and should be trained on a trellis or fence. Pick when the stem of the gourd begins to dry up, wash well, and wax.

EASY

125

Cuphea   *Cupressus*

Cuphea ignea   ANNUAL
CIGAR FLOWER,   FIRECRACKER PLANT
Lythraceae, native to Mexico.

USES: Planters, edgings, rock gardens, house plant.

HABIT: Compact 1' plant bearing summer blooming tubular flowers of bright fiery red with a black and white tip resembling a cigar ash. It is ever-blooming indoors.

GERMINATION: Sow seeds where they are to grow outdoors, but for best results, sow indoors 6-8 weeks before planting outside, not covering seeds which need light to germinate. Maintain a temperature within the medium of 70° during germination which takes 8-10 days.

CULTURE: Plant 9-12" apart in sun or light shade in a light, well drained garden soil. Keep well watered during the season. Indoors, provide at least 4 hours of sun a day, grow cool (50-55° nights), and keep soil evenly moist.

EASY

Cupressus sempervirens var. **Stricta**   TREE
PYRAMIDAL ITALIAN CYPRESS
Cupressaceae, native to Southern Europe.   Zone 7.

USES: Hedges, windbreaks, specimen.

HABIT: Evergreen tree has flattened scale-like leaves and very short branches which form a narrow column. It grows 20-80', has a 1" cone and aromatic foliage.

GERMINATION: Sow outdoors in late fall or early spring for late spring germination, or sow indoors, maintaining a temperature within the medium of 70° during germination which takes 30 days. Germination indoors may be improved by placing seeds in moistened medium and placing in the refrigerator for 3 weeks before sowing.

CULTURE: Plant in full sun and a well drained soil that is not high in fertility. Do not overwater. Little or no pruning is needed.

Cyclamen persicum

Cyclamen species

Cyclamen persicum FLORIST'S CYCLAMEN POT PLANT
SHOOTING STAR
Primulaceae, native to the east Mediterranean. Zone 9, 5.

USES: Greenhouse plant, house plant, bedding in warm climates.

HABIT: Tuberous rooted plants produce light to dark green marbled heart-shaped leaves often with silver markings and stems with 2-4" shooting star-like flowers, single, double or fringed, in white, red, pink, salmon and lavender. It is winter blooming indoors. Most take 18 months to bloom from seed, but the cross 'Puck' takes only 6 months, and is hardy to Zone 5.

GERMINATION: Sow indoors in summer for bloom in winter a year later. Cover well as seeds need darkness to germinate, and maintain a temperature within the medium of 55-60° during germination which takes 50 days.

CULTURE: Indoors, cyclamen must be grown cool (50-55° nights), with a soil rich in humus kept evenly moist, and diffused light. It likes high humidity, so keep in a greenhouse or mist foliage regularly. When flowers fade, withhold water until foliage dies. Keep nearly dry, with the pot placed on its side outdoors in a shady location. Repot in fall and return indoors. Outdoors in warmer climates, plant in fall for winter and spring bloom, and treat as an annual.

Cyclamen species CYCLAMEN PERENNIAL
Primulaceae, native to the Mediterranean. Zones 5-7.

USES: Borders, woodland gardens, ground cover, rock garden.

HABIT: Hardy cyclamen are low growing with nodding flowers with reflexed petals. *C. cilicium* is 3" tall, with round leaves marbled silver above, and fragrant flowers of pink. It is hardy to Zone 7. *C. coum* has round green leaves with red-purple underneath and pink to deep rose flowers. It grows to 3" and is hardy to Zone 6. *C. hederifolium (C. neapolitanum)* grows 4" tall, has heart shaped leaves marbled green and silver, is hardy to Zone 5 and has rose pink flowers. *C. purpurascens (C. europaeum)* has heart shaped green marbled white leaves, is 4" tall, and has very fragrant flowers of crimson to rose. It is hardy to Zone 5. *C. coum* blooms in early spring; the others bloom in late summer and fall.

GERMINATION: Indoors, sow at a temperature within the medium of 55-60° during germination which takes 21-28 days. Cover seeds well as they must be in total darkness to germinate. Seeds sown in late summer can be wintered over in a protected location, cold frame or cool greenhouse for planting out and bloom the following spring to fall.

CULTURE: Plant in part shade or shade, 3-4" apart, in a very rich soil with excellent drainage. Keep moist during the growing season.

127

Cymbalaria   *Cynoglossum*

Cymbalaria muralis   KENILWORTH IVY   PERENNIAL
(Linaria Cymbalaria)
    Scrophulariaceae, native to central Europe.   Zone 3.

USES: Hanging basket, ground cover, house plant, greenhouse.

HABIT: Kidney shaped waxy leaves are found on this evergreen trailing plant, along with lavender-blue flowers with yellow throats, blooming in summer and looking like miniature snapdragons.

GERMINATION: Sow outdoors where plants are to grow any time in spring or summer up to two months before frost, or sow indoors maintaining a temperature within the medium of 70-75° during germination which takes 20 days.

CULTURE: Grow in sun or part shade in an average soil on the alkaline side. Indoors this plant prefers cool nights (50-55°), diffused light, and a soil kept evenly moist.

Cynoglossum amabile   HOUND'S TONGUE   ANNUAL
                     CHINESE FORGET-ME-NOT
    Boraginaceae, native to eastern Asia.

USES: Bedding, borders, cut flowers, rock gardens.

HABIT: May to frost flowering ¼" forget-me-not fragrant blossoms are borne along graceful, branching sprays 18-24" tall with colors of blue, pink or white. Leaves are soft textured and shaped like a dog's tongue.

GERMINATION: Sow outdoors in early spring as soon as soil can be worked, or sow indoors 6-8 weeks before planting outside, maintaining a temperature within the medium of 65-75° during germination which takes 5-10 days. Cover seeds as they need darkness to germinate.

CULTURE: Plant 9-12" apart in full sun and an average, well drained garden soil. This plant is not fussy and may be grown either wet or dry, warm or cold.

EASY

Cyperus

Cyperus alternifolius   POT PLANT
UMBRELLA PLANT,   UMBRELLA FLATSEDGE
Cyperaceae, native to Africa.   Zone 10.

USES: Pool edges, houseplant, greenhouse.

HABIT: Semi-aquatic 4′ plant with long, narrow, grass-like leaves gracefully radiating from the center of the slender stalk like spines of an umbrella. Small green flowers and fruits are borne in tight clusters in the crowns in late summer.

GERMINATION: Sow indoors at any season, maintaining a temperature within the medium of 70-75° during germination which takes 25-30 days.

CULTURE: Plant 24-30″ apart outdoors in part shade and a rich, porous, moist soil. For indoor use, place plants in light shade or indirect light, grow cool (50-55° nights), keep soil wet at all times by keeping water in the saucer, and mist frequently.

Cyphomandra betacea   TREE TOMATO   POT PLANT
Solanaceae, native to South America.   Zone 9.

USES: Planters, house plant, greenhouse.

HABIT: Perennial tree-like woody plant to 5′ with large, sharp pointed, heart-shaped leaves and small, fragrant ½″ pink flowers followed by 2-3″ edible egg-shaped, smooth red fruits with a tomato flavor.

GERMINATION: For outdoors use, sow in early spring; for indoor use, sow at any season. Maintain a temperature within the medium of 70-75° during germination which takes 20-25 days.

CULTURE: Indoors or out, give a warm location, full sun, a constantly moist soil, and never allow temperatures to go below 50°.

EASY.

129

Cytisus

Dahlia

Cytisus scoparius   PERENNIAL
       BUTCHER'S BROOM   SCOTCH BROOM
       Leguminosae, native to British Isles.   Zone 5.

USES: Banks, beds, rock garden, borders, foundation planting.

HABIT: Fast growing 4-6′ shrub with slender upright or trailing bright green branches which, in April and May, are clothed in tiny dark green leaves and masses of pea-like bright yellow flowers.

GERMINATION: Soak seeds for 24 hours in warm water before sowing. Maintain a temperature within the medium of 70-75° during germination which takes 25-30 days. Sowing may be done in spring or summer.

CULTURE: Plant in full sun in a light, sandy, well drained soil. Brooms tolerate heat and drought. They are difficult to transplant and can be pruned back after flowering.

Dahlia hybrids   DAHLIA   PERENNIAL
       Compositae, native to Mexico.   Zone 9.

USES: Bedding, borders, background exhibition, cut flower.

HABIT: Dahlias from seed produce 12-36″ plants with flowers 1-5″ across blooming from early summer to frost in all colors except blue. Color combinations and flowers in single, double, formal, informal, quill, anemone, cactus and pompom forms are available.

GERMINATION: Seeds may be sown where plants are to grow after all danger of frost has past, but for best results, sow indoors 4-6 weeks prior to planting outside, maintaining a temperature within the medium of 68-86° during germination which takes 5-10 days.

CULTURE: Plant 1-3′ apart in full sun in good, rich soil. Keep well watered and feed heavily. Taller varieties should be staked. After tops have been blackened by frost in fall, dig up tubers and store over the winter in plastic bag of dry peat moss in a cool place. Replant after frost has past in spring.

EASY

Living With Flowers

Daucus   Delphinium

Daucus var. **Carota**   BIENNIAL
QUEEN ANNE'S LACE,   WILD CARROT
Umbelliferae, native to Eurasia.   Zone 3.

USES: Wild flower, cut flower, dried arrangements.

HABIT: Taprooted 2-3′ plant with fern-like finely cut leaves and small white flowers borne in a flattened cluster having a single reddish flower in the center. Blooms June to September.

GERMINATION: Sow outdoors where plants are to bloom after all danger of frost has past, or sow indoors 6-8 weeks before planting outside, maintaining a temperature within the medium of 70° during germination which takes 10-14 days. Do not cover seed which needs light to germinate.

CULTURE: Plant 10-12″ apart in full sun in a light, sandy soil. Although generally thought of as a weed, this plant is airy and graceful and very attractive.

EASY

Delphinium species DELPHINIUM   PERENNIAL
Consolida ambigua LARKSPUR   ANNUAL
(Delphinium ajacis)
Ranunculaceae, native to Siberia, (Delphinium), southern Europe (Larkspur).   Zone 2.

USES: Background, border, cut flower.

HABIT: Tall, stately stalks 1-7′ with beautiful 3″ flowers of blue, white, purple, pink and yellow bloom in June and July on perennial varieties and from June through August on annual forms.

GERMINATION: Sow perennial forms outdoors in spring or summer up to two months before frost, or sow indoors, maintaining a temperature within the medium of 65-75° during germination which takes 8-15 days. Sow annual forms outdoors in early spring, or indoors 6-8 weeks before planting outside, maintaining a temperature within the medium of 65-75° during germination which takes 8-15 days. Be sure to totally cover the seeds as they require darkness to germinate. Seeds of *Delphinium* are not long lived and should not be stored.

CULTURE: Plant 1-3′ apart in full sun and a rich, loose, slightly alkaline soil. Stake taller varieties. Keep well watered and fed, and remove faded flowers to prevent seed formation. Both do best in cool climates.

Dianthus barbatus   Dianthus chinensis

Dianthus species and hybrids   ANNUAL
CHINA PINK,   SWEET WILLIAM
Caryophyllaceae, native to Europe and China.

USES: Edging, borders, bedding, cut flower, pot plant.

HABIT: *Dianthus chinensis,* the China Pink, grows 6-18″ with single or double frilled flowers of white, red, pink, rose or lavender, ½-1″ across, in solids or bicolors, above grey-green foliage. The annual Sweet William, *D. barbatus,* grows 4-12″ tall and has single or double flowers red, pink or white in solids or combinations in rounded clusters over green foliage. The flowers are sweetly fragrant. New *Dianthus* hybrids grow 6-12″, bloom in 3 months from seed, have single to double fringed, lacy flowers over blue-green foliage, and are heat tolerant.

GERMINATION: Sow outdoors in spring after danger of frost has past or sow indoors 6-8 weeks before planting outside, maintaining a temperature within the medium of 70° during germination which takes 5-10 days.

CULTURE: Plant 6-12″ apart in full sun in a rich, light, well drained alkaline soil. Cut back after flowering to insure continuous bloom. For best results, choose one of the newer hybrids as the older species do not like hot and dry summers.

An Early Summer Garden

Dianthus

Dianthus species   PERENNIAL
CARNATION,   PINKS,   SWEET WILLIAM
Caryophyllaceae, native to Europe.   Zone 3, 8.

USES: Borders, beds, edging, rock garden, pot plant, cut flower.

HABIT: These plants have grass-like evergreen foliage and stiff, erect stems with 1½-2″ single, double or frilled flowers in colors of red, pink, white, yellow, lavender, orange and salmon, in solids or bicolors, blooming throughout the summer. *D. X. Allwoodii* has a tufted habit and flowers with dark centers; it grows 6-18″. *D. barbatus* (Sweet William) grows 6-24″ with flat flowers in rounded clusters; although it is a perennial, it should be treated as an annual or a biennial. *D. Caryophyllus,* the Carnation, grows 1-3′ and forms flowers one to a stem. This is the species of *D. deltoides* (Maiden Pink) grows 4-12″ and forms a dense mat, making a good ground cover. Its flowers have lacy petals and a red center. *D. gratianopolitanus* (Cheddar Pink) is mat forming with grey leaves and fragrant flowrs. *D. plumarium* (Cottage Pink, Grass Pink) is 12-18″ tall with grey tufted foliage and fragrant flowers. *D. superbus* (Fringed Pink) is 2-3′ tall with rosy fragrant flowers, deeply fringed, and is best treated as a biennial. Except for the Carnation, the perennial *Dianthis* are hardy to Zone 3.

GERMINATION: Sow outdoors in spring or summer, up to two months before frost, or sow indoors, maintaining a temperature within the medium of 70° during germination which takes 14-21 days. *D. barbatus* may be treated as an annual and if so should be started indoors in early spring; it germinates in 5-10 days.

CULTURE: Plant outdoors 6-12″ apart in full sun and a light, sandy, well drained soil that is slightly alkaline. These plants are not long lived and should be replaced frequently. They prefer a cool, damp climate.

EASY

Dicentra   Dichondra

Dicentra spectabilis BLEEDING HEART   PERENNIAL
Fumariaceae, native to Japan.   Zone 2.

USES: Border, rock garden, wild flower garden.

HABIT: Mounded 2½-3' plants have finely cut, soft, blue-green foliage and graceful, arching stems covered with 1" heart shaped flowers of deep pink or white in May.

GERMINATION: Sow outdoors in late fall or early winter for spring germination. Indoors, place seeds in moistened medium and freeze for 6 weeks, followed by germination at a temperature within the medium of 55-60°. Germination takes 30 days or more.

CULTURE: Plant 2' apart in partial shade and a rich, light, fertile soil with excellent drainage. Keep moist throughout the growing season. *Dicentra spectabilis* foliage dies to the ground after flowering, making a perfect spot for shade loving annuals or house plants.

Dichondra micrantha DICHONDRA   PERENNIAL
Convolvulaceae, native to West Indies.   Zone 10.

USES: Lawn substitute, ground cover, hanging basket.

HABIT: *Dichondra* is a low growing (1-2") creeping perennial that spreads by underground runners. Leaves are dark green, kidney shaped, and of a neat, velvety appearance.

GERMINATION: Sow outdoors from March to May on a prepared seed bed, lightly covering and keeping moist. Seed will germinate in 7-14 days. For quickest coverage, sow 2 pounds per 1000 sq. ft.

CULTURE: *Dichondra* will grow in sun or shade, and requires less water than a grass lawn. It rarely needs to be mowed, except in shaded areas and areas with low traffic. As a hanging basket, grow with 55° nights and 70° days, in full sun and an average potting soil kept evenly moist.

EASY

Dictamnus   *Digitalis*

Dictamnus albus   GAS PLANT   PERENNIAL
Rutaceae, native from southern Europe to northern China.   Zone 2.

USES: Border, bed, cut flower.

HABIT: *Dictamnus* grows 2-3' tall and has pinnately compound, leathery, dark green leaves that give off a lemon scent when rubbed. Spikes 10-12" high of loose, fragrant, 1½-2" purple, pink or white flowers appear in June and July. The plant exudes a volatile oil which may be ignited on a calm night.

GERMINATION: Sow outdoors in late fall or early winter for spring germination, or sow indoors following a 4-6 week stratification in the refrigerator. Maintain a temperature within the medium of 55-60° during germination which takes 30-40 days.

CULTURE: Plant 3' apart in full sun and average, well drained garden soil. *Dictamnus* will tolerate light shade and some drought.

DIDISCUS, see **Trachymene coerulea**

Digitalis species   FOXGLOVE   BIENNIAL,   PERENNIAL
Scrophulariaceae, native to Europe.   Zone 4.

USES: Border, background, cut flower, medicinal.

HABIT: Plants with 1-6' spikes of 1-3" nodding bell shaped flowers of white, yellow, pink, purple or red bloom in late spring and early summer. Flowers resemble the end of a glove finger; some are spotted.

GERMINATION: Sow outdoors in spring or summer up to two months before frost for bloom the following year, or sow indoors, maintaining a temperature within the medium of 70° during germination which takes 15-20 days.

CULTURE: Set out 15-24" apart in a rich, loose soil with excellent drainage, in part shade. Plant in permanent position in fall and mulch under the foliage.

136

Dimorphotheca   *Diplocyclos*

Dimorphotheca sinuata   ANNUAL
CAPE MARIGOLD,   STAR OF THE VELDT
(D. aurantiaca)
Compositae, native to South Africa.

USES: Bedding, borders, cut flowers, greenhouse.

HABIT: Gay 4-12″ annual with 2½-3½″ daisy-like flowers in white, yellow, salmon and pink with petal undersides of blue and lavender and contrasting dark centers. Blooms appear from summer to frost and close at night.

GERMINATION: Sow seeds where the plants are to grow after all danger of frost has past, or, for best results, sow indoors 4-5 weeks before planting outside, maintaining a temperature within the medium of 60-70° during germination which takes 10-15 days. Sow in fall for spring color in the greenhouse. Seeds are not long lived and should not be stored.

CULTURE: Plant after frost has past in full sun and a light, sandy, well drained soil. It does best where temperatures are cool. In the greenhouse, grow in average potting soil kept evenly moist and in full sun. Night temperatures should be 45-50°.

Diplocyclos palmatus   MARBLE VINE   ANNUAL
(Bryonopsis laciniosa)
Cucurbitaceae, native to tropical Asia and Pacific Islands.

USES: Vine, screen.

HABIT: This is a fast growing vine with insignificant blooms in summer followed by fruits the size and shape of a marble, apple green with white stripes changing with age to orange-red with cream.

GERMINATION: Sow outdoors where plants are to bloom after all danger of frost has past. Germination will occur in 8-10 days.

CULTURE: Grow in full sun in average, well drained garden soil. Provide a trellis or other support.

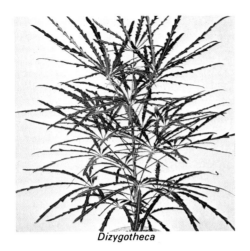

Dizygotheca   Dodecatheon

Dizygotheca elegantissima FALSE ARALIA   POT PLANT
Araliaceae, native to Pacific Islands.

USES: Houseplant, greenhouse plant.

HABIT: Upright growing tree-like plant, to 5' with graceful, narrow leathery notched leaves which are copper as they unfold, turning to blackish green.

GERMINATION: Sow indoors at any season, maintaining a temperature within the medium of 70° during germination which takes 20-30 days. Do not cover the seeds as light aids germination.

CULTURE: Grow in bright indirect light with a night temperature of 70° and a daytime temperature of 75-85°. Keep the soil barely moist at all times, and feed regularly from early spring to early fall.

Dodecatheon Meadia SHOOTING STAR   PERENNIAL
Primulaceae, native to the eastern United States.   Zone 3.

USES: Rock garden, wildflower, greenhouse, ground cover.

HABIT: Free flowering perennial 6-20″ tall with ground hugging mounds of leathery, wavy-margined leaves of green with reddish bases from which slender purple spotted stalks arise bearing clusters of small cyclamen-like flowers of deep rose with purple stamens. Flowers appear from April to June.

GERMINATION: Outdoors, sow in late fall or early winter for germination the following spring. Indoors, place in a moistened medium and put in the freezer for 3 weeks, followed by germination at a temperature within the medium of 60-70°, which takes 30 days or more.

CULTURE: Outdoors, plant in a moist, rich acid soil with excellent drainage in a shady spot. Indoors, grow with 45-50° nights in diffused light and an evenly moist soil. Cut down on watering after bloom.

Dombeya   Doronicum

Dombeya Burgessiae DOMBEYA   POT PLANT
Byttneriaceae, native to tropical Africa.   Zone 10.

USES: House plant, greenhouse plant, outdoors in warm climates.

HABIT: Soft, evergreen, rough, hairy kidney shaped leaves clothe 10-30′ stems bearing 3-4″ drooping ball-like clusters of fragrant, pale centered, rose-pink or white flowers in summer. *Dombeya* can be winter blooming indoors.

GERMINATION: Sow indoors at any season, not covering the seeds which need light to germinate. Maintain a temperature within the medium of 70-75° during germination which takes 14-21 days.

CULTURE: Indoors, place in diffused or filtered sunlight, and give night temperatures of 65°. *Dombeya* likes high humidity, so take necessary steps to provide it, or grow it in the greenhouse. Water well, and then allow the soil to go dry between waterings. Outdoors, grow in full sun in a rich, well drained soil.

Doronicum cordatum LEOPARD'S BANE   PERENNIAL
Compositae, native to Sicily and Asia Minor.   Zone 4.

USES: Bedding, border, rock garden, cut flower.

HABIT: Hardy 18-24″ perennial plants with heart shaped leaves and 2-3″ bright yellow daisy-like flowers in May and June.

GERMINATION: Sow seeds outdoors in spring or summer up to two months before frost, or sow indoors maintaining a temperature within the medium of 70° during germination which takes 15-20 days. Do not cover seed as light is beneficial to germination.

CULTURE: Plant 12-15″ apart in light shade in a rich, moist, well drained soil. The foliage diminishes in summer but increases again in fall.

Dryas   Echeveria

Dryas octopetala   MOUNTAIN AVENS   PERENNIAL
Rosaceae, native to North Temperate zones.   Zone 2.

USES: Edging, walls, ground cover, borders, rock gardens.

HABIT: Evergreen creeping shrubby 3-6″ plants with leathery green leaves with grey undersides bear 1½″ strawberry-like, 8 petaled white flowers from May to July.

GERMINATION: Sow outdoors in late fall or early spring for late spring germination, or sow indoors, maintaining a temperature within the medium of 60-70° during germination which takes 50 days or more.

CULTURE: Plant 12-15″ apart in full sun or light shade in a sandy soil with good drainage.

DUSTY MILLER, see **Chrysanthemum ptarmiciflorum, Senecio Cineraria, Senecio Vira-Vira**

Echeveria X derenosa hybrids   ECHEVERIA   POT PLANT
Crassulaceae, native to North and Central America.   Zone 10.

USES: Houseplant, greenhouse, bedding in warmer climates.

HABIT: Symmetrical succulent rosettes of ground-hugging green or blue-grey often tinged pink leaves with long stems topped with yellow, red or pink tubular flowers in spring and summer.

GERMINATION: Sow at any season indoors, maintaining a temperature within the medium of 70-80° during germination which takes 15-30 days. Do not cover the very fine seed.

CULTURE: Pot in a rich, sandy medium and give at least 4 hours of direct sun a day. This plant does best with 50-60° nights and 70-75° days. Allow the soil to become dry between waterings spring through fall; in winter, water enough only to prevent shriveling. Other echeverias may be grown from seed, but the seeds are not as readily available.

Echinacea

Echinops

Echinacea purpurea   PURPLE CONEFLOWER   PERENNIAL
Compositae, native to North America.   Zone 3.

USES: Borders, bedding, cut flower.

HABIT: Large daisy flowers measure to 4″ across with prominent cone-like dark purple centers and lavender petals drooping downward. Flowers bloom during July and August on 2-3′ stiff hairy stems.

GERMINATION: Sow seeds outdoors in spring or summer up to two months before frost, or sow indoors, maintaining a temperature within the medium of 70-75° during germination which takes 10-20 days. Started early, it blooms the first year.

CULTURE: Plant in spring or fall 18-24″ apart, in full sun to light shade in an average, well drained garden soil. It tolerates dry soil and wind.

Echinops Ritro   GLOBE THISTLE   PERENNIAL
Compositae, native to Eastern Europe and Western Asia.   Zone 3.

USES: Border, background, cut flower, dried flower.

HABIT: Globular 2-3″ heads of spiny, sharp blue flowers bloom in July on 5′ spiny stalks clothed with prickly, rugged leaves with white undersides.

GERMINATION: Sow outdoors in spring or summer up to two months before frost, or sow indoors, maintaining a temperature within the medium of 65-75° during germination which takes 15-20 days.

CULTURE: Plant 24″ apart in full sun, in a dry, light, well drained soil.

EASY

Echium

Elaeagnus

Echium species   BUGLOSS   ANNUAL
Boraginaceae, native to southern Europe.

USES: Borders, rock garden.

HABIT: Shrubby annual with broad, hairy tongue-shaped leaves and showy bell shaped ½" flowers of blue, lavender, rose and white on 1-2' spikes which are covered with bristly grey hairs. Flowers bloom in summer.

GERMINATION: Sow outdoors in early spring as soon as the soil can be worked, or sow indoors, maintaining a temperature within the medium of 70° during germination which takes 7-14 days.

CULTURE: Plant 12-15" apart in full sun and a dry, well drained, somewhat poor soil. In rich soil the plants produce foliage and very few flowers.

EASY

Elaeagnus angustifolia   RUSSIAN OLIVE   SHRUB
Elaeagnaceae, native to Europe and Asia.   Zone 3.

USES: Hedges, specimens.

HABIT: Multiple-trunk deciduous shrub has dark brown shredding bark and grey-green leaves with undersides of silver. Fragrant, 3", silvery yellow flowers appear in June and are followed in late summer to early fall with ½" edible sweet yellow berries covered with silvery scales.

GERMINATION: Sow outdoors in fall or early winter for germination the following spring. Indoors, place in moist medium and put in the refrigerator for 90 days. Germination should be at a temperature within the medium of 70-75° and takes 30 days.

CULTURE: Plant in full sun and a well drained, average garden soil. *Elaeagnus* tolerates drought and high winds.

Emilia   *Ensete*

Emilia javanica   PAINT BRUSH,   ANNUAL
                  TASSEL FLOWER,   CASTLE FLOWER
Compositae, native to the tropics.

USES: Border, cut flower, dried flower.

HABIT: Tassel-like flowers ½" across of orange-red or yellow-gold are
borne in summer on wiry 12-24" stems above a mound of grey-green leaves.

GERMINATION: Sow outdoors where plants are to grow after all danger of frost has past, or
sow indoors 4-6 weeks before planting outside, maintaining a temperature within the medium of
70° during germination which takes 8-15 days.

CULTURE: Plant 6-10" apart in full sun and a dry, sandy soil with good drainage.

EASY

Ensete ventricosum   BANANA   POT PLANT
(Musa Ensete, Musa Arnoldiana)
Musaceae, native to Ethiopia.   Zone 9.

USES: House plant, greenhouse plant, planters in warmer climates.

HABIT: Vigorous, exotic tree-like plants with 10-16' paddle-shaped leaves
with an arching habit and showy, hanging clusters of flower bracts in green,
purple or red, and 6" fruits (bananas) which are inedible.

GERMINATION: Soak seeds in warm water for 24 hours before germination. Plant 1" deep
with seed scar up, and maintain a temperature within the medium of 75-85° during germination
which takes 14-21 days.

CULTURE: Outdoors, give full sun, a rich soil, heavy feeding, and keep moist at all times. It
does best where nights do not go below 65° and the humidity is high. Indoors, give full sun in
winter and part shade in summer, grow in a rich soil kept evenly moist, give 65° nights and 80-
85° days, and provide high humidity.

Episcia

Episcia

Episcia species   POT PLANT
FLAME VIOLET,   PEACOCK PLANT
Gesneriaceae, native to South America.

USES: House plant, greenhouse, terrariums, hanging baskets.

HABIT: Handsome 2-3″ exotic leaves varying in colors, markings and textures, with interesting veining, adorn trailing plants which bear ½-1½″ white, pink, yellow, violet or red flowers from early spring to early fall.

GERMINATION: Sow dust-like seeds at any season, not covering the seeds. Maintain a temperature within the medium of 70-80° during germination which takes 25-40 days.

CULTURE: Pot in a mix rich in humus with excellent drainage, keeping fairly moist at all times. Avoid wetting the leaves when watering. Place in indirect or curtained sunlight, keep the humidity high, and give 65° nights.

Trial Garden at G. W. Park Seed Co.

Erigeron

Erigeron species   PERENNIAL
MIDSUMMER ASTER, FLEABANE
Compositae   Zone 3

USES: Rock gardens, borders, cut flowers

HABIT: *Erigeron* are fine-petaled, daisy-like flowers blooming in early summer. *Erigeron aurantiacus* (Double Orange Daisy) grows 10-12″ high, has orange flowers, and is native to Turkestan. *Erigeron X hybridus* and *E. speciosus* are native to North America. *Erigeron X hybridus* is bushy, 1-2′ high, with pink flowers that are yellow centered; *E. speciosus* is 2½′ high with flowers of violet-blue.

GERMINATION: Sow outdoors in late fall or early spring for late spring germination, or sow indoors, maintaining a temperature within the medium of 55° during germination which takes 15-20 days.

CULTURE: Plant 12″ apart in full sun and a light, sandy, well drained, average to poor soil. Keep faded flowers picked and feed only lightly.

EASY

145

Erinus   *Eryngium*

Erinus alpinus   ALPINE BALSAM   PERENNIAL
Scrophulariaceae, native to central Europe.   Zone 4.

USES: Rock garden, walls.

HABIT: Trailing 4-6″ plant with ½″ pink, purple or white flowers in 2½″ racemes in May and June over dense tufts of deeply toothed dark green leaves.

GERMINATION: Sow outdoors where plants are to grow in early spring, or sow indoors, maintaining a temperature within the medium of 65-75° during germination which takes 20-25 days.

CULTURE: Plant 8-10″ apart in a light, sandy, well drained soil. It is best located in a shaded situation. It is not a long lived plant so is best sown annually.

EASY

Eryngium Bourgatii, E. planum   SEA HOLLY   PERENNIAL
Umbelliferae, native to Europe and Asia.   Zone 5.

USES: Border, wildflower garden, dried flower, cut flower.

HABIT: Bushy 1½-2½′ plant has many branched stems topped with ½″ fluffy, spiny, thistle-like blue flowers in July and August over heart shaped leaves.

GERMINATION: Sow outdoors in early spring through summer up to two months before frost or, for best results, sow indoors, maintaining a temperature within the medium of 65-75° during germination which takes 5-10 days.

CULTURE: Plant 12-18″ apart in full sun in a dry, sandy, poor soil with excellent drainage, kept lightly watered.

Erythrina

Erythrina crista-galli   COCKSPUR CORAL TREE   POT PLANT
Leguminosae, native to Brazil.   Zone 10.

USES: House plant, greenhouse plant, patio tubs.

HABIT: Handsome free flowering 3′ tree-like plant with thorny stems, leathery leaves and butterfly or bird-like waxy flowers in dense racemes of deep scarlet appearing before the foliage in mid winter to early spring.

GERMINATION: Soak seeds for 24 hours in warm water before sowing. Sow indoors at any season, maintaining a temperature within the medium of 70-75° during germination which takes 10-15 days.

CULTURE: Plant outdoors in full sun or light shade in a well drained, average soil. In all but the warmest climates, it must overwinter indoors. Give full sun, 65° nights, average well drained soil, and allow to dry out between watering. Prune back in late fall.

A Terrace Garden

147

Eschscholzia

Eucalyptus

Eschscholzia californica CALIFORNIA POPPY   ANNUAL
Papaveraceae, native to California.

USES: Bedding, borders, rock gardens, planters.

HABIT: Silky 2-3″ saucer shaped double, semi double or single flowers with crinkled petals in shades of gold, yellow, bronze, orange, scarlet, rose or white are borne summer to frost on 1-2′ stems above mounds of finely cut silvery-grey foliage.

GERMINATION: Sow outdoors in early spring, where plants are to bloom. They are hard to transplant, and should be sown indoors only if they can be transplanted very carefully. Maintain a temperature within the medium of 55-60° during germination which takes 10-12 days.

CULTURE: Plant 6-8″ apart in full sun and a sandy, light, well drained soil. In warmer climates it may act as a perennial from self sowing. Keep faded flowers picked off to prolong the flowering season. It does well in hot and dry areas and poor soil.

EASY

Eucalyptus cinerea SILVER DOLLAR TREE   POT PLANT
Eucalyptus Globulus BLUE GUM
Myrtaceae, native to Australia.   Zone 9.

USES: House plant, greenhouse plant, tree in warmer climates, dried arrangements, medicinal.

HABIT: *Eucalyptus* are evergreen trees with simple, entire leaves which grow outdoors in the warmer climates and also make excellent pot plants. *E. cinerea* has unusual 3″ round silvery leaves pierced through the center by the stems; *E. Globulus* has young fuzzy white leaves and mature blue-green glaucous leaves and stems.

GERMINATION: Sow indoors at any season maintaining a temperature within the medium of 70-75° during germination which takes 14-21 days.

CULTURE: For outdoor use, plant 6-8′ apart when seedlings are 8-10″ tall. For indoor use, plant in average potting soil with excellent drainage. Keep in bright indirect light or curtain filtered sunlight with a night temperature of 60-65° and a daytime temperature of 70-75°. Fertilize weekly from late winter to early fall and keep soil evenly moist. During the winter, grow cooler and give just enough water to keep the soil from drying out completely. They withstand dry air as long as sufficient water is given.

148

Eucnide   Eucomis

Eucnide bartonioides ROCK NETTLE,   ANNUAL
                          MICROSPERMA
Loasaceae, native to Texas and Mexico.

USES: House plant, pot plant, border.

HABIT: This spreading, multi-branched plant grows 9-12" with primrose-like foliage and 2" upward facing yellow trumpet shaped flowers which open only in full sun.

GERMINATION: Sow indoors at any season for indoor use, or start indoors 6-8 weeks before last frost for outdoor use, maintaining a temperature within the medium of 70-80° during germination which takes 15-20 days.

CULTURE: Outdoors, plant in full sun in average to dry well drained soil. Indoors, give 55° nights, full sun or part shade and a soil that is allowed to become dry between waterings.

Eucomis bicolor PINEAPPLE LILY   POT PLANT
Liliaceae, native to South Africa.   Zone 7.

USES: House plant, greenhouse plant, bedding and borders in warmer climates.

HABIT: Bulbous plant 2½' tall with long, attractive, light green, shiny sword-like leaves with purple spotted undersides surrounding flower stalks upon which are borne dense spikes of pale green to cream star shaped flowers with purple stamens topped by a cluster of leaves similar to a pineapple's. It flowers in summer.

GERMINATION: Sow indoors in early spring for outdoor use and at any time for indoor use. Maintain a temperature within the medium of 70-75° during germination which takes 20-25 days.

CULTURE: Outdoors, plant 10-12" apart or in tubs using a well drained, light, sandy soil, in full sun. Keep moist spring to fall, but dry in winter. Below Zone 7, dig and store bulbs in fall in a cool, dry area. Indoors, grow with a night temperature of 55° in full sun with the soil kept evenly moist. In the winter, when it goes dormant, water only slightly.

EASY

Euphorbia marginata   *Euphorbia epithymoides*

Euphorbia cyathophora ANNUAL POINSETTIA ANNUAL
MEXICAN FIRE PLANT
(Euphorbia heterophylla)
Euphorbia marginata SNOW-ON-THE-MOUNTAIN
(Euphorbia variegata)
   Euphorbiaceae, native to Mexico and the United States.

USES: Bedding, border.

HABIT: Both of these annuals grow to 2'. *E. cyathophora* has upper bracts
of red over green glossy leaves like the Christmas favorite; *E. marginata* is
similar with white bracts. Stems have milky juices which may irritate the skin and eyes.

GERMINATION: Sow outdoors where plants are to bloom in spring after all danger of frost
has past, or sow indoors 6-8 weeks before planting outside maintaining a temperature within
the medium of 70-75° during germination which takes 10-15 days.

CULTURE: Plant 8-12" apart in full sun or part shade. These plants grow anywhere, even in the
poorest of soils, and withstands heat and drought.

Euphorbia epithymoides SPURGE, PERENNIAL
CUSHION EUPHORBIA
(Euphorbia polychroma)
Euphorbia Myrsinites SPURGE, MYRTLE EUPHORBIA
   Euphorbiaceae, native to Southern Europe. Zone 4.

USES: Bedding, border, rock garden, house plant.

HABIT: These succulents both have yellow bracts in umbels in spring. *E.
Myrsinites* is a 4-8" trailing plant with fleshy blue-green glaucous leaves in
spirals; *E. epithymoides* is a 12-16" hemispherical clump of dark green, hairy
leaves which turn red in fall.

GERMINATION: Sow outdoors in early spring, or sow indoors, maintaining a temperature
within the medium of 65-70° during germination which takes 15-20 days.

CULTURE: Outdoors, plant in full sun in a well drained, dry soil. Indoors, place in a warm spot
in full sun, and allow the soil to become dry between waterings.

150

Exacum   Fatsia

Exacum affine   BIENNIAL
GERMAN VIOLET,   PERSIAN VIOLET
Gentianaceae, native to India and Ceylon.

USES: Edgings, hanging basket, pot plant, house plant.

HABIT: Small, mounded, 2′ plant with small heart shaped leaves and ½″ fragrant, star shaped purple, blue or white flowers with yellow stamens blooming in late summer and fall outdoors and fall and winter indoors.

GERMINATION: Sow dust-like seeds indoors in early spring for outdoor use and at any season for indoor use, not covering the seeds which need light to germinate. Maintain a temperature within the medium of 70-75° during germination which takes 15-20 days.

CULTURE: Outdoors, plant in a warm spot in part shade. Indoors, give diffused sunlight, night temperatures of 60-65° and day temperatures of 70° or higher, and soil kept moist at all times.

EASY

Fatsia japonica   JAPANESE ARALIA   POT PLANT
Araliaceae, native to Japan.   Zone 8.

USES: House plant, greenhouse plant.

HABIT: Handsome evergreen beehive shaped plant to 5′ with flexible stems and large, glossy, green, thin leathery leaves which are deeply lobed bears round clusters of small white flowers in fall, followed by shiny blue-black fruits.

GERMINATION: Sow at any time of year indoors, maintaining a temperature within the medium of 70-75° during germination which takes 15-20 days.

CULTURE: Place in curtain filtered or bright indirect light, keep night temperatures 50-60° and daytime temperatures 65-75°, and keep the soil barely moist at all times. Frequent misting in the house is beneficial.

151

Felicia   Ficus

Felicia amelloides BLUE DAISY, BLUE MARGUERITE   ANNUAL
(Agathaea coelestis)
Felicia Bergerana   KINGFISHER DAISY
Compositae, native to South Africa.

USES: Bedding, borders, edging, planters, greenhouse plant.

HABIT: These plants have slender stems clothed with hairy green leaves. *Felicia amelloides* is 2-3' tall with sky-blue daisy-like flowers from July to frost. *Felicia Bergerana* reaches only 6-8" in height, is bushy, and has bright blue daisy-like flowers with yellow centers, also from July to frost.

GERMINATION: Sow seeds of *F. amelloides* outdoors in early spring as soon as the soil can be worked, or sow indoors, maintaining a temperature within the medium of 55° during germination which takes 30 days. Germination may be improved by refrigerating seeds in moistened medium for 3 weeks prior to sowing. Sow seeds of *F. Bergerana* outdoors in early spring or indoors, maintaining a temperature within the medium of 70° during germination which takes 30 days. Sow in the greenhouse in early fall for spring flowering.

CULTURE: Plant in full sun and a dry, gravelly, slightly rich soil. Water moderately during dry weather. Lift plants from the garden before frost to grow in the greenhouse, giving 55° nights, full sun and a soil allowed to dry slightly between waterings.

Ficus species   FIG   POT PLANT
Moraceae, native to the tropics.   Zone 10.

USES: House plant, greenhouse plant.

HABIT: *Ficus* is a large genus of decorative foliage plants with shiny, waxy leaves. *Ficus auriculata (F. Roxburghii)* has 16", round or heart shaped leaves that are mahogany when young. The plant has a spreading habit and produces white, silky figs. *Ficus benghalensis* (Banyan Tree) has large, leathery, succulent leaves 8" long with prominent yellow-green veining and spotting and orange-red figs. *Ficus benjamina* (Weeping Fig) has pointed, oval, shiny, leathery 5" leaves on drooping branches. *Ficus elastica* 'Decora' (Rubber Plant) is an erect plant with dark green leaves that are oval, pointed and 12" long, with an ivory midrib and a red reverse. Fruits are yellow. *Ficus macrophylla* (Australian Banyan) is bushy, similar to *F. elastica* but not as stiff. Leaves are 6-12", dark green with a silver reverse and oblong. Figs are red-purple. *Ficus religiosa* (Sacred Fig) has smooth round leaves that have a tail half as long as the body. The foliage is open and delicate; figs are purple.

GERMINATION: Sow indoors at any season, maintaining a temperature within the medium of 70-80° during germination which takes 15-20 days. Do not cover the seeds as they need light to germinate.

CULTURE: Place in bright indirect or curtain filtered light and keep the well drained soil slightly moist at all times. Provide 65° nights. *Ficus* go partially dormant in the winter and will need less water at that time.

Franklinia   *Freesia*

FORGET-ME-NOT, see **Myosotis**

Franklinia Alatamaha   FRANKLIN TREE   TREE
(Gordonia Alatamaha)
    Theaceae, native to Georgia.   Zone 5.

    USES: Ornamental tree.

    HABIT: Deciduous, multi-stemed, rare and beautiful tree which grows to 20-30' has 5-6" shiny, leathery dark green leaves that turn bright orange-red in fall. Fragrant, cup shaped, 2-3" white flowers bloom in August and September.

GERMINATION: Sow outdoors in late fall or early winter for spring germination. Indoors, place in moistened medium and place in the freezer for 3-4 weeks, followed by germination at a temperature within the medium of 70-75° taking 25-30 days. Seeds are not long lived and should be stored in the refrigerator.

CULTURE: Plant in full sun to light shade in a rich, moist, acid soil. Pruning is rarely needed.

FOUR O'CLOCK, see **Mirabilis**

Freesia X hybrida   FREESIA   POT PLANT
    Iridaceae, native to South Africa.   Zone 9.

    USES: House plant, greenhouse plant, cut flower, summer borders.

    HABIT: Tender corm-forming plant with slender sword-shaped leaves surround 1-1½" wiry stems atop which are borne 2" single or double fragrant funnel shaped flowers of yellow, lilac, blue, orange and red in clusters at right angles to the stem.

GERMINATION: Soak seeds for 24 hours before sowing. For indoor use, sow any time; for outdoor use, sow in early fall. Plants will bloom in 8-12 months. Maintain a temperature within the medium of 65-75° during germination which takes 25-30 days.

CULTURE: Indoors, grow at 50° nights, provide ample air circulation, and place in full sun. Water liberally and feed every week while in growth and flower. After foliage yellows, cease feeding and gradually withhold water until foliage turns brown. Store in a cool dry area. Outdoors, plant after all danger of frost is past, in a light, sandy, rich, well drained soil, in full sun. After foliage dies, dig corms and store in a cool dry area until next spring, or pot in fall for winter bloom indoors.

EASY

Fuchsia   *Gaillardia*

Fuchsia X hybrida   FUCHSIA,   POT PLANT
                          LADY'S-EARDROPS
Onagraceae, native to Central and South America.   Zone 10.

USES: House plant, greenhouse plant, hanging basket, outdoors in warm areas.

HABIT: Plants with 1-4′ stems, crisp oval leaves, and delicate, drooping, hoop-skirt shaped flowers in pink, red, white, lavender, blue, orange and yellow or combinations of colors with long showy stamens. It blooms in summer outdoors and is everblooming indoors.

GERMINATION: Sow at any season and do not cover seed as light aids in germination. Maintain a temperature within the medium of 70-75° during germination which takes 21-28 days.

CULTURE: Indoors, grow with 50-55° nights and 70° days, in a shaded location, with soil kept evenly moist. Feed heavily during growth and flowering, and keep the humidity high. Cut back heavily in fall, do not feed, and cut back on water. Outdoors, grow in partial shade or shade in a rich soil with perfect drainage, and syringe frequently.

Gaillardia X grandiflora   BLANKET FLOWER   PERENNIAL
(Gaillardia aristata)
Gaillardia pulchella   ANNUAL
Compositae, native to the United States.   Perennial: Zone 2.

USES: Borders, planters, cut flower.

HABIT: *Gaillardia* X *grandiflora* is a perennial; *G. pulchella* is an annual. The perennial form blooms from June to frost with daisy like flowers of yellow, red, orange or yellow with red bands, on plants 12-30″ tall. The annual *Gaillardia* is 10-18″ high with 2½″ ball shaped double flowers of yellow, red, or red, tipped with yellow, all summer to frost.

GERMINATION: Sow perennial types in spring or summer up to two months before frost; sow annual types where they are to grow outdoors after all danger of frost is past, or indoors 4-6 weeks before planting outside. Maintain a temperature within the medium of 70° during germination which takes 15-20 days. Perennial type seeds should not be covered as light aids in germination, and will make blooming plants the first year if started early.

CULTURE: Plant 8-15″ apart in full sun and a light, sandy, well drained soil. *Gaillardia* tolerates heat, drought and poor soil. Remove faded flowers to prolong bloom.

EASY

154

Galtonia

Gardenia

Galtonia candicans SUMMER HYACINTH   PERENNIAL
                       CAPE HYACINTH
Liliaceae, native to South Africa.   Zone 8.

USES: Greenhouse plant, cut flower, borders, background.

HABIT: Bulbous plants with thick, fleshy, strap-like leaves bear racemes of small, white, fragrant flowers resembling a hyacinth on 2-4' stalks in July and August.

GERMINATION: Sow outdoors from early spring through summer up to two months before frost. Indoors, maintain a temperature within the medium of 70° during germination which takes 15-20 days.

CULTURE: Plant in full sun, 15" apart, in a rich, moist soil with excellent drainage. In Zone 7 and colder, bulbs may be dug after frost and stored over the winter in a cool, dry area. Indoors, grow in a cool greenhouse (55° nights and 70° days), in full sun and average potting soil that is allowed to become dry between waterings. The plants will go dormant during winter.

Gardenia jasminoides CAPE JASMINE, GARDENIA   POT PLANT
Rubiaceae, native to China.   Zone 9.

USES: House plant, greenhouse plant, patio tubs.

HABIT: Tender evergreen generally growing to 4' with waxy, white, single or double sweet scented 3" flowers blooming indoors in spring on branches clothed with shiny, dark green leaves.

GERMINATION: Sow indoors at any season, maintaining a temperature within the medium of 70-75° during germination which takes 25-30 days.

CULTURE: Indoors, grow at a night temperature of 65°, away from drafts, and keep the humidity high. The soil should be rich, acid, well drained, and kept evenly moist. Place in full sun. Outdoors, place in a warm, sunny spot, and keep the soil moist and the humidity high.

Gazania   Gentiana

Gazania rigens   TREASURE FLOWER   ANNUAL
Compositae, native to South Africa.

USES: Ground cover, edging, bedding, planters, house plant.

HABIT: Stalks 6-15″ long arise from 6-9″, thick, dark green leaves with felty white undersides and bear single daisy-like flowers 3-5″ across in bright colors of yellow, gold, cream, orange, pink or red, with dark centers. It flowers in summer, and is winter blooming indoors. The blossoms close at night and in cloudy weather.

GERMINATION: Sow outdoors where the plant is to grow after all danger of frost is past, or sow indooors 4-6 weeks before planting outside. Maintain a temperature within the medium of 68-86° during germination which takes 8-14 days. Cover seeds well as darkness aids in germination.

CULTURE: Plant 8-12″ apart in full sun in a light, sandy soil. *Gazania* tolerates drought and does best where summer temperatures are high. Plants may be lifted and brought indoors in winter; give full sun, 60° nights, and average potting soil that is allowed to dry out between waterings.

EASY

Gentiana acaulis   GENTIAN   PERENNIAL
Gentiana lagodechiana   Zone 3.
Gentianaceae, native to mountainous temperate regions.

USES: Rock garden, borders, wildflower garden.

HABIT: *Gentiana acaulis* (Stemless Gentian) grows 4-6″ tall and is a tufted plant with 2″ deep blue trumpet shaped flowers spotted inside, blooming in May and June. *Gentiana lagodechiana* grows 10-15″ tall, with deep blue 1-1½″ flowers with white throats over dense, heart shaped leaves. It blooms in late summer and early fall.

GERMINATION: Sow outdoors in late fall or early winter for spring germination. Indoors, place in moistened medium and freeze for 3 weeks, followed by germination at a temperature within the medium of 70-75° which takes 14-28 days.

CULTURE: Plant 12-18″ apart in full sun to light shade in a rich, moist, acid soil with excellent drainage. *Gentiana* prefers cool climates and likes heavy watering. They are difficult plants to establish, but once established, are well worth it.

Geranium

Gerbera

Geranium sanguineum CRANESBILL   PERENNIAL
   Geraniaceae, native to Eurasia   Zone 3.

USES: Rock garden, border, ground cover.

HABIT: The "true" geranium has 1½-2" flowers of red-purple, pink or white in spring and summer on trailing stems clothed with a dense mat of lobed leaves. The plant reaches 1-1½' in height.

GERMINATION: Sow outdoors in spring, or indoors, maintaining a temperature within the medium of 70° during germination which takes from 20-40 days. Seeds are not long lived and should not be stored.

CULTURE: Plant 10-12" apart in full sun or part shade in average, well drained garden soil.

GERANIUM, see also **Pelargonium**

Gerbera Jamesonii hybrids TRANSVAAL DAISY   PERENNIAL
   Compositae, native to South Africa.
USES: Border, bedding, greenhouse plant, cut flower.   Zone 8.

HABIT:*Gerbera* produces up to 10" dark green leaves with white woolly undersides and solitary daisy-like flowers of orange, red, pink, white, yellow, salmon and lavender, 4-5" across, on strong, leafless, 12-18" stems. It flowers in summer outdoors and in winter in the greenhouse.

GERMINATION: Sow in early spring indoors for summer bloom the same year, placing the sharp end of the seed down, but not covering completely as light is necessary for germination. Maintain a temperature within the medium of 70-75° during germination which takes 15-25 days. Use fresh seed; do not attempt to store it.

CULTURE: Outdoors, grow in full sun spaced 12-18" apart in moist, slightly acid soil that is well drained. In the greenhouse, grow with cool (50-55°) nights, in a sunny, airy, moist atmosphere. Feed twice a month during growth, withhold fertilizer and cut down on water during late fall and winter resting period.

EASY

157

Geum   Ginkgo

Geum Quellyou, Geum reptans AVENS   PERENNIAL
Rosaceae, native to Chile, Europe.

USES: Borders, rock gardens, cut flower.

HABIT:*Geum Quellyou,* a native of Chile, grows 1-2' and flowers in May to July with 1" blooms of scarlet, yellow or orange. *Geum reptans* grows only to 6-8", and has 1½" yellow flowers with purple styles. Both have deeply lobed and toothed foliage. *Geum Quellyou* is hardy to Zone 6; *Geun reptans* a native of Europe, is hardy to Zone 5.

GERMINATION: Sow seeds outdoors in spring or summer up to two months before frost, or sow indoors, maintaining a temperature within the medium of 68-86° during germination which takes 21-28 days.

CULTURE: Plant 12-18" apart in full sun or very light shade in a rich, moist, well drained soil.

EASY

Gilia rubra, see Ipomopsis rubra

Ginkgo biloba MAIDENHAIR TREE   TREE
Ginkgoaceae, native to China.   Zone 5.

USES: Street tree, specimen tree.

HABIT: Slow growing, deciduous tree reaching 50-80' is wide spreading and open with bright green fan-like 2½-3½" leaves turning a clear yellow in fall. Flowers are inconspicuous; the round, 1" fruit on the female tree is bright yellow and has an obnoxious odor.

GERMINATION: Seeds are shipped fresh and wet and must be sown immediately. Sow outdoors in late fall or early winter for spring germination, or, indoors, place the seeds in moistened medium and refrigerate for 8-10 weeks, followed by germination using a temperature in the medium of 70-75°. Germination will take 30 days.

CULTURE: Plant in full sun in almost any garden soil as long as it has good drainage.

Gladiolus   *Gladiolus*

Gladiolus X hortulanus   GARDEN GLADIOLUS   PERENNIAL
Iridaceae, native to the tropics.   Zone 9.

USES: Bedding, borders, cut flowers, greenhouse plant.

HABIT: Sword shaped foliage is surrounded by spikes 3-5' high of funnel shaped flowers of almost all colors. Some are ruffled or bicolored.

GERMINATION: Sow outdoors where plants are to grow, or sow indoors in late winter, maintaining a temperature within the medium of 70° during germination which takes 20-40 days. Small cormels will form the first year which will bloom the second year.

CULTURE: Plant in full sun in a deep, rich, well drained soil that is slightly acid. Keep well fed and watered. Lift corms before frost and store in a cool dry area during winter until planting out after frost the following spring. In the greenhouse, provide 50° nights, full sun and a rich soil kept evenly moist. Plant in succession every week for maximum blooming effect, and stake taller varieties.

Globularia cordifolia   BLUE GLOBE DAISY   PERENNIAL
Globulariaceae, native to southern Europe.   Zone 9.

USES: Rock garden, ground cover.

HABIT: Small, cushion-like plant 2-6" tall has leathery, dark green foliage topped with button shaped ½" flowers of azure blue, blooming in May and June.

GERMINATION: Sow outdoors in late fall or early spring for spring germination, or sow indoors, maintaining a temperature within the medium of 55° during germination which takes 10-12 days. Germination may be improved by refrigerating seeds in moistened medium for 3 weeks before sowing.

CULTURE: Plant 12" apart in part shade in a light, limey, well drained soil.

Gloriosa

Gloxinia

Gloriosa species   GLORIOSA LILY

Liliaceae, native to tropical Asia and Africa.

POT PLANT

Zone 8.

USES: Bedding, border, greenhouse plant, cut flower.

HABIT: This tuberous, limp, 3-8' vining plant has lily-like foliage and reflexed lily-like flowers at the leaf axils in colors of red, yellow or purple, brightly variegated, and with prominent curved stamens. It blooms in summer outdoors and in winter in the greenhouse.

GERMINATION: Sow seeds indoors at any season, maintaining a temperature within the medium of 70-75° during germination which takes 30 days.

CULTURE: Outdoors, plant in full sun in a very rich, well drained soil. Provide plants with a trellis or other support. In areas colder than Zone 8, plant outdoors after all danger of frost has past. When cool weather turns the foliage yellow in fall, dig the tubers and store until the following spring in a 55-60° area. Indoors, grow in a warm (65-70° nights and 70-85° days) greenhouse, mist frequently, give full sun, and keep the rich soil evenly moist. Withhold water and fertilizer after flowering, allow the plants to go dormant, lift and store for four months.

Gloxinia gymnostoma   GLOXINIA

Gesneriaceae, native to Argentina.

POT PLANT

USES: House plant, hanging basket, greenhouse plant.

HABIT: This spreading plant has 3" long, thick, deep rich green leaves and pouch-like 1" scarlet-red flowers with fluted openings and a yellow spotted throat. It is almost everblooming indoors.

GERMINATION: Sow indoors at any season, maintaining a temperature within the medium of 70-75° during germination which takes 15-20 days. Do not cover the fine seeds which need light to germinate.

CULTURE: Place in indirect or diffused light in a very humid (70%) atmosphere. Give 60-65° nights and a very rich soil kept evenly moist. During the dormant period, withhold water and lower temperature.

Gomphrena   *Gossypium*

GLOXINIA, see **Sinningia speciosa**

Gomphrena globosa, Gomphrena Haageana   ANNUAL
GLOBE AMARANTH
Amaranthaceae.

USES: Bedding, edging, planters, cut flower, dried flower.

HABIT: *Gomphrena globosa* is native to the tropics of the Eastern Hemisphere and is a 1½-2½' mounded free blooming plant covered with round, 1", papery clover-like flowers in purple, white, lavender, orange, pink or yellow, blooming in summer and early fall. *Gomphrena Haageana* is native of Texas and Mexico and is similar but with red bracts and yellow florets.

GERMINATION: Sow outdoors where plants are to grow after all danger of frost has past, or sow indoors 6-8 weeks before planting outside, maintaining a temperature within the medium of 70-75° during germination which takes 15-20 days.

CULTURE: Plant 10-15" apart in full sun and a sandy, light, well drained soil. It tolerates drought and heat.

EASY

Gossypium hirsutum   ORNAMENTAL COTTON   ANNUAL
Malvaceae, native to Central America.

USES: Cut branches, specimen.

HABIT: Attractive 2' bushy plants have pink buds, creamy blossoms in May and June, white balls of cotton and lobed leaves.

GERMINATION: Sow seeds outdoors where plants are to grow after all danger of frost has past, or sow indoors 6-8 weeks before planting outside, maintaining a temperature within the medium of 68-86° during germination which takes 8-10 days.

CULTURE: Plant 12-18" apart in full sun and a rich, moist soil. *Gossypium* likes abundant water and a long growing season.

EASY

Grevillea   *Gypsophila*

GOURDS, see **Cucurbita Pepo ovifera, Lagenaria leucantha, Luffa aegyptiaca**

Grevillea robusta   SILK OAK   POT PLANT
Proteaceae, native to Australia.   Zone 10.

USES: House plant, greenhouse plant, street tree in Zone 10.

HABIT: Small, narrow, fern-like and woolly coated leaves are found on this plant which flowers in 4″ clusters of golden yellow and orange in April.

GERMINATION: Soak seeds in warm water for 24 hours before sowing. Sow at any season indoors, not covering the seeds which need light to germinate. Maintain a temperature within the medium of 75-80° during germination which takes 20-25 days.

CULTURE: Indoors, give full sun, cool (50°) nights, and allow the soil to become dry between waterings. Plants may be pruned in early spring to induce branching. Outdoors, grow in full sun, in either a rich or poor soil. *Grevillea* withstands heat and drought.

Gypsophila species   BABY'S BREATH   ANNUAL, PERENNIAL
Caryophyllaceae, native to Europe and Asia.   Zone 3.

USES: Border, rock garden, walls, ground cover, cut flower, dried flower.

HABIT: *Gypsophila* has a delicate, light, airy appearance; the plants are mounded with slender stems and are multi-branched. *Gypsophila elegans* is an annual that grows 8-18″ tall, with lance shaped 3″ leaves and clouds of white, pink or red flowers from June to frost. *Gypsophila pacifica* is a perennial 3′ tall with thousands of tiny pink flowers in summer. Another perennial is *Gypsophila repens*, only 6-10″ tall, with 1″ narrow leaves, a dwarf creeping habit, and single or double white, pink or purple flowers. *Gypsophila paniculata* blooms in June and July and will bloom through October if sheared after the flowers fade. It grows 3′ tall, has 3″ pointed leaves, and many tiny single or double white flowers.

GERMINATION: Perennial forms may be sown outdoors anytime in spring or summer up to two months before frost; annual *Gypsophila* should be sown where it is to grow in early to mid spring. Either may be sown indoors, maintaining a temperature within the medium of 70° during germination which takes 10-15 days. For best effects, make successive sowings of the annual *Gypsophila* two weeks apart throughout spring.

CULTURE: Plant 18-24″ apart in open and well drained alkaline soil, in full sun. Annual *Gypsophila* may also be grown in a cool (50° nights) greenhouse, in full sun, with the soil allowed to dry out between waterings.

Harpephyllum

Harpephyllum caffrum KAFFIR PLUM   POT PLANT
Anacardiaceae, native to South Africa.   Zone 10.

USES: House plant, greenhouse plant, outdoors in warm climates.

HABIT: Tough, leathery, evergreen pinnate leaves and flowers of white or green are found on this plant which can reach 30' outdoors. Dark red edible fruits form after flowering and are the size of olives.

GERMINATION: Sow indoors at any season, maintaining a temperature within the medium of 70-75° during germination which takes 10-15 days.

CULTURE: Outdoors, plant in sun or shade. *Harpephyllum* is fast growing and tolerates wind and heat. Indoors, grow in full sun, with night temperatures of 60° and an average soil that is allowed to become dry between waterings. This plant is easily trained and shaped, with a neat appearance, and makes a good Bonsai.

HEATHER, see **Calluna vulgaris**

Hedychium coccineum   POT PLANT
             BUTTERFLY LILY,   GINGER LILY
Zingiberaceae, native to India.   Zone 10.

USES: House plant, greenhouse plant, border in warm climates.

HABIT: This tender perennial grows 4-6' from thick, fleshy rhizomes. Leaves are 2' long, glossy and oval; long slender stems bear 10" upright spikes of red flowers in summer.

GERMINATION: Sow indoors at any season, maintaining a temperature within the medium of 70-75° during germination which takes 20-25 days.

CULTURE: Outdoors, plant in sun or part shade in a rich, well drained soil. After frost has killed the tops in areas colder than Zone 10, dig the rhizomes and store them in a cool, dry place until the following spring. Indoors, grow warm (65° nights and 80° days), in filtered light, in average potting soil kept evenly moist. Humidity should be 50%, and water reduced after blooming.

163

Helenium

Helianthemum

Helenium autumnale, Helenium Hoopesii   PERENNIAL
SNEEZEWEED
Compositae, native to North America.   Zone 3.

USES: Borders, bedding, cut flower.

HABIT: Late summer and early fall blooming 2-4' perennials bear tall, stiff stems and clusters of 2″ daisy-like flowers in yellow, bronze, red, brown and mahogany.

GERMINATION: Sow outdoors any time in spring or summer up to two months before frost, or sow indoors, maintaining a temperature within the medium of 70° during germination which takes 7-10 days.

CULTURE: Plant 12-18″ apart in full sun in a rich, moist soil. Plants grow naturally in swamps and wet meadows. Remove faded flowers to induce bushiness and more blooms.

Helianthemum nummularium 'Mutabile' SUN ROSE PERENNIAL
Cistaceae, native to the Mediterranean.   Zone 5.

USES: Rock garden, borders, ground cover, edging.

HABIT: Low, trailing, mounded evergreen plant has attractive foliage and 1″ flowers resembling wild roses in yellow, pink, lavender or white from May to July. Its height is 12-18″.

GERMINATION: Sow outdoors in spring or summer up to two months before frost, or sow indoors, maintaining a temperature within the medium of 70-75° during germination which takes 15-20 days.

CULTURE: Plant 12-18″ apart in full sun and a soil on the dry, gravely and poor side, which is slightly alkaline. Prune in early spring to keep compact.

Helianthus

Helichrysum

Helianthus species   SUNFLOWER   ANNUAL
Compositae, native to North America.

USES: Background, screen, border, edible seeds.

HABIT: *Helianthus* has coarse, rough, hairy, somewhat sticky leaves and daisy or chrysanthemum-like flowers. *Helianthus annuus* (Common Sunflower) grows 4-6' and has single yellow flowers with dark red, brown or purple centers or double flowers of gold in late summer. Dwarf forms are available which grow to 15". *Helianthus debilis* grows 4-5' and has 3" single flowers of yellow or white with red-purple centers from July to frost. *Helianthus giganteus* (Giant Sunflower) is 9-12' tall with light yellow to gold flowers up to 1' across in late summer and fall. It is actually a perennial to Zone 3, but should be grown as an annual.

GERMINATION: Sow seeds outdoors after all danger of frost is past where the plants are to grow. Seeds may be started indoors at a temperature within the medium of 68-86° and will germinate in 10-14 days, but the plants are so rapid growing that is unnecessary.

CULTURE: Plant 2-4' apart in full sun in a light, dry, well drained soil. *Helianthus* will do well on poor soils. Stake to support the plants.

Helichrysum bracteatum 'Monstrosum'   ANNUAL
STRAWFLOWER
Compositae, native to Australia.

USES: Border, rock garden, cut flower, dried flower.

HABIT: Branched plants growing 12-30" have narrow leaves and wiry stems which bear flowers of red, salmon, purple, yellow, pink or white from July to frost. The colored parts of the flower are actually bracts, with the true flowers in the center.

GERMINATION: Sow outdoors where plants are to grow after all danger of frost has past, or, for best results, sow indoors 4-6 weeks before planting outside, maintaining a temperature within the medium of 70° during germination which takes 7-10 days. Do not cover the seeds as they need light to germinate.

CULTURE: Plant in full sun, 9-15" apart, in a porous, well drained soil. *Helichrysum* loves long, hot summers.

EASY

Heliopsis

Heliopsis helianthoides SUNFLOWER HELIOPSIS PERENNIAL
Compositae, native to North America.   Zone 3.

USES: Border, cut flower.

HABIT: Double or semi-double 3-4″ sunflower-like flowers with brown centers and yellow or orange petals are found on this 3′ plant from July to September.

GERMINATION: Sow outdoors in spring or summer up to two months before frost, or sow indoors, maintaining a temperature within the medium of 70° during germination which takes 10-15 days. *Heliopsis* will bloom the first year if started early enough.

CULTURE: Plant 24″ apart in full sun and a rich, moist, well drained soil. It is slow to appear in the spring.

A Late Summer Garden

Helleborus   *Helleborus*

Helipterum Humboldtianum   ANNUAL
(H. Sandfordii)   EVERLASTING, STRAWFLOWER
Helipterum Manglesii
(Rhodanthe Manglesii)
Helipterum roseum
(Acrolinium roseum)
   Compositae, native to western Australia.

USES: Bedding, cut flower, dried flower.

HABIT: *Helipterum roseum* is a branching 2′ plant with 2″ daisy-like flowers of pink, salmon, apricot or white; *H. Humboldtianum* is 15-18″ tall, with white woolly leaves and yellow papery flowers in clusters. *Helipterum Manglesii* (Swan River Everlasting) is 18″ tall with 1½″ flowers of pink or violet with golden centers.

GERMINATION: *Helipterum Humboldtianum* and *H. Manglesii* may be sown outdoors where the plants are to grow after all danger of frost is past, or started indoors 6-8 weeks before planting outside, maintaining a temperture within the medium of 68-86° during germination which takes 14-20 days. *Helipterum roseum* may be started indoors in the same manner, but with a temperature within the medium of 65-75°, or sown outdoors in early spring.

CULTURE: Plant 6-12″ apart in full sun and a dry, sandy soil with excellent drainage.

EASY

Helleborus niger   CHRISTMAS ROSE   PERENNIAL
   Ranunculaceae, native to Europe.   Zone 3.

USES: Border, rock garden, cut flower.

HABIT: Evergreen, seven parted leaves that are leathery and 2-4″ white or pink flowers that bloom in late winter are found on this 12-15″ plant.

GERMINATION: Sow seeds outdoors in late fall or early winter for spring germination. Indoors, place in moistened medium in the freezer for 3 weeks, followed by germination using a temperature within the medium of 70-75°. Germination requires 30 to 60 days at least; seeds may not germinate unless they go through two winters outdoors or two periods of indoor freezing.

CULTURE: Plant in partial shade in a moist, rich, well drained soil that is slightly alkaline. Do not divide or transplant as it resents being disturbed.

EASY

Hemerocallis   *Hemerocallis*

Hemerocallis hybrids   DAYLILY   PERENNIAL
Liliaceae, native to Europe and the Orient.   Zone 3.

USES: Borders, cut flower.

HABIT: Sturdy clumps are 2-5′ high, with long, narrow leaves that gracefully arch. Lily-like flowers of yellow, orange, red, pink and lavender bloom in summer. Each flower lasts one day, quickly followed by another flower on the same stalk.

GERMINATION: Sow seeds outdoors in late fall or early spring for late spring germination. Indoors, place seeds in moistened medium and refrigerate for 6 weeks, followed by germination at a temperature within the medium of 60-70°. Germination time varies between 3 and 7 weeks.

CULTURE: Plant in light shade, 18-36″ apart, in a rich, well drained soil. Plants will survive in shade but will bloom only sparsely. It will withstand tremendous neglect.

Herniaria glabra   RUPTUREWORT   PERENNIAL
Caryophyllaceae, native to Europe.   Zone 4.

USES: Rock gardens, ground cover, walls, edging

HABIT: Creeping 4-6″ plant has a moss-like, fresh green appearance and small insignificant white to green flowers in summer. Leaves turn bronze-red in winter.

GERMINATION: Sow outdoors in spring or summer up to two months before frost, or sow indoors, maintaining a temperature within the medium of 70° during germination which takes 10-12 days.

CULTURE: Plant 4-6″ apart in sun or light shade in average, well drained soil.

168

Hesperis

Heuchera

Hesperis matronalis SWEET ROCKET   PERENNIAL
  Cruciferae, native to Europe.   Zone 3.

USES: Borders, cut flowers.

HABIT: A coarse plant with toothed leaves. *Hesperis* has lilac or white fragrant flowers in clusters in May and June atop 3′ stems.

GERMINATION: Sow outdoors in spring or summer up to two months before frost, or sow indoors, maintaining a temperature within the medium of 68-86° during germination which takes 20-25 days. Do not cover seeds as they need light to germinate. It blooms the first year if started early.

CULTURE: Plant 15-18″ apart in full sun or part shade in average, well-drained soil. Shear flowers as they fade to prolong the flowering season. *Hesperis* will tolerate poor soil, but at best is a short-lived plant.

EASY

Heuchera sanguinea CORAL BELLS   PERENNIAL
  Saxifragaceae, native to New Mexico and Arizona.   Zone 3.

USES: Borders, rock gardens, edging, cut flower.

HABIT: Mounds of heart-shaped, scalloped leaves below 15-24″ wiry stems bear clusters of ½″ brightly colored, bell-shaped flowers in pink and red from May to July. Foliage is bronze colored and is evergreen.

GERMINATION: Sow seeds outdoors in late fall or early spring for late spring germination. Indoors, sow and maintain a temperature within the medium of 55° during germination which takes 10-15 days.

CULTURE: Plant 9-15″ apart in full sun to part shade in a rich, moist soil with excellent drainage.

Hibiscus

Hippeastrum

Hibiscus Acetosella   ANNUAL, PERENNIAL
Hibiscus Moscheutos   HIBISCUS, MALLOW
Abelmoschus Manihot (Hibiscus Manihot)
   Malvaceae, native to Europe, Asia.   Perennial: Zone 5.

USES: Hedges, backgrounds, cut flowers.

HABIT: *Hibiscus* is a narrow growing shrubby plant with funnel-shaped single flowers. *Hibiscus Acetosella* is an annual with red leaves that are shiny, deeply lobed, maple-like and dense. It grows to 5' with flowers of purple-red or yellow, and is heat resistant. *Hibiscus Moscheutos* (Rose Mallow) is a perennial, 4-8' tall, with downy stems and hairy leaves, flowering in August and September. Blooms are 5-10" wide, in shades of pink, red or white. *Abelmoschus Manihot* (Sunset Hibiscus) is an annual, 5-6' high, with 6" yellow flowers with dark brown centers in late summer.

GERMINATION: Clip seeds before sowing, or soak them in water and they will sink when ready to be planted. Sow perennial *Hibiscus* outdoors in spring or summer up to two months before frost, or indoors maintaining a temperature within the medium of 70-75° during germination which takes 15-30 days. Annual *Hibiscus* may be sown outdoors where it is to grow after all danger of frost is past, or indoors 6-8 weeks before planting outside, germinating as above.

CULTURE: Plant in full sun or light shade in a rich, well-drained, moist soil.

Hippeastrum hybrids   AMARYLLIS   POT PLANT
   Amaryllidaceae, native to tropical South America.   Zone 10.

USES: House plant, greenhouse plant, cut flower, borders.

HABIT: Bulbous plant with flat, slender, strap-like leaves has 12-24" stems and 2-4" lily-like trumpet-shaped flowers per stem. Colors are red, pink, orange, salmon, white and brown on flowers usually appearing before the leaves.

GERMINATION: Sow seeds on their sides indoors at any season, maintaining a temperature within the medium of 70-75° during germination which takes 4-6 weeks.

CULTURE: Outdoors, grow in full sun in a rich, moist, well-drained soil. In areas colder than Zone 10, dig the bulbs before frost after the foliage has browned and store in a cool, dry area. Indoors, place in full sun, give 60° nights and days to 80°, and keep the rich soil evenly moist while growing. After blooming, allow the foliage to grow until it turns brown, and store the bulb in the pot in a cool, dry area. Amaryllis blooms best when pot bound.

170

Hosta

Hordeum jubatum SQUIRREL TAIL GRASS PERENNIAL
Gramineae, native to north temperate regions. Zone 3.

USES: Ornamental grass, dried branches.

HABIT: Abundant ornamental drooping spikes are 4″ long and appear in late spring and early summer on a 2-2½′ plant.

GERMINATION: Sow seeds outdoors in spring or summer to two months before frost, or sow indoors, maintaining a temperature within the medium of 70° during germination which takes 30-50 days.

CULTURE: Plant in full sun, 12″ apart, in a well-drained, slightly alkaline soil. It can become a weedy plant.

Hosta ventricosa BLUE PLANTAIN LILY PERENNIAL
(Hosta caerulea)
Liliaceae, native to eastern Asia. Zone 3.

USES: Borders, ground cover, edging.

HABIT: Ornamental foliage plant has bold, showy, heart-shaped leaves 9″ long that are dark-green and shiny, and 36″ spikes of 2″ bell-shaped dark violet flowers with darker veins borne in summer in loose racemes.

GERMINATION: Sow outdoors in spring or summer up to two months before frost, or sow indoors, maintaining a temperature within the medium of 70° during germination which takes 15-20 days. Other species of *Hosta* may be germinated in the same manner, but the seeds are not as readily available.

CULTURE: Plant in part shade or shade, 12″ apart, in a rich, moist, well-drained soil.

Hoya   Humulus

Hoya carnosa WAX PLANT   POT PLANT
Asclepiadaceae, native to southern China and Australia.   Zone 10.

USES: House plant, greenhouse plant, hanging basket.

HABIT: Semi-succulent vine has rope-like stems, thick, shiny, dark-green
3″ leaves, and ½″ fragrant pink, red or white waxy flowers in spring and
summer in dense heads.

GERMINATION: Sow indoors at any season, maintaining a temperature within the medium of
70-75° during germination which takes 10-15 days.

CULTURE: Plant in a light, rich, well-drained soil, keeping well watered in spring and summer
and only moist enough to prevent shriveling in fall and winter. Grow cool in the winter,
increasing temperatures in summer to 65° at night and to 80-85° in the day. Grow in part shade
or diffused light. Do not remove the short flowering spurs or there will be no bloom, and prune
little, if any. Grow pot bound.

Humulus japonicus 'Variegatus'   ANNUAL
                        VARIEGATED JAPANESE HOP
Cannabaceae, native to the Orient.

USES: Vine, screen, trellis.

HABIT: This clinging vine grows 25′ per year and has bright green, deeply
lobed, rough foliage that is streaked and mottled with white. Male flowers
are greenish, borne in hanging clusters 6-10″ long, while female flowers (on
separate plants) are in pairs under long, narrow bracts. The cones (fruits) on
the female of other species of *Humulus* than this one are the hops used in
brewing.

GERMINATION: Sow outdoors where plants are to grow after all danger of frost is past, or
sow indoors, maintaining a temperature within the medium of 70-75° during germination which
takes 25-30 days.

CULTURE: Plant 3-5′ apart in full sun or part shade in a light, rich, well-drained soil. Provide a
sturdy lattice or other support. All *Humulus* do best in hot areas and will tolerate dry soils.

Hunnemannia   *Hypericum*

Hunnemannia fumariifolia   MEXICAN TULIP POPPY ANNUAL
Papaveraceae, native to Mexico.

USES: Border, cut flower.

HABIT: Downy, smooth, finely divided blue-green leaves are topped with
3″ yellow flowers resembling a ruffled-edged tulip. The plant grows to 2′.

GERMINATION: Sow outdoors where plants are to grow after all danger of frost is past, or
sow indoors 4-6 weeks before planting outside, maintaining a temperature within the medium of
70-75° during germination which takes 15-20 days.

CULTURE: Plant 9-12″ apart in a warm location and full sun in a light, dry well-drained soil
that is slightly alkaline. Do not overwater. *Hunnemannia* is drought resistant.

EASY

Hypericum calycinum   ST. JOHN'S WORT   PERENNIAL
Hypericum olympicum
Hypericaceae, native to Europe and Asia Minor.   Zone 5.

USES: Border, rock garden, ground cover, edging.

HABIT: Showy shrubby plant 1-2′ tall has 3″ cupped yellow flowers in the
summer. The 3-4″ leaves turn purplish in the fall. *Hypericum olympicum*
has a more spreading habit than *H. calycinum.*

GERMINATION: Sow outdoors in spring or summer up to two months before frost, or sow
indoors, maintaining a temperature within the medium of 70° during germination which takes
25-30 days.

CULTURE: Plant in full sun or light shade in a light soil with excellent drainage. *Hypericum*
will tolerate sandy, poor soil and heat. Prune back hard in early spring for compact growth.

173

Hypoestes   *Iberis*

Hypoestes phyllostachya   POLKA DOT PLANT   POT PLANT
(Hypoestes sanguinolenta)
Acanthaceae, native to South Africa.   Zone 10.

USES: House plant, terrariums, borders, beds.

HABIT: Tender plants 6-24″ high have pink and white spotted dark-green hairy leaves. It is generally grown for its foliage, although it does produce lilac flowers in late summer when grown outdoors.

GERMINATION: Sow indoors at any season for house-plant use, or in early spring for outdoors use. Maintain a temperature within the medium of 70-75° during germination which takes 10-12 days.

CULTURE: Outdoors, plant 12″ apart in sun or light shade in an average garden soil with excellent drainage. Indoors, grow in diffused or filtered bright light, at 65° nights and 75-85° days, in a very rich soil kept evenly moist. Do not fertilize. Pinch plants to induce bushiness. *Hypoestes* likes high humidity, so mist daily.

EASY

Iberis amara   ROCKET CANDYTUFT   ANNUAL
Iberis umbellata   GLOBE CANDYTUFT
   Cruciferae, native to Europe.

USES: Beds, borders, edging, cut flower.

HABIT: *Iberis amara* grows 12-18″ tall and is covered with umbels of fragrant white flowers from early summer to frost. *Iberis umbellata* is a more bushy plant of about the same height, with flowers all summer until frost in colors of red, pink, rose, lavender and white above dark-green leaves.

GERMINATION: Sow outdoors where plants are to grow after all danger of frost is past, or sow indoors 6-8 weeks before planting outside, maintaining a temperature within the medium of 68-86° during germination which takes 10-15 days.

CULTURE: Plant 6-12″ apart in average, well-drained garden soil, in full sun. Water when dry, and cut off faded flowers to prolong bloom.

174

Iberis

Ilex

Iberis sempervirens EDGING CANDYTUFT   PERENNIAL
Aethionema cordifolium STONE CRESS
(Iberis jucunda) LEBANON CRESS
   Cruciferae.

USES: Edging, border, rock garden, ground cover.

HABIT: *Iberis sempervirens*, native to southern Europe, has 1½" evergreen dark-green leaves on a 6-12" compact, mat-forming plant. Racemes of white flowers bloom in May. *Aethionema cordifolium* is also evergreen, but with blue-green leaves, and dainty spikes of ½" pink flowers in May and June. This native of Turkey and Lebanon grows to 6". *Iberis sempervirens* is hardy to Zone 3; *Aethionema cordifolium* is hardy to Zone 5.

GERMINATION: Sow outdoors in early spring, or sow indoors, maintaining a temperature within the medium of 55-65° during germination which takes 16-20 days.

CULTURE: Plant in full sun (*Iberis sempervirens* will tolerate light shade) in a light, sandy, well-drained soil, 6-9" apart. Shear after blooming.

ICE PLANT, see **Mesembryanthemum crystallinum**

Ilex Aquifolium ENGLISH HOLLY   TREE
Ilex crenata JAPANESE HOLLY   SHRUB
   Aquifoliaceae.   Zone 6.

USES: Hedges, specimen.

HABIT: *Ilex Aquifolium* grows to 50' with thick, leathery, shiny, dark-green leaves, most of which are spiny. Bright red ¼" berries appear in fall. *Ilex crenata* is smaller, reaching 6' at most, and has 1" leaves and dense, twiggy branching. Small black berries are almost inconspicuous. Both of these evergreens have separate male and female plants. *Ilex Aquifolium* is native to Europe, West Asia and North Africa; *I. crenata* is a native of Japan.

GERMINATION: Sow seeds of either outdoors in late fall or early winter. *Ilex crenata* may be sown indoors and germinated at a temperature within the medium of 70° in 20-25 days. Seeds of *Ilex Aquifolium* should be placed in moistened medium and refrigerated for 3 months, followed by germination at a temperature within the medium of 70°. Germination is slow and may take from 3 months to much longer. If no germination is seen in 6 months, return the seeds to the refrigerator for another 3 months, and repeat the process.

CULTURE: Plant in full sun or part shade in a spot protected from winter sun and wind. Soil should be fertile, rich, moist and well-drained. If pruning is necessary, do so in early spring before growth begins.

175

Impatiens Balsamina   *Impatiens Wallerana*

Impatiens Balsamina   GARDEN BALSAM   ANNUAL
Balsaminaceae, native to Asian tropics.

USES: Bedding, borders, planters.

HABIT: This everblooming annual has either single or double flowers that are waxy, borne close to the stem, and look like roses in shades of pink, red, white, lavender and yellow from early summer to frost. Flowers are solid colors or spotted on a 12-36″ plant clothed with 6″ pointed, toothed leaves.

GERMINATION: Sow outdoors where plants are to grow after all danger of frost has past, or sow indoors 6-8 weeks before planting outside, maintaining a temperature within the medium of 70° during germination which takes 8-14 days.

CULTURE: Plant 10-18″ apart in full sun or part shade, in a rich, fertile, sandy soil. Balsam loves heat and plenty of water.

EASY

Impatiens Wallerana   IMPATIENS, PATIENT PLANT ANNUAL
(I. Holstii, I. Sultanii)   BUSY LIZZIE
Balsaminaceae, native to East Africa.

USES: Borders, planters, bedding, hanging basket, house plant.

HABIT: Open faced 1-2″ single or double flowers of white, pink, orange, salmon, red and lavender, in solids and bicolors, bloom from early summer to frost on 6-30″ compact mounded plants.

GERMINATION: Sow indoors at any season for indoor use, or 12 weeks before planting outside for outdoor use. Do not cover the seed as light is necessary for germination. Maintain a temperature within the medium of 70-75° during germination which takes 15-20 days.

CULTURE: Plant 12-15″ apart in a rich, sandy, moist, well-drained soil in part shade or shade. Pinch plants to promote bushiness. Indoors, grow in full sun or bright light in a very rich soil kept evenly moist. Give 60° nights and 70-75° days.

EASY

176

Incarvillea   *Ipomoea alba*

Incarvillea Delavayi HARDY GLOXINIA   PERENNIAL
Bignoniaceae, native to China.   Zone 6.

USES: Beds, borders, pot plant.

HABIT: Trumpet-shaped 2-3″ flowers of rosy purple with a yellow throat bloom in May and June on 1-2′ stems above lacy, fern-like foliage.

GERMINATION: Sow outdoors in late fall or early spring for late spring germination, or sow indoors, maintaining a temperature within the medium of 55-65° during germination which takes 25-30 days.

CULTURE: Plant in full sun, 12-15″ apart, in a rich, deeply worked, well-drained soil that is slightly acid. Water well during the growing season. Remove faded flowers to prolong bloom. In areas colder than Zone 6, the fleshy roots can be lifted after frost in fall and stored over the winter in a cool, dry place. Indoors, grow in full sun, in a cool place (50° nights), and allow the soil to become dry between waterings.

Ipomoea alba MOON VINE   ANNUAL
(Calonyction aculeatum)
Ipomoea X multifida CARDINAL CLIMBER
(Quamoclit sloteri)
Ipomoea Quamoclit CYPRESS VINE
  Convolvulaceae, native to the Tropics.
USES: Vine, screen.
HABIT: *Ipomoea alba* climbs to 15′, is clothed with handsome, bright, shiny green leaves, and bears fragrant, white, trumpet-shaped flowers from July to September that open in the evening. *Ipomoea X multifida* grows to 30′, has fernlike foliage and flowers in summer with 2″ tubular red flowers with white throats. *Ipomoea Quamoclit* reaches 25′, has airy, thread-like foliage, and has 1½″ bright red flowers in summer and early fall that remain open all day.

GERMINATION: Clip or notch the seed or soak in warm water for 24 hours before sowing. Seeds may be sown outdoors where plants are to grow after all danger of frost has past, but for best results, sow indoors 6-8 weeks before planting outside, maintaining a temperature within the medium of 68-86° during germination which takes 5-10 days. *Ipomoea X multifida* and *I. Quamoclit* do not like to be disturbed, so transplant into their permanent location with extreme care.

CULTURE: Plant in full sun in a light, rich, sandy soil. Keep well-watered, and provide a trellis or other support.

177

Ipomoea   *Ipomopsis*

Ipomoea Nil, Ipomoea purpurea, MORNING GLORY   ANNUAL
Ipomoea tricolor, Ipomoea leptophylla,
Convolvulus tricolor
 Convolvulaceae, native to the Tropics.
USES: Vine, screen, trellis.

HABIT: *Ipomoea Nil, I. purpurea* and *I. tricolor* are the well-known vines which grow 8-10', have heart-shaped leaves, and have showy, funnel-shaped flowers that are single or double in colors of blue, purple, pink, red or white. The flowers bloom from July to frost, opening in early morning and fading by afternoon, and are solid, striped or bicolored. The Bush Morning Glory, *I. leptophylla,* is 3', bushy, and has 3" flowers of rosy-pink deeping to purple. *Convolvulus tricolor* (Dwarf Morning Glory) is a 12" plant with bright royal blue flowers. Several of the Morning Glories are perennials, but all should be treated as annuals as they self-sow easily and can become weedy.

GERMINATION: Nick the seed carefully, or soak in warm water for 24 hours before sowing. Sow outdoors where plants are to grow after all danger of frost is past, or sow indoors 4-6 weeks before planting outside, maintaining a temperature within the medium of 68-86° during germination which takes 5-7 days.

CULTURE: Plant in full sun, in a light, sandy, well-drained soil. Soil that is too rich or too fertile will not produce flowers. Provide a trellis or other support for the vining types. Water only moderately, for Morning Glory will tolerate dry soil.

Ipomopsis rubra SKYROCKET,   BIENNIAL
(Gilia coronopifolia) STANDING CYPRESS
Gilia rubra
 Polemoniaceae, native to eastern United States.

USES: Edging, border, planters, cut flower.

HABIT: Narrow 1-2" flowers that are red outside and yellow and dotted red inside appear in spikes in summer above dainty, feathery foliage on a 4-6' plant.

GERMINATION: Sow outdoors in spring or summer for bloom the following year. Seeds may be sown indoors, but must be transplanted very carefully, as *Ipomopsis* does not move well. Maintain a temperature within the medium of 55-65° during germination which takes 10-15 days. Germination is adversely affected by temperatures in the medium in excess of 65° F.

CULTURE: Plant 12-18" apart in full sun and a dry to average light, well-drained soil. Stake taller plants.

Iris

Jacaranda

Iris Kaempferi   IRIS   PERENNIAL
Iris kamaonensis
Iradaceae.   Zone 4.

USES: Beds, borders, rock gardens, cut flowers.

HABIT: *Iris Kaempferi,* the Japanese Iris, is a native of Japan, growing to 2'
with sword-shaped leaves and single or double flowers predominantly red or
purple. The flowers measure to 8" across, open flat, and appear in June and
July. *Iris kamaonensis* is more compact, with 6-8" leaves and blue-purple
flowers mottled with white on short stems in May. It is a native of the
Himalayas.

GERMINATION: Sow outdoors in late fall or early winter for spring germination. Indoors,
place seeds in moistened medium in the refrigerator for 6 weeks, followed by germination at a
temperature within the medium of 65-75° which takes 3-5 weeks or more. Germination is often
slow and irregular.

CULTURE: Plant *Iris Kaempferi* 18" apart in sun or part shade in a rich, slightly acid, very
moist soil. It does well by the side of pools or streams. *Iris kamaonensis* should be planted 6"
apart in full sun and average soil with excellent drainage. It does best in cool climates.

Jacaranda mimosifolia   GREEN EBONY   POT PLANT
   Bignoniaceae, native to Argentina.   Zone 10.

USES: House plant, greenhouse plant, screen, outdoors in warm climates.

HABIT: This graceful tree grows to 3' indoors and to 50' outdoors, with
elegant finely cut fern-like foliage and 8" clusters of 2" flowers that are
funnel shaped, fragrant and bloom from April to June.

GERMINATION: Sow in early spring for outdoor use and anytime for indoor use, maintaining
a temperature within the medium of 68-86° during germination which takes 10-15 days.

CULTURE: Plant outdoors in full sun or light shade in a sandy, moist, well drained soil,
keeping well watered. Indoors, provide 65° nights and day temperatures to 85°, and provide
high humidity or grow in the greenhouse. Give bright light and allow the soil to become
somewhat dry between waterings. Prune in early spring to shape and contain size. *Jacaranda* is
difficult to bloom indoors.

Jasione

Jasminum

Jasione perennis   SHEEP'S BIT,   PERENNIAL
                     SHEPHERD'S SCABIOSA
Campanulaceae, native to southern Europe.   Zone 5.

USES: Borders, walls, rock gardens.

HABIT: Tiny, sky blue, bell-shaped flowers in dense 2″ globular heads bloom in May and June above 12-18″ plants. Foliage is small, hairy and tufted.

GERMINATION: Sow outdoors in spring or summer up to two months before frost, or sow indoors, maintaining a temperature within the medium of 70° during germination which takes 10-15 days.

CULTURE: Plant 12″ apart in sun or light shade in average, well drained, somewhat dry and sandy soil. In rich soil, *Jasione* becomes floppy.

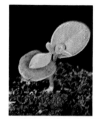

Jasminum humile JASMINE   PERENNIAL
  Oleaceae, native to the Himalayas.   Zone 8.

USES: Vine, screen, greenhouse plant.

HABIT: This climbing evergreen grows to 20′ forming a shrubby plant with pinnately compound leaves and clusters of fragrant, starry, bright yellow flowers in June and July. The foliage is shiny and dark green.

GERMINATION: For best results, sow indoors in early spring, maintaining a temperature within the medium of 70-75° during germination which takes 20-25 days. Sow any time of year for greenhouse use.

CULTURE: Plant 4-6′ apart in sun or part shade in a light, rich, well drained soil. Provide a trellis or other support. Pruning should be done immediately after flowering. Indoors, *Jasminum* will grow in either a warm or cool greenhouse, in full sun, with the soil kept evenly moist.

Justicia

Kalanchoe

JEWELS OF OPAR, see **Talinum paniculatum**

Justicia aurea KING'S CROWN   POT PLANT
(Jacobinia aurea, Justicia umbrosa)
Acanthaceae, native to Mexico and Central America.   Zone 10.

USES: House plant, greenhouse plant, outdoors in warm climates.

HABIT: This tropical looking perennial has 12″ downy green leaves and 12″ dense terminal panicles of yellow, curving, tubular flowers, blooming in late summer and fall.

GERMINATION: Sow indoors at any season, not covering the seed which needs light to germinate. Maintain a temperature within the medium of 70° during germination which takes 20-25 days.

CULTURE: Outdoors, grow in full sun or part shade in a rich, well drained, slightly acid soil. Cut back in spring as growth starts. Indoors, provide night temperatures of 65° and day temperatures to 85°. Place in indirect light from spring to fall and in direct sun in winter. Soil should be kept evenly moist and humidity high. Fertilize heavily during the growing season.

Kalanchoe Blossfeldiana KALANCHOE   POT PLANT
      Crassulaceae, native to Madagascar.   Zone 10.

USES: House plant, greenhouse plant.

HABIT: This succulent has oval, waxy leaves and clusters of tiny red or yellow flowers in winter.

GERMINATION: Sow indoors in spring for bloom the following winter. Do not cover the fine seeds which need light for germination. Maintain a temperature within the medium of 70-75° during germination which takes 10 days.

CULTURE: *Kalanchoe* likes normal house conditions. Give 60-65° nights and 70-75° days, place in full sun, and allow the soil to become dry between waterings. Be sure the atmosphere is not too humid. *Kalanchoe* blooms on long nights; they will not initiate flower buds if the nights are shorter than 12 hours.

Kalmia   *Kniphofia*

KALE, FLOWERING, see **Brassica oleracea** Acerphala

Kalmia latifolia   MOUNTAIN LAUREL   SHRUB
Ericaceae, native to eastern North America.   Zone 4.

USES: Foundation planting, specimen.

HABIT: Leathery, glossy, oval leaves and pink to white flowers that are spotted inside and bloom in June are found on this shrub that grows to 10'. The flowers are 1″ across and bloom in clusters.

GERMINATION: Sow outdoors in late fall or early winter for spring germination, or place seeds in moistened medium in the refrigerator for 3 months, followed by germination at a temperature within the medium of 70°. Germination is varied but will take approximately 30 days.

CULTURE: Plant in part shade in moist, acid, sandy or peaty soil. Water regularly and do not cultivate around the shallow roots.

Kniphofia Uvaria   RED HOT POKER, TRITOMA   PERENNIAL
Liliaceae, native to South Africa.   Zone 6.

USES: Borders, rock gardens, cut flowers.

HABIT: This 3' plant has 12″ strap-like broad leaves tufted at the base of erect, stiff flower stalks which terminate in poker shaped clusters of drooping tubular flowers in graduating colors of yellow to fiery red at the top in early summer.

GERMINATION: Sow outdoors in spring or summer up to two months before frost, or sow indoors, maintaining a temperature within the medium of 70-75° during germination which takes 10-20 days.

CULTURE: Plant 18-24″ apart in full sun and a sandy, well drained soil. Disturb the plants as little as possible.

EASY

Kochia

Laburnum

Kochia scoparia forma **trichophylla** Cv. **Childsii** ANNUAL
BURNING BUSH, SUMMER CYPRESS
(Kochia Childsii)
Chenopodiaceae, native to Eurasia.

USES: Hedge, border, screen, accent.

HABIT: Dense, globe shaped 2½-3′ plants are green during summer and turn bright red in the fall. The foliage is narrow and feathery, the green flowers insignificant.

GERMINATION: Sow outdoors after all danger of frost is past, or sow indoors 4-6 weeks before planting outside, maintaining a temperature within the medium of 70-75° during germination which takes 10-15 days. Do not cover seed as it needs light to germinate. Seeds are not long lived and should not be stored.

CULTURE: Plant 18-24″ apart in full sun and a dry soil with excellent drainage. *Kochia* tolerates hot weather and is slow to develop in cool weather. It may be sheared, and it self sows readily.

EASY

Laburnum anagyroides   GOLDEN-CHAIN   TREE
(Laburnum vulgare)
Leguminosae, native to Europe.   Zone 5.

USES: Specimen.

HABIT: Deciduous tree 20-30′ bears compound leaves and 6-12″ racemes of yellow pea-like flowers in late spring that resemble *Wisteria.*

GERMINATION: Sow outdoors in spring, or sow indoors, maintaining a temperature within the medium of 55-70° during germination which takes 30-60 days. Soak seeds for 24 hours in warm water or nick the seed coat before sowing.

CULTURE: Plant in light shade in an area protected from wind in a moist, deeply prepared, well drained soil. Prune after flowering to encourage the next season's bloom.

Lagenaria   Lagerstroemia

Lagenaria siceraria WHITE FLOWERED GOURDS   ANNUAL
Cucurbitaceae, native to the Old World Tropics.

USES: Screen, decorative fruits.

HABIT: This vine grows to 30', with cordate leaves and showy, fragrant, funnel shaped flowers. The hard shelled fruits are decorative, colored green, white or orange, or combinations of these colors, in interesting shapes and sizes from 3" to 3'. These gourds are larger than the Yellow Flowered Gourd (*Cucurbita Pepo ovifera*).

GERMINATION: Seeds may be sown in hills outdoors after all danger of frost has past where the plants are to grow, but since *Lagenaria* needs such a long growing season, should be sown indoors 6-8 weeks before last frost. Soak seeds for 24 hours before sowing, and maintain a temperature within the medium of 70° during germination which takes 8-14 days.

CULTURE: Set plants 2' apart in full sun in a rich, well drained soil suitable for growing vegetables. Train on a trellis or other support and provide ample water throughout the summer. *Lagenaria* needs a long growing season and may not mature in the north. Pick gourds as the stem starts to dry (pick the white ones as they start to yellow), wash well and wax.

EASY

Lagerstroemia indica CRAPE MYRTLETTES   PERENNIAL
Lythraceae, native to China.   Zone 7.

USES: Borders, hedges, planters, greenhouse plant.

HABIT: These dwarf plants reach 4', are deciduous, and have crinkled flowers of white, rose, pink, red and lavender borne in clusters in summer.

GERMINATION: Sow outdoors after all danger of frost has past, or sow indoors 6-8 weeks before last frost, maintaining a temperature within the medium of 70-75° during germination which takes 15-20 days. Do not cover seed as light aids in germination.

CULTURE: Plant in full sun in a rich, sandy, well drained soil, and feed monthly during the growing season. Plant 2' apart if used as a hedge. Prune in early spring to shape and uniform the plants. Crape Myrtlettes love the sun and heat and therefore do best in the south. Indoors, provide 50° nights, good air circulation, average soil kept evenly moist and full sun.

Lagurus

Lantana

Lagurus ovatus   HARE'S TAIL GRASS   ANNUAL
Gramineae, native to the Mediterranean.

USES: Ornamental grass, dried branches.

HABIT: Dense, woolly, pale, feathery heads 2″ long that resemble rabbit's tails appear in fall on 1-2′ plants.

GERMINATION: Sow outdoors in spring where plants are to grow, or sow indoors 6-8 weeks before planting outside, maintaining a temperature within the medium of 55° during germination which takes 15-20 days.

CULTURE: Plant 1′ apart in full sun and average, well drained garden soil.

Lantana Camara   LANTANA   POT PLANT
Verbenaceae, native to the West Indies.   Zone 9.

USES: Planters, cut flower, greenhouse plant.

HABIT: Grey-green oval leaves are found on this plant, along with flowers in a dense, neatly flat-topped head 2″ across, opening pink, yellow or orange and changing to white, red or orange, often with all colors on the same flower. It is summer blooming outdoors and winter blooming indoors. It can be trained to an attractive standard.

GERMINATION: Sow indoors at any season for indoor use, or indoors 12 weeks before last frost for outdoor use. Maintain a temperature within the medium of 70-75 ° during germination which takes 6-8 weeks.

CULTURE: Plant outdoors in a warm spot in full sun and in a rich, loamy, well drained soil. Water deeply but infrequently and feed lightly. Prune back hard in spring in warm areas where it is used as a perennial. Indoors, provide 60° nights, bright sun, and allow the soil to become dry between waterings.

EASY

Lathyrus latifolius   *Lathyrus odoratus*

LARKSPUR, see **Delphinium**

Lathyrus latifolius   PERENNIAL PEA   PERENNIAL
     Leguminosae, native to southern Europe.   Zone 3.

USES: Vine, screen, cut flower.

HABIT: *Lathyrus latifolius* climbs to 6-9', has winged stems, compound leaves, and 3-5" clusters of 1½" flowers, borne many to a stem in colors of purple, rose, white, red, blue and pink.

GERMINATION: Sow outdoors in early fall in Zones 8-10 and in early spring in colder zones, planting 2" deep. Prepare the soil in fall for spring planting. It may also be sown indoors 4-6 weeks before planting outside, maintaining a temperature within the medium of 55-65° during germination which takes 20-30 days. Soak seeds for 24 hours in warm water or file the seed coats before sowing.

CULTURE: Soil for *Lathyrus latifolius* must be deeply prepared, rich, fertile and slightly alkaline. This plant does not do well in hot climates, preferring a cool, moist climate. Provide a support such as a trellis, and keep flowers cut after fading to prolong bloom. Mulch the plants to retain moisture and keep the roots cool. Give full sun.

Lathyrus odoratus   SWEET PEA   ANNUAL
     Leguminosae, native to Italy.

USES: Vine, planters, borders, beds, screens.

HABIT: This much improved old-fashioned annual has climbing versions that grow to 6' and bush types that reach 2½'. The 2" flowers are borne 1-4 per stem, are fragrant, and are in colors of purple, rose, red, white, pink and blue. It blooms in spring and early summer, and the improved types are heat tolerant and will bloom throughout the summer.

GERMINATION: Sow outdoors in early spring, or in late fall in Zones 8-10. Prepare the soil in the fall if spring planting. Outdoors, sow 2" deep. It may also be sown indoors 4-6 weeks before planting outside, maintaining a temperature within the medium of 55-65° during germination which takes 10-14 days. Soak the seeds for 24 hours or file the seed coat before planting. Be sure to cover the seeds well as germination is aided by darkness.

CULTURE: Plant in full sun in a deeply prepared, rich, fertile, slightly alkaline soil. Provide a trellis or other support for climbing types. Give plenty of water, mulch the soil to keep the roots cool, and cut back to stimulate growth and flowering. Position away from drying winds.

EASY

Lavatera   *Layia*

Lavatera hybrids   TREE MALLOW   ANNUAL
Malvaceae, native to the Mediterranean.

USES: Borders, backgrounds, hedges, screens, cut flowers, greenhouse plant.

HABIT: During summer 2½-3″ flowers, cup-like in pink or white and resembling hollyhocks, are borne on 2½-4′ hairy stemmed plants with maple-like leaves.

GERMINATION: *Lavatera* may be sown indoors 6-8 weeks before planting outside, maintaining a temperature within the medium of 70° during germination which takes 15-20 days, but it is difficult to transplant, so is better sown outdoors in early spring. Sow indoors in fall for winter and spring bloom in the greenhouse.

CULTURE: Outdoors, plant in full sun, 24″ apart, in average, well drained soil. Feed monthly with a balanced fertilizer. Keep faded flowers removed to prolong bloom. Indoors, provide 50-55° nights, full sun, and a rich, porous soil that is allowed to dry out between waterings.

LAVENDER, see Chapter "Growing Edibles from Seed"

Layia platyglossa   TIDY TIPS   ANNUAL
Compositae, native to California.

USES: Borders, planters, cut flowers.

HABIT: A solid mound 12-24″ high of 2″ clear yellow, white tipped, single daisy-like flowers blooms in summer, hiding small, narrow, grass-like leaves.

GERMINATION: Sow outdoors after all danger of frost is past where plants are to grow, or sow indoors 6-8 weeks before planting outside, maintaining a temperature within the medium of 70-75° during germination which takes 8-12 days.

CULTURE: Plant 12-15″ apart in full sun and a light, rich, well drained soil kept moist. Feed every other month with a balanced fertilizer. *Layia* does best where summers are cool.

EASY

Leontopodium

LAZY DAISY, see **Aphanostephus skirhobasis**

Leontopodium alpinum   EDELWEISS   PERENNIAL
Leontopodium leontopodioides
(L. sibiricum)
   Compositae, native to European and Asian mountains.   Zone 5.

USES: Rock gardens, walls, planters, greenhouse plant.

HABIT: Woolly, tufted, dwarf plant 6-12″ high have a silvery-white appearance and several erect stems, each carrying star shaped "flowers" composed of white leaf bracts in the center of which are tiny yellow flowers, blooming in July and August. *Leontopodium leontopodioides* has smaller flowers, but there are more of them.

GERMINATION: Sow outdoors in early spring, or sow indoors maintaining a temperature within the medium of 55° during germination which takes 10-14 days. Do not cover seed as light is necessary for germination. Seeds may also be placed in moistened medium in the refrigerator for 3 weeks, followed by germination at a temperature within the medium of 70°.

CULTURE: Plant 3-6″ apart in full sun and a dry, alkaline, sandy, well drained soil. The lighter and poorer the soil and the sunnier the location, the more typically silver this plant will be. *Leontopodium leontopodioides* will take more summer heat and is easier to grow. In the greenhouse, provide 50° nights, full sun, and allow the soil to become dry between waterings.

Lewisia rediviva   BITTER ROOT   PERENNIAL
   Portulacaceae, native to western United States mountains.   Zone 4.

USES: Rock gardens, borders, greenhouse plant.

HABIT: Fleshy strap-like leaves 6″ long and topped with 1″ starry flowers in pearly pink or white in early spring. The foliage disappears after flowering and reappears in fall.

GERMINATION: Sow outdoors in late fall or early winter for spring germination, or place seeds in moistened medium in the freezer for 3 weeks, followed by germination at a temperature within the medium of 70° which will take 30 days.

CULTURE: Plant 10-12″ apart in full sun or light shade in a light, sandy soil with excellent drainage. It will tolerate a dry and rocky soil, although it does like to be well watered while in flower. Give it a warm spot in a sheltered position. Indoors, give 50° nights, full sun, and allow the soil to become dry between waterings.

Liatris   *Liatris*

Liatris scariosa   GAYFEATHER   PERENNIAL
Liatris spicata
Compositae, native to North America.   Zone 3.

USES: Borders, cut flowers, wild gardens.

HABIT: Over basal tufts of narrow, grassy leaves, spikes 1½-4' bloom with tiny, fuzzy flowers opening from the top down in July or August. Flowers of *Liatris scariosa* are white; those of *L. spicata* are rosy-purple.

GERMINATION: Sow outdoors from early spring through summer up to two months before frost, or sow indoors. *Liatris* will germinate successfully at a wide temperature range within the medium of 55-75° and germination takes 20-25 days.

CULTURE: Plant 12-15" apart in full sun or light shade in a sandy, rich, well drained soil. Roots must not be wet in northern states in the winter. *Liatris* will withstand heat, drought, cold and poor soil.

EASY

G. W. Park Seed Co. Gardens

189

Lilium   *Lilium*

Lilium species LILY   PERENNIAL
Liliaceae.

USES: Border, pot plant, cut flower, greenhouse plant.

HABIT: Lilies are bulbous plants which bear spikes of magnificent flowers in summer. *Lilium auratum* (Gold Banded Lily) grows 4-6' and has saucer shaped 10-12" flowers in August that are very fragrant. Blooms are white with yellow striping and maroon dots. From Japan, it is hardy to Zone 4. *Lilium Davidii* var. *Willmottiae* is native to west China and hardy to Zone 4, with 6" reflexed orange blooms with brown spotting. The plant grows 4-7' and is relatively rare. It blooms from June to August. *Lilium x formolongi* is a hybrid hardy to Zone 6 with trumpets of white on a 3' plant. *Lilium formosanum* is also white, with fragrant trumpets that look like the Easter Lily. Flowers are 5-8" long and bloom in August and September on a 2-5' plant. From Taiwan, it is hardy to Zone 5. *Lilium Henryi* blooms atop 4-8' bronze flecking in August. It is hardy to Zone 4 and native to Central China. *Lilium Kelloggii* is a more difficult plant to grow, reaching 2-4' with dainty, graceful 1½-2" fragrant flowers of pink spotted with purple-black. It blooms in June, is hardy to Zone 7, and comes to us from northwest California. *Lilium longiflorum* (Trumpet Lily, Easter Lily), from Japan, is hardy to Zone 8, with 7" fragrant trumpets of white on 18-36" plants. *Lilium Martagon* (Turban Lily) is from Europe and Asia and hardy to Zone 3. Recurved purple waxy flowers are spotted with black and are ill scented, appearing in July and August on a 4-6' plant. *Lilium occidentale* (Western Lily) is from southern Oregon and the northern California coast and hardy to Zone 8. Nodding, 2½", recurved flowers of orange-red with a maroon spotted throat bloom in July on 2-6' plants. *Lilium pumilum (L. tenuifolium),* known as the Siberian Lily or the Coral Lily, has waxy, recurved, scarlet fragrant flowers, 2" across atop, 1½-2' wiry stems. It is from Siberia and China and is hardy to Zone 3. *Lilium regale* (Royal Lily) grows 3-6' with 6" trumpets of ivory white flowers flushed purple-rose with a yellow throat. Blooms are fragrant and appear in July. The plant is native to west China and hardy to Zone 3. *Cardiocrinum giganteum (L. giganteum Takeshima)* grows to 12' with fragrant 6" flowers of white tinged green on the outside and red on the inside. It is from the Himalayas and Tibet, hardy to Zone 6, and is also more difficult to grow. There are also many hybrids with new and varied colors and large, exotic flowers.

GERMINATION: Seeds of all except *L. auratum, L. Martagon and C. giganteum* may be sown outdoors in early spring, or sown indoors, maintaining a temperature of 70° within the medium during germination which takes from 3-6 weeks in most cases. The others should be sown outdoors in late summer for germination the following spring. Indoors, maintain a temperature within the medium of 70° for 3 months, then refrigerate for 6 weeks, followed by germination within the medium of 70° which will take 3-6 weeks. Seeds of *L. regale* are not long lived and should not be stored.

CULTURE: Grow outdoors, preferably in full sun, in a light, fertile, deep, slightly acid soil with perfect drainage. Lilies require ample moisture all year and should be mulched to keep the soil moist, cool and shaded. Stake tall varieties. Remove faded flowers immediately and allow the foliage to die off naturally. In the greenhouse, grow at 50-55° nights in full to filtered light and a soil kept evenly moist.

Limonium

Limonium Bonduellii   ANNUAL
Limonium latifolium   PERENNIAL
Liminium sinuatum SEA LAVENDER, STATICE   BIENNIAL
Goniolimon tataricum (Limonium tataricum)
Psylliostachys Suworowii (Limonium Suworowii)
  Plumbaginaceae

USES: Beds, borders, rock gardens, cut flowers, dried flowers.

HABIT: Delicate, light, airy flower stalks are hidden beneath broad billows of tiny, funnel-shaped flowers in clusters during the summer. The foliage is long and leathery and in basal rosettes. *Limonium Bonduellii* grows 2-3′, has yellow flowers, is an annual or biennial and is commonly known as Algerian Sea Lavender after its native habitat; *L. latifolium* (Wideleaf Sea Lavender) is a native of southern Europe, a perennial to Zone 3 with lavender, white or pink flowers on 2-3′ plants; *L. sinuatum* (Notch Leaf Sea Lavender) is a biennial or annual from the Mediterranean area with flowers of white, blue, yellow or red on 12-30″ plants; *Goniolimon tataricum* is a perennial to Zone 6 with flowers of red, pink or white on 12-20″ plants. From Europe, it is known as Tatarian Sea Lavender. *Phylliostachys Suworowii*, the Russian Statice, is an annual from eastern Europe with lavender, pink or white flowers on an 18-30″ plant.

GERMINATION: Annual forms may be sown outdoors where the plants are to grow after all danger of frost has past, but for best results, sow indoors 8-10 weeks before planting outside, maintaining a temperature within the medium of 70° during germination which takes 15-20 days. Perennial and biennial forms should be sown outdoors in late fall or early spring for earliest bloom, or indoors in the same manner as for the annuals. Be sure to completely cover the seeds of *Psylliostachys Suworowii* as they need darkness to germinate.

CULTURE: Plant 18-24″ apart in full sun and a sandy, light, well drained soil. These plants tolerate drought, heat and salt spray.

191

Linaria

Linaria maroccana TOADFLAX ANNUAL
  Scrophulariaceae, native to Morocco.

USES: Border, bedding, rock gardens, edging, greenhouse plant, cut flower.

HABIT: Mounded 8-12″ plant with hairy leaves bears ½″ miniature snapdragon-like brightly colored blossoms of yellow, blue, lavender, pink, red, salmon, bronze, white and multi-colors during summer.

GERMINATION: Sow outdoors where plants are to grow in early spring as soon as soil can be worked, or sow indoors, maintaining a temperature within the medium of 55-60° during germination which takes 10-15 days.

CULTURE: Plant 6-10″ apart in rich, porous, sandy soil with excellent drainage in full sun or light shade. Water moderately. *Linaria* does best in cooler climates. In the greenhouse, give 50° nights, full sun and a soil kept evenly moist.

EASY

Linum flavum 'Compactum' GOLDEN FLAX PERENNIAL
Linum perenne PERENNIAL FLAX
  Linaceae, native to central and southern Europe. Zone 4, 5.

USES: Border, bedding, rock gardens.

HABIT: *Linum flavum* 'Compactum' is a dwarf (6″) plant with myriads of dainty 1½″ yellow flowers that bloom continually through the summer even though the individual flowers last only one day. Plants have needle-like fluted green foliage. *Linum perenne* grows to 2′, with deep blue silky flowers 1″ across borne in gracefully arching, multi-branched panicles from May to August. The former is hardy to Zone 5, the latter to Zone 4.

GERMINATION: Sow outdoors where plants are to grow in spring or summer up to two months before frost. Seeds may be sown indoors maintaining a temperature within the medium of 70° during germination which takes 20-25 days, but move to the garden carefully as *Linum* does not like to be transplanted.

CULTURE: Plant 12″ apart in full sun and a light, well drained soil. Feed monthly with a balanced fertilizer. Flax blooms best where summers are cool and does not like to be divided.

EASY

192

Liriope

Lithops

Liriope Muscari var. **exiliflora** LILYTURF   PERENNIAL
Liliaceae, native to China and Japan.   Zone 6.

USES: Ground cover, border, rock garden, cut flower.

HABIT: Tufted clumps of grass-like leaves of dark green or variegated with white or yellow, give rise to 6-12″ spikes of ¼″ grape hyacinth-like flowers (but larger) in purple or white, blooming late summer and fall. The foliage is evergreen in the south.

GERMINATION: Soak seeds in warm water for 24 hours before sowing. Seeds may be sown outdoors anytime from late spring through summer up to two months before frost, or sown indoors, maintaining a temperature within the medium of 65-70° during germination which takes 30 days.

CULTURE: Plant 6-12″ apart in light shade or shade in average, well drained garden soil. It will tolerate sun if additional moisture is provided. Cut off old foliage in early spring to encourage new growth.

Lithops species LIVING STONES   POT PLANT
Aizoaceae, native of South Africa.   Zone 10.

USES: House plant, greenhouse plant.

HABIT: Curious succulent plants with silvery or blue cast on clumps that resemble stones. Blooms of daisy-like yellow or white flowers appear from fissures in the "stones" in late summer and early fall. There are other genera of succulents known as Living Stones and their germination and culture is identical.

GERMINATION: Sow indoors at any season, maintaining a temperature within the medium of 70-75° during germination which takes 10-15 days.

CULTURE: Grow in full sun in a gravelly, well drained soil that is allowed to become dry between waterings. In winter, water only enough to prevent shrivelling. Pots may also be sunk in gravel. Night temperatures should be 55-60°.

Lobelia

Livistona chinensis   CHINESE FAN PALM   POT PLANT
Palmae, native of China.   Zone 9.

USES: House plant, greenhouse plant, outdoors in warm climates.

HABIT: Glossy green, fan shaped leaves are partially incised in narrow segments which gracefully hang like fringe. This plant will grow to 30′ outdoors and to 10′ in the house, with leaves growing to 6′ across.

GERMINATION: Sow indoors at any season, maintaining a temperature within the medium of 70-75° during germination which takes 2-6 months. Do not attempt to store seeds for a long period of time as they are short lived.

CULTURE: Grow in part shade or filtered sunlight in a rich, well drained soil that is kept quite moist. High humidity or a greenhouse is required. Give warm (60°) nights and days to 80°.

Lobelia species   LOBELIA   ANNUAL, PERENNIAL
   Lobeliaceae

USES: Bedding, edging, borders, baskets, greenhouse plant

HABIT: *Lobelia Erinus,* edging Lobelia, is a trailing annual with profuse flowers, growing 4-8″ high. It is native to South Africa. Flowers may be blue, white, or red and bloom all summer. *Lobelia Cardinalis,* Cardinal Flower, is a perennial hardy to Zone 2 that has spikes of red flowers in late summer on a 3′ plant. It is native to the eastern United States. *Lobelia splendens* is similar to *L. Cardinalis* and is native to Mexico. There is also a blue form of perennial *Lobelia.*

GERMINATION: Sow annual types 10-12 weeks before last frost, maintaining a temperature within the medium of 70-75° during germination which takes 15-20 days. Sow perennial types outdoors in late fall for spring germination, or sow indoors, following 3 months in the refrigerator in moistened medium. Maintain a temperature within the medium of 70° during germination which takes 15-20 days.

CULTURE: Plant annual types 4-6″ apart in full sun or light shade in a rich, sandy soil. Plant perennial *Lobelia* 15-18″ apart in a very rich, moist, well drained soil in full sun or part shade. Remove flower spikes after bloom to encourage further growth. Indoors, grow at 55° nights in indirect light and a very rich soil kept evenly moist.

194

Lobularia   Lonas

Lobularia maritima   SWEET ALYSSUM   ANNUAL
Cruciferae, native to the Mediterranean.

USES: Borders, edgings, rock gardens, planters, greenhouse plant.

HABIT: Tiny clusters of sweet smelling flowers bloom from June to frost in colors of lavender, pink, rose, purple or white on 3-6" multi-branching mounds which spread to 6-12". Foliage is linear. In Zones 9 and 10, it will act as a perennial and bloom year round.

GERMINATION: Seeds may be sown outdoors in early spring where plants are to grow, or sown indoors 4-6 weeks before last frost, maintaining a temperature within the medium of 65-70° during germination which takes 8-15 days. Do not cover seeds as light is necessary for germination.

CULTURE: Plant 5-8" apart in full sun and average, well drained garden soil. Sweet Alyssums prefer to be kept moist but will tolerate drought and heat. Shear back occasionally to encourage more flowers. Lift and take indoors for winter flowering, providing cool (50-55°) nights, full sun, good air circulation, and a soil kept evenly moist.

EASY

Lonas annua (Lonas inodora)   GOLDEN AGERATUM   ANNUAL
Compositae, native to Italy and N.W. Africa.

USES: Edging, borders, wildflower gardens.

HABIT: Wide, fluffy, ¼" yellow flowers bloom in 2" clusters and resemble ageratum. Flowers appear from June through frost on 10-12" plants over finely cut leaves.

GERMINATION: Sow outdoors after all danger of frost has past where plants are to grow, or sow indoors 6-8 weeks before last frost, maintaining a temperature within the medium of 70° during germination which takes 5-7 days. Cover seeds completely as they need darkness to germinate.

CULTURE: Plant 6" apart in full sun and average, well drained garden soil. *Lonas* will tolerate wind and seashore conditions.

EASY

195

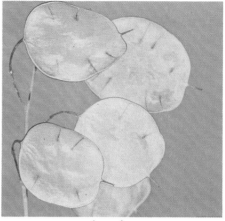

Luffa   Lunaria

Luffa aegyptiaca   DISHRAG GOURD   ANNUAL
Cucurbitaceae, native to the Old World Tropics.

USES: Screen, fiber from fruit.

HABIT: This vine grows 10-15', has white or yellow flowers, lobed leaves, and a fruit in fall with a dry, papery rind and an interior fiber that is used as a dishrag or a sponge.

GERMINATION: Seeds may be sown outdoors in hills after all danger of frost has past where the plants are to grow, but since *Luffa* needs a long growing season, it is best to sow them indoors 6-8 weeks before last frost, maintaining a temperature within the medium of 70° during germination which takes 8-10 days.

CULTURE: Plant 2' apart in full sun and a rich soil suitable for growing vetetables. Train on a trellis or other support and provide ample water during the growing season.

EASY

Lunaria annua   MONEY PLANT   BIENNIAL
Cruciferae, native to southern Europe.

USES: Bedding, cut flower, dried seed pods.

HABIT: This old fashioned plant grows to 3' and is best known for its flat, round, silvery, translucent seed pods which appear the second year. Flowers are fragrant, purple, pink or white, and appear in clusters in late spring and early summer. The stems are clothed with coarsely toothed, heart shaped leaves.

GERMINATION: Sow outdoors in mid-summer for biennial use; if started early enough in the spring in an area with a long growing season, it may be treated as an annual. Seeds may also be sown indoors, maintaining a temperature within the medium of 70° during germination which takes 10-14 days.

CULTURE: Plant 12-15" apart in full sun or light shade in any garden soil as long as drainage is excellent. *Lunaria* self sows readily and can become weedy. When used as a biennial, the plants are larger and more colorful.

EASY

Lupinus

Lychnis

Lupinus subcarnosus TEXAS BLUEBONNET ANNUAL
Lupinus Russell hybrids LUPINES PERENNIAL
Leguminosae, native to southwestern and western United States.

USES: Borders, bedding, backgrounds, cut flowers.

HABIT: *Lupinus subcarnosus* is a 1' annual with compound, silky leaves and flowers of blue with a white or yellow spot, blooming in spring and early summer. Russell hybrids form stately spires of yellow, purple, red, orange, white, pink or blue, 1' long on 3' stems over palmately compound foliage in May and June. There are also dwarf forms of the Russell hybrids which grow to only 18". *Lupinus polyphyllus* is an important ancestor of the Russell hybrids. All Lupines have flowers that are dense spikes of pea-like blooms. The perennial is hardy to Zone 3.

GERMINATION: Soak seeds for 24 hours in warm water or nick or clip the hard seed coats before sowing. Sow outdoors in early spring where plants are to grow, or sow indoors, maintaining a temperature within the medium of 55-70° during germination. The annual will germinate in 15-20 days; the perennial will take about 5 days longer. Move to the garden carefully as Lupines resent transplanting because of their long tap root.

CULTURE: Plant 18-24" apart in full sun or light shade. Lupines do best where summers are cool and humidity high; in warmer areas, mulch the roots to keep cool. Soil should be well drained and slightly alkaline; otherwise they do well in almost any soil.

Lychnis chalcedonica MALTESE CROSS, CAMPION PERENNIAL
Caryophyllaceae, native to Russia. Zone 3.

USES: Beds, borders, cut flowers, rock gardens.

HABIT: Erect dark green, hairy spikes are topped with clusters of white or bright scarlet 1" flowers in June. The flowers are cross shaped, and so the name for this 2-3' plant.

GERMINATION: Sow outdoors in spring or summer up to two months before frost, or sow indoors, maintaining a temperature within the medium of 70° during germination which takes 21-25 days. Do not cover seeds as light is necessary for germination. *Lychnis* will bloom the first year if started early.

CULTURE: Plant 12-15" apart in full sun in any well drained garden soil. It will not tolerate "wet feet" in winter. If cut back immediately after flowering, it may bloom again in fall.

EASY

Lythrum   Machaeranthera

Lythrum Salicaria 'Roseum Superbum'   PERENNIAL
                   LOOSESTRIFE
Lythraceae, native to the Old World.   Zone 3.

USES: Background, border, wild gardens, cut flower.

HABIT: This is a woody, shrubby plant growing 3-6′ with willow-like leaves and erect stems bearing slender 16″ spikes of 1″ blossoms in rose-purple in summer.

GERMINATION: Seeds may be sown outdoors in early spring, or indoors, maintaining a temperature within the medium of 65-70° during germination which takes 15-20 days.

CULTURE: Plant 18-24″ apart in full sun or light shade and almost any type of garden soil. *Lythrum* tolerates dry, poor soils, rich moist ones, heavy ones. Keep faded blooms removed to extend flowering season.

EASY

Machaeranthera tanacetifolia   TAHOKA DAISY   ANNUAL
Compositae, native of western North America.

USES: Border, cut flower.

HABIT: Pure blue and lavender flowers 2½″ across with gold centers bloom in clusters from June to frost on 12-24″ plants with bristly, ferny leaves.

GERMINATION: Sow outdoors in early spring or sow indoors after placing seeds in moistened medium in the refrigerator for 2 weeks. Sow seeds indoors 6-8 weeks before last frost, maintaining a temperature within the medium of 70° during germination which takes 25-30 days.

CULTURE: Plant 9″ apart in full sun and average, well drained garden soil. It does best in cool climates.

EASY

Magnolia   *Malva*

Magnolia grandiflora SOUTHERN MAGNOLIA   TREE
Magnoliaceae, native to eastern North America.   Zone 7.

USES: Specimen.

HABIT: Decorative tree reaches 90' and has glossy, dark green leaves 5-8" long that are evergreen and 8", 6 petaled, waxy, white, fragrant flowers. Cone-like fruits 4" long appear in early fall.

GERMINATION: Sow outdoors in late fall or early winter for spring germination, or sow indoors after placing seeds in moistened medium in the refrigerator for 12-16 weeks. Maintain a temperature within the medium of 70° during germination which may take 1-2 months. The seeds are not long lived and if stored before sowing, must be stored in the refrigerator.

CULTURE: Plant in full sun or light shade in a moist, rich, slightly acid soil that is deeply worked. Always move with a ball of soil around the roots. Keep well watered, and do minimal pruning after blooming in spring.

MALTESE CROSS, see **Lychnis chalcedonica**

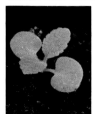

Malva Alcea var. **fastigiata**   MALLOW   PERENNIAL
Malvaceae, native of India.   Zone 4.

USES: Border, wildflower gardens.

HABIT: From mid-summer to fall, bushy masses of 2" hollyhock-like flowers bloom in bright rose, pink or white atop 2-4' stems clothed with downy, palm shaped foliage.

GERMINATION: Sow outdoors in spring or summer up to months before frost, or sow indoors, maintaining a temperature within the medium of 70° during germination which takes 5-10 days.

CULTURE: Plant 12-24" apart in full sun or light shade in average garden soil that is well drained. Keep well watered and fertilize. Clumps may be left undisturbed almost indefinitely.

EASY

MARIGOLD, see **Tagetes**

MARTYNIA, see **Proboscidea louisianica**

Matthiola

MATRICARIA, see **Chrysanthemum parthenium**

Matthiola incana STOCK   ANNUAL
Matthiola longipetala   EVENING SCENTED STOCK
(Matthiola bicornis)
   Cruciferae, native to the Mediterranean.

USES: Borders, bedding, edging, planters, greenhouse plant, cut flower.

HABIT: Stock is a 12-30″ plant grown as an annual with narrow, lance shaped bluish gray leaves and spikes of cross shaped single or double 1″ flowers of white, cream, pink, rose, red, blue or purple in summer and fall. The blooms are fragrant and are winter blooming indoors. There are 7 and 10 week strains. *Matthiola longipetala* grows 12-18″ with small, lilac or pink flowers that are fragrant and open at night.

GERMINATION: Sow outdoors after all danger of frost has past where plants are to grow, or, for best results, sow indoors 6-8 weeks before last frost, maintaining a temperature within the medium of 70° during germination which takes 7-10 days. In Zones 9 and 10, sow seeds in early fall for late winter and spring bloom. Sowing for greenhouse plants may be done at any season. Do not cover the seed as light is necessary for germination.

CULTURE: Plant 12-15″ apart in light, sandy, fertile, rich, moist soil. Feed monthly with a balanced fertilizer. Stocks do best where summers are cool. Indoors, grow at 50° nights, in full sun, with evenly moist soil, and feed weekly.

Meconopsis betonicifolia   BLUE POPPY   PERENNIAL
(Meconopsis Baileyi)
   Papaveraceae, native to China.   Zone 6.

USES: Beds, borders, planters, rock gardens.

HABIT: Clusters of glistening sky blue, gold centered, 2-3″, silky, single or double poppy-like flowers bloom in late summer on 5-6′ plants with 6″ hairy leaves.

GERMINATION: Sow outdoors in late fall or early spring for late spring germination, or sow indoors, maintaining a temperature within the medium of 65-70° during germination which takes 20-25 days. Seeds may be sown indoors in fall if plants can be carried over the winter in a cold frame or cool greenhouse.

CULTURE: Plant in light shade, 12-15″ apart, in a rich, acid, very well drained soil. It will not survive with "wet feet" in the winter, and does not do well in areas with hot summers and hot, drying winds. Do not allow this plant to flower until its third year.

EASY

Mentzelia   Merremia

Mentzelia Lindleyi BLAZING STAR   ANNUAL
(Bartonia aurea)

Loasaceae, native to California.

USES: Bedding, borders, cut flowers.

HABIT: Summer flowering fragrant 2½″ golden yellow, 5 petaled flowers with a vermilion base adorn 12-24″ plants. The flowers open in the evening and last until the following noon.

GERMINATION: Sow outdoors where the plants are to grow in early spring, or sow indoors, maintaining a temperature within the medium of 55-60° during germination which takes 5-10 days.

CULTURE: Plant 8-10″ apart in full sun with a light, rich, sandy soil with excellent drainage.

EASY

Merremia tuberosa WOODROSE   ANNUAL
(Ipomoea tuberosa)

Convolvulaceae, native to the American tropics.

USES: Screen, dried fruits.

HABIT: A somewhat untidy, vigorous vine with 7 lobed leaves and yellow funnel shaped, 2″ flowers that resemble a morning glory and bloom in late summer. It grows to 8′ and develops fruit that looks like a carved wooden rose.

GERMINATION: Soak seeds for 24 hours in warm water or file the hard seed coat before sowing. Seeds may be sown outdoors where plants are to grow after all danger of frost has past, but for best results, sow indoors 6-8 weeks before planting outside, maintaining a temperature within the medium of 70-75° during germination which takes 8-10 days. The jar and peat system may also be used: fill a glass jar with moistened peatmoss and place the seeds against the glass. Place the jar in a location that is 70-75°. As the seeds germinate, remove them and place them in individual pots.

CULTURE: Plant in full sun in a rich, sandy, well drained soil. *Merremia* will tolerate a dry and infertile soil. In areas colder than Zone 10, winter the plants over in a warm greenhouse or sun porch, watering only enough to keep the plants from shriveling.

201

Mesembryanthemum

Mesembryanthemum chrystallinum   ICE PLANT   ANNUAL
Dorotheanthus bellidiformis   LIVINGSTONE DAISY
(Mesembryanthemum criniflorum)
Aizoaceae, native to South Africa.

USES: Ground cover, bedding, edging, planters.

HABIT: These succulents are low growing, resembling rocks or stones, and have bright and showy daisy like flowers in spring and early summer. Ice Plant grows 8″ tall and spreads to 15″ across, has 1¼″ white to rose flowers, and leaves covered with glistening ice-like lumps. Livingstone Daisy is 3″ tall, with ½-1″ flowers of pink, red or white in a spreading carpet. It is perennial in Zone 10 and most popular in the southwest.

GERMINATION: Sow seeds indoors 10-12 weeks before last frost, maintaining a temperature within the medium of 65-75° during germination which takes 15-20 days. Place seed flats in a dark location as the seed germinates best in the absence of light. Seeds are very fine and should not be covered.

CULTURE: Plant 6-12″ apart in full sun and a dry, average garden soil. Water only sparingly. These plants tolerate drought and salt spray.

Mimosa   Mimulus

MIGNONETTE, see **Reseda odorata**

Mimosa pudica   SENSITIVE PLANT   POT PLANT
Leguminosae, native to tropical America.   Zone 9.

USES: Greenhouse plant, edging, borders, planters.

HABIT: A low, spreading, spiny plant with pretty, pinnately compound leaves that react to the touch by folding up and drooping. Dainty, pink, mimosa-like flowers appear in late summer on this 12-24" plant.

GERMINATION: Sow at any season for indoor use; for outdoor use, sow where plants are to grow after all danger of frost has past, or indoors 10-12 weeks before last frost. Maintain a temperature within the medium of 70-80° during germination which takes 8-12 days. Cover the seeds well as darkness is needed for germination.

CULTURE: Outdoors, plant in full sun and a rich, well drained garden soil. Feed every month with a balanced fertilizer. Indoors, provide diffused sunlight, high humidity, 65° nights and to 80° days, and a soil kept evenly moist.

EASY

Mimulus cupreus   MONKEY FLOWER   ANNUAL
Mimulus X hybridus 'Grandiflorus'
Scrophulariaceae, native to Chile

USES: Bedding, borders, rock garden, planters, greenhouse plant.

HABIT: Both of these plants grow 6-8", are mounded, and have 2" flowers of yellows and reds that are spotted and resemble monkeys' faces, blooming in summer. Flowers of *M. X hybridus 'Grandiflorus'* are larger and more brightly colored.

GERMINATION: Sow indoors 10-12 weeks before last frost for outdoors use; for indoor use, sow in fall for spring bloom or in winter for summer bloom. Maintain a temperature within the medium of 70-75° during germination which takes 7-14 days. Do not cover the fine seeds.

CULTURE: Plant outdoors in shade in a rich, moist, well drained soil, 6" apart. *Mimulus* does well by the side of ponds or streams, and prefers a cool area. Indoors, provide 50° nights, diffused light and an evenly moist soil.

Mina   *Mirabilis*

Mina lobata   FLAG OF SPAIN   ANNUAL
(Quamoclit lobata)
Convolvulaceae, native to Mexico, Central and South America.

USES: Vine, screen.

HABIT: This is actually a perennial but should be treated as an annual. It grows 15-20', with 3-lobed heart-shaped leaves and long racemes of ¾" crimson flowers fading to yellow, blooming in late summer and early fall.

GERMINATION: Soak seeds in warm water for 24 hours before sowing, or file or nick the hard seed coat. Sow outdoors where plants are to grow after the soil is warm, or sow indoors, maintaining a temperature within the medium of 70° during germination which takes 20-25 days.

CULTURE: Plant in full sun in a warm sheltered location in a rich, well drained soil kept heavily watered. Provide a trellis or other support.

Mirabilis Jalapa   FOUR-O-CLOCK, MARVEL OF PERU ANNUAL
Nyctaginaceae, native to tropical America.

USES: Beds, borders, hedge.

HABIT: This tuberous rooted, heavily branched plant has 1-2" trumpet or funnel shaped flowers in white, red, yellow, pink or violet borne on 1½-3' soft, succulent stems and opening late in the afternoon until the next morning. Flowers appear summer through frost and are open all day in cloudy weather.

GERMINATION: Sow outdoors where plants are to grow after all danger of frost has past, or sow indoors 4-6 weeks before last frost, maintaining a temperature within the medium of 70° during germination which takes 7-10 days.

CULTURE: Plant 1-1½' apart in full sun and a light, well drained soil. It tolerates poor soil and summer heat. Feed monthly with a balanced fertilizer. The roots may be dug after the tops are blackened by frost and stored over the winter in a cool, dry area. *Mirabilis* also self sows freely.

EASY

Moluccella   *Monarda*

Moluccella laevis   BELLS OF IRELAND   ANNUAL
Labiatae, native to Asia Minor.

USES: Borders, cut flowers, dried flowers.

HABIT: White veined, 1″ crisp, green, bell shaped bracts appear in late summer and cling to hairy stems that grow 2-3′. The actual flowers are tiny, fragrant and white, and are found deep within the base of the green bracts.

GERMINATION: Sow outdoors in early spring where plants are to grow, or sow indoors, maintaining a temperature within the medium of 55° during germination which takes 25-35 days. Do not cover the seeds as light is necessary for germination.

CULTURE: Plant 12″ apart in full sun or light shade in average garden soil with good drainage. Give moderate watering and monthly feeding with a balanced fertilizer. This plant self sows readily.

EASY

Monarda didyma   BEEBALM, BERGAMOT   PERENNIAL
Labiatae, native to North America.   Zone 4.

USES: Borders, cut flower, wildflower garden.

HABIT: Coarse, rough, hairy-leaved 2-3′ plants give off a minty fragrance and bear slender tubular flowers in 2-3″ whorls in red, pink or white during July and August. *Monarda* attracts bees and hummingbirds.

GERMINATION: Sow seeds outdoors from early spring through summer up to two months before frost, or sow indoors, maintaining a temperature within the medium of 60-70° during germination which takes 15-20 days.

CULTURE: Plant 12-15″ apart in full sun or light shade in a light, rich, moist but well drained soil. Remove faded flowers to prolong bloom. *Monarda* can become weedy.

EASY

Monstera   Myosotis

Monstera deliciosa SWISS CHEESE PLANT,   POT PLANT
CUT LEAF PHILODENDRON
Araceae, native to tropical America.   Zone 10.

USES: House plant, greenhouse plant.

HABIT: This tropical plant grows to 3′ indoors and has glossy, green, leathery leaves that are at first entire but later become deeply cut, often with holes.

GERMINATION: Seeds are shipped fresh and wet and must be sown immediately. Sow indoors, maintaining a temperature within the medium of 75-80° during germination which takes 15-20 days.

CULTURE: *Monstera* is a perfect house plant because it tolerates dry air and low light. Give it 65° nights, rich soil kept evenly moist and indirect light. Clean the leaves from time to time.

MORNING GLORY, see **Ipomoea**

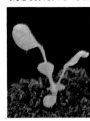

Myosotis scorpioides FORGET-ME-NOT   PERENNIAL
(Myosotis palustris)
Myosotis sylvatica   BIENNIAL
(Myosotis alpestris)
Boraginaceae, native to temperate zones of Europe and Asia.   Zone 3.

USES: Ground cover, border, edging, planters, greenhouse plant.

HABIT: Tiny but profuse flowers bloom on these 6-12″ plants. *Myosotis sylvatica* has ½″ flowers of mostly blue, but also white and pink. It blooms in spring over tufted foliage. *Myosotis scorpioides* blooms in summer with bright blue flowers with a center of yellow, pink or white.

GERMINATION: Outdoors, sow seeds in late summer to bloom the following year. Indoors, sow in early spring, maintaining a temperature within the medium of 55-70° during germination which takes 8-14 days. *Myosotis sylvatica* will bloom in fall from early spring sowing and self seeds easily. Cover seeds well as they require darkness to germinate.

CULTURE: Plant 8-12″ apart in light shade in a very rich, moist, well drained soil. It is an excellent plant for wet soil conditions and does best where summers are cool. Lift plants before frost and bring them inside for winter bloom, providing 50° nights, filtered sunlight, and a soil kept thoroughly wet.

EASY

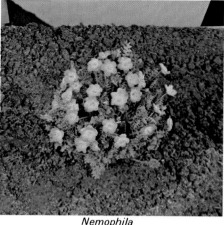

Nemesia   *Nemophila*

NASTURTIUM, see **Tropaeolum**

Nemesia strumosa   POUCH NEMESIA   ANNUAL
Scrophulariaceae, native to South Africa.

USES: Edging, border, rock gardens, planters, cut flower.

HABIT: Masses of ¾" tubular, cup-like flowers are in 3-4" racemes. The flowers are white, yellow, bronze, pink, cream and lavender with a pouch at the base, blooming from summer to frost on 12-18" plants.

GERMINATION: Sow outdoors where plants are to grow after all danger of frost has past, or, for best results, sow indoors 4-6 weeks before last frost, maintaining a temperature within the medium of 55-70° during germination which takes 7-14 days. Cover seeds well as they require darkness to germinate. Sow in early fall for winter bloom in the greenhouse.

CULTURE: Plant 6" apart in full sun and a rich, moist, well drained soil. Pinch back to induce bushiness. They must be grown where summers are cool as they do not tolerate extreme heat or high humidity. Indoors, give night temperatures of 55-60°, bright sun and a soil kept evenly moist.

Nemophila Menziesii   BABY BLUE EYES   ANNUAL
(Nemophila insignis)
Hydropyllaceae, native to California.

USES: Beds, borders, rock gardens, ground cover, edging, greenhouse plant.

HABIT: Mounded plants 6-12" high are clothed with tufted ornamental leaves and long, almost prostrate stems at the ends of which are delicate blue, trumpet-shaped 1½" flowers with white centers. The flowers are highly fragrant and bloom in summer.

GERMINATION: Sow outdoors in early spring as soon as the soil can be worked. In Zone 9 and 10, sow in late fall for winter and spring bloom. Indoors, maintain a temperature within the medium of 55° during germination which takes 7-12 days.

CULTURE: Plant 6-9" apart in full sun or light shade in a light, sandy soil which is well drained. It self sows readily. In the greenhouse, grow in full sun, at 50° nights, in a soil kept evenly moist.

EASY

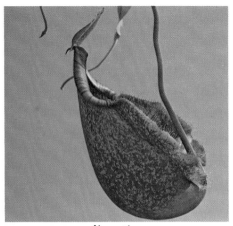

Nepenthes
(Courtesy of Longwood Gardens)

Nephrolepsis

Nepenthes khasiana   PITCHER PLANT   POT PLANT
Nepenthaceae, native to Assam.

USES: Greenhouse plant, hanging basket.

HABIT: Slender, green pitchers, 3-7″ long, in which insects are caught, are found in early spring on this plant with narrow green leaves.

GERMINATION: Sow indoors at any season, maintaining a temperature within the medium of 70-75° during germination which takes 30 days or more.

CULTURE: Grow in a shaded position in a very rich soil kept thoroughly moist. Provide high humidity and minimum night temperature of 65°.

Nephrolepis exaltata   SWORD FERN   POT PLANT
Polypodiaceae, native to the Tropics.

USES: House plant, greenhouse plant, hanging basket.

HABIT: Medium green, slowly tapering, pendulous fronds that grow to 3-5′ when mature, are narrow and pinnately compound. *Nephrolepis exaltata* sired the popular Boston Fern and its many variations.

GERMINATION: Moisten sterile medium being sure to use a sterile container. Firm the medium and sow the dust-like spores on the surface, not covering them. Cover the container with a piece of plastic or glass and set in a saucer of water, maintaining a temperature within the medium of 60-70°. Germination is long and varied. For complete instructions, see the section on "Ferns from Spores".

CULTURE: Provide 60-65° nights and 65-70° days, a humid atmosphere, a rich soil kept evenly moist, and diffused sunlight. *Nephrolepis* can take sun in winter.

Nertera

Nertera granadensis BEADPLANT   POT PLANT
Rubiaceae, native to South America, New Zealand and Tasmania. Zone 9

USES: Greenhouse plant, terrariums, ground cover, rock garden, edging.

HABIT: This creeping plant grows 3″ high and 10″ across with matted, tiny, leathery, oval, smooth, bright green leaves, small greenish flowers in spring, and pea sized orange or scarlet berries in late summer.

GERMINATION: Sow indoors at any season for greenhouse use, or in early spring for outdoor use. Maintain a temperature within the medium of 65-70° during germination which takes 20-25 days. Cover seeds well as they need darkness to germinate.

CULTURE: Plant 12″ apart in part shade and a rich, light, sandy, well drained soil. Keep soil moist during summer or no berries will be produced. It does best where summers are cool and humidity high. Indoors, grow at 50° nights, in filtered sun, with high humidity and a soil kept evenly moist.

Nicandra Physalodes   SHOO-FLY PLANT   ANNUAL
Solanaceae, native to Peru.

USES: Borders, specimen.

HABIT: Toothed 1′ leaves on this branching plant clothe the 3-4′ stems which bear delicate, 1″, round, blue flowers in summer followed by papery 5-winged "envelopes" enclosing small berries. It is said that insects feeding on the sap are destroyed.

GERMINATION: Sow outdoors in hills 2′ apart after all danger of frost has past, or sow indoors 8-10 weeks before planting outside, maintaining a temperature within the medium of 70-75° during germination which takes 15-20 days.

CULTURE: Plant 2′ apart or thin the hills to the strongest plant. Give full sun, and any ordinary garden soil with good drainage. Feed every other month with a balanced fertilizer.

Nicotiana   *Nierembergia*

Nicotiana alata   FLOWERING TOBACCO   ANNUAL
   Solanaceae, native to South America.

USES: Border, bedding, pot plants.

HABIT: Bushy 12-36″ plants have star shaped trumpet-like flowers 2″ wide which are sweetly scented and bloom from summer to frost in white, green, pink, red and lavender. The newer hybrids are open during the day as opposed to the older varieties which opened only at night.

GERMINATION: Sow outdoors where plants are to grow after all danger of frost has past, or sow indoors 6-8 weeks before last frost, maintaining a temperature within the medium of 68-86° during germination which takes 10-20 days. Do not cover the seeds as they need light to germinate.

CULTURE: Plant in light shade in a rich, moist, well drained soil, 10-12″ apart. *Nicotiana* will tolerate full sun. It self sows readily and is a perennial in Zone 10. Indoors, give 55° nights, full sun, and keep the soil evenly moist.

EASY

Nierembergia hippomanica   CUPFLOWER   PERENNIAL
Nierembergia scoparia
(Nierembergia frutescens)
   Solanaceae, native to Argentina.   Zone 7.

USES: Bedding, edging, borders, rock gardens, planters.

HABIT: Mounded hairy plants bear continous masses of 1″ cup shaped flowers during summer. *Nierembergia hippomanica* grows 6-12″, is compact and is smothered in hundreds of blue-violet flowers; *N. scoparia* is 2-3′ tall, shrubby, and filled with blue-tinted white flowers.

GERMINATION: Sow in spring or summer up to two months before frost, or sow indoors, maintaining a temperature within the medium of 70-75° during germination which takes 15-20 days. In northern areas, use as an annual, and sow indoors 10-12 weeks before last frost.

CULTURE: Plant in sun to light shade in a rich, light, moist, well drained soil.

EASY

Nigella

Nymphaea

Nigella damascena   LOVE-IN-A-MIST   ANNUAL
Ranunculaceae, native to southern Europe and northern Africa.

USES: Border, cut flower, dried fruits, bedding.

HABIT: Many branched 12-24″ plants bear 1½″ cornflower-like blooms of blue and white amid thread-like foliage which also forms a collar under the flower. Flowers are followed by pine green, globular seed pods which have reddish brown markings. Pungent seeds are used in flavoring foods.

GERMINATION: Make successive sowings outdoors from early spring to early summer for continual bloom. Seeds may also be sown indoors 4-6 weeks before planting outside, but *Nigella* resents transplanting, so use extreme care when moving to the garden. Maintain a temperature within the medium of 65-70° during germination which takes 10-15 days.

CULTURE: Plant 8″ apart in full sun and ordinary garden soil with excellent drainage. Water when dry and fertilize monthly. *Nigella* self seeds readily.

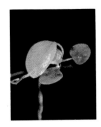

Nymphaea species   WATER LILY   PERENNIAL
Nymphaea Lotus   EGYPTIAN LOTUS
   Nymphaceae.   Zone 10.

USES: Water gardens.

HABIT: These are floating aquatic plants whose roots are anchored under the water. Water Lilies have huge, round, floating leaves and flowers of white, pink, yellow, red or blue, some day blooming, others night blooming. Egyptian Lotus has 12-20″ dark green, round, waxy leaves and 5-10″ double flowers of white shaded with red or pink. It is night blooming. Both flower all summer to frost. Water Lilies have mixed origin; Egyptian Lotus is a native of Egypt.

GERMINATION: Sow Water Lily seeds on top of germinating medium with a very light cover of sand and immerse in water so that they are covered by ½-1″ of water, taking care not to wash the small seeds away. Sow Lotus seeds 1″ deep in a pot of germinating medium covered with 1″ of sand and immerse in water so that it is covered by 2-3″. Maintain water temperature of 70-75° during germination which takes 15-20 days. Nick or file the Lotus seeds before sowing. If grown as an annual, sow outdoors after frost, or indoors 4-6 weeks before last frost.

CULTURE: The pool where these plants are to grow should be in full sun, away from the wind, and about 2′ deep. Plant in a container with very rich soil to which 1 lb. of all purpose fertilizer has been added. Cover the soil with sand and plunge in water. Tubers may be overwintered in moist sand in a cool area, or the plants grown as annuals.

Oenothera   *Oxypetalum*

Oenothera species SUNDROP,   PERENNIAL
EVENING PRIMROSE
Onagraceae, native to the United States.   Zone 3, 4.

USES: Borders, rock gardens, wildflower gardens.

HABIT: Bright, attractive, sweetly scented, cup-like flowers during the summer bloom in shades of yellow over rosettes of basal leaves. *Oenothera erythrosepala* (Evening Scented Primrose) is 3′ tall with 1″ flowers opening in evening; *O. missourensis* (Ozark Sundrop) is a trailing 1′ plant with 5″ tissue paper-like flowers opening in evening; *O. tetragona (O. fruticosa Youngii)* is day flowering, with 1½″ blooms on 18-24″ stems. *Oenothera tetragona* is hardy to Zone 3; the others are hardy to Zone 4.

GERMINATION: Sow outdoors in late summer, fall or early spring, or sow indoors in early spring, maintaining a temperature within the medium of 68-86° during germination which takes 15-20 days.

CULTURE: Plant 6-12″ apart in full sun or light shade in almost any well drained garden soil, although it does best in rich soils. *Oenothera* tolerates dry soil and reseeds readily.

EASY

Oxypetalum caeruleum SOUTHERN STAR   ANNUAL
Asclepiadaceae, native to Brazil and Uruguay.

USES: Borders, edgings, bedding, greenhouse plant.

HABIT: Shrubby plant treated as an annual grows 15-18″ with heart shaped downy leaves and pink buds developing into silvery-blue ½-1″ 5-pointed flowers which turn purple as they fade. The flowers appear from June to frost on arching sprays and are winter blooming indoors.

GERMINATION: Sow outdoors where plants are to grow after all danger of frost has past, or, for best results, sow indoors 6-8 weeks before last frost, maintaining a temperature within the medium of 70° during germination which takes 10-15 days.

CULTURE: Plant 6-8″ apart in full sun and a rich, well drained soil. Dig plants before frost for winter blooming in the greenhouse. Give 55° nights, filtered light, and keep the soil evenly moist.

EASY

Paeonia   Paeonia

Paeonia suffruticosa   TREE PEONY   PERENNIAL
Paeoniaceae, native to Asia.   Zone 5.

USES: Borders, hedges, specimen, cut flower.

HABIT: Large, showy, fragrant, 6-10″ flowers of rose, pink, red, white or yellow, either single or double, bloom in May and June on a 2-4′ plant. The branches of the Tree Peony become woody and the plant actually becomes more of a shrub.

GERMINATION: Sow outdoors in early fall for germination the following spring. Indoors, sow seeds and maintain a temperature within the medium of 70° until roots develop. Then refrigerate or place the seed flat outdoors (if it is cold) for 8-10 weeks, followed by germination at a temperature within the medium of 70°, which may take up to two months.

CULTURE: Plant in full sun in a location that is shaded from the hot afternoon sun. Soil should be slightly acid, rich, fertile and well drained, and kept moist all summer. Prune just before new growth starts in the spring. Tree Peony should be protected from the wind and mulched after the ground freezes.

A Fall Garden

213

Papaver   *Papaver*

PANSY, see **Viola X Wittrockiana**

Papaver species   POPPY   ANNUAL, PERENNIAL
Papaveraceae.

USES: Borders, rock gardens.

HABIT: *Papaver Alpinum* (Alpine Poppy) is a perennial hardy to Zone 5, growing 5-10″ high, with 1½″ flowers of white, yellow or pink in spring over blue-green leaves. *Papaver nudicaule* (Iceland Poppy) grows 1-2′ tall over coarse, divided, basal leaves. Flowers are fragrant, 1-4″ across, single or double, cup shaped, and colored white with yellow, red, orange, rose or apricot. This native of North America blooms from May to August and is a perennial hardy to Zone 2. *Papaver orientale,* also a perennial hardy to Zone 2, is native to southwest Asia and known as the Oriental Poppy. Leaves are 2-4′ long, coarse and pinnately compound. Flowers have 4-6 petals, bloom in May and June, and are colored white, orange, pink red or salmon with a black center. They are 3″ across. The foliage of Oriental Poppy disappears after blooming and reappears in early fall. *Papaver Rhoeas* (Shirley Poppy) is an annual, erect, branched and 2-3′ tall. Flowers are 2″ across, colored red, purple, white, pink, salmon or orange. This European native flowers in summer.

GERMINATION: Sow any poppy outdoors in late fall or early spring for spring germination where the plants are to grow. Seeds may also sown indoors, maintaining a temperature within the medium of 55° during germination which takes 10-15 days, but extreme care must be taken when moving to the garden as poppies do not like to be transplanted. The fine seeds of *P. orientale* should not be covered as they need light to germinate. Others like to germinate in darkness, so place the seed flat in a darkened location or cover with black plastic. Outdoors, make sure seed is completely covered.

CULTURE: All poppies like full sun and prefer a cool climate. Soil should be rich and have excellent drainage. *Papaver Alpinum* is planted 6″ apart and tolerates poor soil; *P. nudicaule* is planted 10″ apart and can be a biennial; *P. orientale* is planted 18″ apart, must have a dry soil, and should be moved only when dormant; *P. Rhoeas* is planted 9-12″ apart and should be sown successively for best results and effect.

214

Passiflora   Passiflora

Passiflora caerulea PASSION FLOWER   POT PLANT
Passiflora edulis PURPLE GRANADILLA
   Passifloraceae, native to Brazil.   Zone 10.

USES: Vine, screen, greenhouse plant.

HABIT: Either of these vines grow to 20-35' outdoors and 6' indoors and have outstanding flowers during June to September, followed by an egg shaped fruit. *Passiflora caerulea* has blue to white 4" flowers that are thought by many to symbolize the Crucifixion. *Passiflora edulis* has 2" flowers of white edged with purple, and edible fruit. It is more hardy than *P. caerulea* (Zone 8).

GERMINATION: Sow seeds outdoors after all danger of frost has past, but for best results, sow indoors 8 weeks before last frost, maintaining a temperature within the medium of 70-75° during germination which takes 30-45 days. For greenhouse use, sow at any season. Seeds are not long lived and should not be stored.

CULTURE: Plant in sun or light shade in a deeply worked, moist, rich, sandy soil that is well drained. Provide a sturdy trellis or other support. In areas where *Passiflora* is a perennial, prune back heavily during fall or early spring. Indoors, grow at 55-60° nights, in full sun and keep soil evenly moist. Prune and allow to go slightly dormant after blooming.

215

Pelargonium   *Pelargonium*

Pelargonium species   GERANIUM   POT PLANT, ANNUAL
Geraniaceae, native to South Africa.   Zone 10.

USES: Border, ground cover, bedding, planters, baskets, house plant, greenhouse plant.

HABIT: *Pelargonium X hortorum* and its hybrids are the well known Geraniums of the garden, with 5″ heads of pink, salmon, red and white on 15-24″ plants. Foliage is 3-5″ across, heart shaped, scalloped and often zoned. Apple Geranium, *Pelargonium odoratissimum,* is a trailing plant with apple scented moss green, 1″, ruffled leaves and flowers of pink or white veined with red. *Pelargonium tomentosum,* the Peppermint or Woolly Geranium, is a shrubby plant reaching 3′, with 3″, 3-lobed, heart shaped, velvety white leaves that have a mint fragrance. Flowers are white splotched with red. The Coconut Geranium, *P. grossularioides,* is a trailing basket plant with a somewhat rangy habit and a coconut scent. Flowers are a deep rosy-purple. The Crowfoot Geranium, *P. radens* 'Dr. Livingston', has a lemon fragrance to its deeply lobed, hairy, lacy leaves. The plant is bushy, grows to 3′, and the flowers are rose. *Pelargonium quercifolium* 'Prostratum', the Oak Leaved Geranium, is an excellent ground cover with sweet scented, deeply lobed, ruffled and toothed leaves, like those of the oak. Flowers are 2″, lavender veined purple. The Martha Washington Geranium, *P. X domesticum,* has large, bell shaped flowers of rose, red, lilac, pink or white in clusters on an 18″ plant with lobed leaves. It is a good greenhouse plant.

GERMINATION: Seed is scarified before shipping. Sow seeds of *P. X hortorum* indoors 12-16 weeks before last frost, maintaining a temperature within the medium of 75° during germination which takes 5-15 days. Seeds of scented geraniums should be sown at a temperature within the medium of 68-86° during germination which takes 20-50 days, and should be started indoors 12 weeks before last frost for best results.

CULTURE: Outdoors, grow in full sun in a slightly acid, well drained, rich soil. Flowers should be removed regularly as they fade. Geraniums like to be well fed and well watered. Indoors, grow in full sun in a cool location (50-55°) that has good air circulation. Soil should be slightly acid and allowed to dry out between waterings. Feed twice a month while in active growth, and keep pot-bound. Plant of *P. X hortorum* may be stored dormant over the winter, but they become woody and less productive for the following year; therefore, this practice is not recommended.

Pennisetum   Penstemon

Pennisetum setaceum   FOUNTAIN GRASS   PERENNIAL
Gramineae, native to Africa.   Zone 7.

USES: Ornamental grass, dried branches.

HABIT: Strongly colored spikes of purple, rose or coppery-red that are 1′ long nod in a fountain effect on this 2-4′ plant.

GERMINATION: Sow seeds outdoors in spring or summer up to two months before frost, or sow indoors, maintaining a temperature within the medium of 70° during germination which takes 15-20 days. If started in early spring, *Pennisetum* will produce flower spikes by fall.

CULTURE: Plant 2-3′ apart in full sun and average, well drained garden soil.

Penstemon hybrids   BEARD-TONGUE   PERENNIAL, ANNUAL
Scrophulariaceae

USES: Bedding, borders, rock gardens, cut flower

HABIT: *Penstemon* have low clumps of dark green foliage from which arise thin spikes of tube shaped flowers. A cross between *P. Hartwegii* and *P. Cobaea,* known as *P. gloxinoides,* is an annual growing 2½′ high with flowers of red, rose, pink and lavender. A cross of *P. gentianoides* and *P. Hartwegii* is a perennial to Zone 7 with blue flowers, 2′ high.

GERMINATION: Sow outdoors in late fall or early spring, or sow indoors, maintaining a temperature within the medium of 55° during germination which takes 10-15 days for the annual type and 30 days for the perennial.

CULTURE: Plant 12-18″ apart in full sun in a light, rich, acid, perfectly drained soil. Penstemon does best in cool climates.

217

Pentas   Peperomia

Pentas lanceolata   EGYPTIAN STAR CLUSTER   POT PLANT
Rubiaceae, native to Africa and Arabia.   Zone 10.

USES: House plant, greenhouse plant, bedding.

HABIT: Almost continuous blooming 18″, bushy plant with downy, slender branches and soft, bright green, hairy leaves bears 1½″ tubular flowers that are waxy, long lasting and star shaped, formed in dense heads of purple, white, rose, pink and salmon.

GERMINATION: Sow at any season for indoor use, or in early spring indoors for outdoor use. Maintain a temperature within the medium of 70-75° during germination which takes 20-25 days.

CULTURE: Outdoors, grow in sun or light shade in a deep, rich, well drained soil. Feed monthly with a balanced fertilizer. Indoors, grow warm (65° nights and 80° days), in full sun with the soil kept evenly moist. In the house, mist frequently or take other means to keep the humidity high.

Peperomia maculosa   PEPEROMIA   POT PLANT
Piperaceae, native to tropical Americas.

USES: House plant, greenhouse plant.

HABIT: Small, tropical, usually succulent plants form the peperomia group. *Peperomia maculosa* grows to 12″ with fleshy, narrow, egg shaped, waxy gray-green leaves with silver veins.

GERMINATION: Sow indoors at any season, maintaining a temperature within the medium of 70-75° during germination which takes 15-20 days.

CULTURE: *Peperomia* is ideally suited to normal house conditions, liking 65° nights and dry air. Place in indirect light and allow the soil to become dry between waterings. Other *Peperomia* species may also be grown from seed.

Perilla

Petunia

Perilla frutescens   BEEFSTEAK PLANT   ANNUAL
Labiatae, native to India.

USES: Borders, beds, planters, house plants, herb.

HABIT: Crisp, deeply cut, reddish purple foliage with a metallic, bronzy sheen grows 18-36″ and bears pale lavender-pink and white flowers in 3-6″ racemes in late summer. It is primarily grown for its foliage.

GERMINATION: Sow outdoors where plants are to grow after all danger of frost has past, or sow indoors 4-6 weeks before last frost, maintaining a temperature within the medium of 65-75° during germination which takes 15-20 days. Do not cover the seeds as light is necessary for germination. Transplant with extra care to the permanent place in the garden as *Perilla* resents being moved.

CULTURE: Plant 12-15″ apart in full sun or light shade in an average to dry garden soil with good drainage. Pinch when 6″ high to induce bushiness. It self sows readily. Indoors, provide 55° nights, full sun, and a soil kept evenly moist.

EASY

PERIWINKLE, see **Catharanthus roseus**

Petunia X **hybrida**   PETUNIA   ANNUAL
Solanaceae, native to Argentina.

USES: Bedding, borders, planters, hanging basket, greenhouse plant.

HABIT: These annuals grow 10-18″ tall with a spreading or cascading habit. Blooming from June to frost, the funnel shaped, slightly fragrant flowers are double or single, some ruffled, in colors of violet, blue, pink, rose, salmon, red, yellow or white, solids or bicolors. The grandiflora Petunias have flowers to 7″ across; the multiflora Petunias have more flowers per plant, but smaller flowers (2-3″). The newer F_1 hybrids are more vigorous, more uniform in color, height and habit, and are hand pollinated and therefore more expensive.

GERMINATION: Sow seeds indoors 10-12 weeks before last frost, maintaining a temperature within the medium of 70-75° during germination which takes 10 days. Seeds of doubles and F_1 hybrids may require a temperature within the medium of 80° to germinate. Do not cover seeds as light is required for germination. Petunia is one of the few seeds that can be germinated in full sun.

CULTURE: Plant 12″ apart in full sun and a rich, light, sandy soil that has excellent drainage. Pinch back plants when 6″ high and again after the first flush of bloom. Feed monthly with a balanced fertilizer. The single Petunias will tolerate poor and alkaline soil; the multifloras are more weather tolerant than the grandifloras. In the greenhouse, give 50° nights, full sun, and allow the soil to become dry between waterings.

EASY

219

Philodendron   Phlox

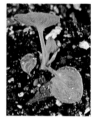

Philodendron species   LOVE PLANT   POT PLANT
Araceae, native to tropical America.

USES: House plant, greenhouse plant.

HABIT: These handsome and popular foliage plants have leathery, usually glossy leaves which are often entire in the juvenile stages, becoming lobed with maturity. *Philodendron bipinnatifidum* has large elephant ear leaves which are deeply cut; *P. Lundii* is similar upon maturity, with leaves ruffled and shaped like an arrow-head; *P. Selloum* is also very similar with large, deeply cut, forest green leaves. *P. Tuxla* has oxblood furls which open to reveal 1′ bright green leaves. *P. Wendlandii* forms a rosette of thick, waxy, long leaves that have a thick mid-rib, resembling the Bird's Nest Fern.

GERMINATION: Maintain a temperature within the medium of 75-80° during germination which takes 15-30 days.

CULTURE: Philodendrons are popular house plants because they take low light and dry atmospheric conditions. Provide 60-65° nights and a rich soil kept evenly moist. They prefer to be slightly pot bound; the climbing types should be supported on a bark slab or other similar device.

Phlox Drummondii   ANNUAL PHLOX   ANNUAL
Polemoniaceae, native to Texas.

USES: Bedding, border, edging, planters, rock gardens, cut flowers.

HABIT: Moundlike plants 8-15″ high are covered with 1½″ flowers in clusters in colors of pink, red, lavender and white during the summer.

GERMINATION: Sow seeds outdoors in early spring as soon as soil can be worked, or sow indoors, maintaining a temperature within the medium of 55-65° during germination which takes 10-15 days. It is best to sow directly into pots as it resents transplanting. Cover the seeds completely as they need darkness to germinate. The weakest seedlings often give the best colors.

CULTURE: Plant 6″ apart in full sun and a rich, light, sandy soil with excellent drainage. Keep moist during the growing season, feed heavily, and keep faded flowers removed. It is heat tolerant.

EASY

Phlox   Phygelius

Phlox paniculata PERENNIAL PHLOX,   PERENNIAL
GARDEN PHLOX
Polemoniaceae, native to the eastern United States.   Zone 3.

USES: Borders, bedding, cut flowers.

HABIT: Brightly colored flowers of pink, purple, magenta, white, salmon, rose or pink are 1″ across and appear in clusters during July and August. Plants grow 3-4′ tall.

GERMINATION: Sow outdoors in late fall for spring germination, or sow indoors after placing the seeds in moistened medium in the refrigerator for 3-4 weeks. Maintain a temperature within the medium of 70° during germination which takes 25-30 days. Be sure to cover the seeds completely as they need darkness to germinate.

CULTURE: Plant 2-3′ apart in full sun and a rich, fertile, moist, well drained soil. Remove faded flowers. Do not allow plants to self sow as they will revert to the magenta Phlox. Provide good air circulation.

Phygelius capensis CAPE FUCHSIA   PERENNIAL
Scrophulariaceae, native to South Africa.   Zone 7.

USES: Borders, beds, planters, greenhouse plant.

HABIT: Leaves 1-5″ long are 5-lobed and found on this 2-3′ shrubby plant along with 2″ drooping, tubular, scarlet or orange flowers in 18″ panicles. Cape Fuchsia blooms during July and August.

GERMINATION: Sow outdoors in spring or summer up to two months before frost, or sow indoors, maintaining a temperature within the medium of 70-75° during germination which takes 10-14 days.

CULTURE: Plant 3′ apart in sun or shade in a light, sandy soil with good drainage. *Phygelius* withstands heat and drought. It may be potted up and brought into the greenhouse in winter - provide 55° nights, full sun and an evenly moist soil.

221

Physalis   Physostegia

Physalis Alkekengi   CHINESE LANTERN   PERENNIAL
(Physalis Franchetii)
  Solanaceae, native to Asia and Europe.   Zone 2.

USES: Dried branches.

HABIT: Inconspicuous white flowers in early summer are followed by inflated orange-red seed pods resembling Chinese lanterns which are bright, hollow and papery. *Physalis* creeps by underground stems.

GERMINATION: Sow outdoors in spring or summer up to two months before frost, or sow indoors, maintaining a temperature within the medium of 70-75° during germination which takes 20-25 days. If used as an annual, sow in early spring indoors or outdoors. Do not cover seeds as light is necessary for germination.

CULTURE: Plant 2' apart in full sun or light shade in average garden soil that is well drained. *Physalis* spreads quickly, especially in rich soils, and can become weedy, so it should be grown as an annual.

Physostegia virginiana   FALSE DRAGONHEAD,   PERENNIAL
                             OBEDIENT PLANT
  Labiatae, native to eastern North America.   Zone 2.

USES: Border, wildflower garden, cut flower.

HABIT: Spreading plants grow 2-3½' with erect stems bearing white, purple or rose snapdragon-like flowers in late summer and fall surrounded by dark green, willow-like leaves.

GERMINATION: Sow outdoors in spring or summer up to two months before frost, or sow indoors, maintaining a temperature within the medium of 70-75° during germination which takes 20-25 days.

CULTURE: Plant 15-18" apart in rich, moist, slightly acid soil, in full sun or part shade. Light, dry soil checks spreading and provides stiffer stems.

Picea

Picea Abies NORWAY SPRUCE   TREE
   Pinaceae, native to the cooler parts of Europe.   Zone 2.

USES: Specimen, windbreak.

HABIT: This evergreen can grow as tall as 150' and takes on a stiff, rigid, triangular shape. Needles are ¾" long, shiny and dark green; cones are 7" long. Both are found on characteristic drooping branchlets.

GERMINATION: Sow outdoors in late fall or early spring for late spring germination, or sow indoors, maintaining a temperature within the medium of 55° during germination which takes 30 days. Other species of *Picea* may be grown from seed, but in most cases the seed will have to be stratified for 1-3 months.

CULTURE: *Picea Abies* does best in full sun and a rich, moist, well drained soil. It is not suitable for city planting or small property. Its best performance is in cool climates.

Pinus   Pittosporum

PINEAPPLE LILY, see **Eucomis bicolor**

Pinus Mugo   SWISS MOUNTAIN PINE   SHRUB
Pinaceae, native to the mountains of Spain and central Europe.   Zone 2.

USES: Specimen.

HABIT: This prostrate shrub grows only 2-3′ tall and has bright green 2″ needles, 2 to a bundle, and 2″ cones.

GERMINATION: Sow outdoors in spring or summer in a shaded seed bed, or sow indoors, maintaining a temperature within the medium of 70° during germination which takes 30 days. If seed is not fresh, it will need stratification for 30-90 days.

CULTURE: Plant in full sun in average, well drained garden soil. *Pinus* tolerates poor and infertile soils and needs little food. Prune candles to half their length to control height and density.

Pittosporum Tobira   JAPANESE PITTOSPORUM   SHRUB
Pittosporaceae, native to China and Japan.   Zone 8.

USES: Specimen, hedge, house plant, greenhouse plant.

HABIT: This warm climate evergreen has shiny, leathery, green leaves, an attractive branching habit and ½″ creamy white flowers in clusters in late spring and early summer.

GERMINATION: Sow indoors, maintaining a temperature within the medium of 55° during germination which takes 30 days.

CULTURE: Outdoors, plant in full sun or half shade. *Pittosporum* prefers a moist, rich soil but will tolerate slight drought. It should be fed in spring and summer, and needs little or no pruning. Indoors, grow at 50° nights in full sun, and allow the soil to become dry between waterings.

Platycodon   *Plumbago*

Platycodon grandiflorus BALLOON FLOWER,   PERENNIAL
                             CHINESE BELLFLOWER
Campanulaceae, native to eastern Asia.   Zone 3.

USES: Borders, beds, rock gardens.

HABIT: Swelling, balloon-like flower buds of pink, blue or white burst open into 2-3″ bell shaped, pointed flowers in July and August. The plant grows 2′ high.

GERMINATION: Sow outdoors in spring or summer up to two months before frost, or sow indoors, maintaining a temperature within the medium of 70° during germination which takes 10-15 days. Do not cover seeds as light is necessary for germination.

CULTURE: Plant 12-18″ apart in full sun or light shade in a rich, well drained soil. Remove faded flowers to lengthen blooming season. *Platycodon* is difficult to divide because of its long tap root.

EASY

Plumbago auriculata CAPE LEADWORT   ANNUAL
   Plumbaginaceae, native to South Africa.

USES: Ground cover, house plant, greenhouse plant.

HABIT: This shrubby, semi-climbing plant grows 1′ tall and may become a spreading bush. Soft, light green foliage is complemented with pale blue 1″, phlox-like flowers in clusters from June to frost. Indoors, it is everblooming.

GERMINATION: Sow seeds indoors at any season for indoor use, and in early spring for outdoor use, maintaining a temperature within the medium of 70-75° during germination which takes 25-30 days.

CULTURE: Plant 18-24″ apart in full sun and a light, sandy soil which is somewhat dry and has excellent drainage. A support may be provided to grow *Plumbago* as a vine. In Zone 10, where it is a perennial, prune back hard in spring. Indoors, provide 60-65° nights, full sun, and a soil kept evenly moist.

Polemonium   *Polygonum*

POINCIANA, see **Caesalpina Gilliensii**

Polemonium caeruleum   JACOB'S LADDER   PERENNIAL
Polemoniaceae, native to Europe and Asia.   Zone 2.

USES: Borders, rock gardens.

HABIT: Mounds 2-3′ high of feathery, fern-like leaves are topped from late spring to early summer with soft clusters of dainty, cup-shaped, 1″, sky blue flowers with yellow stamens.

GERMINATION: Sow outdoors in late fall or early spring for late spring germination, or sow indoors, maintaining a temperature within the medium of 70° during germination which takes 20-25 days.

CULTURE: Plant 18″ apart in full sun or light shade and a very rich, moist, well drained soil. *Polemonium* prefers a cool spot.

EASY

Polygonum capitatum   FLEECEFLOWER,   PERENNIAL
KNOTWEED
Polygonaceae, native to the Himalayas.   Zone 6.

USES: Borders, edging, ground cover, hanging basket, rock gardens.

HABIT: Vining plant with ¾″ rose pink flowers in dense heads blooms in summer. This vigorous, creeping plant grows only 3-4″ tall and has heart shaped leaves which are tinged with pink.

GERMINATION: Sow outdoors where plants are to grow after all danger of frost has past. For best results, especially when using as an annual, sow indoors 6-8 weeks before last frost, maintaining a temperature within the medium of 70-75° during germination which takes 20-25 days.

CULTURE: Plant 18-24″ apart in full sun or light shade and a rich, light, well drained soil. Provide a good supply of water. *Polygonum* roots and reseeds freely and can become invasive.

POPPY, CALIFORNIA, see **Eschscholtzia californica**

Portulaca   Potentilla

POPPY; ICELAND, ORIENTAL, SHIRLEY, ALPINE, see **Papaver** species

Portulaca grandiflora ROSE MOSS   ANNUAL
Portulacaceae, native to South America.

USES: Bedding, border, edging, rock garden.

HABIT: Mound shaped, 4-6″ plant that spreads to 2′ across has needle-like leaves and 2½″ ruffled flowers of pink, red, gold, yellow, cream, rose, white or salmon. The flowers are single and cup shaped or double and resemble roses. They open in the sun and close in shade, at night or in cloudy weather.

GERMINATION: Sow seeds outdoors where plants are to grow after all danger of frost has past, or sow indoors, maintaining a temperature within the medium of 68-86° during germination which takes 10-15 days.

CULTURE: These succulent plants should be spaced 12-24″ apart in full sun and a sandy, dry, well drained soil. *Portulaca* withstands heat and drought and should be watered only scantly. It self seeds readily.

EASY

Potentilla nepalensis CINQUEFOIL   PERENNIAL
Rosaceae, native to the Himalayas.   Zone 5.

USES: Borders, rock garden, shrub.

HABIT: Colorful 12-18″ plant with 5-part leaves and 1″ single, brilliant rose-red flowers with a darker center blooms in clusters from June to August.

GERMINATION: Sow outdoors in late fall or early spring for late spring germination, or sow indoors, maintaining a temperature within the medium of 65-70° during germination which takes 15-20 days. Seeds are not long lived and should not be stored.

CULTURE: Plant 18″ apart in full sun and a sandy, well drained soil. *Potentilla* thrives in difficult places, dry soil, poor soil or heat.

227

Primula   Primula

Primula species   PRIMROSE   POT PLANT, PERENNIAL
Primulaceae, native to North Temperate zones.

USES: Bedding, borders, rock garden, edging, greenhouse plant.

HABIT: *Primula Auricula,* from the Alps, is hardy to Zone 2. It grows 6-9″ tall, has 4″ evergreen, powdery leaves and flowers in April and May with 1″ fragrant blooms of yellow, purple, rose, cream or brown appearing in clusters. *Primula X kewensis* is a greenhouse plant that grows 12-18″ tall, has 4-8″ toothed, wavy leaves covered with silvery, white powder and has fragrant yellow flowers, each ¾″ wide, blooming in clusters one above the other. *Primula malacoides* (Baby Primrose) is also a greenhouse plant or outdoor plant in Zones 8-10. It grows 4-8″ high, with 3″ light green, papery, toothed leaves and has ½″ flowers of rose, lavender, white, red, or purple in superimposed clusters. *Primula obconica* 'Gigantea' (German Primrose) is an outdoor plant in Zones 8-10 or a greenhouse plant. It reaches 12″ in height and has 10″ round leaves. Flowers are 1″ across in red, purple, lilac, blue or pink, in umbels. It is from China. *Primula X polyantha* (Polyanthus) is a perennial hardy to Zone 3, with many 1-2″ orange, blue, white, apricot, pink, rose, yellow or red flowers in clusters. It blooms in spring on a 12″ plant. *Primula sinensis* (Chinese Primrose) is a greenhouse plant hardy to Zone 8, growing 12″ tall above 3-5″ leaves. The 1½″ flowers appear in clusters in colors of red, orange, pink, rose, purple or blue. It is a native of China. *Primula vulgaris (P. acaulis)* is 6″ high with 10″ wrinkled, tufted leaves and ½″ flowers in 2½″ clusters in colors of yellow, purple, blue, red and white with a yellow eye in April and May. A native of Europe, it is hardy to Zone 5 and is commonly known as English Primrose.

GERMINATION: Sow hardy types outdoors in late fall or early spring for late spring germination, or sow indoors after placing in the refrigerator for 3-4 weeks in moistened medium, followed by germination at a temperature within the medium of 70°. Germination will take from 21-40 days. Greenhouse varieties should be sown in summer for bloom the following winter and spring. Maintain a temperature within the medium of 70° during germination which takes 20-25 days. Do not cover the fine seeds. All need light to germinate except *P. sinensis* which requires darkness.

CULTURE: Hardy varieties of primrose prefer a spot in part shade in a rich, cool, slightly acid soil that is heavily watered but still well drained. Mulch to keep roots cool in warmer climates. In the greenhouse, provide 50-60° nights, high humidity, filtered sunlight and an evenly moist soil.

228

Proboscidea

Proboscidea Flower Detail

Proboscidea louisianica   UNICORN PLANT   ANNUAL
(Martynia Proboscidea)
    Martyniaceae, native to southeast United States.

USES: Dried fruits.

HABIT: A somewhat trailing, 18″ tall, rank growing, ill scented plant with sticky heart shaped leaves has 5-lobed, 2″ lavender, pink or white flowers. The good part of this plant is the 4-12″ fruit which looks like a bird's curved beak.

GERMINATION: Sow outdoors where plants are to grow after all danger of frost has past, or sow indoors 6-8 weeks before last frost, maintaining a temperature within the medium of 70-75° during germination which takes 20-25 days.

CULTURE: Plant 5′ away from the flower garden in full sun and a rich, light, well drained soil.

A Colorful Garden

229

Pteris

Pueraria

Pteris cretica 'Albo-lineata'   BRAKE FERN   POT PLANT
Polypodiaceae, native to the Tropics and Subtropics.

USES: House plant, greenhouse plant.

HABIT: This strikingly beautiful fern has leathery fronds that grow to 18″ and have a broad, creamy white center stripe.

GERMINATION: Moisten sterile medium being careful to use a sterile container. Firm the medium and sow the dust-like spores on the surface, not covering them. Cover the container with a piece of glass or plastic and set in a saucer of water, maintaining a temperature within the medium of 60-70°. Germination is long and varied. For complete instructions see the section on "Ferns from Spores".

CULTURE: Place in indirect light and away from the sun. Plant in a rich soil kept evenly moist, provide 50% humidity and give 55-60° nights. Mist frequently if low humidity exists.

Pueraria lobata   KUDZU VINE   PERENNIAL
Leguminosae, native to China and Japan.   Zone 6.

USES: Trellis, screens.

HABIT: Extremely fast growing woody vine to 60-75′ has 6″ bean-like foliage and violet-purple bean-like fragrant flowers in 4″ racemes during July and August.

GERMINATION: Soak seeds for 24 hours in warm water before sowing, or clip or file the hard seed coat. Sow outdoors where the plants are to grow after all danger of frost has past, or sow indoors 6-8 weeks before last frost, maintaining a temperature within the medium of 70-75° during germination which takes 20-30 days.

CULTURE: Plant in full sun to part shade in any well drained garden soil. Kudzu vine tolerates drought and wind. It dies to the ground in the winter in almost any area, and can become weedy.

Punica   Ranunculus

Punica Granatum 'Nana' POMEGRANATE   PERENNIAL
Punicaceae, native to south Asia, southeast Europe.   Zone 8.

USES: Edging, borders, house plant, planters, Bonsai, greenhouse plant.

HABIT: This dwarf pomegranate grows to 12″ and has showy, small, willow-like green leaves. Vivid pink or scarlet 1″ flowers appear in May and June followed by a red, hard skinned fruit.

GERMINATION: Sow indoors in early spring, maintaining a temperature within the medium of 70--75° during germination which takes 20-25 days. Do not cover seeds as they need light to germinate.

CULTURE: Plant 12″ apart in a rich, deep, heavy, well drained soil. *Punica* is most popular in the southwest as it does best in hot, semi-arid areas and tolerates alkaline soil. Indoors, grow at 55° nights in full sun. Allow the soil to become dry between waterings. Humidity should be 50%; the leaves naturally fall in winter.

PYRETHRUM, see **Chrysanthemum coccineum**

Ranunculus asiaticus PERSIAN RANUNCULUS,   PERENNIAL
                                PERSIAN BUTTERCUP
Ranunculaceae, Native to southwest Europe and southeast Asia.   Zone 8.

USES: Borders, rock garden, greenhouse plant.

HABIT: Semi-double and fully double camellia-like 3-5″ flowers of pink, red, white, yellow, orange, gold or rose bloom in late spring outdoors on 12-18″ plants with 1-4 flowers per stem. It may be forced into bloom at any time in the greenhouse.

GERMINATION: Seeds may be sown outdoors after all danger of frost has past where plants are to grow, but for best results, sow indoors 6-8 weeks before last frost, maintaining a temperature within the medium of 70° during germination which takes 10-15 days. Sow in winter in the greenhouse for blooms the following winter.

CULTURE: Plant outdoors in full sun and a rich, sandy, moist soil with perfect drainage. They prefer a cool location. In more severe climates than Zone 8, lift tuberous roots after the foliage dies out and store over the winter in a cool, dry place. Replant after frost the following spring. In the greenhouse, give 50° nights, full sun and a soil kept evenly moist. After blooming when the foliage yellows, give a rest period.

Rehmannia   *Reseda*

Rehmannia elata BEVERLY BELLS   PERENNIAL
(Rehmannia angulata)
   Gesneriaceae, native to China.   Zone 10.

USES: Bedding, cut flower, greenhouse plant.

HABIT: Terminal racemes of 3″ trumpet shaped flowers bloom from spring through fall in colors of rose-red or orchid-pink with yellow throats. The flowers are often spotted with red or purple and are reminiscent of Foxgloves. The foliage is broad, hairy and coarse, 10″ long and 4″ wide.

GERMINATION: Sow outdoors after all danger of frost has past, or sow indoors 6-8 weeks before last frost, maintaining a temperature within the medium of 70-75° during germination which takes 15-20 days.

CULTURE: Plant in sun or part shade in a rich soil that is heavily watered. In the greenhouse, grow at 50° nights in diffused light and a soil kept evenly moist.

Reseda odorata MIGNONETTE   ANNUAL
   Resedaceae, native to North Africa.

USES: Bedding, planters, cut flower, greenhouse plant.

HABIT: This highly fragrant annual is 1-1½′ in height and bears 6-10″ thick spikes of greenish-yellow, yellowish-brown or yellowish-white small flowers in summer.

GERMINATION: Sow outdoors in early spring as soon as soil can be worked, or sow indoors, maintaining a temperature within the medium of 70° during germination which takes 5-10 days. Do not cover the seeds as light is necessary for germination. *Reseda* resents transplanting, so take extra precautions when moving into the permanent place in the garden. In Zones 9-10, sow in late fall for early spring bloom.

CULTURE: Plant 10-12″ apart in full sun or light shade in a rich, somewhat moist, well drained soil. *Reseda* does best in cool climates. In the greenhouse, give 50° nights, indirect light and a soil kept evenly moist.

EASY

Rhododendron

Rhynchelytrum

Rhododendron species and hybrids   AZALEA   SHRUB
                                      RHODODENDRON
Ericaceae, native to the Northern Hemisphere.

USES: Foundation planting, hedges, specimen, rock garden, planters.

HABIT: Azaleas are species of *Rhododendron.* They are evergreen or deciduous, grow 3-15′ tall and flower in many shades in spring and early summer. Exbury hybrids are deciduous, with 2-3″ flowers of white, pink, orange, red or yellow in large clusters. Mollis hybrids (*Rhododendron X Kosteranum*) are also deciduous, with 2-3″ flowers in 5-6″ clusters in shades of yellow and orange. Both grow to 6′ and are hardy through Zone 5. Rhododendrons, mainly evergreen, with large clusters of flowers in late spring or summer, range in height from 1½-8′ and bloom in tones of white, pink, red, lavender, purple, orange, yellow and almost blue. *Rhododendron ferrugineum,* the Alpine Rose, grows to 4′ and has clusters of funnel shaped flowers of scarlet to pink in summer. It is hardy to Zone 4; other *Rhododendrons* have varying degrees of hardiness.

GERMINATION: Sow outdoors in late winter or early spring, or indoors about the same time, maintaining a temperature within the medium of 55-60° during germination which takes 50-60 days. Do not cover the very fine, light seeds, and keep shaded from direct sun.

CULTURE: Plant in light shade in a cool, moist, rich, fertile, well drained soil. Both have shallow roots and so should not be cultivated; a mulch is beneficial.

Rhynchelytrum repens   RUBY GRASS, NATAL GRASS, ANNUAL
Gramineae, native to South Africa.

USES: Border, ornamental grass, dried branches.

HABIT: This grass grows 3-4′ tall and has slender 8″ leaves and shining, open panicles 6-10″ long of pink, rosy-purple or red brown. Looking at this grass is like looking through a rosy haze.

GERMINATION: Sow outdoors where plants are to grow after all danger of frost has past, or sow indoors, maintaining a temperature within the medium of 70° during germination which takes 20-25 days. Seeds should be started indoors 6-8 weeks before last frost.

CULTURE: Plant in full sun in a fertile, sandy, well drained soil.

Ricinus   Ricinus Seed Pods

Ricinus communis   CASTOR BEAN   ANNUAL
Euphorbiaceae, native to tropical Africa.

USES: Background, screen, seed pod.

HABIT: Tropical, branching, shrubby plants grow 5-8′ and have 3′ deeply lobed, palm-like leaves. Young leaves have a red and bronze tinge. Insignificant reddish-brown or white flowers are borne in 1-2′ clusters. The seeds of Castor Bean are toxic.

GERMINATION: Sow outdoors where plants are to bloom after all danger of frost has past, or sow indoors 6-8 weeks before last frost, maintaining a temperature within the medium of 70-75° during germination which takes 15-20 days.

CULTURE: Plant 4-5′ apart in full sun and a rich, well drained, sandy or clay soil. *Ricinus* likes heat and moisture. In Zones 8-10, it will act as a perennial.

EASY

Living with Flowers

Rosa   *Rudbeckia*

Rosa species   ROSE   PERENNIAL
Rosaceae, native to China, Japan.

USES: Beds, hedges, miniatures, rock garden, edging, ground cover, house plant, greenhouse plant.

HABIT: *Rosa multiflora,* the Japanese Rose, is a vigorous, thorny bush growing to 10'. Its arching canes are covered with clusters of small white flowers in mid June. Its main use is as an understock for modern hybrids; it is hardy to Zone 5. *Rose X Rehderana,* the Baby Rose or Polyantha Rose, has sweetly scented single and semi-double flowers of white and pink on a 3' spreading plant. *Rosa chinensis* 'Minima' *(R. Rouletti),* the Fairy Rose, grows 10-18" high with 1-1½" flowers of white or pink in June and scattered throughout the summer. It is hardy to Zone 7, and is the fore-runner of the modern miniature rose.

GERMINATION: Most of today's garden roses are hybrids and therefore will not come true from seed; the above and other species of roses may be sown in this manner and are reliably true. Sow outdoors in late fall or early spring for late spring germination, or sow indoors, maintaining a temperature within the medium of 55° during germination which takes 21-25 days. Germination may be aided by stratification at 40° for 6-12 weeks.

CULTURE: Plant in full sun in a rich, fertile, well drained soil. *Rosa multiflora* needs plenty of room and will need frequent pruning to keep it shapely and attractive. Indoors, grow the smaller roses in full sun and an evenly moist soil; night temperatures should be 55-60°.

Rudbeckia hirta 'Gloriosa Daisy'   GLORIOSA DAISY   PERENNIAL
Compositae, native to eastern United States.   Zone 4.

USES: Beds, borders, cut flower.

HABIT: This cultivar of the old-fashioned Black Eyed Susan grows 2-3' tall with an upright branching habit and 3-6" flowers of gold, yellow, bronze, orange, brown or mahogany, often zoned or banded, with brown, yellow or black cone shaped centers. Flowers can be single or double.

GERMINATION: Sow outdoors in spring or summer up to two months before frost, or sow indoors, maintaining a temperature within the medium of 70-75° during germination which takes 5-10 days. Plants will bloom the first year from seed if started early enough.

CULTURE: Plant in full sun or part shade, 12-24" apart, in any well drained garden soil. *Rudbeckia* loves the heat and will tolerate drought and poor soil, although it will perform best in a rich soil kept adequately moist.

EASY

Sagina   *Saintpaulia*

Sagina subulata PEARLWORT   PERENNIAL
Caryophyliaceae, native to west and central Europe.   Zone 4.

USES: Edging, rock gardens, bedding, ground cover, walls.

HABIT: Moss-like, evergreen 2-4″ plants have densely tufted, ¼″, narrow bright green leaves and small, white round flowers in late summer.

GERMINATION: Sow outdoors in early spring as soon as the soil can be worked, or sow indoors, maintaining a temperature within the medium of 55° during germination which takes 10-15 days.

CULTURE: Plant 3-4″ apart in full sun or part shade and a light, well drained soil. *Sagina* prefers dry, sandy, rocky spots and may be mowed like a lawn.

Saintpaulia ionantha AFRICAN VIOLET   POT PLANT
Gesneriaceae, native to Tanzania.

USES: House plant, greenhouse plant.

HABIT: Thousands of varieties of this popular plant exist, all having bronze-coppery green, velvety 2-3″ leaves formed in a rosette. Year round clusters of single or double flowers are in shades of pink, blue, purple, white or rose. Flowers may be bicolored, ruffled or frilled.

GERMINATION: Sow indoors at any season, maintaining a temperature within the medium of 70-75° during germination which takes 20-25 days. Do not cover the fine seeds which need light to germinate.

CULTURE: African violets thrive in bright indirect or filtered light, and can withstand the winter sun. Grow at 60-65° nights. Soil should be very rich and well drained, and kept just moist at all times, watering only with warm water. Humidity should be 40-60% and may be kept at that level with pebble trays. Water should never touch the leaves and therefore bottom watering is often recommended.

Salpiglossis

Salpiglossis

Salpiglossis sinuata PAINTED TONGUE ANNUAL
Solanaceae, native to Chile.

USES: Borders, backgrounds, cut flower, greenhouse plant.

HABIT: This 2-3′ handsome plant bears veined, tubular, trumpet shaped, 2½″ flowers from July to frost in velvety shades of purple, red, yellow, blue and rose.

GERMINATION: Sow outdoors after all danger of frost has past where plants are to grow, or, for best results, sow indoors 8 weeks before last frost, maintaining a temperature within the medium of 70-75° during germination which takes 15-20 days. Seeds are fine and should not be covered. They also need darkness to germinate, so place the seed flat away from light or cover with black plastic until germination. Sow in early fall for winter bloom in the greenhouse.

CULTURE: Plant 8-12″ apart in full sun and a rich, light soil with excellent drainage. Plants may need support. *Salpiglossis* does best where summers are cool. In the greenhouse, give 50° nights, full sun and an evenly moist soil.

A Study in Contrast

Salvia

Salvia

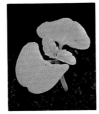

Salvia species   SALVIA, SAGE   PERENNIAL, BIENNIAL
Labiatae.   ANNUAL

USES: Border, bedding, edging, planters.

HABIT: *Salvia splendens* is the well known annual, Scarlet Sage, with spikes of flowers from early summer to frost, primarily in red but also in white, purple, pink, rose and lavender. Plants grow from 6-36″, are native to southern Brazil and have deep green, glossy leaves. Clary, *S. Sclarea turkestanica,* is a biennial from Turkestan which blooms in summer and fall with bright pink flowers on a 36″ plant. *S. X superba* is a perennial to Zone 5, compact, growing to 12″ and having deep blue to purple flowers. Baby salvia, *S. microphylla,* is 15″ tall, shrubby and has small red flowers. It is a perennial to Zone 5 and native to Mexico. *S. farinacea* is a perennial to Zone 8, native to New Mexico and Texas, with grey-green leaves on a bushy plant and spikes of blue flowers. It grows from 18-36″, and can be treated as an annual. *S. viridis (S. Horminum)* is an annual or biennial growing 18″ high with flowers of rose, purple, blue, pink or white. It comes to us from southern Europe.

GERMINATION: For best results with annual varieties, sow indoors 6-8 weeks before last frost, maintaining a temperature within the medium of 70° during germination which takes 12-15 days. If treating *S. farinacea* as an annual, start indoors 12 weeks before last frost. Red flowering salvias need light to germinate, so do not cover the seeds. Biennial forms should be sown outdoors in late summer and fall for bloom the following summer. Perennial forms should be sown outdoors from spring through summer up to two months before frost, or sown indoors as above. Perennials will bloom the first year if started early enough. Seeds of *S. splendens* are not long lived and should not be stored.

CULTURE: Perennial forms will grow in full sun or light shade; pastel annuals are best in part shade. Others should be grown in full sun, in a rich, well drained soil. All will perform best when well watered, but they will tolerate a slightly dry soil.

For Garden Sage *(S. officianalis),* see the Chapter "Growing Edibles from Seed".

EASY

Santolina | Sanvitalia

Santolina Chamaecyparissus   LAVENDER COTTON PERENNIAL
Compositae, native to the Mediterranean.   Zone 6.

USES: Borders, edging, groundcover, herb knot garden.

HABIT: This woody stemmed evergreen has mounds of aromatic, woolly, silvery-grey, fern-like foliage. It grows 15-24" high and bears ¾" button-like flowers of yellow-gold in July and August.

GERMINATION: Sow outdoors in spring or summer up to two months before frost, or sow indoors, maintaining a temperature within the medium of 65-70° during germination which takes 15-20 days. Start in early spring to use as an annual.

CULTURE: Plant 18-20" apart in full sun and any garden soil with excellent drainage. *Santolina* does very well in dry, poor or sandy soils. Prune to 4-6" every year to encourage new growth.

Sanvitalia procumbens   CREEPING ZINNIA   ANNUAL
Compositae, native to Mexico.

USES: Edging, bedding, rock gardens, hanging baskets.

HABIT: Daisy-like ¾" double flowers of golden yellow with purple centers appear from summer through frost on 6" plants with trailing stems.

GERMINATION: Sow outdoors where plants are to grow after all danger of frost has past, or sow indoors 4-6 weeks before last frost, maintaining a temperature within the medium of 70° during germination which takes 10-15 days. *Sanvitalia* resents transplanting, so care must be taken in placing plants in their permanent positions. Do not cover the seeds as light is necessary for germination.

CULTURE: Plant 5-6" apart in full sun and a light, open, well drained soil.

EASY

Saponaria   *Saxifraga*

Saponaria Ocymoides   SOAPWORT   PERENNIAL
Caryophyllaceae, native to southwest and central Europe.   Zone 2.

USES: Groundcover, walls, edging, rock garden, borders.

HABIT: Trailing to 3′ across, *Saponaria* grows 10-12″ high and has thick, oval, dark green, succulent leaves which, when bruised, produce a soap-like lather when stirred in warm water. The plants are dotted with single pink, rose or reddish flowers in May and June.

GERMINATION: Sow outdoors in spring or summer up to two months before frost, or sow indoors, maintaining a temperature within the medium of 70° during germination which takes 10-15 days. Cover seeds completely as they need darkness to germinate.

CULTURE: Plant 6-8″ apart in full sun and a light, sandy, rich, well drained soil. *Saponaria* tolerates poor soil and self sows readily. Prune back severely after bloom to keep neat and compact.

EASY

Saxifraga species   ROCKFOIL   PERENNIAL
Saxifragaceae, native to mountainous areas.   Zone 6, 7.

USES: Border, edging, rock garden, walls, hanging basket, house plant, greenhouse plant.

HABIT: This low growing plant has foliage that ranges from moss-like to thick leaved succulents and racemes of pink, red, white, purple or yellow flowers in late spring or early summer. Most species are hardy to Zone 6. Flowers generally reach 12″ above the basal rosettes of leaves. *Saxifraga stolonifera (S. sarmentosa),* the Strawberry Geranium or Mother of Thousands, is a creeping plant with leaves that are veined white with reddish undersides. Young plantlets form at the end of thin runners. Flowers are tiny and white, appearing in racemes on 12-24″ stems. It is hardy to Zone 7.

GERMINATION: Sow outdoors where plants are to grow after all danger of frost has past, or sow indoors, maintaining a temperature within the medium of 65-75° during germination which takes 15-20 days. For interior use, sow seeds at any season.

CULTURE: Outdoors, grow in light shade, 6-12″ apart, in a moist, excellently drained soil. *Saxifraga* does well in soil that is rocky, alkaline and cool. Indoors, give 50° nights, high humidity, full sun and a soil kept moist in summer and allowed to dry between waterings in winter.

Scabiosa

Schefflera

Scabiosa species   PINCUSHION FLOWER, ANNUAL, PERENNIAL
Dipsacaceae, native to the Mediterranean.

USES: Borders, bedding, cut flower.

HABIT: Both the annual and the perennial form have pincushion-like flowers from which extend dark silvery grey pollen-bearing filaments appearing like pins from June to September. *Scabiosa atropurpurea* (Sweet Scabious) is an annual with 2-4" purple, rose, white, pink, red or blue fragrant double flowers on 18-36" slender stems. *Scabiosa caucasica* is a perennial to Zone 2 with flowers of blue primarily but also lavender or white that are 3" across. Some flowers are fringed or ruffled; all appear atop 2-3' slender stems.

GERMINATION: Sow perennial types outdoors in spring or summer; sow annual types outdoors after all danger of frost has past. Either may be sown indoors, maintaining a temperature within the medium of 70-75° during germination which takes 10-15 days. The annual *Scabiosa* will do best if started indoors 4-5 weeks before last frost. Perennial *Scabiosa* may also be sown outdoors in fall for bloom the following summer.

CULTURE: Plant 10-15" apart in full sun and a rich, well drained soil. It prefers an alkaline soil. Drainage must be perfect in winter.   EASY

Schefflera digitata   UMBRELLA TREE   POT PLANT
Brassaia actinophylla
(S. actinophylla)
Araliaceae, native to Australia and New Zealand.   Zone 10.

USES: House plant, greenhouse plant.

HABIT: This long-lived house plant grows approximately 5-6' indoors and has dark green, palmately compound leaves. *Schefflera digitata's* new leaves are yellowish and hairy; the mature leaves are dull and satiny. There are 7-10 leaflets per leaf, greenish yellow flowers and purple-black berries. *Brassaia actinophylla* has 6-16 leaflets per leaf that are 6-12" long, a shiny, dark green color, and dark red flowers upon maturity.

GERMINATION: Sow seeds indoors at any season, maintaining a temperature within the medium of 75° during germination which takes 20-25 days.

CULTURE: Place either one in indirect light and allow the soil to become dry between waterings. Both make good house plants as they will tolerate dry atmosphere. *Brassaia actinophylla* likes a night temperature of 55-65°; *Schefflera digitata* prefers it a little cooler.

Schizanthus   *Sedum*

Schizanthus X wisetonensis   BUTTERFLY FLOWER,   ANNUAL
POOR MAN'S ORCHID
Solanaceae, native to Chile.

USES: Beds, borders, cut flower, planters, greenhouse plant.

HABIT: This free branching 12-24″ plant has finely cut fern-like foliage and profusely borne clusters of 1½″ purple to yellow delicate orchid-like flowers with markings of white, rose, gold, red and violet in late summer.

GERMINATION: Sow indoors 12 weeks before last frost, maintaining a temperature within the medium of 60-70° during germination which requires 20-25 days. Do not cover the fine seeds. Darkness is helpful in germination, so place the seed flat away from light or cover with black plastic until germination occurs. Sow indoors in fall for greenhouse bloom in winter and spring.

CULTURE: Outdoors, place 12″ apart in full sun to light shade in a rich, moist soil with excellent drainage. *Schizanthus* does best outdoors in cool climates. Indoors, give 55° nights, full sun and a soil kept evenly moist. *Schizanthus* does not make a good house plant as it needs greenhouse conditions. It flowers best when pot bound.

EASY

Sedum species   STONECROP   POT PLANT, PERENNIAL
Crassulaceae, native to the Northern Hemisphere.

USES: Ground cover, rock gardens, borders, edging, house plants.

HABIT: *Sedum* species are low growing, fleshy leaved succulents. There are several species suitable for outdoor growing and hardy to Zone 3: *Sedum acre* (Goldmoss), which is a creeping, mat forming plant 2-3″ tall with light green pointed leaves and bright yellow flowers in May and June; *Sedum reflexum* which grows to 8″ with vari-colored rosettes and ½″ yellow flowers in summer; *Sedum Selskianum,* which forms 4″ grayish cushions and has yellow flowers ½″ across in July and August; *Sedum spurium* which grows 6″ tall with 1″ long, thick bronzy dark green leaves and rose-pink flowers in July and August. There are also species hardy to Zone 10 which make excellent plants for the house and dish gardens.

GERMINATION: Sow indoors, maintaining a temperature within the medium of 70-80° during germination which takes 15-30 days.

CULTURE: Outdoors, grow in full sun and a thin, poor, gritty soil with excellent drainage. Indoors, give full sun, 50-55° nights and allow the soil to become dry between waterings.

242

Sempervivum   *Senecio*

Sempervivum species   HOUSELEEK,   PERENNIAL
                                LIVE FOREVER
Crassulaceae, native to Europe, Morocco, west Asia.   Zone 4, 5.

USES: Edging, border, rock gardens, house plant.

HABIT: *Sempervivum* are small, fleshy rosettes of succulent leaves surrounding 3-12″ stems on which are borne flowers of yellow, red, white, pink or purple. Blooms are tiny and star shaped and appear in clusters in late summer and fall. *Sempervivum tectorum* is the most common and best known, the Hens and Chicks.

GERMINATION: Sow indoors in spring or summer, maintaining a temperature within the medium of 75-85° during germination which takes 15-30 days.

CULTURE: Plant in full sun in a light, well drained soil. *Sempervivum* does well in poor, dry and unfertilized soils. Indoors, grow in full sun at 50° nights in a sandy soil allowed to dry out between waterings.

Senecio Cineraria   DUSTY MILLER   PERENNIAL
Senecio Vira-vira
   Compositae.   Zone 6.

USES: Edgings, beds, borders, planters.

HABIT: *Senecio Cineraria* grows to 2½′ with stiff branches, compact habit and white, woolly leaves. The pinnately cut leaves are broad and blunt. Flowers are 1½″ across, appearing in terminal clusters in late summer, daisy-like and yellow or cream colored. *Senecio Vira-vira* is similarly colored a silvery white, but the foliage is more finely cut. The plants grow from 8-24″ and have white flowers in terminal clusters in late summer. The flowers also differ from those of *S. Cineraria* as they have no rays (petals). *S. Cineraria* is native to the Mediterranean and *S. Vira-vira* to Argentina.

GERMINATION: Sow outdoors in spring or summer up to two months before frost, or sow indoors, maintaining a temperature within the medium of 65-75° during germination which takes 10-15 days. These plants may be treated as annuals by starting them indoors 8-10 weeks before last frost.

CULTURE: Plant 8-10″ apart in full sun and a light, well drained soil. Water lightly throughout the growing season. They may be sheared to prevent legginess.

EASY

Senecio   *Setaria*

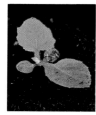

Senecio X hybridus   CINERARIA   POT PLANT
Compositae, native to the Canary Islands.   Zone 10.

USES: House plant, greenhouse plant.

HABIT: Cineraria grows 6-18″ high and across, with single or double daisy-like flowers of red, scarlet, crimson, pink, blue, purple, violet or white, 3-5″, some with light center. The foliage is large but attractive.

GERMINATION: For spring flowering plants, sow seeds indoors in the fall. Maintain a temperature within the medium of 70° during germination which takes 10-15 days.

CULTURE: Bring into bloom in a 50° greenhouse being careful not to overwater. While the plants are in bud and bloom, grow at 50-55° nights in a rich soil watered generously. Keep almost potbound for best flowering. Cineraria may be grown in the house if the night temperatures are cool enough. Place in full sun or filtered light and feed twice a month.

EASY

SENSITIVE PLANT, see **Mimosa pudica**

Setaria macrochaeta   PLAINS BRISTLE GRASS   ANNUAL
Gramineae, native to southwest United States.

USES: Ornamental grass, dried branches.

HABIT: Nodding 10″ spikes with dense heads sway in a graceful air on 3-4′ dense plants.

GERMINATION: Sow outdoors where plants are to grow in spring, or sow indoors, maintaining a temperature within the medium of 70° during germination which takes 10-15 days.

CULTURE: Plant 3′ apart in full sun and a light, well drained soil that is never allowed to completely dry out.

Silene   *Sinningia*

SHASTA DAISY, see **Chrysanthemum X superbum**

Silene vulgaris subsp. **maritima**   SEA CAMPION   PERENNIAL
Caryophyllaceae, native to the west coast of Europe.   Zone 4.

USES: Borders, rock gardens, walls, accent.

HABIT: Dense, trailing stems clothed with silver, grey-green tufted leaves form a plant 8-12″ high. White or pink ¾″ flowers appear in clusters in July and August.

GERMINATION: Sow seeds outdoors any time from early spring through late fall. Those sown early enough will bloom the first year. Seeds may also be sown indoors, maintaining a temperature within the medium of 70° during germination which takes 15-20 days.

CULTURE: Plant 6-10″ apart in full sun and a rich, sandy, moist, well drained soil.

EASY

Sinningia species   SINNINGIA   POT PLANT
Gesneriaceae, native to Brazil.

USES: House plant, greenhouse plant, terrariums.

HABIT: These everblooming favorites have trumpet shaped floweis. *Sinningia cardinalis* (Cardinal Flower) has downy leaves 6″ long and 4″ wide, grows 6-12″ high, and has 2″ bright scarlet flowers. One group within *Sinningia speciosa* is called Slipper Gloxinia, with olive green leaves and nodding, graceful flowers shaped like Cinderella's slipper; another group within the same species is the well known Gloxinia, with fuzzy leaves 8″ long and 6″ wide. Bell shaped flowers are 1½-5″, single or double, in shades of white, pink, rose, red, blue, yellow, purple or lavender. Some flowers are spotted, some ruffled, others have a contrasting edge or throat. *Sinningia verticillata* has hairy leaves 8″ long and 4″ wide that are toothed. This plant grows to 24″, with 1½″ flowers of pale pink with wine colored markings. There are also interspecific hybrids which are miniature, growing to only 4″, with 1½″ long flowers of lavender, purple, peach or pink.

GERMINATION: Sow indoors at any season, maintaining a temperature within the medium of 70° during germination which takes 15-20 days. Do not cover the fine seeds which need light to germinate.

CULTURE: Place in bright indirect or filtered light; they can take winter sun. Grow at 65° nights in an atmosphere with high humidity. Soil should be very rich and kept evenly moist. Do not wet the leaves when watering. After flowering, dry off graduallly and allow the plant to go dormant. Store in the pot at 50° for several months, followed by repotting and new growth.

Smithiantha   *Solanum*

Smithiantha zebrina   NAEGELIA,   POT PLANT
                          TEMPLE BELLS
Gesneriaceae, native to Mexico.   Zone 10.

USES: House plant, greenhouse plant.

HABIT: Fleshy stems are surrounded by 3-4″ velvety leaves that are round to heart shaped and have purple, red or brown veins. Flowers are red, yellow or spotted, drooping, tubular and bloom in spikes.

GERMINATION: Sow indoors at any season, maintaining a temperature within the medium of 70-75° during germination which takes 15-20 days. Do not cover the seeds as they are fine and need light to germinate.

CULTURE: Place in an east or south window and provide 65° nights. The humidity should be 60-70%; therefore *Smithiantha* does best in the greenhouse. Soil should be light, very rich, well drained and kept evenly moist during the growing season. Leaves will become limp and the plant will go dormant in winter. Store the scaly rhizomes in the pot in a cool, shaded, dry place. Repot in three months, ½″ deep.

SNAPDRAGON, see **Antirrhinum majus**

Solanum Melongena   ORNAMENTAL EGGPLANT   ANNUAL
Solanaceae, native to Africa and Asia.

USES: Specimen.

HABIT: Lobed foliage to 9″ long is formed on this 12-36″ bushy plant. Lavender flowers are 1½″ and are followed by inedible, white egg shaped fruits.

GERMINATION: Sow indoors 8-10 weeks before last frost, maintaining a temperature within the medium of 70° during germination which takes 10-15 days. Ornamental Eggplant requires a long growing season.

CULTURE: Plant 2-3′ apart in full sun and a rich, neutral, well drained soil.

EASY

Solanum   *Sophora*

Solanum Pseudocapsicum   JERUSALEM CHERRY, POT PLANT
CHRISTMAS CHERRY
Solanaceae, native to the Old World.   Zone 9.

USES: House plant, greenhouse plant, outdoors in warm climates.

HABIT: Semi-woody plants grow 8-24″ and bear small, star shaped, white flowers in summer, followed by round scarlet, yellow or orange berries in fall. Leaves are glossy and deep green; berries are 1″ across and remain on the plant for several months. The berries are not edible.

GERMINATION: Sow indoors in late winter for plants the following Christmas. Maintain a temperature within the medium of 70° during germination which takes 15-20 days. Do not cover the seeds as light aids in germination.

CULTURE: Grow at 60-65° nights and mist frequently until all danger of frost is past in late spring, when the plants should be placed outside in full sun. Feed weekly with house plant fertilizer. Before frost, return to a sunny location indoors, growing at 50-55° nights and with an evenly moist soil. This plant is usually grown as an annual, but may be cut back after berries have dropped and moved outdoors after frost in spring, repeating the above cycle.

Sophora japonica 'Pendula'   JAPANESE PAGODA TREE   TREE
Leguminosae, native to China and Korea.   Zone 4.

USES: Shade, specimen.

HABIT: This deciduous tree grows to 15′ and has a densely rounded, globe shaped head with weeping branches. Leaves are 6-10″ long and pinnately compound. This weeping variety rarely flowers; when it does, the blooms are 10-15″ clusters of ½″ yellowish white pea-like flowers and appear in August.

GERMINATION: Nick or file the seed coat before sowing seeds. Sow outdoors in late fall or early spring, or sow indoors, maintaining a temperature within the medium of 68-86° during germination which takes 10-15 days. Seeds are not long lived and if stored, must be stored in the refrigerator.

CULTURE: Plant in full sun in average, moist, well drained soil. Soil should be deeply prepared to accommodate the long root system.

Stachys   *Stephanotis*

Stachys byzantina   LAMB'S EARS   PERENNIAL
(S. lanata)
Labiatae, native to Caucasus.   Zone 4.

USES: Borders, edging, accent.

HABIT: This perennial is clothed with dense, white, woolly 4-6″ leaves and small purple or pink flowers on 12″ spikes in late spring and early summer.

GERMINATION: Sow outdoors in spring or summer up to two months before frost, or sow indoors, maintaining a temperature within the medium of 70° during germination which takes 15-20 days.

CULTURE: Plant 10-18″ apart in full sun or light shade and a light, rich soil with excellent drainage. *Stachys* will tolerate poor soil and drought.

Stephanotis floribunda   MADAGASCAR JASMINE POT PLANT
Asclepiadaceae, native to Madagascar.   Zone 10.

USES: Vine, greenhouse plant.

HABIT: This evergreen climbs to 10′ or more. The leaves are smooth, shiny, thick, oval and deep green; the flowers are 2″, white, tubular, star shaped, heavily scented and in clusters of 6-8. The long lasting blooms appear from April to October.

GERMINATION: Sow seeds indoors at any season, maintaining a temperature within the medium of 70-75° during germination which takes 30 days.

CULTURE: Grow in the greenhouse in full sun with 65° nights and a soil kept evenly moist. If grown in a planter, it may be summered outdoors in a spot in part shade.

Stokesia

Stipa pennata   FEATHER GRASS   PERENNIAL
   Gramineae, native to Eurasia.   Zone 5.

USES: Ornamental grass, borders, dried branches.

HABIT: Narrow leaves and 3' tufted spears are adorned with 1' panicles that are yellowish, very thin, and very graceful, like a narrow feather.

GERMINATION: Sow outdoors in spring or summer up to two months before frost, or sow indoors, maintaining a temperature within the medium of 70° during germination which takes 30 days.

CULTURE: Plant 15" apart in full sun and an open, fertile, well drained soil.

STOCK, see **Matthiola**

Stokesia laevis   STOKES ASTER   PERENNIAL
   Compositae, native to southeast United States.   Zone 5.

USES: Border, cut flower.

HABIT: This sprawling perennial grows 12-18" and has 2-8" long, slender, pointed, grey-green leaves. Stiff, erect stems bear 4" blue, white, pink, purple or yellow aster-like flowers from July to September.

GERMINATION: Sow outdoors in spring or summer up to two months before frost, or sow indoors, maintaining a temperature within the medium of 70° during germination which takes 25-30 days. *Stokesia* will bloom the first year if started early enough.

CULTURE: Plant 12-15" apart in an average, well drained soil and full sun.

EASY

Strelitzia   Streptocarpus

Strelitzia reginae   BIRD OF PARADISE   POT PLANT
Strelitziaceae, native to South Africa.   Zone 10.

USES: House plant, greenhouse plant, outdoors in warmest climates, cut flower.

HABIT: Banana-like or spear shaped leaves have pale or red midribs and are 12-24″ long. Several long, strong stalks bear orange and blue exotic flowers shaped like the heads of birds. The plant grows 3-6′ indoors.

GERMINATION: Sow seeds immediately upon receipt as they must be fresh. Maintain a temperature within the medium of 85-90° during germination which starts in 30 days and continues intermittantly for up to 6 months or a year. Germination may be improved by soaking the seeds for 3-4 days in warm water, changing the water daily. The soaking will also help eliminate seed and root rot which can strike *Strelitzia.*

CULTURE: Place in full to partial sun indoors, keeping a night temperature of 55°. Use a rich, sterile medium with excellent drainage. Keep evenly moist except in late fall and winter when the medium should be allowed to dry out between waterings. Fertilize twice monthly in spring and summer, and keep the humidity high.

Streptocarpus species   CAPE PRIMROSE   POT PLANT
Gesneriaceae, native to south and east Africa.   Zone 10.

USES: House plant, greenhouse plant.

HABIT: *Streptocarpus X hybridus* are hybrids chiefly developed from *S. Rexii.* They have primrose-like foliage which is narrow, 6-12″ long, quilted, hairy and forms ground hugging rosettes. Flowers are 2-5″, trumpet shaped, pink, white, rose, blue or purple, and bloom all year. They often have frilled edges or throats splashed with contrasting colors. *Streptocarpus saxorum* is a trailing species with succulent, waxy, bright green leaves and 1½″ lavender or blue flowers. Both species bear their flowers on slender, stiff, 12-24″ stems.

GERMINATION: Sow indoors at any season, maintaining a temperature within the medium of 75° during germination which takes 15-20 days. Do not cover the seeds as they are fine and need light to germinate.

CULTURE: Place in indirect or filtered light and pot in a very rich soil. In summer, provide 60° nights and keep the soil evenly moist; in winter, nights should be 50° and the soil kept drier. *Streptocarpus* likes high humidity and monthly feeding while in growth. *Streptocarpus X hybridus* goes through a dormant period in winter when no food and little or no water should be given. Repot when new growth starts.

SUNFLOWER, see **Helianthus** species

SWEET PEA, see **Lathyrus odoratus**

Tagetes   Talinum

SWEET PEA, PERENNIAL, see **Lathyrus latifolius**

Tagetes species   MARIGOLD   ANNUAL
Compositae, native to Mexico.

USES: Bedding, borders, edging, cut flower, planters.

HABIT: *Tagetes erecta* is the tall growing African Marigold that reaches 3′ and has solitary 2-5″ double flowers of yellow-orange. *T. patula* is the lower growing French Marigold that is 6-24″ high with 1½-2″ single or double flowers of yellow or orange often marked with red. There are many hybrids from 18-30″ with 3-3½″ flowers in many colors; the newer triploid hybrids are more dwarf (12-15″), very vigorous, and have sustained bloom of 2-2½″ flowers of yellow, orange and gold shades. Irish Lace *(T. filifolia)* grows 6-12″ high and has tiny white flowers above very finely cut foliage.

GERMINATION: Seeds may be sown outdoors where plants are to grow after all danger of frost has past, or sown indoors 4-6 weeks before last frost, maintaining a temperature within the medium of 70-75° during germination which takes 5-7 days. African Marigolds should be started indoors since they take a long time to come into bloom.

CULTURE: Plant 6-18″ apart in full sun and average garden soil with good drainage. Keep faded flowers picked off to induce bushiness and prolong flowering.
EASY

Talinum paniculatum   JEWELS OF OPAR   PERENNIAL
Portulacaceae, native to southern United States to   Zone 6.
Central America.

USES: Border, rock gardens, planters, cut flower.

HABIT: Fleshy, bright green, waxy, 3″ leaves adorn 12-24″ plants. Airy panicles carry small, bright pink flowers from late spring through summer. The flowers last but one day, but are produced in succession.

GERMINATION: Sow seeds outdoors where plants are to bloom after all danger of frost has past, or sow indoors 6-8 weeks before last frost, maintaining a temperature within the medium of 65-75° during germination which takes 15-20 days.

CULTURE: Plant 12-15″ apart in full sun and a light, sandy, well drained soil. *Talinum* tolerates heat and drought. It self sows readily.

EASY

251

Taxus   Tetranema

Taxus baccata ENGLISH YEW   TREE
Taxaceae, native to Europe, north Africa, west Asia.   Zone 6.

USES: Specimen, hedge.

HABIT: *Taxus baccata* is an evergreen tree with small, shiny, dark green, narrow, flat, needle-like leaves. The plant grows to 60′ in a dense, pyramidal form. The berries are red, fleshy and juicy when ripe, and are said to be toxic.

GERMINATION: Sow outdoors in late fall or early winter for germination the second spring. Indoors, place seed in moistened medium at 70° for 3 months, followed by refrigeration for 4 months. Seeds should then germinate at a temperature within the medium of 70°, but the process may be long and erratic.

CULTURE: Plant in full sun to light shade out of the way of winter winds and sun in a moist, rich, neutral to slightly alkaline well drained soil. Yews will tolerate slight drought and may be sheared or heavily pruned. Other species of *Taxus* may be grown from seed and cared for in the same manner.

Tetranema roseum MEXICAN FOXGLOVE,   POT PLANT
                        RED VIOLET
(Tetranema mexicanum, Allophyton mexicanum)
Scrophulariaceae, native to Mexico and Guatemala.   Zone 10.

USES: Greenhouse plant, house plant, terrariums.

HABIT: Flower stalks 6-8″ high appear from the center of compact rosettes of large, dark green, leathery leaves and bear dainty ½″ pink to purple violet-like, trumpet shaped nodding flowers all year.

GERMINATION: Sow indoors at any season, maintaining a temperature within the medium of 75° during germination which takes 10-15 days.

CULTURE: Place in diffused or indirect light with a soil kept evenly moist. Night temperatures should be 55°. Fertilize twice monthly. *Tetranema* prefers high humidity and is therefore a better greenhouse plant or terrarium specimen than a house plant.

Teucrium   Thallictrum

Teucrium Chamaedrys GERMANDER   PERENNIAL
  Labiatae, native to Europe and southwest Asia.   Zone 5.

USES: Groundcover, hedge, edging, rock garden.

HABIT: This glossy leaved, dense, evergreen shrub grows 10-12″ high and spreads to 24″. Flowers of purple or rose appear on loose spikes in summer.

GERMINATION: Sow outdoors in spring or summer up to two months before frost, or sow indoors, maintaining a temperature within the medium of 70° during germination which takes 25-30 days.

CULTURE: Plant 12-24″ apart in full sun and a rich soil with excellent drainage. Plants may be sheared to size and shape. It may suffer some winter kill in Zones 5-6 but will recover quickly. *Teucrium* tolerates sun, heat, rocks and poor soil.

Thallictrum aquilegifolium MEADOW RUE   PERENNIAL
  Ranunculaceae, native to Europe and Asia.   Zone 5.

USES: Borders, beds, cut flowers.

HABIT: This graceful perennial grows 2-3′ and has deeply cut grey-green leaves that resemble those of columbine. Flowers appear in panicles in early summer, and are colored purple, pink or white. The flowers have no petals but do have prominent stamens and colored sepals in large, open clusters that make a showy, airy, mass effect.

GERMINATION: Seeds may be sown outdoors in late fall or spring or sown indoors, maintaining a temperature within the medium of 70° during germination which takes 15-30 days.

CULTURE: Plant in full sun or light shade in a rich, moist, well drained soil in a spot protected from the wind.

Thermopsis   *Thunbergia*

Thermopsis caroliniana   CAROLINA LUPINE   PERENNIAL
Leguminosae, native to southeast United States.   Zone 3.

USES: Borders, beds, backgrounds, cut flower.

HABIT: Three part grey-green leaves appear below stiff, erect 4-5′ stems which bear 8-12″ spikes of yellow, pea-like flowers in July and August.

GERMINATION: Soak seeds in warm water, or clip or file the seed coats before sowing. Sow outdoors in spring or summer up to two months before frost, or sow indoors, maintaining a temperature within the medium of 70° during germination which takes 15-20 days.

CULTURE: Plant 3-4′ apart in full sun and a deep, light, rich, moist, well drained soil. *Thermopsis* is difficult to transplant because of its long tap root. The plants will need to be staked.

EASY

Thunbergia alata   BLACK-EYED SUSAN VINE   ANNUAL
Thunbergia Gregorii
Acanthaceae, native to tropical Africa.

USES: Screen, ground cover, hanging basket, planter.

HABIT: These vines can grow to 6′ and have dense, dark green, arrowhead shaped leaves. They both bloom in the summer outdoors and in the greenhouse in winter. *Thunbergia alata* has 1½″ bell shaped, tubular flowers of white, orange-yellow or yellow with a purple or black throat; *T. Gregorii* has an abundance of waxy, tubular 2½″ deep orange flowers with a dark center.

GERMINATION: Sow outdoors where plants are to bloom after all danger of frost has past, or sow indoors, maintaining a temperature within the medium of 70-75° during germination which takes 10-15 days. Indoor seeds should be started 6-8 weeks before last frost.

CULTURE: Plant in full sun or very light shade in a light, rich, moist, well drained soil. Provide a trellis or other support for these rapidly growing plants. Do not prune during the growing season. *Thunbergia* does not like excessive heat.

EASY

Thymus

Tigridia

Thymus praecox subsp. **arcticus**   PERENNIAL
MOTHER OF THYME
(Thymus Serphyllum)
Labiatae, native of western Europe.   Zone 3.

USES: Edging, rock garden, ground cover, border.

HABIT: This creeping evergreen grows only 2″ tall and forms mats of ¼″, dark green, round, sweet scented foliage. Purple flowers in terminal clusters bloom in summer.

GERMINATION: Sow outdoors in late fall or early spring for late spring germination, or sow indoors, maintaining a temperature within the medium of 55° during germination which takes 15-20 days.

CULTURE: Plant in sun or part shade in a warm, light, dry, well drained soil. *Thymus* withstands neglect, and may be pruned hard if necessary to keep it within bounds. For other Thymes, see Chapter on "Growing Edibles from Seed".

EASY

Tigridia Pavonia   TIGER FLOWER   PERENNIAL
Iridaceae, native to Mexico, Guatemala and the Andes.   Zone 6.

USES: Bedding, border, rock garden.

HABIT: Sword shaped, ribbed leaves grow from this bulbous plant and reach 2′ in height. Triangular shaped flowers of white, red, rose or yellow are 3-5″ across and have 3 petals and 3 sepals. Flowers last only one day but are produced in succession for 4 weeks in late summer.

GERMINATION: Sow outdoors where plants are to grow after all danger of frost has past, or sow indoors 6-8 weeks before last frost, maintaining a temperature within the medium of 65-75° during germination which takes 20-25 days.

CULTURE: Plant in full sun, or part shade in very hot climates. Soil should be light, sandy, rich and well drained. Water regularly while in growth and fertilize every 2 weeks. Lift bulbs before frost and store in a dry place until after frost the following spring.

Tithonia   Torenia

Tithonia rotundifolia   MEXICAN SUNFLOWER   ANNUAL
Compositae, native to Mexico and Central America.

USES: Borders, backgrounds, hedges, specimen, cut flower.

HABIT: Velvety, grey 6-12″ leaves clothe this 4-6′ coarse, shrubby plant. Large dahlia-like flowers of orange-red bloom in summer and early fall.

GERMINATION: Sow outdoors where plants are to grow after all danger of frost has past, or sow indoors 6-8 weeks before last frost, maintaining a temperature within the medium of 70° during germination which takes 5-10 days. Light may be beneficial to germination.

CULTURE: Plant 2′ apart in full sun and average garden soil. *Tithonia* is heat and drought resistant but does require good drainage.

EASY

Torenia Fournieri   WISHBONE FLOWER   ANNUAL
Scrophulariaceae, native to Asia and Africa.

USES: Bedding, edging, borders, planters, house plant, greenhouse plant.

HABIT: Toothed leaves and racemes of trumpet shaped flowers that look like miniature gloxinias grace this 8-12″ plant. The flowers have a light violet upper lip, dark purple lower lip and a yellow or white throat, and appear from summer to frost. In the throat is a pair of stamens that looks like a wishbone.

GERMINATION: Sow indoors at any season for indoor use, or 10-12 weeks before last frost for outdoor use. Maintain a temperature within the medium of 70-75° during germination which takes 15-20 days.

CULTURE: Plant 6-8″ apart in a shady location and a rich, moist, well drained soil. *Torenia* will take full sun only in cool climates. Indoors, grow at 60° nights, provide high humidity, diffused light and a very rich soil kept evenly moist.

EASY

Trachymene   Tradescantia

Trachymene coerulea BLUE LACE FLOWER   ANNUAL
(Didiscus coeruleus)
Umbelliferae, native to Australia.

USES: Borders, beds, cut flower.

HABIT: Tiny, sky blue lacy summer flowers in sweet scented, flat topped clusters look like blue Queen Anne's Lace or 2-3″ umbrellas. Erect stems 2-2½′ tall are clothed with finely divided leaves.

GERMINATION: Sow outdoors where plants are to grow after all danger of frost is past, or sow indoors 6-8 weeks before last frost, maintaining a temperature within the medium of 70° during germination which takes 15-20 days. Make sure the seeds are fully covered as they require darkness to germinate. *Trachymene* resents transplanting, so move to its final position in the garden very carefully.

CULTURE: Plant 12″ apart in full sun and a light, rich, sandy, well drained soil. *Trachymene* does not like hot weather.

EASY

Tradescantia X Andersoniana SPIDERWORT   PERENNIAL
Tradescantia virginiana
Commelinaceae, native to eastern United States.   Zone 4.

USES: Border.

HABIT: *Tradescantia* grows with a spreading habit, with erect stems 2-3′ high sheathed with delicate, linear leaves. Flowers are single, with 3 petals and 3 sepals, and appear in clusters in late summer and fall. They last but one day, but appear in succession. *Tradescantia X Andersoniana* has pink and white flowers; *T. virginiana* has flowers of blue and purple.

GERMINATION: Sow outdoors from early spring through summer up to two months before frost, or sow indoors, maintaining a temperature within the medium of 70° during germination which takes 30 days.

CULTURE: Plant 12-15″ apart in light to part shade and a rich, moist, well drained soil. *Tradescantia* will take poor soil conditions and self sows readily.

EASY

Trillium

Trifolium procumbens SHAMROCK   PERENNIAL
(T. dubium)
Leguminosae, native to south Europe.   Zone 3.

USES: House plant, bedding.

HABIT: This plant that St. Patrick used to symbolize the Trinity has 3 leaflet leaves, grows 12″ high, and blooms in late spring and early summer. Flowers are yellow, ½″ across, and appear in loose, oval heads.

GERMINATION: Sow indoors, maintaining a temperature within the medium of 65-70° during germination which takes 7-10 days. Cover the seeds completely as they need darkness to germinate. Sow in late December for 2″ plants by St. Patrick's Day.

CULTURE: Plant outdoors in full sun and a heavy clay soil. Indoors, give 50° nights, full sun, and a heavy soil kept evenly moist.

EASY

Trillium ovatum WAKE ROBIN   PERENNIAL
Liliaceae, native of the west coast of Canada and the United States.
     Zone 8.

USES: Edging, border, wildflower garden.

HABIT: Three part foliage 6″ long appears in whorls. Flowers bloom in early spring on 1-2″ stems and are 2″ across, 3 petaled, waxy and white, turning to rose-purple.

GERMINATION: Outdoors, sow in late fall for germination the second spring. Indoors, place in moistened medium in the refrigerator for 3 months, followed by holding at 60-70° for 3 months, followed by refrigeration for 3 months again. Germinate at a temperature within the medium of 60-70°; germination is long and varied.

CULTURE: Plant in part to full shade, 12″ apart, in a rich, acid, moist, fertile soil.

Tropaeolum   *Tropaeolum*

TRITOMA, see **Kniphofia Uvaria**

Tropaeolum majus   NASTURTIUM   ANNUAL
Tropaeolaceae, native to the Andes.

USES: Beds, walls, edging, screen, hanging basket.

HABIT: Nasturtium is a rapid growing, vining plant with brilliant yellow, orange or red funnel shaped and spurred flowers in singles and doubles, blooming from early summer to frost. Some of the 2-2½" flowers are fragrant. Leaves are round, 2-7" across, dull green, and often used in salads. Plants vary in height from 12" and bushy to 8' and climbing.

GERMINATION: Sow outdoors after all danger of frost has past where plants are to grow. Seeds may be started indoors, but it is not necessary, and Nasturtium does not transplant well. Maintain a temperature within the medium of 65° during germination which takes 7-12 days. Seeds must be completely covered as they need darkness to germinate.

CULTURE: Plant 8-12" apart in full sun to light shade in a light, sandy, dry, poor, well drained soil. Rich soil causes lush foliage and no flowers. Nasturtium does best in cool, dry summers.

EASY

A Colorful Corner

Valeriana   Venidium

Valeriana officinalis   HELIOTROPE   PERENNIAL
Valerianaceae, native to Europe and west Asia.   Zone 3.

USES: Borders, bedding, pot plant, greenhouse plant, cut flower.

HABIT: Clusters 1' across of dark purple are found on this 2' plant from May to September. The flowers are very fragrant, with a vanilla-like odor. *Valeriana* is winter blooming indoors.

GERMINATION: Sow indoors at any season for greenhouse use; sow indoors 10-12 weeks before planting outside for annual use. Maintain a temperature within the medium of 70° during germination which takes 21-25 days.

CULTURE: Plant 1' apart in full sun and a rich, well drained soil. When grown in pots outdoors, place in light shade. Indoors give 60° nights and 70-75° days, fresh circulating air, diffused light, and a rich soil kept evenly moist. It can also be grown as a standard.

EASY

Venidium fastuosum   MONARCH OF THE VELDT,   ANNUAL
                             CAPE DAISY
  Compositae, native to South Africa.

USES: Borders, bedding, greenhouse plant, cut flower.

HABIT: This annual grows 2' tall and sparkles with 4-5" daisy-like brilliant flowers of orange, white, ivory, cream, salmon and red with an inner zone of purple-black and a center of shiny black. Flowers appear from summer to frost atop flower stems that are covered with silvery white feather-like hairy leaves which give the appearance of being covered with finely spun cobwebs.

GERMINATION: Sow outdoors after all danger of frost has past where plants are to grow, or sow indoors 6-8 weeks before last frost, maintaining a temperature within the medium of 70-75° during germination which takes 15-25 days. Do not cover the seeds as they need light to germinate. Sow in September in the greenhouse for winter bloom.

CULTURE: Plant 12" apart in full sun and a light, sandy, well drained soil. *Venidium* loves heat, drought, sun and difficult spots. In the greenhouse, grow in full sun at 55° nights, and allow the soil to become dry between waterings.

Verbascum

Verbena

Verbascum bombyciferum MULLEIN   BIENNIAL
Scrophulariaceae, native to Asia Minor.   Zone 6.

USES: Borders, background.

HABIT: Stately many branched plants have 16", fuzzy grey-white leaves appearing in low clumps from which rise 3-6' stout, erect stems laden with 1" yellow flowers from mid-summer to early fall.

GERMINATION: Sow outdoors in spring or summer up to two months before frost for flowering the following year, or sow indoors, maintaining a temperature within the medium of 75-85° during germination which takes 15-20 days.

CULTURE: Plant 12-18" apart in full sun and average, slightly alkaline soil with excellent drainage, especially in winter. It self sows readily.

EASY

Verbena species VERVAIN   PERENNIAL, ANNUAL
Verbenaceae.

USES: Bedding, edging, borders, cut flowers, greenhouse plant.

HABIT: *Verbena* have lobed or toothed leaves and small tubular flowers in spiked or rounded terminal clusters. *Verbena bipinnatifida* (Dakota Verbena) is a perennial to Zone 3 with dark green, deeply lobed leaves and flowers of light purple - lavender blue. It is a native of the mid-western United States and is prostrate growing to a height of 15". Garden Verbena, *V. X hybrida (V. hortensis)* is an annual growing 6-18" high with fragrant flowers of blue, red, white, purple, lilac, pink or yellow with a contrasting white eye. *Verbena rigida (V. venosa)* is a perennial hardy to Zone 8, a spreading plant reaching 12-24" in height and bearing deep blue to purple flowers. It is a native of South America.

GERMINATION: Sow indoors 12-14 weeks before last frost, maintaining a temperature within the medium of 70-75° during germination which takes 20-25 days. Cover the seed flat with black plastic since darkness is needed for germination.

CULTURE: Plant 12" apart in full sun in a rich, light, well drained soil. Perennials can become straggly, so prune back severely or renew from seed each year. In the greenhouse, provide 55° nights, full sun, and allow the soil to become dry between waterings.

261

Verbesina

Veronica

Verbesina encelioides   BUTTER DAISY   ANNUAL
Compositae, native to western United States and Mexico.

USES: Borders, cut flower.

HABIT: *Verbesina* grows 2-3' and bears 2" daisy-like golden yellow flowers with cushiony centers from summer to frost. Leaves are 4", toothed, hairy and grey-green.

GERMINATION: Sow seeds outdoors where plants are to grow after all danger of frost has past, or sow indoors, 6-8 weeks before last frost, maintaining a temperature within the medium of 70° during germination which takes 8-10 days. *Verbesina* is difficult to transplant.

CULTURE: Plant 18-24" apart in full sun and excellently drained garden soil.

EASY

Veronica species   SPEEDWELL   PERENNIAL
Scrophulariaceae.

USES: Borders, edging, rock garden, ground cover, cut flower.

HABIT: *Veronica* bears 6-8" spikes of tiny flowers throughout summer. *Veronica incana (V. candida),* Woolly Speedwell, grows 9-24" high and has white to silver woolly, matted 3" leaves. Native to north Asia and Russia, it is hardy to Zone 3. Flowers are violet-blue. *V. latifolia* reaches 18-24" and has bright blue or reddish flowers in early summer. From Europe, it is hardy to Zone 3 and makes a good ground cover; *V. longifolia* grows 2½-3½' tall with deep blue flowers. It is native to Europe and Asia and hardy to Zone 4. Creeping Speedwell, *V. repens,* is only 2-4" high, mat forming, with moss-like shiny leaves. Flowers of rose or light blue appear in early summer. From Corsica and Spain, it is hardy to Zone 5. *V. spicata* 'Rosea' is a rare form from Northern Europe and Asia that grows 12-18" tall and has flowers of rose-pink. It is hardy to Zone 3.

GERMINATION: Sow seeds outdoors in spring or summer, up to two months before frost, or sow indoors, maintaining a temperature within the medium of 70° during germination which takes 15-20 days.

CULTURE: Plant 12-15" apart in full sun and average, well drained garden soil. Keep well watered and fed.

EASY

Viburnum

Viburnum Opulus 'Roseum'   SNOWBALL BUSH   SHRUB
Caprifoliaceae, native to north Africa and north Asia.   Zone 3.

USES: Specimen, hedge.

HABIT: This strong, dense plant has 3 lobed, maple-like leaves 2-4″ long which turn orange-red in fall. Creamy white flat 4″ clusters of flowers appear in May. The vivid scarlet berries are edible but very tart.

GERMINATION: Sow outdoors in late summer for germination the following spring. Indoors, sow and maintain a temperature within the medium of 70° for 3 months, followed by refrigeration for 3 months. Again maintain a temperature within the medium of 70° during germination which may take 2 months. If seeds must be stored, store at 40°. Other species of *Viburnum* may be sown in a similar manner.

CULTURE: Plant in sun or light shade in a heavy, rich, well drained soil that should be kept from drying out. If pruning is necessary, do it after flowering. *Viburnum* will tolerate heat and either acid or alkaline soil.

Viola   Viola

Viola species   VIOLET, VIOLA, PANSY   PERENNIAL, ANNUAL
Violaceae.

USES: Bedding, borders, rock garden, edging, planters.
HABIT: Members of the *Viola* genus have dainty, flat, single flowers. *Viola cornuta* (Viola) has 1-2″ flowers of yellow, blue, purple, red and apricot in solids and bicolors in early spring on 6-12″ neat, compact, tufted plants. Hardy to Zone 6, Viola is a perennial from Spain and the Pyrenees. Also a perennial to Zone 6, *V. odorata,* the Sweet Violet or English Violet, has clear, bright or deep blue flowers up to 1″ across that have a sweet fragrance. The plant is 4″ high and tufted; the leaves are heart shaped. Bloom is in spring on this native of Europe, Asia and Africa. *V. tricolor,* the Johnny Jump Up, has purple and yellow flowers in spring over lobed leaves on a 7-12″ tufted plant. This perennial is hardy to Zone 4. The popular Pansy, *V. X Wittrockiana (V. tricolor hortensis)* blooms in early spring and will bloom throughout the summer if conditions are right. Flowers are 3-4″ in colors of red, purple, blue, bronze, yellow, white, pink, lavender or orange, blotched or faced, atop a 7-9″ plant whose foliage stays green all winter. It is grown as an annual.

GERMINATION: Sow perennial seeds anytime spring through fall outdoors. Fall sown seeds will germinate the following spring; those started in early spring will bloom the first year. Indoors, maintain a temperature within the medium of 70° during germination which takes 10-20 days. Pansy is sown in summer, overwintered in a cold frame or in place, or sown indoors in mid-winter as with perennial Violas. All need darkness to germinate and may benefit by placing in moistened medium in the refrigerator for several days prior to starting germination.

CULTURE: All Violas prefer a moist, rich soil. All but the *V. odorata* prefer full sun in all but the hottest sections of the country, where they need part shade. *V. odorata* should be grown in part shade in most locations and in full shade in hot climates. Pansies generally do best where summers are cool, although the newer hybrids are more heat resistant. Mulch Violas in summer to keep soil cool and moist.

EASY

Washingtonia   *Wisteria*

Washingtonia robusta   MEXICAN FAN PALM   POT PLANT
  Palmae, native to the Baja.   Zone 10.

USES: House plant, greenhouse plant, street tree in Zone 10.

HABIT: Shiny, bright green, plaited, fan shaped leaves are stiff and lightly cut. Young plants bear fibrous threads on the foliage. The stem is shaggy.

GERMINATION: Sow indoors at any season, maintaining a temperature within the medium of 75-80° during germination which takes 2-6 months.

CULTURE: Grow in full sun or bright light in an evenly moist soil. Give 55° nights and feed heavily. Outdoors, it will tolerate poor soil or drought.

Wisteria sinensis   CHINESE WISTERIA   PERENNIAL
  Leguminosae, native to China.   Zone 5.

USES: Vine, screen, specimen.

HABIT: This vigorous, deciduous, twisting vine has 12″ racemes of blue-violet, slightly fragrant flowers that appear in late May before the foliage and open all at once. The lacy, fern-like leaves are light green.

GERMINATION: File, nick or clip the hard seed coats before sowing. Soaking in hot water for 24 hours may also benefit germination. Maintain a temperature within the medium of 55-65° during germination which takes 30-35 days.

CULTURE: Plant in full sun or part shade in a deep, rich, moist, well drained soil. Keep heavily watered and do not feed with a high nitrogen fertilizer. Provide a trellis or other support. Prune after flowering each year and avoid transplanting.

Worsleya

Xanthisma

Worsleya Rayneri BLUE AMARYLLIS POT PLANT
Amaryllidaceae, native to Brazil. Zone 10.

USES: House plant, greenhouse plant, outdoors in warm climates.

HABIT: This rare bulbous plant has 6-8 light blue flowers flecked with amethyst, each 5½-6½" long, in an umbel atop a 16" stem. Foliage is strap-like, 12-36" long, is green all year, and is drooping.

GERMINATION: Sow indoors at any season, maintaining a temperature within the medium of 70-75° during germination which takes 30 days.

CULTURE: Place in full sun indoors and pot in a very fibrous soil with excellent drainage. Planting medium should be acid, kept evenly moist and watered with soft water or rain water. Night temperatures should be 55-60°. Outdoors, grow in full sun in a rich, acid, well drained soil and treat as above. This plant is a relic of unknown plant families extinct for probably thousands of years, and is challenging to grow.

Xanthisma texana STAR OF TEXAS ANNUAL
Compositae, native to Texas.

USES: Border, bedding, cut flower.

HABIT: This neat, bushy 18-30" plant bears 2-3" yellow daisy-like flowers during summer on branching stems clothed with narrow grey-green leaves. The flowers close at night.

GERMINATION: Sow outdoors where plants are to grow anytime from late fall through spring. Seeds may also be sown indoors, maintaining a temperature within the medium of 70-75° during germination which takes 25-30 days.

CULTURE: Plant 6" apart in poor, dry, well drained soil. Stake to hold flowers upright.

EASY

Xeranthemum   *Yucca*

Xeranthemum annuum   IMMORTELLE   ANNUAL
Compositae, native to the Mediterranean.

USES: Cut flower, border, dried flower.

HABIT: Silvery-white plants grow 2-3' tall and produce 1½" single or double daisy-like flowers with a papery texture in red, pink, purple and white in late summer and fall.

GERMINATION: Sow outdoors where plants are to grow after all danger of frost has past, or sow indoors 6-8 weeks before last frost, maintaining a temperature within the medium of 70° during germination which takes 10-15 days. *Xeranthemum* is difficult to transplant, so take the necessary precautions.

CULTURE: Plant 8-10" apart in full sun and a light, rich, well drained soil.

EASY

Yucca aloifolia   SPANISH BAYONET   PERENNIAL
Yucca filamentosa   ADAM'S NEEDLE
Agavaceae.

USES: Specimen, borders.

HABIT: *Yucca* have long, pointed, strap shaped leaves in large clumps from which arise erect stems bearing white, waxy, drooping, bell shaped flowers. *Yucca aloifolia* is a native of southern United States, Mexico and the West Indies and is hardy to Zone 8. It blooms in late summer. *Yucca filamentosa* is hardy to Zone 4, native to eastern United States and blooms in June and July.

GERMINATION: Sow outdoors in early spring; *Y. aloifolia* may be sown throughout the summer. Indoors, maintain a temperature within the medium of 70-75° during germination for *Y. aloifolia* and 55° for *Y. filamentosa*. *Yucca aloifolia* will germinate in 20-25 days; *Y. filamentosa* in 30-35 days.

CULTURE: Plant 2-4' apart in full sun and an open, sandy, well drained soil. *Yucca* will tolerate drought.

Zantedeschia   Zea

Zantedeschia species   CALLA LILY   POT PLANT
   Araceae, native to South Africa.   Zone 10.

USES: Bedding, house plant, greenhouse plant, cut flower.

HABIT: Huge arrow shaped green leaves surround 1-5' flower stalks. *Zantedeschia aethiopica* reaches 3-5' and has 18" leaves. The spathe is pure white and 5-10" long; the spadix is yellow. *Z. albomaculata* (Spotted Calla) grows to 2' with 18" mottled white leaves and 4½" flowers of creamy white with a purple throat. *Z. Elliottiana* (Golden Calla) is 2½' tall, with dark green leaves and white translucent spots and 6" bright golden yellow flowers. *Z. Rehmannii* 'Superba' (Pink Calla) is the smallest, 1' high with narrow leaves with translucent white spots. Flowers are 3-5" and pale rosy-purple to light pink.

GERMINATION: Sow indoors in early spring, maintaining a temperature within the medium of 70-75° during germination which takes 30-35 days. Do not cover the seeds.

CULTURE: Plant in full sun except in hot areas where light shade is better. Soil should be very rich, moist, well drained and kept mulched. Rhizomes may be dug before frost and stored until the next spring in a cool, dry place. Indoors, grow at 50° nights until roots develop, then grow at 60-65°. Keep the soil barely damp until growth begins, then water to keep constantly moist. All except *Z. aethiopica* require a 3 month dormant period during which the plants should be allowed to wither and then stored in their pots.

Zea Mays var. **japonica**   ORNAMENTAL CORN   ANNUAL
   Gramineae, native to tropical America.

USES: Specimen, dried arrangements, accent.

HABIT: Plants reach to 15' and develop ears with kernels of black, gold, white, purple or red.

GERMINATION: Sow seeds outdoors where the plants are to grow after all danger of frost has past. Seeds will germinate in 5-7 days.

CULTURE: Plant in full sun in a fertile, well drained soil that is well watered. To get all colors on a single ear, hand pollinate.

EASY

Zinnia

Zinnia

Zinnia species   ZINNIA   ANNUAL
Compositae, native to Mexico.

USES: Borders, edging, planters, bedding, cut flower.

HABIT: *Zinnia elegans,* the Common Zinnia or Youth and Old Age, grows 6-40″ tall and bears stiff single or double flowers from 1-7″ across in shades of pink, rose, cherry, lavender, purple, red, orange, salmon, gold, yellow, white, cream or light green. Flowers are solid, multi-colored or zoned, in shapes of chrysanthemums, dahlias, cactus, round or ball and bloom from early summer to frost. *Zinnia Haageana,* the Mexican Zinnia, grows from 12-18″, has narrow leaves and single or double flowers 1-2½″ across in tones of red, mahogany, yellow and orange, in solids or two-tones. *Zinnia angustifolia (Z. linearis)* reaches 12″ in height and bears single flowers of golden-orange and yellow stripes.

GERMINATION: Sow outdoors where plants are to grow after all danger of frost has past, or sow indoors 4 weeks before planting outside after frost, maintaining a temperature within the medium of 70-75° during germination which takes 5-7 days. Double flowered types often revert to singles when transplanted, and for this reason sowing directly into the garden is recommended.

CULTURE: Plant 6-12″ apart in a rich, fertile, well drained garden soil. Pinch plants to induce bushiness. It is better to water Zinnias at ground level than to water overhead. Zinnias thrive in heat and in dry places.

EASY

CHAPTER VI

GROWING EDIBLES

FROM SEED

On the following pages are the edibles of the garden; the vegetables, the fruits and the herbs that season our cooking. Also included in these pages are those herbs that are not really edible, but used for their qualities of fragrance.

The format is the same as in Chapter V, with the inclusion of harvesting information. Picking vegetables, fruit or herbs at the peak of freshness and flavor is what makes growing them really worth the effort.

Abelmoschus   *Agaricus*

Abelmoschus esculentus   OKRA   VEGETABLE
Malvaceae, native to the tropics

HABIT: This exotic looking plant grows 3-6' and produces maroon centered, pale yellow 2-3″ flowers followed by pointed, ribbed, edible pods.

GERMINATION: Soak seeds for 24 hours in warm water before germination. Start seeds indoors 4-6 weeks before planting outside, maintaining a temperature within the medium of 70° during germination which takes 10-14 days. Seeds may be sown ½-¾″ deep in garden rows spaced 3' apart after night temperatures will remain above 50°. Okra needs a long and warm growing season, so seeds should be started indoors in all but the warmest climates and not set out until the soil is fairly warm.

CULTURE: Plant in full sun, 15-18″ apart, in a rich, neutral, well drained soil. Fertilize prior to planting and again when plants are 12″ tall, and when they begin to flower.

HARVESTING: Pick when pods are no more than 3″ long, and pick them daily whether they are to be used or not as plants cease to produce when pods are allowed to ripen.

Agaricus bisporus   MUSHROOM   VEGETABLE
Agaricaceae, native to Eurasia and North Africa

HABIT: Mushrooms are edible fungi that grow from slender white threads called mycelia.

GERMINATION AND CULTURE: The first step is to prepare compost using fresh horse manure, containing a fair amount of straw. Make a pile 3-5′ high, wet it and let it ferment 7-21 days, then turn the pile and wet again. Set in a bed 6-8″ deep and allow to reach 125-140° F. When the temperature drops to 75° (7-10 days), it is ready to use.

Plant the mycelium containing spawn 8-10″ apart by lifting the manure to a depth of 2″ and spreading a teaspoon of spawn over an area of 2 sq. in. Do not water unless the manure starts to dry out. For the first 2 weeks, keep the bed at 72-75°, dropping slowly after that to 68-70°. In another 2 weeks the bed should contain many white threads, and the temperature should be dropped to 60-62°.

At this time, cover the beds with a light soil, 1″ deep, and firm gently. This casing soil should be slightly basic and never dry out. Expect mushrooms to appear in 2-3 weeks. If a slow crop is desired, drop the temperature to 52-56°. Mushrooms require plenty of fresh air but must not be in drafts. The bed temperature should not go over 68° and the air should be 56-58° and have a high moisture content. Lightly water every day. Beds will produce for 3-8 months.

271

Allium Ampeloprasum   *Allium Cepa*

Allium Ampeloprasum, Porrum Group   LEEK   VEGETABLE
Allium Cepa, Cepa Group   ONION
  Amaryllidaceae

HABIT: Onions are bulbous plants to 20″ grown for the edible enlarged bulbous portion which may be white, red or yellow. Leeks are hardy to Zone 4 and do not develop bulbs but rather are grown for the milder flavored stems and base. Leeks are native to Europe, North Africa and Asia, while Onions are known only in cultivation.

GERMINATION: Sow Onions outdoors as soon as the soil can be worked in early spring, or sow indoors in late winter, maintaining a temperature within the medium of 70-75° during germination which takes 10-14 days. Leeks may be treated in the same manner, but since they have a longer growing season than Onions, must be started indoors in late winter in the north. In areas of Zone 8 or warmer, Onions and Leeks may be sown outdoors in fall.

  For outdoor sowing, plant ¼″ deep in rows 12-18″ apart. Thin when 2-3″ high to 2″ apart and again when 6″ high to 4″ apart. Use the thinnings as soup flavorings. Seedlings started indoors may be moved outside as soon as soil can be worked, set out 4″ apart.

CULTURE: Grow in full sun in a light, fertile, deeply prepared, rich soil. Water regularly and feed again in mid summer. Cultivate lightly.

HARVESTING: Harvest scallions (green under-developed onions) when the bulbs are an inch across or less. Harvest bunching Onions (*A. fistulosum*), which do not develop bulbs, at any time. When the tops of Onions begin to bend over, pin them to the ground to hasten maturity and pull in 2-3 days. Allow to dry before storing. Leeks may be harvested in fall when mature; hilling soil against their "stems" when fairly mature produces long, white "stems".

Allium Schoenoprasum   *Anethum*

Allium Schoenoprasum   CHIVES   PERENNIAL HERB
Amaryllidaceae, native to Europe and Asia   Zone 3

HABIT: Bulbous perennial plants grow 8-12″ high in neat, close tufts of slender, tubular grass-like leaves and small globular heads of pale purple flowers in early summer. Leaves have a delicate onion flavor.

GERMINATION: Sow outdoors in spring as soon as soil can be worked, or sow indoors, maintaining a temperature within the medium of 60-70° during germination which takes 10-14 days.

CULTURE: Plant in sun or light shade, 6″ apart, in a rich, moist, well drained soil. Clumps may be lifted in the fall and grown indoors during winter in a sunny windowsill.

HARVESTING: Snip leaves for flavoring at any time.

EASY

Anethum graveolens   DILL   ANNUAL HERB
Umbelliferae, native to southwest Asia

HABIT: Plants 2-3′ tall have finely divided, light green foliage and bear flat topped clusters of tiny yellow flowers in mid-summer. The flowers produce small flat seeds used for flavoring and pickling.

GERMINATION: Sow outdoors where plants are to grow in early spring, or sow indoors, maintaining a temperature within the medium of 60-70° during germination which takes 21-25 days. Sow in individual pots or transplant carefully, as Dill resents being disturbed. Do not cover the seeds which need light to germinate.

CULTURE: Plant 8-12″ apart in full sun and well drained, average garden soil, which should be slightly acid. Keep well watered.

HARVESTING: Pick leaves at any time for fresh use or drying. Harvest the seeds when they turn brown or place the stalks upside down in a bag to collect the seeds as they ripen.

EASY

Angelica

Angelica Archangelica ANGELICA BIENNIAL HERB
Umbelliferae, native to Europe and Asia

HABIT: This aromatic herb grows 5' high with large, 3-part, compound leaves and rounded umbels of greenish-white flowers appearing in July.

GERMINATION: Sow outdoors in late fall for spring germination, or sow indoors after placing in the refrigerator for 6-8 weeks, followed by germination at 60-70° within the medium which takes 21-25 days. Seeds are not long lived and should not be stored.

CULTURE: Plant in sun or light shade, 3' apart, in a rich, fertile, well drained soil. It does best in moist soil and a cool climate.

HARVESTING: Cut leaves at any time for flavoring or use as a vegetable. For candied stems, cut the stalks in the second year just before the flowers begin to open.

Anthriscus Cerefolium CHERVIL ANNUAL HERB
Umbelliferae, native to southeast Europe and western Asia

HABIT: A dainty 12-18" plant has finely cut and richly aromatic soft, light green leaves surrounding flower stalks which bear tiny white flowers in flat umbels in May. Leaves have a slight licorice flavor and are often used in place of Parsley.

GERMINATION: Sow outdoors in early spring or sow indoors, maintaining a temperature within the medium of 60-70° during germination which takes 7-14 days. Sow indoors in individual pots or move carefully as Chervil resents transplanting.

CULTURE: Plant in part shade or shade, 8" apart, in a rich, well drained, sandy soil. Chervil may be grown indoors in full sun, 55° nights and with a medium kept evenly moist. Outdoors, Chervil prefers cool climates.

HARVESTING: Cut leaves at any time for fresh use and just before flowers open for drying or freezing.

Apium

Arachis

Apium graveolens var. **dulce**   CELERY   VEGETABLE
Umbelliferae, widely distributed

HABIT: Edible, elongated leaf stalks grow to 30".

GERMINATION: Sow seeds indoors 10-12 weeks before planting outside, maintaining a temperature within the medium of 70-75° during germination which takes 21-25 days. Never let seedlings' temperature drop below 65°.

CULTURE: Celery is a difficult crop to grow. It prefers a long, cool growing season and should therefore be grown as a winter and spring crop in the south and a summer and fall crop in the north. Soil must be extremely rich and moist, almost like a muck, but with good drainage. Set plants in full sun, 12" apart, in rows 12" apart, after frost has past. Keep plants constantly moist, applying water to the ground and not the foliage, and feed every 2-3 weeks with a soluble fertilizer. Cultivate carefully.

HARVESTING: Blanching of the Celery leaf stalks, once a common practice, is no longer recommended because it reduces flavor and vitamin content while it is reducing color. Harvest as soon as mature, cutting the plant off with a knife just below soil level.

Arachis hypogaea   PEANUT   VEGETABLE
Leguminosae, native to southern Brazil

HABIT: This annual plant with trailing stems, grows 12-18" high with clover-like leaves, yellow pea-like flowers and a dozen or more underground "nuts" growing at the ends of above ground stalks, known as pegs. After the flowers have withered, the stalks which bore them become longer and bend down and push their way into the soil, where they develop into Peanuts. Peanuts are not for the small home garden.

GERMINATION: Sow seeds outdoors where plants are to grow after all danger of frost has past, 1" deep, shelled or unshelled. Germination takes 18-21 days.

CULTURE: Plant in full sun and a well drained, deeply worked, sandy light soil that is slightly alkaline. Peanuts require a long hot growing season to develop.

HARVESTING: Lift entire plant before frost when foliage yellows and soil is fairly dry. Shake free of dirt, and dry in a warm, shady, well ventilated area for 2-3 weeks.

EASY

275

Artemisia Absinthium

Artemisia Dracunculus

Artemisia Absinthium   PERENNIAL HERB
WORMWOOD, ABSINTHE
Compositae, native to Europe   Zone 2

HABIT: Coarse, white, hairy, deeply divided leaves cover 4' plants. The yellow to purple flowers on long wiry branches are tiny and insignificant.

GERMINATION: Sow in place outdoors in spring; germination will take 7-10 days.

CULTURE: Plant in full sun or light shade, 18" apart, in average garden soil with excellent drainage. *Artemisia* can tolerate dry, poor soil. Prune back to keep in an attractive shape.

HARVESTING: Cut fresh leaves at any time to flavor vermouth or poultry dishes; cut leaves for drying as the flowers appear.

Artemisia Dracunculus   PERENNIAL HERB
SIBERIAN TARRAGON
(Artemisia Redowski)
Compositae, native to southern Europe, Asia, western U. S.   Zone 5

HABIT: A woody 3-5' plant has lance-like, dark green leaves that are anise-flavored. The flowers are inconspicuous, greenish-white and in clusters. This is not to be confused with French Tarragon which does not set seeds and must be propagated by cuttings.

GERMINATION: Sow outdoors in spring or sow indoors, maintaining a temperature within the medium of 60-70° during germination which takes 20-25 days.

CULTURE: Plant 18" apart in full sun or light shade in a light, well drained soil. Fertilize in early spring and again in early summer.

HARVESTING: Cut leaves at any time for fresh use; for drying, cut just before flowers open.

276

Asparagus officinalis   *Beta vulgaris (Cicla)*

Asparagus officinalis   ASPARAGUS   PERENNIAL VEGETABLE
Liliaceae, native to Europe, Asia and North Africa   Zone 3

HABIT: Delicate fern-like foliage growing to 3′ produces edible stalks 6-10″ high in spring.

GERMINATION: Soak seeds for 48 hours in very warm water prior to sowing. Sow indoors in midwinter, or outdoors after the soil has warmed up, maintaining a temperature within the medium of 75-80° during germination which takes 14-21 days.

CULTURE: Set plants 3-5″ apart in full sun and a well prepared, deep, rich, loose, well limed soil. In the second year, transplant to 15″ apart. Fertilize before growth starts in spring and again after the crop is harvested. Keep well watered. Let foliage brown and die down in the fall. Choose rust resistant varieties for best results.

HARVESTING: Snap or cut spears when 6-8″ high at or just below ground level, being careful not to injure any underground shoots. Do not harvest Asparagus until the plants are three years old.

Beta vulgaris, Cicla Group   SWISS CHARD   VEGETABLE
Chenopodiaceae, native to coastal Europe

HABIT: Vigorous, coarse leaved vegetable is related to the Beet, but does not produce a thickened, edible root. The plants are 12-18″ high with red or green deeply crinkled leaves and prominent central ribs. If grown as a biennial, it produces a long, edible stalk the second year.

GERMINATION: Sow outdoors as soon as soil can be worked in early spring (fall sowing may be done in Zones 9 and 10), 1″ deep in rows·15-18″ apart. Germination takes 7-10 days.

CULTURE: Thin to 4″-6″ apart (use thinnings as soup or salad greens). Grow in full sun or very light shade in a loose, rich, well drained soil. Fertilize prior to planting and again every six weeks. Water well. Swiss Chard tolerates summer heat.

HARVESTING: In approximately two months after sowing, leaves may be picked. Cut them off at the base of the plant, allowing the undisturbed inner leaves to grow. Pick flower stalks the second year before flowers open.

EASY

277

Beta vulgaris (Crassa)	Borago

Beta vulgaris, Crassa Group   VEGETABLE
GARDEN BEET, SUGAR BEET
Chenopodiaceae, native to southern Europe

HABIT: Biennials grown as annuals produce globular or tapering edible roots and reddish-green leafy edible tops, both high in iron.

GERMINATION: Sow outdoors as soon a soil can be worked in early spring, following soaking in warm water for 24 hours. Sow ½" deep in rows 18-24" apart. Germination takes 10-14 days. The "seeds" that you buy and plant are actually fruits and contain several seeds, so the seedlings will have to be thinned immediately.

CULTURE: Thin to 4" apart. Grow in full sun in a deep, rich, sandy soil that is neutral (pH 7.0). Fertilize prior to planting and again when Beets are 3-4" tall. Keep cultivated and well watered. For a continuous supply, sow successively at three week intervals. Beets, especially Sugar Beets, prefer cool temperatures.

HARVESTING: Dig when Beets are 2-3" across for best flavor. Beet greens may also be harvested and cooked at that time.

Borago officinalis   BORAGE   ANNUAL HERB
Boraginaceae, native to Europe and North Africa

HABIT: This decorative plant has drooping clusters of 1½" blue or purple star shaped flowers in summer on 2' stems clothed with hairy, coarse leaves. It is a good source of bee forage.

GERMINATION: Sow outdoors in fall or very early spring, covering the seed completely, as it needs darkness to germinate. It is best sown in place, as it is very difficult to transplant. Germination takes 7-10 days.

CULTURE: Plant 10-12" apart in full sun or light shade in a dry, poor soil.

HARVESTING: Immature leaves are tender and are used in iced drinks and salads. Flowers may be cut as they start to open, floated on drinks or used candied on cakes, etc.

EASY

278

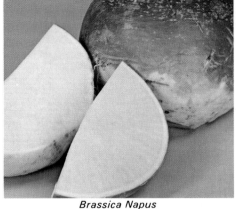

Brassica juncea   *Brassica Napus*

Brassica juncea var. **crispifolia**   MUSTARD   VEGETABLE
Brassica Rapa, Perviridis Group
Cruciferae, native to the Mediterranean

HABIT: This spinach-like annual grows 10-12″ high, and its cluster of basal leaves is used as greens. *Brassica juncea* var. *crispifolia* has cut, curled and crisped leaves; *B. Rapa,* Perviridis Group (Tendergreen, Spinach Mustard) has smooth, thick, glossy, dark green leaves that are less pungent.

GERMINATION: Sow outdoors where plants are to grow in early spring and again 3-4 weeks later. Sow again 6-8 weeks before first fall frost. In Zone 8 and warmer, sow in fall for winter use. Sow ¼″ deep, 1-2″ apart in rows 12-15″ apart. Germination takes 9-12 days.

CULTURE: Grow in full sun in a rich, moist, well drained soil. Thin to 6-8″ apart and use the thinnings for flavorings. Fertilize prior to planting and again 3 weeks later. Mulch to keep soil moist and cool. Mustard is a cool weather crop; Tendergreen is more heat and drought tolerant.

HARVESTING: Cut outside leaves when 3-4″ long and still tender.
EASY

Brassica Napus, Napobrassica Group   VEGETABLE
                    RUTABAGA, SWEDISH TURNIP
Cruciferae, nativity unknown

HABIT: This vegetable is much like the Turnip, but differs from it in having a distinct leafy neck, smooth waxy leaves that are bluish-green, and larger and finer roots that are globe shaped and light yellow.

GERMINATION: Rutabaga is a cool fall crop. Sow it outdoors 3-3½ months before first fall frost. Sow ½″ deep in rows 18-24″ apart. Germination takes 7-10 days.

CULTURE: Grow in full sun, 6-8″ apart in a light, rich, neutral, well drained soil. Fertilize prior to planting and again when plants are 4-6″ tall. Keep well watered and cultivated.

HARVESTING: Harvest when 3-4″ across or more, or mulch and leave in the ground until needed as long as the ground does not freeze. Rutabagas have a long storage life if kept cool. Greens are edible but are strongly flavored.

EASY

Brassica oleracea (Acephala)   *Brassica oleracea (Botrytis)*

Brassica oleracea, Acephala Group   VEGETABLE
COLLARDS, KALE
Cruciferae, native to coastal Europe

HABIT: These relatives of the Cabbage do not produce heads, but grow in stalks that bear blue-green leaves that are finely cut or curly, like those of a Cabbage. Kale grows to 2½'; Collards to 3'.

GERMINATION: Seeds may be started indoors in midwinter for transplanting outdoors as soon as soil can be worked in spring, maintaining a temperature within the medium of 70-75° during germination which takes 10-14 days. Seeds can also be directly sown into the ground in early spring, ½" deep for Collards and ¼" deep for Kale, in rows 18-24" apart. In Zone 8 and warmer, sow in late summer or early fall for winter and spring crops. A sowing may also be made in cooler areas in midsummer for fall harvesting.

CULTURE: Grow in full sun, 12-15" apart, in a rich, sandy, well drained soil. Fertilize prior to planting and again every 3-4 weeks. Keep the soil moist and mulch to keep it cool and weed-free. Kale is a cool weather plant, while Collards will tolerate summer heat.

HARVESTING: Pick leaves as needed, not disturbing the growing point of the plant. Frost will improve the flavor of both Collards and Kale, and both are relatively hardy.

Brassica oleracea, Botrytis Group CAULIFLOWER   VEGETABLE
Cruciferae, native to coastal Europe

HABIT: A head of tightly clustered flower buds is white, purple or green and surrounded by large blue-green leaves. The plant grows to 2-2½'.

GERMINATION: Seedlings should be planted into the garden 2 weeks before last spring frost; start them indoors 5-7 weeks before that date, maintaining a temperature within the medium of 70-75° during germination which takes 8-10 days. Cauliflower is a cool weather crop and will not head under hot or dry conditions. A fall crop may be planted 3-3½ months before first fall frost by sowing seeds directly into the garden, ½" deep in rows 3' apart. In Zone 8 and warmer, seeds may be sown in late summer for a winter crop.

CULTURE: Plant in full sun, 18-24" apart in a deep, rich, moist, well drained soil. Fertilize prior to planting and again every 4 weeks during growth. Keep well watered. Mulch to conserve moisture. White Cauliflower that is not self blanching may be blanched by tying outer leaves over the heads when they are 2" across. Do not blanch purple or green varieties.

HARVESTING: Harvest while buds are still tight by cutting the stalk below the head.

280

Brassica oleracea (Capitata)   *Brassica oleracea (Gemmifera)*

Brassica oleracea, Capitata Group   CABBAGE   VEGETABLE
Cruciferae, native to coastal Europe

HABIT: This leafy vegetable forms globular heads to 15" of compressed, edible leaves. There are three types: green foliaged, with smooth green leaves; Red Cabbage with smooth purplish red leaves; Savoy Cabbage with crinkled green leaves.

GERMINATION: Set plants outdoors as soon as soil can be worked in early spring. Sow the seeds indoors 5-7 weeks before that date, maintaining a temperature within the medium of 70-75° during germination which takes 10-14 days. In areas with cold winters, also sow seeds directly into the ground in midsummer for a fall crop, ½" deep in rows 24-30" apart. In Zone 8 and warmer, sow in early fall for a winter crop.

CULTURE: Plant in full sun, 15-18" apart, in a rich, fertile, deep, moist, well drained soil. Fertilize prior to planting and again every 4 weeks with 5-10-5 or better, nitrate of soda. Cabbage is a cool weather crop.

HARVESTING: Harvest when heads are well formed and firm. Cabbage will withstand considerable frost.

Brassica oleracea, Gemmifera Group   VEGETABLE
BRUSSELS SPROUTS
Cruciferae, native to Belgium

HABIT: Plant 2-3' tall produces 1-2" cabbage-like buds at each leaf axil.

GERMINATION: Brussels Sprouts is best grown as a fall crop. Sow seeds indoors 6-8 weeks before planting time, which is 4 months before first fall frost, maintaining a temperature within the medium of 70-75° during germination which takes 10-14 days. Seeds may also be sown at the same time in seed beds, ¼" deep in rows 30-36" apart. In Zone 8 and warmer, seeds may be sown in early fall for a winter crop.

CULTURE: Plant in full sun, 18-24" apart, in a rich, moist, fertile, well drained soil. Fertilize prior to planting and again when plants are 6-8" high, 12-15" high, and when sprouts begin to form. Keep well watered and mulch to conserve moisture and keep the soil cool.

HARVESTING: As sprouts begin to touch each other, remove the lower leaves. Do not remove upper leaves unless you want to speed the development of a late crop, when the terminal tip should be removed. Harvest sprouts from the bottom up as they mature. Flavor is improved by frost.

Brassica oleracea (Gongylodes)   *Brassica oleracea (Italica)*

Brassica oleracea, Gongylodes Group   VEGETABLE
         KOHLRABI

Cruciferae, nativity unknown

HABIT: This vegetable produces a turnip-like lower portion of the stem which rests on the soil surface and has leaves sprouting from all over.

GERMINATION: Sow indoors 4-6 weeks before planting outside, which should be done as soon as the soil can be worked. Maintain a temperature within the medium of 70-75° during germination which takes 12-15 days. Seeds may also be sown outdoors, ¼″ deep in rows 15-18″ apart. Sow at two week intervals up to one month before first fall frost for successive harvesting. In Zone 8 and warmer, sow in late summer and fall for late fall and winter harvest.

CULTURE: Plant in full sun or moderate shade in a deep, rich, moist, well drained soil, 4-6″ apart. Fertilize prior to planting and again every 3 weeks. Keep well watered and mulch to conserve moisture, keep roots cool and eliminate the need for weeding. Kohlrabi prefers cool weather.

HARVESTING: Harvest in approximately 8 weeks when 2-2½″ across.

Brassica oleracea, Italica Group   BROCCOLI   VEGETABLE
     Cruciferae, native to coastal Europe

HABIT: Although there are some types of Broccoli that belong to the Botrytis Group, the ones generally grown in the garden are in the Italica Group and do not form a solid head. Plants grow to 2′ and produce clusters of flower buds which are edible along with the stems and upper leaves.

GERMINATION: Plants should be set into the garden 2 weeks before last spring frost; start seeds indoors 5-7 weeks before that date, maintaining a temperature within the medium of 70-75° during germination which takes 10-14 days. In Zone 8 and warmer, sow seeds outdoors in early fall for a late fall and winter crop, ½″ deep in rows 2½-3′ apart. Broccoli is a cool weather crop.

CULTURE: Plant in full sun, 18-24″ apart, in a rich, moist, well drained soil. Fertilize prior to planting and again when plants are 6-8″ tall, 12-15″ tall and when buds form. Keep well watered and mulch to keep the ground moist and cool.

HARVESTING: Harvest just before the buds open, cutting the stem 6″ below the cluster of buds. Side branches will continue to produce for another 2-2½ months.

EASY

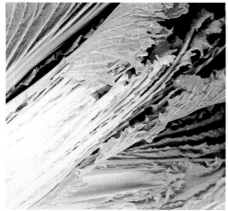

Brassica Rapa (Pekinensis)   *Brassica Rapa (Rapifera)*

Brassica Rapa, Pekinensis Group   VEGETABLE
CHINESE CABBAGE
Cruciferae, native to Asia

HABIT: This 18″ plant resembles a cross between Cabbage and Celery, with leaves in loose egg shaped or vase shaped clusters.

GERMINATION: Chinese Cabbage is best grown as a fall crop as it must have cool weather. Sow seeds 2½-3 months before first fall frost, either indoors maintaining a temperature of 70-75° within the medium during germination which takes 10-14 days, or outdoors, ½″ deep in rows 18-24″ apart.

CULTURE: Grow in full sun, 12-18″ apart, in a rich, moist, well drained soil. Fertilize prior to planting and again 3 weeks later with 5-10-5 or nitrate of soda. Keep well watered and mulch to conserve moisture and eliminate weeding. Be careful not to splash soil up into loose heads.

HARVESTING: Harvest when mature by pulling up plants, cutting off roots and peeling away the outer leaves.

Brassica Rapa, Rapifera Group   TURNIP   VEGETABLE
Cruciferae, native to Eurasia

HABIT: A rough and hairy leaved vegetable producing enlarged, edible roots with white or yellow flesh.

GERMINATION: Sow outdoors in early spring, as soon as soil can be worked, ½″ deep in rows 15-18″ apart, and make successive sowings until 5 weeks before 80° days. Turnip is a cool crop, so seeds may be sown again in late summer for fall harvest. In Zone 8 and warmer, sow in early fall through early spring for continuous winter crops. Germination takes 7-10 days.

CULTURE: Plant in full sun 3-5″ apart in a fertile, moist, rich, well drained soil. Fertilize prior to planting and again when plants are 4″ tall. Keep well watered.

HARVESTING: Harvest when 2″ across. Greens may be harvested at any time, but are most tender when young.

EASY

Capsicum

Capsicum

Capparis spinosa   CAPER BUSH   ANNUAL HERB
Capparaceae, native to the Mediterranean

HABIT: Caper Bush is a spiny, shrubby plant growing 3-5' high, with 2" round leaves and 2-3" flowers.

GERMINATION: Sow indoors in late winter, maintaining a temperature within the medium of 55° at night and 85° by day, during germination which takes 3 months.

CULTURE: Grow 3' apart in full sun in a sandy, well drained soil. Caper Bush does well in rocky soil and tolerates drought.

HARVESTING: For pickling, pick flower buds before they open.

EASY

Capsicum annuum var. **annuum,**   PEPPERS   VEGETABLE
Grossum and Longum Groups
Solanaceae, native to tropical America

HABIT: Shrubby plants grow to 30" and bear edible fruits of varying sizes, shapes and colors of red, green or gold, which are sweet or hot in taste.

GERMINATION: In all but the warmest parts of the country, sow Peppers indoors 6-8 weeks before night temperatures remain above 55°. Maintain a temperature within the medium of 75-80° during germination which takes 10 days.

CULTURE: Plant in full sun 18-24" apart in rows 30-36" apart. Soil should be rich and well drained. Fertilize prior to planting and again lightly after 6 weeks. Keep plants moist and mulch to conserve moisture.

HARVESTING: Both hot and sweet Peppers will turn red at maturity, but sweet Peppers are usually picked when green as soon as they are firm.

284

Carthamus   Carum

Carthamus tinctorius   ANNUAL HERB
SAFFLOWER, FALSE SAFFRON
Compositae, native to Eurasia

HABIT: The 3′ plant has 2-2½″ thistle-like leaves studded with short, prickly orange hairs and thistle-like flowers of deep yellow to orange. White seeds that resemble teeth are stained with brown and follow the flowers.

GERMINATION: Sow outdoors where plants are to grow after all danger of frost has past, or, for best results, sow indoors 8 weeks before last frost, maintaining a temperature within the medium of 65-70° during germination which takes 10-14 days.

CULTURE: Plant 12″ apart in full sun and a well drained, average garden soil. Safflower tolerates poor and dry soil but does best when kept moderately moist.

HARVESTING: Pick fresh flowers to use as natural dyes; collect seeds for flavoring. The flavor is almost identical to Saffron.

Carum Carvi   CARAWAY   BIENNIAL HERB
Umbelliferae, native to Europe   Zone 3

HABIT: Mounded plants are clothed with finely cut, dark green leaves which are practically evergreen. Flower stalks 2′ high are topped with clusters of tiny white flowers in June and July, followed by brown anise-flavored seeds.

GERMINATION: Since Caraway is difficult to transplant, it is best sown in place. Sow in fall to have seeds by the following summer; seeds sown in spring will not grow into seed-producing plants until the second summer. Germination takes 10-14 days.

CULTURE: Plant 10-12″ apart in full sun and a well drained garden soil.

HARVESTING: Harvest seeds when they turn brown in midsummer.

EASY

285

Chenopodium   Cicer

Chenopodium Botrys   ANNUAL HERB
AMBROSIA, FEATHER GERANIUM
Chenopodiaceae, native to Europe, Asia, Africa

HABIT: This herb grows 1½' high and has miniature oak-like leaves often hidden by 2' feathery sprays of yellow-green, very tiny blossoms in July. Leaves are reddish before turning light green, and the flower stems are covered with a sticky substance. The entire plant is intensely scented.

GERMINATION: Sow outdoors in early spring, or sow indoors, maintaining a temperature within the medium of 70° during germination which takes 20-25 days.

CULTURE: Plant in full sun, 10-12" apart, and keep well watered. The plant does best in gravelly or sandy soils.

HARVESTING: Cut leaves for scenting or drying at any time.

Cicer arietinum CHICK PEA, GARBANZO BEAN   VEGETABLE
Leguminosae, native to southwest Asia

HABIT: This 2' bushy plant has deeply cut leaves and produces small, round, light brown beans.

GERMINATION: Sow outdoors after all danger of frost is past, 8-12" apart in rows 2' apart. Germination takes 6-10 days. Innoculate with nitrogen fixing bacteria prior to sowing.

CULTURE: Grow in full sun in a rich, light, sandy, well drained soil. Fertilize prior to planting and again when plants are 6" high. Keep well watered.

HARVESTING: Pick when green for fresh use, or allow beans to ripen for dried use.

EASY

286

Cichorium Endiva   *Cichorium Intybus*

Cichorium Endiva   ENDIVE   VEGETABLE
Compositae, native to India

HABIT: This lettuce-like annual or biennial forms a flat rosette of slender, curled, cut or lobed leaves up to 18″ across. Escarole is similar but with broad, flat leaves.

GERMINATION: Endive is best grown as a fall crop. Sow seeds outdoors 3-3½ months before first fall frost, ¼″ deep in rows 18-24″ apart. Seeds may also be started indoors, maintaining a temperature within the medium of 70-75° during germination which takes 7-14 days. In Zone 8 and warmer, start seeds in fall for winter harvest.

CULTURE: Space 8-12″ apart in full sun in a rich, well drained soil. Fertilize prior to planting and again every 3-4 weeks. Mulch plants to conserve moisture, keep the soil cool and reduce the need for weeding. Keep well watered.

HARVESTING: When plants are well formed and 15″ across, blanch to reduce bitterness by gathering the outer leaves together over the crown and tying with a rubber band or twist-em. To prevent decay, uncover the plants and let them dry out after any rainfall. Blanch for 2 weeks and pick any time after that.

Cichorium Intybus   CHICORY   PERENNIAL VEGETABLE
Compositae, native to the Mediterranean   Zone 3

HABIT: This lettuce-like plant has oblong basal leaves and 3½-5′ stems which bear blue daisy-like flowers from June to frost. It is best grown as an annual, as it can become weedy. Roots are often used as a coffee substitute.

GERMINATION: Sow outdoors in early mid-spring, ¼″ deep in rows 18″ apart. Seeds may also be sown indoors, maintaining a temperature within the medium of 70° during germination which takes 7-14 days.

CULTURE: Space 6″ apart in full sun and a rich, well drained soil. Fertilize prior to planting and again every 3-4 weeks. Keep well watered.

HARVESTING: Chicory can be used as a salad plant as-is, but is usually grown to produce witloof. Dig roots after frost, cut the tops off 2″ above the crown and store in a cool place. Force at 60-70°, setting roots cut to 6-9″ long upright in a box and covered with moist sand. In about 1 month, the tops will be produced and ready for harvesting.

287

Citrullus

Citrullus

Citrullus lanatus   WATERMELON   ANNUAL FRUIT
Cucurbitaceae, native to Africa

HABIT: Watermelon is a large, sprawling vine with hairy leaves and fruits that are round, oblong or oval. The skin is smooth and varies from light to dark green, often with stripes, and the flesh is red, yellow or white.

GERMINATION: In areas with long growing seasons, seeds may be sown outdoors 2 weeks after all danger of frost has past, 1″ deep in hills 6-8′ apart. Otherwise, start seeds indoors 3-4 weeks before night temperatures remain above 55°, maintaining a temperature within the medium of 75° during germination which takes 5-7 days. Sow in individual pots as they do not like to be transplanted.

CULTURE: Plant in full sun in a light, rich, sandy soil with excellent drainage. Thin to 3 plants per hill or space 2′ apart in rows 6-8′ apart. Keep well watered during the growing season, cutting down when the fruit is ripening. Watermelon needs the longest growing season of all the melons.

HARVESTING: It is difficult to tell when watermelons are ripe. Rapping the side of the fruit should produce a dull rather than a sharp sound, and the bottom spot where the melon touches the ground will darken from light to golden yellow when the melon is ripe.

Coriandrum sativum   CORIANDER   ANNUAL HERB
Umbelliferae, native to southern Europe

HABIT: Large, coarse plants have finely divided, soft green leaves and 12-30″ stems topped with flat clusters of tiny white or pale pink flowers in late summer. Lemon flavored white seeds that resemble peppercorns follow the flowers.

GERMINATION: For best results, sow in place in early spring, completely covering the seeds which need darkness to germinate. Germination takes 10-14 days.

CULTURE: Plant 8-10″ apart in full sun and average garden soil with good drainage.

HARVESTING: Pick leaves at any time for salad. When the seeds begin to brown, cut stem and place it upside down in a paper bag to collect the seeds.

EASY

288

Cucumis Melo   *Cucumis Melo*

Cucumis Melo   MELONS   ANNUAL FRUIT
Cucurbitaceae, native to western Africa

HABIT: What we call the Cantaloupe is actually Muskmelon, *C. Melo,* Reticulatus Group. The true Cantaloupe is not grown in the United States. Melons are sprawling, vining plants to 10' that bear fruit with edible inner flesh. There are new dwarf varieties available that do not send out long runners and so are perfect for the small garden. Muskmelon is round or oval, ribbed, with netting on the skin. The flesh is usually orange or salmon. Honeydew, *Cucumis Melo* Inodorus Group, is round or slightly elongated, with smooth skin and a light green flesh.

GERMINATION: In areas with long and hot growing seasons, seeds may be sown outdoors 2 weeks after danger of frost has past, ½" deep in hills 4-6' apart or in rows 4' apart. Otherwise, start seeds indoors 3-4 weeks before night temperatures remain above 55°, maintaining a temperature within the medium of 75° during germination which takes 5-7 days. Melons do not like to be transplanted, so sow in individual pots.

CULTURE: Plant in full sun in a light, rich, sandy, well drained soil. Space plants 12" apart in rows 4' apart or thin to 3 plants per hill. Small Melons may be grown on a fence if supported. Keep well watered, and mulch with black plastic to eliminate weeds, conserve moisture and speed harvesting. Fertilize prior to planting and again every 4 weeks. Melons can only be grown in long and hot seasons. They like to be well watered while growing, but on the dry side when ripening. Some new varieties are early maturing, making it possible to grow Melons in the north. Honeydew needs a longer growing season than Muskmelon.

HARVESTING: Harvest Muskmelons when the stem slips easily from the melon with slight pressure. Honeydew is picked when the skin turns yellow.

Cucumis sativus

Cucumis sativus

Cucumis sativus   CUCUMBER   VEGETABLE
*Cucurbitaceae,*native to southern Asia

HABIT: This rough, vining annual grows up to 8', produces 1" yellow flowers, and bears elongated green, white or yellow fruits.Slicing Cucumbers are generally used when 6-8" long and pickling Cucumbers when 1½-3" long. There are dwarf varieties which do not produce long runners and are excellent for container culture.

GERMINATION: Seeds may be sown outdoors where plants are to grow 1-2 weeks after all danger of frost has past, ½" deep in rows or hills 4' apart. Seeds may be started indoors 4-6 weeks before planting outside, maintaining a temperature within the medium of 70° during germination which takes 7-10 days. Grow in individual pots so the roots are not disturbed during transplanting.

CULTURE: Plant in full sun, 12" apart in rows, or 4' apart in hills, with 4 plants per hill. Soil should be light, rich, fertile and well drained. Fertilize prior to planting and again every 3 weeks. Keep well watered and cultivate carefully.

HARVESTING: Pick Cucumbers while they are dark green; if they turn yellow, the plants will stop producing. Cut them, rather than break them off.

290

Cucurbita   Cucurbita

Cucurbita species   PUMPKIN, SQUASH   VEGETABLE
Cucurbitaceae, of cultivated American origin

HABIT: Pumpkins and Squash are bushy or vining annuals that bear fruits with white, yellow or orange edible flesh. Pumpkins are yellow or orange, round, from small to immense sizes, and produced on sprawling vines. They are very similar to Winter Squash which is eaten when the fruit is mature in fall, produced on a vining plant. Summer Squash, on the other hand, is eaten when immature. Most Summer Squash are bush plants, and are produced in a range of colors, sizes and shapes and include the popular Zucchini. Essentially all Summer Squash are *Cucurbita Pepo,* but not all *C. Pepo* are Summer Squash. Cultivars known as Winter Squash and Pumpkin are found in *C. Pepo, C. maxima, C. mixta,* and *C. moschata.* Vegetable Spaghetti and edible Gourds are also found in this grouping.

GERMINATION: After all danger of frost has past, sow seeds outdoors in hills 4' apart for bush types and 8' apart for vining types. Seeds may also be started indoors 3 weeks before planting outside, maintaining a temperature within the medium of 70-75° during germination which takes 7-10 days.

CULTURE: Plant in full sun in a very rich, sandy, well drained soil. Thin to 2 plants per hill or space bush types 2-3' apart in rows 4-6' apart and vining types 3-4' apart in rows 8-12' apart. Keep weeded and well watered. Fertilize prior to planting and every 3 weeks until harvest. The vining types are too large for many home gardens.

HARVESTING: Pick Summer Squash when immature, when a thumbnail easily pierces the skin. Pick when ready to keep the vine producing. Pick Winter Squash and Pumpkin when fully mature or after the first light frost when the rind is hard.

Cynara

Cuminum Cyminum   CUMIN   ANNUAL HERB
Umbelliferae, native to the Mediterranean

HABIT: This spreading plant grows 6" high and has thread-like leaves and umbels of tiny white or rose flowers followed by flavorful seeds.

GERMINATION: Plant outdoors in spring after all danger of frost has past, or start seeds indoors 6-8 weeks before last frost, maintaining a temperature within the medium of 70° during germination which takes 10-14 days.

CULTURE: Plant 2' apart in full sun and average, well drained soil. Cumin prefers a mild climate and needs a long growing season.

HARVESTING: Harvest when seeds begin to dry; the stems may be cut and placed upside down in a bag to collect the seeds.

Cynara Scolymus   ARTICHOKE   PERENNIAL VEGETABLE
Compositae, native to the Mediterranean   Zone 8.

HABIT: Large, spreading plants have silvery-green, fern-like foliage and 4-5' stems which carry edible flower buds with thick and heavy scales. If the buds are not cut, they open into 6-8" thistle-like, purple-blue flowers.

GERMINATION: Sow seeds indoors 6-8 weeks before last frost in spring, maintaining a temperature within the medium of 60-70° during germination which takes 12-15 days.

CULTURE: Plant in full sun, 4' apart in all directions, in a rich, well drained soil. Water heavily throughout the season. Fertilize prior to planting and again when the plants are 24" high. Artichokes do best in areas with long, cool summers, such as the mid-California coastline. If started early enough, Artichokes will be produced the first year.

HARVESTING: Cut stems 1-2" below the base of the bud when the bud is 4" in diameter, tight yet plump. After harvest, cut stalks to ground level for a second crop.

Daucus   *Daucus*

Daucus Carota var. **Sativus**   CARROT   VEGETABLE
Umbelliferae, of cultivated origin

HABIT: Hardy biennial grown as an annual reaches 20″ with bright green, fern-like foliage and edible yellow or orange roots.

GERMINATION: Sow seeds outdoors in early spring as soon as soil can be worked, ½″ deep in rows 12″ apart. Germination takes 14-21 days, so Radishes are often sown with Carrots to mark the rows. Make successive sowings every three weeks until early summer.

CULTURE: Grow in full sun and a rich, loose, deeply worked, sandy soil with excellent drainage, thinning to 2″ apart. Fertilize prior to sowing and again when plants are 6-8″ tall. Mound soil slightly at the tops of the Carrots to prevent them from turning green.

HARVESTING: Harvest when Carrots are between finger size and 2″ in diameter.

Eruca vesicaria subsp. **sativa**   ROCKET   ANNUAL HERB
Cruciferae, native to the Mediterranean

HABIT: This herb is grown as a salad plant for its strong, peppery tasting foliage. It grows quickly to 2½′ and has flowers of white with purple veins.

GERMINATION: Sow outdoors in early spring as soon as the soil can be worked, or sow indoors, maintaining a temperature within the medium of 60-70° during germination which takes 5-8 days.

CULTURE: Plant 12″ apart in full sun and a light, sandy, rich, moist, well drained soil. Rocket does best in cool weather.

HARVESTING: Cut leaves frequently to keep them from becoming bitter.

Foeniculum   *Fragaria*

Foeniculum vulgare FENNEL, SWEET FENNEL   ANNUAL HERB
Foeniculum vulgare var. **azoricum** FLORENCE FENNEL
    Umbelliferae, native to southern Europe

HABIT: Fennel is a 4-5′ annual herb with thread-like, bright yellow-green foliage, similar to dill, but coarser. The stems bear flat and large yellow umbels of flowers in summer, which are followed by light tan ribbed seeds. Florence Fennel, also known as Finocchio or Anise, is similar but lower growing and with a thickened base. It has a licorice or anise flavor.

GERMINATION: Sow Fennel outdoors after all danger of frost has past, or sow indoors, maintaining a temperature within the medium of 65° during germination which takes 10-14 days. Cover seeds completely, as darkness is required for germination. It is best sown into individual pots if started indoors as it is difficult to transplant. Florence Fennel is best sown in early summer and treated as a fall crop.

CULTURE: Plant in full sun, 8-12″ apart, in a dry, rich, fertile, limey soil that is well drained.

HARVESTING: Cut leaves from either while flowers are in bloom; seeds from either are harvested when they begin to turn brown. Celery-like stalks of Florence Fennel may be blanched by piling up soil around them for 2-3 weeks, followed by harvesting just before flowers open.

Fragaria Vesca   STRAWBERRY   PERENNIAL FRUIT
    Rosaceae, native to the Americas   Zone 5

HABIT: Strawberries are deciduous plants with 3-leaflet leaves and are often spread by runners. White ½-1″ flowers in spring are followed by red edible fruits. Some varieties produce fruit only once per year; others, the everbearing, produce in spring and in late summer through frost. The everbearing Strawberries are usually runnerless.

GERMINATION: Sow seeds outdoors in late fall or early spring, or sow indoors, maintaining a temperature within the medium of 55° during germination which takes 30 days.

CULTURE: Plant in full sun in a fertile, sandy, rich soil that has excellent drainage. Fertilize in spring. Keep well watered and mulch to conserve moisture and keep the fruit from rotting. Plant single crop Strawberries 2½′ apart in rows 3′ apart; plant everbearing ones 12″ apart in rows 2′ apart. Remove the blossoms from first year plants to promote vigorous growth.

HARVESTING: Pick in the morning when fruits are red or pink.

Glycine   *Helianthus*

Glycine Max   SOYBEAN   VEGETABLE
Leguminosae, native to southeast Asia

HABIT: This hairy, bushy annual reaches 6' in height, has inconspicuous white flowers and 3" beans that have a nutty flavor.

GERMINATION: Sow outdoors after all danger of frost has past when soil is warm, 1½" deep in rows 24-30" apart. Innoculate with nitrogen fixing bacteria prior to sowing. Germination takes 12-15 days.

CULTURE: Thin to 2-3" apart and grow in full sun in a rich, well drained soil. Keep well watered. Fertilize prior to planting and again when plants are 8-10" high. Soybeans require a long, warm growing season.

HARVESTING: Pick immature beans when the pods are plump and the seeds full size, but still green. Beans may also be left on the plant until mature and used dried.

Helianthus tuberosus   PERENNIAL VEGETABLE
JERUSALEM ARTICHOKE
Compositae, native to eastern Canada and United States   Zone 4

HABIT: This coarse sunflower-like plant grows 8-12' tall, has 3½" yellow flowers in late summer and produces edible potato-like tubers.

GERMINATION: Tubers, not seeds, are the means of propagating Jerusalem Artichoke. Plant whole small tubers or larger tubers cut up, so they have at least one eye. Plant 4" deep, 15-24" apart in rows 30" apart in spring or fall.

CULTURE: Grow in full sun in average, well drained garden soil. The better the soil, the weedier the plant becomes, so it is better grown as an annual. If the top 12-18" of stem is cut off as flowers form, the tubers will be larger.

HARVESTING: Dig tubers when mature in fall, either before or after frost.

EASY

Hyssopus   *Ipomoea*

Hyssopus officinalis   HYSSOP   PERENNIAL HERB
Labiatae, native to south and east Europe   Zone 3

HABIT: This 1½' shrubby perennial evergreen has square stems and aromatic dark green leaves. Small blue-violet mint-like flowers bloom on 2½-5" spikes during June.

GERMINATION: Sow outdoors where plants are to bloom in early spring, or sow indoors, maintaining a temperature within the medium of 60-70° during germination which takes 7-10 days. If started early, Hyssop will flower the first year.

CULTURE: Plant 18" apart in full sun or light shade in average, well drained soil that is slightly alkaline. Hyssop does well in dry and rocky places.

HARVESTING: Pick leaves at any time for drying and use in scents.

Ipomoea Batatas   SWEET POTATO   VEGETABLE
Convolvulaceae, native to tropical America   Zone 8

HABIT: This perennial vining plant is usually cultured as an annual and forms a low growing ground cover. Spindle or fist shaped edible roots have flesh of white, yellow or orange. There are two types: a dry-fleshed type and a moist-fleshed type which is more delicious and is erroneously called Yam. There are also vineless or bush varieties.

GERMINATION: Sweet Potatoes are not propagated from seed, but from shoots grown from certified "seed potatoes". Roots are laid horizontally in a hot bed and covered with 3-4 inches of soil. When sprouts are 6-8", they are pulled and rooted.

CULTURE: Shape soil into 6-10" high ridges 18-24" wide with ridges 4-5" apart. Plant 4" deep and 12-15" apart in the center of the ridge. Soil must be acid, light, sandy and well drained. Fertilize 2 weeks prior to planting. Sweet Potatoes require a long, warm growing season. Sweet Potatoes grow too large for many home gardens.

HARVESTING: Dig in late fall or when tops are blackened by frost. Handle carefully as skins are tender and bruise easily. Store at 75-85° for 2 weeks, then at 50-55°.

Lactuca

Lactuca

Lactuca sativa   LETTUCE   VEGETABLE
Compositae, native to the Mediterranean

HABIT: This leafy annual comes in 4 basic types. The Crisphead is the Lettuce of the supermarket and not the home garden, with a firm, tight ball. Butterhead forms an open but distinct head of crisp but fleshy and delicate leaves. Cos or Romaine is tall, slender and upright, forming heads not quite as tight as Crispheads. Leaf Lettuce produces a round, loose rosette of leaves.

GERMINATION: Sow seeds outdoors as soon as soil can be worked in early spring, not covering the seeds, in rows 12-18" apart. As Lettuce is a cool weather crop, seeds may also be sown in late summer for a fall crop. In Zone 8 and warmer, sow in early fall for winter crops. Seeds may also be started indoors 4 weeks before planting outside, not covering the seeds which need light to germinate and maintaining a temperature within the medium of 65-70° during germination which takes 7-10 days. Young Lettuce seedlings should be transplanted carefully to avoid placing them in shock. Plant only what you can use and make successive sowings as long as the temperature is below 80°.

CULTURE: Soil should be light, sandy, rich, moist, fertile, neutral and well drained. Plant leaf types 4-6" apart and head types 10-12" apart. Fertilize prior to planting and again lightly every 3 weeks. Keep soil moist at all times.

HARVESTING: Harvest head Lettuce when the center is firm. Cut outer leaves from leaf Lettuce as the plant develops and cut off the entire plant when it becomes mature.

Lavandula   *Lepidium*

Lavandula angustifolia   LAVENDER   PERENNIAL HERB
subsp. **angustifolia**
(L. officinalis)
Labiatae, native to the Mediterranean   Zone 5

HABIT: Lavender is an aromatic perennial, deciduous to semi-evergreen, many branched with blue-violet flowers in whorled clusters in early summer. Foliage is gray-green. Typical Lavender is 2' in height; 'Munstead' grows 12-18" high and is early blooming.

GERMINATION: Sow outdoors in late fall or early spring. Indoors, place in moistened medium in the refrigerator for 4-6 weeks, followed by germination at a temperature within the medium of 70° which takes 15-20 days.

CULTURE: Plant 12" apart in full sun in a light, rich, limey, well drained soil. Prune back after flowering to keep the plants compact.

HARVESTING: Cut flower spikes as the buds begin to open and dry in a cool, shady place.

Lepidium sativum   GARDEN CRESS   ANNUAL HERB
Cruciferae, native to Egypt and western Asia

HABIT: Curled and crisped bright green leaves surround 2' stems bearing tiny greenish-white flowers in racemes. This plant is also known as peppergrass.

GERMINATION: Sow outdoors in early spring as soon as soil can be worked, and sow successively every 2 weeks until early summer. Resume sowings again in late summer. Germination takes 7-10 days.
CULTURE: Grow in a stream, pond or bog. If that is unavailable, grow in the shade, 3" apart, in an area that is very rich and can be kept constantly wet. Watercress may also be grown in tanks or tubs by placing a few inches of rich soil in the bottom, setting the plants in the soil, and filling the tank with water to the tips of the shoots. If the water does not run constantly, change it once a week. Watercress prefers cold water.

HARVESTING: Cut shoots at any time.
EASY

298

Levisticum

Lycopersicon

Levisticum officinale   LOVAGE   PERENNIAL HERB
Umbelliferae, native to southern Europe   Zone 3

HABIT: Mounded, tropical looking plants grow 2-3' tall with Celery flavored leaves and hollow stalks up to 6' which carry clusters of small greenish-yellow flowers followed by light tan, aromatic seeds.

GERMINATION: Sow outdoors in fall or indoors in early spring, maintaining a temperature within the medium of 60-70° during germination which takes 10-14 days.

CULTURE: Plant 30-36" apart in full sun or part shade in rich, moist garden loam.

HARVESTING: Cut leaves at any time for fresh use. For dried leaves, cut stems above the second set of leaves and hang upside down. Seeds may be collected for use as flavorings. Cut fresh stalks and substitute for Celery.

EASY

Lycopersicon Lycopersicum   TOMATO   VEGETABLE
Solanaceae, native to the Andes
HABIT: This shrubby or vining plant grows to 6' or more and bears edible fruits, primarily red, in round, oblong or pear shapes. There are two types: determinate Tomatoes which are compact, 12-24", and stop height growth when they reach their inherent size, and indeterminate, which are the vining types which produce until killed by frost.
GERMINATION: Except in warm and long growing seasons when seeds can be started outdoors after all danger of frost has past, sow seeds indoors 5-7 weeks before last frost, maintaining a temperature within the medium of 70-75° during germination which takes 5-8 days.

CULTURE: Plant in full sun, in a rich, fertile, deep, well drained soil, 18-24" apart if they are to be staked and further apart if they are allowed to sprawl on the ground. Set plants out after nights are above 55°, and plant 2" deeper than they previously grew. Fertilize prior to planting and again lightly every month. Provide a stake, set at planting time, for indeterminate varieties. Mulch with organic matter or black plastic. Fruit set may be improved by spraying hormones on blossoms.

HARVESTING: Pick when red and juicy and keep picked to keep the vine producing. Green Tomatoes should be picked before frost and allowed to ripen indoors.

Marrubium *Matricaria*

Marrubium vulgare HOREHOUND PERENNIAL HERB
Labiatae, native to the Mediterranean Zone 3

HABIT: The spreading plant grows 18-24″ high and has deeply veined, wrinkled, woolly, aromatic leaves covering square stems. The stems, themselves covered in gray down, bear small, white, sharply lobed, tubular flowers in whorls from June to August.

GERMINATION: Sow outdoors anytime from early spring, up to two months before frost. Germination takes 10-14 days.

CULTURE: Plant in full sun, 12-15″ apart, in an average, well drained garden soil. Horehound is difficult to transplant. It tolerates hot and dry situations and poor soil, and tends to be weedy.

HARVESTING: Harvest leaves at any time.

EASY

Matricaria recutita CHAMOMILE ANNUAL HERB
Compositae, native to Europe and west Asia

HABIT: This sweet-scented, many branched plant grows 2-2½′ high and has finely cut leaves and daisy-like flowers with yellow discs and white rays (petals).

GERMINATION: Sow where plants are to grow outdoors in early spring as soon as soil can be worked, or sow indoors, maintaining a temperature within the medium of 55° during germination which takes 10-12 days.

CULTURE: Plant 6-12″ apart in full sun and a dry, light, sandy, well drained soil.

HARVESTING: Cut foliage for scenting purposes at any time; cut dried flower heads for tea.

Melissa   *Mentha*

Melissa officinalis   BALM, LEMON BALM   PERENNIAL HERB
Labiatae, native to southern Europe   Zone 4

HABIT: This hardy perennial grows to 2' with lemon scented, rough leaves of deep green that are heart shaped and deeply veined on square stems. Yellow buds open into tiny white flowers during summer. It is a good source of bee forage.

GERMINATION: Sow outdoors in early spring as soon as soil can be worked, or sow indoors, maintaining a temperature within the medium of 70° during germination which takes 14 days. Do not cover the seed.

CULTURE: Plant 12" apart in light shade in a poor, light, sandy, well drained soil. Balm tolerates dry soil but does better if kept moderately moist. It tends to be weedy. Shear back after flowering to keep compact.

HARVESTING: Pick leaves at any time for fresh use or drying.

Mentha species   MINT   PERENNIAL HERB
Labiatae, native to temperate Europe   Zone 3

HABIT: Mints are aromatic herbs with square stems and flowers produced in a circle around the stem. They increase by underground runners. *Mentha aquatica* var. *crispa* grows 3' high, has crisped or crinkled leaves and purple flowers in summer. *Mentha* X *piperita,* 2-3' tall, has purple tinged, pointed leaves and purple flowers in late summer and fall. *Mentha spicata* grows 1-2' high, is sprawling, has bright green pointed leaves and lavender flowers. *Mentha aquatica* var. *crispa* is commonly known as Curled Mint; *M. X piperita* as Peppermint; *M. spicata* as Spearmint.

GERMINATION: Sow seeds outdoors in spring through summer up to two months before frost. Indoors, maintain a temperature within the medium of 70° during germination which takes 12-16 days.

CULTURE: Plant 12" apart in full sun or part shade, in a rich, light, moist, well drained soil. Mint can become an invasive pest.

HARVESTING: Pick leaves at any time for fresh use. For drying, pick just before flowers open and hang upside down in a dry, dark place.

301

Nepeta

Nasturtium officinale   WATERCRESS   PERENNIAL HERB
Cruciferae, native to Europe   Zone 4

HABIT: Watercress is an aquatic plant with thin, divided leaves and terminal tufts of 4-petaled flowers. It has a pungent flavor and odor.

GERMINATION: Sow outdoors in early spring through summer in a source of water such as a stream, bog or pond. Indoors, sow in medium kept constantly wet and at a temperature of 55° during germination which takes 7-10 days. Do not cover the seed.

CULTURE: Grow in a stream, pond or bog. If that is unavailable, grow in the shade in an area that is very rich and can be kept constantly wet, 3″ apart. Watercress may also be grown in tanks or tubs by placing a few inches of rich soil in the bottom, setting the plants in the soil, and filling the tank with water to the tips of the shoots. If the water does not run constantly, change it once a week. Watercress prefers cold water.

HARVESTING: Cut shoots at any time.

Nepeta species   CATMINT   PERENNIAL HERB
Labiatae, native to Eurasia   Zone 3

HABIT: *Nepeta* grows in mounds of aromatic, silvery-grey foliage covered during summer with tiny flowers on square stems. *Nepeta Cataria,* also known as Catnip, grows to 3′ with spikes of white flowers that have pale purple spots. *Nepeta Mussinii* is a spreading plant, 1′ high, with loose racemes of lavender-blue flowers. Cats love this plant, which is good or bad, depending on your feelings about cats.

GERMINATION: Sow outdoors in early spring as soon as soil can be worked, or sow indoors, maintaining a temperature within the medium of 60-70° during germination which takes 7-10 days.

CULTURE: Plant 6-15″ apart in full sun and almost any well drained garden soil. *Nepeta* thrives in hot, dry, poor, sandy soils. To encourage a second bloom, cut flower stalks back to the foliage after the first flowers have faded. It can become weedy.

HARVESTING: Cut leaves and shoots at any time.

Ocimum

Origanum

Ocimum Basilicum   BASIL   ANNUAL HERB
Labiatae, native to the Old World tropics

HABIT: This plant grows 15-24″ high with broad, clove scented leaves. Spikes of white to purplish flowers bloom in summer. The variety 'Dark Opal' has purple leaves, pink flowers and is as useful as an ornamental and as an herb.

GERMINATION: Sow outdoors where plants are to grow after all danger of frost has past, or start indoors 6-8 weeks before last frost, maintaining a temperature within the medium of 70° during germination which takes 7-10 days.

CULTURE: Plant 10-12″ apart in full sun and a dry, light, medium rich, well drained soil. Basil may also be grown indoors in a sunny window.

HARVESTING: Cut leaves anytime for fresh use. For drying, cut leaves as flowers begin to open.

Origanum Majorana   ANNUAL HERB
              MARJORAM, SWEET MARJORAM
(Majorana hortensis)
Labiatae, native to the Mediterranean

HABIT: This 2′ plant has velvety, oval, 1″ aromatic leaves of grey-green and spikes of tiny white or lilac flowers in midsummer.

GERMINATION: Sow outdoors in early spring as soon as soil can be worked, or sow indoors, maintaining a temperature within the medium of 70° during germination which takes 8-14 days.

CULTURE: Plant 6-8″ apart in full sun and a light, slightly rich, sandy, well drained soil.

HARVESTING: Pick leaves and stems at any time for fresh use and just before blooming for dried use.

EASY

303

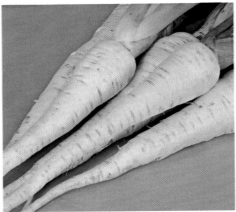

Pastinaca   Petroselinum

Pastinaca sativa   PARSNIPS   VEGETABLE
Umbelliferae, native to Eurasia

HABIT: Parsnips are biennials grown as annuals with thick 18-36" tops and large, carrot-like, white edible roots with a sweet flavor.

GERMINATION: Soak seeds for 24 hours before sowing. Sow outdoors in early spring as soon as soil can be worked, ½" deep in rows 15-18" apart. As they are slow to germinate, taking 21-25 days, seeds may also be sown mixed with Radish seeds. Germination percentage is poor, so sow heavily. Parsnip seed is not long lived and should be stored in the refrigerator. In Zone 8 and warmer, seed may be sown in fall for harvest the following spring.

CULTURE: Soil must be deep, fertile, light, preferably sandy and well drained. Thin to 3-4" apart when 1" tall. Fertilize prior to planting and again mid-way through the season. It is most important to keep Parsnips well weeded. The growing season is a long one. The tale that Parsnips are toxic if allowed to grow a second year is unproved.

HARVESTING: Dig any time after frost and store in a cool place or leave in the ground all winter and dig as needed.

Petroselinum crispum   PARSLEY   ANNUAL HERB
Umbelliferae, native to Europe and west Asia

HABIT: The common Parsley is *P. crispum* var. *crispum,* a biennial grown as an annual. The plant grows 12-18" and has divided, curled, crisped, dark green foliage. Var. *tuberosum,* Hamburg Parsley, is grown for its edible, parsnip-like roots. Its foliage is flat.

GERMINATION: Soak seeds in warm water for 24 hours before sowing. Sow outdoors 2-4 weeks before last frost, ¼" deep in rows 12" apart. In warm climates, sow outdoors in early fall. Seed may also be sown indoors 8 weeks before last frost, maintaining a temperature within the medium of 70-75° during germination which takes 14-21 days. Since Parsley is difficult to transplant, sow into individual pots. Completely cover the seed as darkness aids germination.

CULTURE: Grow in full sun or light shade, 6-8" apart, in a rich, deep, well drained soil. Fertilize when plants are 4" tall and again one month later. Parsley may also be grown indoors on a sunny windowsill.

HARVESTING: Pick leaves at any time. If the plant is allowed to grow a second year, pick leaves before the flowers open. Hamburg Parsley is dug in fall after frost, and is used for flavoring or as a vegetable. Its leaves have little flavor.

Phaseolus limensis   *Phaseolus lunatus*

Phaseolus limensis, LIMA BEAN   VEGETABLE
Phaseolus lunatus
Leguminosae, native to tropical South America

HABIT: This tender annual grows in bush or climbing form and bears long, flat, green pods containing green, white or speckled edible seeds with a meaty consistency and nutty flavor. *Phaseolus lunatus* is also known as Butter Bean.

GERMINATION: Sow 2" deep outdoors after all danger of frost is past and soil is warm. Sow bush varieties 3-6" apart, in rows 18-24" apart, and pole varieties 6-8" apart, in rows 36" apart. Innoculate with a nitrogen fixing bacteria prior to sowing. Germination takes 7-10 days. Seeds can be started indoors 4 weeks before planting outside, maintaining a temperature within the medium of 70°. Start in individual pots.

CULTURE: Grow in full sun in a rich, sandy, well drained soil. Pole varieties may be grown around tripods with 3 plants growing in hills at the base of each leg. If a tripod is not used, a fence, trellis or strings will be needed for support. Fertilize prior to planting and again when plants are 6-8" tall. Keep well watered. Bush Beans will bear earlier than pole varieties, but pole varieties will bear over a longer period. Lima Beans need a longer and milder growing season than Green Beans; the pole varieties may not bear in the north. To keep down chances of disease, don't work in the garden when foliage is wet.

HARVESTING: Pick after seeds are full size but before pods begin to turn yellow, and shell before cooking.

Phaseolus vulgaris   *Phaseolus vulgaris*

Phaseolus vulgaris   GREEN BEAN   VEGETABLE
Leguminosae, native to tropical America

HABIT: This species contains plants known as Green Bean, Snap Bean, French Bean, String Bean, Wax Bean, Kidney Bean and Pinto Bean. Annual plants are in bush or climbing forms with pea-like flowers followed by long yellow, purple or green pods which contain large edible seeds. Unlike the Lima Bean, these Beans are eaten when immature.

GERMINATION: Sow outdoors 1½-2" deep where plants are to grow after all danger of frost has past. Sow bush varieties 2-3" apart in rows 18-24" apart and pole varieties 6-8" apart in rows 36" apart. Innoculate with a nitrogen fixing bacteria prior to sowing. Germination takes 6-10 days. Seeds may also be started indoors in individual pots 3 weeks before planting outside, maintaining a temperature within the medium of 70° during germination. Plant bush varieties successively every 2 weeks until 2 months before frost for a continuous crop.

CULTURE: Grow in full sun in a loose, rich, neutral, well drained soil. Pole varieties must be trained on a tripod, trellis, fence or other support. Fertilize prior to planting and again when plants are 6-8" tall. Keep well watered. Bush Beans will mature faster than Pole Beans, but Pole Beans are more productive. To cut down on disease, don't work in the garden when the foliage is wet.

HARVESTING: Harvest prior to maturity when beans are succulent and keep beans picked or the plants will stop producing. For dried beans, allow the beans to remain on the bush until pods are dry or begin to shatter.

EASY

Pisum   *Pisum*

Pimpinella Anisum   ANISE   ANNUAL HERB
Umbelliferae, native to Greece and Egypt

HABIT: Dainty, spreading herb 18-24″ high has small, lacy leaves and 2″ clusters of tiny white flowers in summer. Following the flowers are small, grey, licorice flavored seeds.

GERMINATION: Sow outdoors after danger of frost has past, or sow indoors, maintaining a temperature within the medium of 70° during germination which takes 20-28 days. Sow in individual pots as Anise resents transplanting. Anise seeds are not long lived and should not be stored.

CULTURE: Plant in full sun, 6-8″ apart, in a dry, light, sandy, rich, slightly acid soil. Support may be needed.

HARVESTING: Cut leaves anytime. Gather seeds as they form and dry in a dark, cool room.

Pisum sativum   PEA   VEGETABLE
Leguminosae, native to Eurasia

HABIT: This shrubby or vining plant grows from 2-6′ and produces white flowers and pods of edible Peas. Peas are classified as smooth or wrinkled, the wrinkled being sweeter and superior. Edible-podded Peas, known as Snow Peas or Sugar Peas, have thicker, softer, edible pods.

GERMINATION: As Peas are a cool and humid weather crop, sow seeds outdoors in early spring as soon as soil can be worked. Sow successively every 10-14 days until 2 months before 75° temperatures. In Zone 8 and warmer, sow in fall for winter crop. Sow seeds 1-2″ deep in rows 18-24″ apart for dwarf varieties and 30-36″ apart for taller, vining types. Innoculate seeds with a nitrogen fixing bacteria prior to sowing. Germination takes 7-10 days.

CULTURE: Grow in a fertile, sandy, rich, deep, well drained soil, thinning to 1-2″ apart. A double row of the vining types can be placed 2-3″ apart with 30″ between the double rows and a trellis between them. Grow in full sun.

HARVESTING: Pick in the morning when pods are fully swollen and round and before the seeds become hard. Edible-podded Peas are picked when young, succulent and still flat.

Poterium   Raphanus

Poterium Sanguisorba   BURNET   PERENNIAL HERB
(Sanguisorba minor)
Rosaceae, native to Europe and west Asia

HABIT: A pretty 1½-2' herb has finely cut leaves bunched at the base of the plant. The stems bear small white or rose clusters in dense, oblong heads in early summer.

GERMINATION: Sow seeds outdoors in spring or summer up to two months before frost, or sow indoors, maintaining a temperature within the medium of 70° during germination which takes 8-10 days.

CULTURE: Plant 12-15" apart in full sun and a poor, infertile, sandy, limey, well drained soil. Burnet self sows readily unless flower heads are removed.

HARVESTING: Snip the cucumber-flavored leaves at any time.

EASY

Raphanus sativus   RADISH   VEGETABLE
Cruciferae, native to Eurasia

HABIT: Annual growing 6-8" high has enlarged edible roots which are round or elongated in white, red or bicolored.

GERMINATION: Sow outdoors as soon as soil can be worked in early spring, ½" deep in rows 6-12" apart. As Radishes are a cool weather crop, sow successively until midspring and start again in late summer. Germination takes 4-6 days. Sow for a fall and winter crop in Zone 8 and warmer.

CULTURE: Grow in full sun, 1-2" apart, in a loose, fertile, sandy, well drained soil. Fertilize prior to planting and again every 2 weeks with liquid fertilizer. Keep well watered.

HARVESTING: Pick when crisp and mildly flavored.

Rosmarinus   *Ruta*

Rosmarinus officinalis   ROSEMARY   PERENNIAL HERB
Labiatae, native to the Mediterranean   Zone 8

HABIT: This 3′ herb is treated as an annual in cooler sections. Leaves and stems have a lasting aromatic fragrance. Pale blue ½″ flowers bloom in winter and early spring and are surrounded by grey-green, needle-like evergreen foliage.

GERMINATION: Sow seeds outdoors in early spring as soon as soil can be worked, or sow indoors, maintaining a temperature within the medium of 55° during germination which takes 18-21 days.

CULTURE: Plant in full sun, 12-18″ apart, in a light, dry, limey, well drained soil. Rosemary will tolerate heat. It may also be grown indoors in full sun at 55° with a soil kept evenly moist.

HARVESTING: Cut leaves for fresh use or drying at any time. In areas where Rosemary is a perennial, cut leaves and stems as flowers open.

Ruta graveolens   RUE   PERENNIAL HERB
Rutaceae, native to southern Europe   Zone 4

HABIT: Evergreen, shrubby plants grow 1½-3′ and have fern-like, unpleasantly fragrant, blue-grey leaves. Small yellow flowers are produced in clusters in July.

GERMINATION: Sow outdoors where plants are to grow in early spring, or sow indoors, maintaining a temperature within the medium of 60-70° during germination which takes 10-14 days.

CULTURE: Plant 6-12″ apart in full sun and a poor, heavy, moist, well drained soil. Keep well watered. Prune back in early spring to induce branching from the base. Leaves are said to possibly cause dermatitis.

HARVESTING: Cut leaves at any time.

Salvia   Satureja

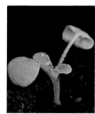

Salvia officinalis   GARDEN SAGE   PERENNIAL HERB
Labiatae, native to the Mediterranean   Zone 3

HABIT: Sage is a semi-shrubby 2-2½' herb with oblong, white, wooly leaves and flowers of violet-blue in spikes.

GERMINATION: Sow outdoors in early spring as soon as soil can be worked, or sow indoors, maintaining a temperature within the medium of 60-70° during germination which takes 14-21 days.

CULTURE: Plant 12-18" apart in full sun and a light, sandy, limey soil with good drainage. Cut back occasionally to induce bushiness.

HARVESTING: Cut the stem and leaves 5-6" long as the flowers are beginning to open and hang in the shade to dry.

Satureja hortensis   SUMMER SAVORY   ANNUAL HERB
Satureja montana   WINTER SAVORY   PERENNIAL HERB
    Labiatae, native to Europe

HABIT: Summer Savory is an annual with grey-green leaves, growing 12-18" high and bushy. The leaves are long and narrow; the flowers are white to pale lavender, blooming in summer. Winter Savory grows 6-12" high and is more spreading and slightly stiffer than Summer Savory. It is evergreen, or nearly so; flowers are pink to white, blooming in summer. Winter Savory is hardy to Zone 5.

GERMINATION: For best results, sow indoors in early spring, maintaining a temperature within the medium of 60-70° during germination which takes 10-15 days. Seeds of perennial types may take a little longer. Do not cover seeds as light is necessary for germination.

CULTURE: Plant in full sun, setting Summer Savory 8-12" apart and winter savory 12-15" apart. Soil should be sandy, light, well worked and with good drainage. Summer Savory prefers a richer soil than Winter Savory. Pinch tips of branches of Winter Savory to induce bushiness and prune back hard in the fall.

HARVESTING: Cut leafy tops when flowers are in bud for drying purposes. For fresh use, cut any time.

EASY

Sesamum   *Solanum*

Sesamum indicum   SESAME   ANNUAL HERB
Pedaliaceae, native to the Tropics

HABIT: This herb grows to 3' and is covered with attractive, long pointed leaves that are dark green and slightly hairy. Pale rose or white 1" flowers that are bell shaped bloom in summer.

GERMINATION: Sow outdoors where plants are to grow after all danger of frost has past, or sow indoors, maintaining a temperature within the medium of 68-86° during germination which takes 5-7 days. Indoor sowing should be done 6-8 weeks before last frost, and sow in individual pots, as Sesame does not like to be transplanted.

CULTURE: Space 8-10" apart in full sun in average, well drained soil. Sesame does best where summers are long and hot.

HARVESTING: Gather seeds when ripe.

Solanum Melongena   EGGPLANT   VEGETABLE
Solanaceae, native to Asia and Africa

HABIT: Bushy 2-3' plants bear 4 or more egg-shaped fruits up to 10" long at maturity. Fruits are generally smooth skinned and deep purple, although there are darker and lighter ones that also vary in shape and size.

GERMINATION: Sow seeds indoors, 8-10 weeks before night temperatures remain above 55°, maintaining a temperature within the medium of 70° during germination which takes 10-15 days. Seeds may be started outdoors only in warm areas with very long growing seasons.

CULTURE: Plant in full sun, 2-3' apart in rows 2½-3' apart. Soil must be rich, deep, loose and fertile. Fertilize prior to planting and again every 4-6 weeks. Keep plants weeded and well watered.

HARVESTING: Pick when 4" in diameter while still very shiny.

311

Solanum

Sorghum

Solanum tuberosum   POTATO   VEGETABLE
Solanaceae, native to Peru

HABIT: This weak stemmed annual grows 30-36″ high and produces edible underground tubers which form at the tip of underground stems and above the roots. Tubers are generally round or oblong and white or red.

GERMINATION: Potatoes are not grown from seed, but from pieces cut from certified "Seed Potatoes". Cut pieces 1½″ square that contain at least one eye and plant them 2-4″ deep and 9-12″ apart in rows 24-36″ apart, 2 weeks before last frost. Sprouts will appear in about 2 weeks.

CULTURE: Plant in full sun in a light, sandy, slightly acid, rich soil with excellent drainage. Fertilize prior to planting. When plants are 6-8″ tall, mound soil around the stem to keep Potatoes from turning green and repeat the mounding when plants are 18″ high. Keep plants well and evenly watered. Cool temperatures aid in the production of tubers.

HARVESTING: "New" Potatoes may be dug when the tops begin to flower. Harvest full size Potatoes 2 weeks after frost has blackened the tops.

Sorghum bicolor   SWEET SORGHUM   VEGETABLE
Saccharatum Group
Gramineae, native to China and South Africa

HABIT: This annual grows to 12′ and is coarse and grassy, resembling Corn. The stems contain a juice which is used to make syrups, as it is very sweet.

GERMINATION: Sow outdoors after all danger of frost has past and the soil is warm, 1″ deep in rows 24-30″ apart. Germination takes 7-10 days.

CULTURE: Grow in full sun, 10-14″ apart, in a deep, rich, sandy, well drained soil. Plant several rows together to insure proper pollination. Fertilize prior to planting and again when plants are 8″ high. Keep well watered.

HARVESTING: Cut the stem before the seeds mature when it is still soft.

EASY

Spinacia   *Thymus*

Spinacia oleracea   SPINACH   VEGETABLE
Chenopodiaceae, native to southwest Asia

HABIT: Spinach is an annual growing 1' high with rosettes of basal, dark green foliage 8-10" across. The leaves may be either smooth or crinkled (savoy).

GERMINATION: Sow outdoors in early spring as soon as soil can be worked and sow successively every 7-10 days until 6 weeks before daytime temperatures are above 75°. Sow again in late summer up to 6 weeks before 20° nights. Sow ½" deep in rows 15-18" apart. To hasten germination, seeds may be placed in the refrigerator in moistened medium for 1 week prior to sowing. Germination takes 8-10 days.

CULTURE: Thin plants to 4-5" apart and grow in full sun in a light, rich soil with excellent drainage. The pH should be as close to neutral as possible. Fertilize prior to planting and again after thinning. Spinach is a cool weather and short day crop so does not do well in summer. Keep well watered.

HARVESTING: Cut entire plant off at soil surface when leaves are 6-8" long and before the flower stalk forms.

Thymus hyemalis   WINTER THYME   PERENNIAL HERB
Thymus vulgaris   COMMON THYME
Labiatae, native to the Mediterranean   Zone 5

HABIT: Winter Thyme grows to 1' and is a shrubby plant with a grey cast and tiny deep rose flowers in dense clusters. Common Thyme is a stiff ground cover, 6-12" high, with ½" aromatic, grey-green leaves and small blue-violet flowers in clusters. The flowers appear in spring and the foliage is evergreen in most sections.

GERMINATION: Sow outdoors in early spring or indoors, maintaining a temperature within the medium of 55° during germination which takes 21-30 days.

CULTURE: Plant 6-8" apart in full sun and a light, sandy, well drained soil that is kept on the dry side. Keep plants clipped to keep them bushy.

313

Vigna radiata   *Vigna unguiculata*

Vigna radiata   MUNG BEAN   VEGETABLE
Leguminosae, native to Indonesia

HABIT: This hairy plant grows to 3' and produces yellow flowers if grown to maturity, but is usually grown for young bean sprouts.

GERMINATION: Rinse seeds in a solution of one tablespoon of household bleach to one quart of water and rinse in water. Germinate in a shallow dish by keeping seeds moist, but not wet. No medium is needed, and a layer of paper towels will help in keeping the moisture level right. Germination takes 3-5 days.

HARVESTING: Beans are ready for eating as soon as fully sprouted.

EASY

Vigna unguiculata   COWPEA   VEGETABLE
Leguminosae, native to the tropics

HABIT: This vine-like plant produces yellow to purple pea-like flowers and 8-12" pods of Peas that have dark "eyes". Black-eyed Peas are a well known part of this species. The Yard-long Bean also belongs here, with 1-3' pods that are used like Snap Beans.

GERMINATION: Sow outdoors where plants are to grow after all danger of frost has past and the soil is warm. Sow ½-1" deep in rows 24-36" apart. Germination takes 7-10 days. Innoculate seeds with a nitrogen fixing bacteria.

CULTURE: Grow in full sun, 3-4" apart, in a deep, rich, fertile, sandy soil. Cowpeas need a long, warm growing season.

HARVESTING: Pick when the shell is green and the seeds developed but not hard. An alternate method is to allow the seeds to ripen and store as for dried beans.

314

Zea Mays   *Zea Mays*

Zea Mays var. **rugosa**   SWEET CORN   VEGETABLE
Gramineae, native to the Americas

HABIT: This annual grows tall to 5-7' and has central stalks surrounded by broad and tapering grass-like leaves. The plant yields ears of Corn with seeds in colors of white, yellow or bicolored. There are also dwarf varieties which reach only several feet and produce ears 4-5" long.

GERMINATION: Sow outdoors after all danger of frost has past and the ground is warm, 1-1½" deep in rows 24-30" apart. Sow every two weeks until early summer for a continuous crop. Seeds may also be started indoors 4 weeks before planting outside, maintaining a temperature within the medium of 70° during germination which takes 5-7 days, but sow in individual pots as Corn does not like to be transplanted.

CULTURE: Grow in full sun, 10-14" apart, in a deep, rich, sandy, well drained soil. Plant several rows together, rather than in one long row, to insure proper pollination. Cultivate often but shallow and mulch to keep down weeds and conserve moisture. Fertilize prior to planting and again lightly when stalks are 8" high and 18" high. Keep well watered, especially from tasseling time to picking. Do not remove suckers.

HARVESTING: Pick Corn when the silks at the end of the ears turn brown and the kernels are filled with a milky juice.

315

APPENDIX

PLANTS FOR EASY CULTIVATION (Perfect for beginners or children)

Abutilon hybridum FLOWERING MAPLE
Acanthus mollis BEAR'S BREECH
Achillea species YARROW
Alcea rosea HOLLYHOCK
Allium Schoenoprasum CHIVES
Alyssum montanum BASKET OF GOLD
Amaranthus species SUMMER POINSETTIA, JOSEPH'S COAT, LOVE-LIES-
  BLEEDING
Ammobium alatum 'Grandiflora' WINGED EVERLASTING
Anchusa species ALKANET, BUGLOSS, SUMMER FORGET-ME-NOT
Anethum graveolens DILL
Anthemis tinctoria 'Kelwayi' GOLDEN MARGUERITE
Anthriscus cerefolium CHERVIL
Antirrhinum majus SNAPDRAGON
Aphanostephus skirrhobasis LAZY DAISY, PRAIRIE DAISY
Arabis species ROCK CRESS, WALL CRESS
Arachis hypogaea PEANUT
Arctotis stoechadifolia AFRICAN DAISY
Armeria maritima THRIFT, SEA PINK
Arnica montana MOUNTAIN ARNICA
Asarina antirrhinifolia MAURANDIA
Asclepias tuberosa BUTTERFLY WEED
Asphodeline lutea KING'S SPEAR, JACOB'S ROD
Avena sterilis ANIMATED OATS
Baptisia australis BLUE WILD INDIGO, FALSE INDIGO
Belamcanda species BLACKBERRY LILY
Bellis perennis ENGLISH DAISY
Beta vulgaris BEET, SWISS CHARD
Borago officinalis BORAGE
Bougainvillea hybrids PAPER FLOWER
Brachycome iberidifolia SWAN RIVER DAISY
Brassica species FLOWERING CABBAGE AND KALE, MUSTARD, TURNIP,
  COLLARDS, KALE, BROCCOLI
Briza maxima QUAKING GRASS
Buddleia Davidii BUTTERFLY BUSH
Calendula officinalis POT MARIGOLD
Campanula species BELLFLOWER
Capsicum annuum var. **annuum** PEPPER
Carum Carvi CARAWAY
Catananche caerulea CUPID'S DART
Catharanthus roseus PERIWINKLE
Celosia cristata COCKSCOMB
Centaurea Cyanus BACHELOR'S BUTTON, CORNFLOWER
Cerastium tomentosum SNOW-IN-SUMMER
Chrysanthemum carinatum and **coronarium** ANNUAL CHRYSANTHEMUM
Chrysanthemum coccineum PYRETHRUM, PAINTED DAISY
Chrysanthemum X morifolium CHRYSANTHEMUM

Chrysanthemum Parthenium   MATRICARIA, FEVERFEW
Chrysanthemum ptarmiciflorum   DUSTY MILLER
Cicer arietinum   CHICK PEA, GARBANZO BEAN
Cirsium japonicum   THISTLE
Cleome Hasslerana   SPIDER FLOWER
Coleus X hybridus   COLEUS
Coreopsis grandiflora   TICKSEED
Coriandrum sativum   CORIANDER
Corynocarpus laevigata   NEW ZEALAND LAUREL
Cosmos species   COSMOS
Crepis rubra   HAWK'S BEARD
Cucurbita Pepo var. **ovifera**   YELLOW FLOWERED GOURDS
Cuphea ignea   CIGAR FLOWER
Cynoglossum amabile   CHINESE FORGET-ME-NOT
Cyphomandra betacea   TREE TOMATO
Dahlia hybrids   DAHLIA
Daucus Carota   CARROT, QUEEN ANNE'S LACE
Dianthus species and hybrids   SWEET WILLIAM, CHINA PINK, CARNATION
Dichondra micrantha   DICHONDRA
Echinops exaltatus   GLOBE THISTLE
Echium species   BUGLOSS
Emilia javanica   PAINT BRUSH
Erigeron species   MIDSUMMER ASTER, FLEABANE
Erinus alpinus   ALPINE BALSAM
Eschscholzia californica   CALIFORNIA POPPY
Eucomis bicolor   PINEAPPLE LILY
Exacum affine   GERMAN VIOLET, PERSIAN VIOLET
Freesia X hybrida   FREESIA
Gaillardia species   BLANKET FLOWER
Gazania rigens   TREASURE FLOWER
Geranium sanguineum   CRANESBILL
Geum species   AVENS
Glycine Max   SOYBEAN
Gomphrena species   GLOBE AMARANTH
Gossypium hirsutum   ORNAMENTAL COTTON
Helianthus species   SUNFLOWER, JERUSALEM ARTICHOKE
Helichrysum bracteatum   STRAWFLOWER
Helipterum species   EVERLASTING, STRAWFLOWER
Hesperis matronalis   SWEET ROCKET
Hunnemannia fumariifolia   MEXICAN TULIP POPPY
Hypoestes phyllostachya   POLKA DOT PLANT
Hyssopus officinalis   HYSSOP
Impatiens Balsamina   GARDEN BALSAM
Impatiens Wallerana   IMPATIENS, PATIENT PLANT
Incarvillea Delavayi   HARDY GLOXINIA
Ipomoea Batatas   SWEET POTATO
Kniphofia Uvaria   RED HOT POKER, TRITOMA
Kochia scoparia   BURNING BUSH
Lagenaria siceraria   WHITE FLOWERED GOURDS
Lantana Camara   LANTANA
Lathyrus latifolius   PERENNIAL PEA
Lathyrus odoratus   SWEET PEA

Lavatera hybrids TREE MALLOW
Layia platyglossa TIDY TIPS
Lepidium sativum GARDEN CRESS
Levisticum officinale LOVAGE
Liatris species GAYFEATHER
Linaria maroccana TOADFLAX
Linum species FLAX
Lobularia maritima SWEET ALYSSUM
Lonas annua GOLDEN AGERATUM
Luffa aegyptiaca DISHRAG GOURD
Lunaria annua MONEY PLANT
Machaeranthera tanacetifolia TAHOKA DAISY
Malva Alcea MALLOW
Marrubium vulgare HOREHOUND
Matthiola species STOCK
Melissa officinalis BALM, LEMON BALM
Mentha species MINT
Mentzelia Lindleyi BLAZING STAR
Mimosa pudica SENSITIVE PLANT
Mirabilis Jalapa FOUR-O-CLOCK
Molucella laevis BELLS-OF-IRELAND
Monarda didyma BEE BALM
Myosotis species FORGET-ME-NOT
Nemophila Menziesii BABY BLUE EYES
Nepeta species CATMINT
Nicotiana alata FLOWERING TOBACCO
Nierembergera species CUPFLOWER
Nigella damascena LOVE-IN-A-MIST
Ocimum Basilicum BASIL
Oenothera species EVENING PRIMROSE
Oxypetalum caeruleum SOUTHERN STAR
Perilla frutescens BEEFSTEAK PLANT
Petroselinum crispum PARSLEY
Petunia X hybrida PETUNIA
Phaseolus species BEANS
Pimpinella Anisum ANISE
Platycodon grandiflorus BALLOON FLOWER
Polemonium caeruleum JACOB'S LADDER
Portulaca grandiflora ROSE MOSS
Poterium Sanguisorba BURNET
Raphanus sativus RADISH
Reseda odorata MIGNONETTE
Ricinus communis CASTOR BEAN
Rudbeckia hirta GLORIOSA DAISY
Salvia species SALVIA, SAGE
Saponaria Ocymoides SOAPWORT
Satureja species SAVORY
Scabiosa species PINCUSHION FLOWER
Schizanthus X wisetonensis BUTTERFLY FLOWER, POOR MAN'S ORCHID
Senecio species DUSTY MILLER, CINERARIA
Sesamum indicum SESAME
Silene vulgaris subsp. **maritima** SEA CAMPION
Solanum Melongena ORNAMENTAL EGGPLANT

Sorghum bicolor SWEET SORGHUM
Stokesia laevis STOKES ASTER
Tagetes species MARIGOLD
Talinum paniculatum JEWELS OF OPAR
Thermopsis caroliniana CAROLINA LUPINE
Thunbergia species BLACK-EYED-SUSAN VINE
Thymus species THYME, MOTHER OF THYME
Torenia Fournieri WISHBONE FLOWER
Trachymene coerulea BLUE LACE FLOWER
Trifolium procumbens SHAMROCK
Tropaeolum majus NASTURTIUM
Verbascum bombyciferum MULLEIN
Verbesina encelioides BUTTER DAISY
Veronica species SPEEDWELL
Vigna radicans MUNG BEAN
Viola species VIOLA, VIOLET, PANSY
Xanthisma texanum STAR OF TEXAS
Xeranthemum annuum IMMORTELLE
Zea Mays CORN
Zinnia species ZINNIA

SEEDS THAT REQUIRE SPECIAL TREATMENT

SEEDS THAT NEED LIGHT TO GERMINATE

Achillea species   YARROW
Ageratum Houstonianum   FLOSS FLOWER
Agrostis nebulosa   CLOUD GRASS
Alyssum montanum   BASKET OF GOLD
Anethum graveolens   DILL
Antirrhinum majus   SNAPDRAGON
Aquilegia species and hybrids   COLUMBINE
Arabis species   ROCK CRESS, WALL CRESS
Begonia species   BEGONIA
Brassica oleracea Acephala   FLOWERING CABBAGE
Browallia speciosa   BROWALLIA
Calceolaria crenatiflora   POCKETBOOK PLANT
Campanula species   BELLFLOWER
Capsicum annuum   ORNAMENTAL PEPPER
Chrysanthemum Parthenium   MATRICARIA, FEVERFEW
Chrysanthemum X superbum   SHASTA DAISY
Coffea arabica   ARABIAN COFFEE PLANT
Coleus X hybridus   COLEUS
Coreopsis grandiflora   TICKSEED
Cortaderia Selloana   PAMPAS GRASS
Crossandra infundibuliformis   CROSSANDRA
Cuphea ignea   CIGAR FLOWER
Daucus Carota   QUEEN ANNE'S LACE
Dizygotheca elegantissima   FALSE ARALIA
Dombeya Burgessiae   DOMBEYA
Doronicum cordatum   LEOPARD'S BANE
Exacum affine   GERMAN VIOLET, PERSIAN VIOLET
Ficus species   FIG
Fuchsia X hybrida   FUCHSIA
Gaillardia X grandiflora   BLANKET FLOWER
Gerbera Jamesonii hybrids   TRANSVAAL DAISY
Gloxinia gymnostoma   GLOXINIA
Grevillea robusta   SILK OAK
Helichrysum bracteatum   STRAWFLOWER
Hesperis matronalis   SWEET ROCKET
Impatiens Wallerana   IMPATIENS, PATIENT PLANT
Justicia aurea   KING'S CROWN
Kalanchoe Blossfeldiana   KALANCHOE
Lactuca sativa   LETTUCE
Lagerstroemia indica   CRAPE MYRTLETTES
Leontopodium species   EDELWEISS
Lobularia maritima   SWEET ALYSSUM
Lychnis chalcedonica   MALTESE CROSS
Matthiola species   STOCK
Molucella laevis   BELLS-OF-IRELAND
Nicotiana alata   FLOWERING TOBACCO
Papaver orientale   ORIENTAL POPPY
Perilla frutescens   BEEFSTEAK PLANT

Petunia X hybrida PETUNIA
Physalis Alkekengi CHINESE LANTERN
Platycodon grandiflorus BALLOON FLOWER
Primula species except **P. sinensis** PRIMROSE
Punica Granatum 'Nana' POMEGRANATE
Reseda odorata MIGNONETTE
Saintpaulia ionantha AFRICAN VIOLET
Sanvitalia procumbens CREEPING ZINNIA
Satureja species SAVORY
Sinningia species SINNINGIA
Smithiantha zebrina NAEGELIA, TEMPLE BELLS
Solanum Pseudocapsicum JERUSALEM CHERRY, CHRISTMAS CHERRY
Streptocarpus species CAPE PRIMROSE
Salvia species SALVIA (Red flowered varieties)
Tithonia rotundifolia MEXICAN SUNFLOWER
Venidium fastuosum MONARCH OF THE VELDT, CAPE DAISY

SEEDS THAT NEED DARKNESS TO GERMINATE

Asparagus asparagoides SMILAX
Borago officinalis BORAGE
Calendula officinalis POT MARIGOLD
Catharanthus roseus PERIWINKLE
Centaurea Cyanus BACHELOR'S BUTTON
Consolida ambigua LARKSPUR
Coriandrum sativum CORIANDER
Cyclamen species CYCLAMEN
Cynoglossum amabile CHINESE FORGET-ME-NOT
Delphinium species DELPHINIUM
Foeniculum species FENNEL
Gazania rigens TREASURE FLOWER
Lathyrus odoratus SWEET PEA
Lonas annua GOLDEN AGERATUM
Mesembryanthemum chrystallinum ICE PLANT
Mimosa pudica SENSITIVE PLANT
Myosotis species FORGET-ME-NOT
Nemesia strumosa POUCH NEMESIA
Nertera granadensis BEAD PLANT
Papaver species except **P. orientale** POPPY
Phlox species PHLOX
Primula sinensis CHINESE PRIMROSE
Psylliostachys Suworowii SEA LAVENDER, STATICE
Salpiglossis sinuata PAINTED TONGUE
Saponaria Ocymoides SOAPWORT
Schizanthus X wisetonensis BUTTERFLY FLOWER, POOR MAN'S ORCHID
Trachymene coerulea BLUE LACE FLOWER
Trifolium procumbens SHAMROCK

Tropaeolum majus NASTURTIUM
Verbena species VERVAIN
Viola species VIOLA, VIOLET, PANSY

SEEDS THAT REQUIRE SOAKING BEFORE SOWING

Abelmoschus esculentus OKRA
Albizia distachya PLUME ACACIA, PLUME ALBIZIA
Armeria maritima THRIFT, SEA PINK
Asparagus species ASPARAGUS, ASPARAGUS FERN, SMILAX
Caesalpina Gilliesii POINCIANA
Camellia Sasanqua SASANQUA CAMELLIA
Camellia sinensis TEA PLANT
Canna X generalis CANNA
Cercis canadensis REDBUD
Chamaedora elegans 'Bella' PARLOR PALM, NEANTA BELLA
Clitoria Ternata BUTTERFLY PEA
Coffea arabica ARABIAN COFFEE PLANT
Coix Lacryma-Jobi JOB'S TEARS
Cucurbita Pepo var. **ovifera** YELLOW FLOWERED GOURDS
Cytisus scoparius SCOTCH BROOM
Ensete ventricosum BANANA
Erythrina crista-galli COCKSPUR CORAL TREE
Freesia X hybrida FREESIA
Grevillea robusta SILK OAK
Hibiscus species MALLOW
Ipomoea species MORNING GLORY et al
Laburnum anagyroides GOLDEN CHAIN
Lagenaria siceraria WHITE FLOWERED GOURDS
Lathyrus latifolius PERENNIAL PEA
Lathyrus odoratus SWEET PEA
Liriope Muscari LILY TURF
Lupinus species LUPINES
Merremia tuberosa WOODROSE
Mina lobata FLAG OF SPAIN
Pastinaca sativa PARSNIPS
Petroselinum crispum PARSLEY
Pueraria lobata KUDZU VINE
Sophora japonica 'Pendula' JAPANESE PAGODA TREE
Strelitzia reginae BIRD OF PARADISE
Thermopsis caroliniana CAROLINE LUPINE
Wisteria sinensis CHINESE WISTERIA

SEEDS THAT NEED STRATIFICATION BEFORE SOWING (Cold Treatment)

Aconitum Carmichaelii and hybrids   MONKSHOOD
Allium species   FLOWERING ONION
Angelica Archangelica   ANGELICA
Aquilegia species and hybrids   COLUMBINE
Brassica Oleracea Acerphala   FLOWERING CABBAGE
Calluna vulgaris   HEATHER
Camellia sinensis   TEA PLANT
Campsis radicans   TRUMPET VINE, TRUMPET CREEPER
Cercis canadensis   REDBUD
Clematis virginiana   VIRGIN'S BOWER
Cornus species   DOGWOOD
Cupressus sempervirens 'Stricta'   PYRAMIDAL ITALIAN CYPRESS
Dicentra spectabilis   BLEEDING HEART
Dictamnus albus   GAS PLANT
Dodecatheon Meadia   SHOOTING STAR
Elaeagnus angustifolius   RUSSIAN OLIVE
Franklinia Alatamaha   FRANKLIN TREE
Gentiana species   GENTIAN
Ginkgo biloba   MAIDENHAIR TREE
Helleborus niger   CHRISTMAS ROSE
Hemerocallis hybrids   DAYLILY
Ilex Aquifolium   ENGLISH HOLLY
Iris species   IRIS
Kalmia latifolia   MOUNTAIN LAUREL
Lavandula angustifolia   LAVENDER
Lewisia rediviva   BITTER ROOT
Lilium (some species)   LILY
Lobelia species   LOBELIA (Perennial)
Machaeranthera tanacetifolia   TAHOKA DAISY
Magnolia grandiflora   SOUTHERN MAGNOLIA

Paeonia suffruticosa   TREE PEONY
Phlox paniculata   PHLOX (perennial)
Picea species   SPRUCE (most species)
Pinus Mugo   SWISS MOUNTAIN PINE
Primula species   PRIMROSE
Rosa species   ROSE
Taxus baccata   ENGLISH YEW
Trillium ovatum   WAKE ROBIN
Trollius europaeus   GLOBEFLOWER
Viburnum Opulus 'Roseum'   SNOWBALL BUSH
Viola species   VIOLA, VIOLET, PANSY

SEEDS THAT MUST BE SCARIFIED BEFORE SOWING (Nicked or filed)

Albizia distachya   PLUME ALBIZIA, PLUME ACACIA
Baptisia australis   BLUE WILD INDIGO, FALSE INDIGO
Canna X generalis   CANNA
Cassia alata   CANDLE BUSH
Clitoria Ternata   BUTTERFLY PEA
Coronilla varia   CROWN VETCH
Hibiscus species   MALLOW
Ipomoea species   MORNING GLORY et al
Laburnum anagyroides   GOLDEN CHAIN
Lathyrus species   PERENNIAL AND SWEET PEA
Lupinus species   LUPINES
Merremia tuberosa   WOODROSE
Mina lobata   FLAG OF SPAIN
Pueraria lobata   KUDZU VINE
Sophora japonica 'Pendula'   JAPANESE PAGODA TREE
Thermopsis caroliniana   CAROLINA LUPINE
Wisteria sinensis   CHINESE WISTERIA

SEEDS THAT NEED COOL TEMPERATURE (55°) TO GERMINATE

Acanthus mollis   BEAR'S BREECH
Agrostis nebulosa   CLOUD GRASS
Alstroemeria aurantiaca hybrids   PERUVIAN LILY
Anaphalis margaritacea   PEARLY EVERLASTING
Arenaria montana   MOUNTAIN SANDWORT
Arnica montana   MOUNTAIN ARNICA
Aubrieta detoidea   FALSE ROCK CRESS, PURPLE ROCK CRESS
Bergenia cordifolia   HEART LEAF BERGENIA
Briza maxima   QUAKING GRASS
Cheiranthus Cheiri   WALLFLOWER
Chiastophyllum oppositifolium   SILVER CROWN
Cytisus scoparius   BROOM
Dictamnus albus   GAS PLANT
Erigeron species   MIDSUMMER ASTER, FLEABANE
Eschscholzia californica   CALIFORNIA POPPY
Felicia amelloides   BLUE DAISY
Fragaria Vesca   STRAWBERRY
Globularia cordifolia   BLUE GLOBE DAISY
Heuchera sanguinea   CORAL BELLS
Iberis sempervirens   CANDYTUFT
Incarvillea Delavayi   HARDY GLOXINIA
Ipomopsis rubra   SKYROCKET

Laburnum anagyroides   GOLDEN CHAIN
Lagurus ovatus   HARE'S TAIL GRASS
Lathyrus latifolius   PERENNIAL PEA
Lathyrus odoratus   SWEET PEA
Leontopodium species   EDELWEISS
Linaria maroccana   TOADFLAX
Matricaria recutita   CHAMOMILE
Mentzelia Lindleyi   BLAZING STAR
Molucella laevis   BELLS-OF-IRELAND
Nemophila Menziesii   BABY BLUE EYES
Papaver species   POPPY
Penstemon hybrids   BEARD-TONGUE

Phlox Drummondi   ANNUAL PHLOX
Picea Abies   NORWAY SPRUCE
Pittosporum Tobira   JAPANESE PITTOSPORUM
Rhododendron species   AZALEA, RHODODENDRON
Rosa species   ROSE
Rosmarinus officinalis   ROSEMARY
Sagina subulata   PEARLWORT
Thymus species   THYME, MOTHER OF THYME
Yucca filamentosa   ADAM'S NEEDLE

SEEDS THAT SHOULD BE SOWN AS SOON AS POSSIBLE (They are not long lived and should not be stored)

Angelica Archangelica   ANGELICA
Anthurium species   FLAMINGO FLOWER
Asparagus species   ASPARAGUS FERN, SMILAX
Chrysanthemum coccineum   PYRETHRUM, PAINTED DAISY
Clivia Belgian hybrids   KAFFIR LILY
Corynocarpus laevigata   NEW ZEALAND LAUREL
Delphinium species   DELPHINIUM
Dimorphoteca sinuata   CAPE MARIGOLD
Franklinia Alatamaha   FRANKLIN TREE
Geranium sanguineum   CRANESBILL
Gerbera Jamesonii hybrids   TRANSVAAL DAISY
Ginkgo biloba   MAIDENHAIR TREE
Kochia scoparia   BURNING BUSH
Lilium regale   ROYAL LILY
Livistona chinensis   CHINESE FAN PALM
Magnolia grandiflora   SOUTHERN MAGNOLIA
Monstera deliciosa   SWISS CHEESE PLANT, CUT LEAF PHILODENDRON
Passiflora species   PASSION FLOWER, PURPLE GRANADILLA
Philodendron species   LOVE PLANT
Potentilla nepalensis   CINQUEFOIL
Salvia splendens   SCARLET SAGE
Sophora japonica 'Pendula' JAPANESE PAGODA TREE
Strelitzia reginae   BIRD OF PARADISE

HARDY ANNUALS (Seeds that may be sown outdoors in early spring as soon as soil can be worked and will not be affected by late spring frosts)

Agrostis nebulosa CLOUD GRASS
Allium Ampeloprasum LEEK
Allium Cepa ONION
Anethum graveolens DILL
Anthriscus Cerefolium CHERVIL
Arctotis species and hybrids AFRICAN DAISY
Beta vulgaris BEET, SWISS CHARD
Borago officinalis BORAGE
Briza maxima QUAKING GRASS
Brassica species BROCCOLI, BRUSSELS SPROUTS, CABBAGE, CAULIFLOWER, CHINESE CABBAGE, COLLARDS, KALE, KOHLRABI, MUSTARD, TURNIP
Centaurea Cyanus BACHELOR'S BUTTON, CORNFLOWER
Chenopodium Botrys AMBROSIA, FEATHER GERANIUM
Consolida Ambigua LARKSPUR
Coriandrum sativum CORIANDER
Cynoglossum amabile CHINESE FORGET-ME-NOT
Daucus Carota var. **sativa** CARROT
Echium species BUGLOSS
Eruca vesicaria ROCKET
Eschscholzia californica CALIFORNIA POPPY
Felicia species BLUE DAISY, BLUE MARGUERITE
Gypsophila species BABY'S BREATH
Helipterum roseum EVERLASTING
Lactuca sativa LETTUCE
Lepidium sativum GARDEN CRESS
Lobularia maritima SWEET ALYSSUM
Machaeranthera tanacetifolia TAHOKA DAISY
Matricaria recutita CHAMOMILE
Mentzelia Lindleyi BLAZING STAR
Molucella laevis BELLS-OF-IRELAND
Nemophila Menziesii BABY BLUE EYES
Nigella damascena LOVE-IN-A-MIST
Origanum Majorana MARJORAM
Pastinaca sativa PARSNIPS

Petroselinum crispum PARSLEY
Phlox Drummondi ANNUAL PHLOX
Pisum sativum PEA
Raphanus sativus RADISH
Reseda odorata MIGNONETTE
Spinacia oleracea SPINACH
Xanthisma texanum STAR OF TEXAS

SEEDLINGS THAT RESENT TRANSPLANTING (Sow seeds where they are to grow or in individual pots)

Anethum graveolens DILL
Anthriscus Cerefolium CHERVIL
Borage officinalis BORAGE
Carum Carvi CARAWAY
Coriandrum sativum CORIANDER
Cucumis Melo MELONS
Cucumis sativus CUCUMBERS
Eschscholtzia californica CALIFORNIA POPPY
Foeniculum species FENNEL
Ipomoea species CARDINAL CLIMBER, CYPRESS VINE
Ipomopsis rubra SKYROCKET, STANDING CYPRESS
Lavatera hybrids TREE MALLOW
Linum species FLAX
Lupinus species LUPINES
Papaver species POPPY
Perilla frutescens BEEFSTEAK PLANT
Petroselinum crispum PARSLEY
Phlox Drummondi ANNUAL PHLOX
Pimpinella Anisum ANISE
Reseda odorata MIGNONETTE
Sanvitalia procumbens CREEPING ZINNIA
Sesamum indicum SESAME
Trachymene coerulea BLUE LACE FLOWER
Tropaeolum majus NASTURTIUM
Verbesina encelioides BUTTER DAISY
Xeranthemum annuum IMMORTELLE
Zea Mays CORN

PLANTS FOR SPECIAL PLACES

PLANTS FOR A COOL GREENHOUSE (50° nights)

Albizia distachya PLUME ALBIZIA, PLUME ACACIA
Allium species FLOWERING ONION
Alstroemeria aurantiaca hybrids PERUVIAN LILY
Antirrhinum majus SNAPDRAGON
Asparagus asparagoides SMILAX
Brachycome iberidifolia SWAN RIVER DAISY
Cacti CACTUS
Calceolaria crenatiflora POCKETBOOK PLANT
Calendula officinalis POT MARIGOLD
Callistephus chinensis ASTER, CHINA ASTER
Camellia Sasanqua SASANQUA CAMELLIA
Cassia alata CANDLE BUSH
Celsia Arcturus CRETAN BEAR'S TAIL
Chrysanthemum X morifolium CHRYSANTHEMUM
Cladanthus arabicus PALM SPRINGS DAISY
Clarkia hybrids ROCKY MOUNTAIN GARLAND
Clivia Belgian hybrids KAFFIR LILY
Cobaea scandens CUP AND SAUCER VINE
Cuphea ignea CIGAR FLOWER
Cyclamen persicum FLORISTS' CYCLAMEN
Cymbalaria muralis KENILWORTH IVY
Cyperus alternifolius UMBRELLA PLANT
Dichondra micrantha DICHONDRA
Dimorphoteca sinuata CAPE MARIGOLD
Dodecatheon Meadia SHOOTING STAR
Freesia X hybrida FREESIA
Fuchsia X hybrida FUCHSIA
Gerbera Jamesonii hybrids TRANSVAAL DAISY
Gladiolus X hortulanus GLADIOLUS
Grevillea robusta SILK OAK
Gypsophila species BABY'S BREATH
Incarvillea Delavayi HARDY GLOXINIA
Lagerstroemia indica CRAPE MYRTLETTES
Leontopodium species EDELWEISS
Lewisia rediviva BITTER ROOT
Lilium species LILY
Linaria maroccana TOADFLAX
Lobularia maritima SWEET ALYSSUM
Mimulus species MONKEY FLOWER
Myosotis species FORGET-ME-NOT
Nemophila Menziesii BABY BLUE EYES
Nertera granadensis BEADPLANT
Petunia X hybrida PETUNIA
Pittosporum Tobira JAPANESE PITTOSPORUM
Primula species PRIMROSE
Ranunculus asiaticus PERSIAN RANUNCULUS, PERSIAN BUTTERCUP
Rehmannia elata BEVERLY BELLS

Reseda odorata MIGNONETTE
Salpiglossis sinuata PAINTED TONGUE
Saxifraga species ROCKFOIL
Sempervivum species HOUSELEEK, LIVE FOREVER
Solanum Pseudocapsicum JERUSALEM CHERRY, CHRISTMAS CHERRY
Trifolium procumbens SHAMROCK

PLANTS FOR AN INTERMEDIATE GREENHOUSE (55° nights)

Abutilon hybridum FLOWERING MAPLE
Acanthus mollis BEAR'S BREECH
Adiantum species MAIDENHAIR FERN
Agapanthus africanus LILY OF THE NILE
Anemone species WINDFLOWER
Arctotis stoechadifolia grandis AFRICAN DAISY
Asarina antirrhinifolia MAURANDIA
Browallia speciosa BROWALLIA
Catharanthus roseus PERIWINKLE
Clitoria Ternata BUTTERFLY PEA
Echeveria X derenosa hybrids ECHEVERIA
Eucnide bartonioides ROCK NETTLE, MICROSPERMA
Eucomis bicolor PINEAPPLY LILY
Fatsia japonica JAPANESE ARALIA
Felicia species BLUE DAISY, BLUE MARGUERITE, KINGFISHER DAISY
Galtonia candicans SUMMER HYACINTH
Lavatera hybrids TREE MALLOW
Lithops species LIVING STONES
Lobelia Erinus LOBELIA
Nicotiana alata FLOWERING TOBACCO
Oxypetalum caeruleum SOUTHERN STAR
Passiflora species PASSION FLOWER, PURPLE GRANADILLA
Perilla frutescens BEEFSTEAK PLANT
Phygelius capensis CAPE FUCHSIA
Pseudopanax Lessonii PSEUDOPANAX
Punica Granatum 'Nana' POMEGRANATE
Sedum species STONECROP
Senecio X hybridus CINERARIA
Strelitzia reginae BIRD OF PARADISE
Tetranema roseum MEXICAN FOXGLOVE, RED VIOLET
Venidium fatuosum MONARCH OF THE VELDT, CAPE DAISY
Washingtonia robusta MEXICAN FAN PALM

PLANTS FOR A WARM GREENHOUSE (60° nights)

Achimenes hybrids   MAGIC FLOWER, NUT ORCHID
Aeschynanthus radicans   LIPSTICK PLANT, ROYAL RED BUGLER
Aloe variegata   TIGER ALOE
Amaranthus species   SUMMER POINSETTIA, JOSEPH'S COAT, LOVE-LIES-
BLEEDING
Anthurium species   FLAMINGO FLOWER
Antigonon leptopus   CORALVINE
Asparagus species   ASPARAGUS FERNS
Asplenium nidus   BIRD'S NEST FERN
Begonia species   BEGONIA
Bougainvillea hybrids   PAPER FLOWER
Caesalpinum Gilliesii   POINCIANA
Capsicum annuum   ORNAMENTAL PEPPER
Celosia cristata COCKSCOMB
Codiaeum variegatum var. **pictum**   CROTON
Coffea arabica   ARABIAN COFFEE PLANT
Coleus X hybridus   COLEUS
Corynocarpus laevigata   NEW ZEALAND LAUREL
Crossandra infundibuliformis   CROSSANDRA
Cyphomandra betacea   TREE TOMATO
Dizygotheca elegantissima   FALSE ARALIA
Dombeya Burgessiae   DOMBEYA
Erythrina crista-galli   COCKSPUR, CORAL TREE
Eucalyptus species   SILVER DOLLAR TREE, BLUE GUM
Ficus species   FIG
Gardenia jasminoides   CAPE JASMINE
Gloriosa species   GLORIOSA LILY
Gloxinia gymnostoma   GLOXINIA
Harpephyllum caffrum   KAFFIR PLUM
Hedychium coccineum   BUTTERFLY LILY
Hippeastrum hybrids   AMARYLLIS
Hoya carnosa   WAX PLANT
Hypoestes phyllostachya   POLKA DOT PLANT
Impatiens Wallerana   IMPATIENS
Jacaranda mimosifolia   GREEN EBONY
Justicia aurea   KING'S CROWN
Kalanchoe Blossfeldiana   KALANCHOE
Lantana Camara   LANTANA
Livistona chinensis   CHINESE FAN PALM
Merremia tuberosa   WOODROSE
Monstera deliciosa   SWISS CHEESE PLANT, CUT LEAF PHILODENDRON
Nemesia strumosa   POUCH NEMESIA
Nepenthes khasiana   PITCHER PLANT
Nephrolepsis exaltata   SWORD FERN
Pentas lanceolata   EGYPTIAN STAR CLUSTER
Peperomia maculosa   PEPEROMIA
Philodendron species   LOVE PLANT
Pilea repens   PILEA
Plumbago auriculata   CAPE LEADWORT
Saintpaulia ionantha   AFRICAN VIOLET

Sinningia species SINNINGIA
Smithiantha zebrina NAEGELIA, TEMPLE BELLS
Stephanotis floribunda MADAGASCAR JASMINE
Streptocarpus species CAPE PRIMROSE
Torenia Fournierii WISHBONE FLOWER
Worsleya Rayneri BLUE AMARYLLIS
Zantedeschia species CALLA LILY

FLOWERING HOUSE PLANTS

Abutilon hybridum FLOWERING MAPLE
Achimenes hybrids MAGIC FLOWER, NUT ORCHID, WIDOW'S TEARS
Aeschynanthus radicans LIPSTICK PLANT
Agapanthus africanus LILY OF THE NILE
Asarina antirrhinifolia MAURANDIA
Begonia species BEGONIA
Browallia speciosa BROWALLIA
Calceolaria crenatiflora POCKETBOOK PLANT
Clivia Belgian hybrids KAFFIR LILY
Crossandra infundibuliformis CROSSANDRA
Cyclamen persicum FLORISTS' CYCLAMEN, SHOOTING STAR
Cymbalaria muralis KENILWORTH IVY
Episcia species FLAME VIOLET
Exacum affine GERMAN VIOLET, PERSIAN VIOLET
Freesia X hybrida FREESIA
Fuchsia X hybrida FUCHSIA
Gardenia jasminoides CAPE JASMINE
Gloxinia gymnostoma GLOXINIA
Hippeastrum hybrids AMARYLLIS
Impatiens Wallerana IMPATIENS, PATIENT PLANT
Justicia aurea KING'S CROWN
Kalanchoe Blossfeldiana KALANCHOE
Pelargonium species GERANIUM
Pentas lanceolata EGYPTIAN STAR CLUSTER
Phygelius capensis CAPE FUCHSIA
Saintpaulia ionantha AFRICAN VIOLET
Saxifraga species ROCKFOIL
Senecio X hybridus CINERARIA
Sinningia species SINNINGIA
Streptocarpus species CAPE PRIMROSE
Worsleya Rayneri BLUE AMARYLLIS

HOUSE PLANTS FOR INDIRECT LIGHT

Abutilon hybridum   FLOWERING MAPLE
Achimenes hybrids   MAGIC FLOWER, NUT ORCHID, WIDOW'S TEARS
Adiantum species   MAIDENHAIR FERN
Aeschynanthus radicans   LIPSTICK PLANT, ROYAL RED BUGLER
Asarina antirrhinifolia   MAURANDIA
Asparagus species   ASPARAGUS FERN, SMILAX
Asplenium nidus   BIRD'S NEST FERN
Begonia species   BEGONIA
Chamaedora elegans 'Bella'   PARLOR PALM, NEANTA BELLA
Clivia Belgian hybrids   KAFFIR LILY
Cyperus alternifolius   UMBRELLA PLANT
Episcia species   FLAME VIOLET
Exacum affine   GERMAN VIOLET, PERSIAN VIOLET
Fatsia japonica   JAPANESE ARALIA
Ficus species   FIG
Fuchsia X hybrida   FUCHSIA
Gloxinia gymnostoma   GLOXINIA
Hedychium coccineum   BUTTERFLY LILY
Hoya carnosa   WAX PLANT
Livistona chinensis   CHINESE FAN PALM
Meryta Sinclairii   PUKA
Mimosa pudica   SENSITIVE PLANT
Nephrolepsis exaltata   SWORD FERN
Philodendron species   LOVE PLANT
Pilea repens   PILEA
Pteris cretica   BRAKE FERN
Saintpaulia ionantha   AFRICAN VIOLET
Streptocarpus species   CAPE PRIMROSE
Tetranema roseum   MEXICAN FOXGLOVE, RED VIOLET

PLANTS FOR PART SHADE OUTDOORS

Ageratum Houstonianum   FLOSS FLOWER
Aquilegia species and hybrids   COLUMBINE
Astilbe X Arendsii   FALSE SPIREA
Aubrieta detoidea   FALSE ROCK CRESS, PURPLE ROCK CRESS
Baptisia australis   BLUE WILD INDIGO, FALSE INDIGO
Begonia species   BEGONIA
Belamcanda species   BLACKBERRY LILY
Bergenia cordifolia   HEART LEAF BERGENIA
Campanula species   BELLFLOWER
Catharanthus roseus   PERIWINKLE
Chrysanthemum X superbum   SHASTA DAISY

Coleus X hybridus COLEUS
Corydalis lutea GOLDEN BLEEDING HEART
Cyclamen species CYCLAMEN
Cymbalaria muralis KENILWORTH IVY
Cyperus alternifolius UMBRELLA PLANT
Dicentra spectabilis BLEEDING HEART
Dichondra micrantha DICHONDRA
Digitalis species FOXGLOVE
Erinus alpinus ALPINE BALSAM
Exacum affine GERMAN VIOLET, PERSIAN VIOLET
Fuchsia X hybrida FUCHSIA
Globularia cordifolia BLUE GLOBE DAISY
Harpephyllum caffrum KAFFIR LILY
Hedychium coccineum BUTTERFLY LILY
Helleborus niger CHRISTMAS ROSE
Heuchera sanguinea CORAL BELLS
Hosta species PLANTAIN LILY
Ilex species HOLLY
Impatiens Balsamina GARDEN BALSAM
Impatiens Wallerana IMPATIENS, PATIENT FLOWER
Iris Kaempferi JAPANESE IRIS

Kalmia latifolia MOUNTAIN LAUREL
Lobelia species LOBELIA
Mimulus species MONKEY FLOWER
Nertera granadensis BEADPLANT
Nicotiana alata FLOWERING TOBACCO
Phygelius capensis CAPE FUCHSIA
Pittosporum Tobira JAPANESE PITTOSPORUM
Primula species PRIMROSE
Rehmannia elata BEVERLY BELLS
Rhododendron species AZALEA, RHODODENDRON
Rudbeckia hirta GLORIOSA DAISY
Sagina subulata PEARLWORT
Thymus species THYME, MOTHER OF THYME
Torenia Fournieri WISHBONE FLOWER
Tradescantia species SPIDERWORT
Trillium ovatum WAKE ROBIN
Trollius europaeus GLOBEFLOWER

PLANTS THAT TOLERATE HOT AND DRY CONDITIONS

Aphanostephus skirrhobasis LAZY DAISY, PRAIRIE DAISY
Arctotis stoechadifolia grandis AFRICAN DAISY
Asclepias tuberosa BUTTERFLY WEED
Capparis spinosa CAPER BUSH
Catananche caerulea CUPID'S DART
Catharanthus roseus PERIWINKLE
Centaurea Cyanus BACHELOR'S BUTTON, CORNFLOWER
Centratherum intermedium MANAOS BEAUTY
Cerastium tomentosum SNOW-IN-SUMMER
Cleome Hasslerana SPIDER FLOWER
Coronilla varia CROWN VETCH
Cosmos species COSMOS
Crepis rubra HAWK'S BEARD
Cytisus scoparius SCOTCH BROOM
Dictamnus albus GAS PLANT
Echium species BUGLOSS
Eleagnus angustifolius RUSSIAN OLIVE
Euphorbia species ANNUAL POINSETTIA, MEXICAN FIRE PLANT,
  SNOW-ON-THE-MOUNTAIN, SPURGE, EUPHORBIA
Gaillardia species BLANKET FLOWER
Gazania rigens TREASURE FLOWER
Gomphrena species GLOBE AMARANTH
Grevillea robusta SILK OAK
Humulus species HOPS
Hunnemannia fumariifolia MEXICAN TULIP POPPY
Hypericum species ST. JOHN'S WORT
Ipomoea species MORNING GLORY
Kochia scoparia BURNING BUSH
Liatris species GAYFEATHER
Lewisia rediviva BITTER ROOT
Limonium species STATICE, SEA LAVENDER
Merremia tuberosa WOODROSE
Mesembryanthemum chrystallinum ICE PLANT
Oenothera species EVENING PRIMROSE
Phygelius capensis CAPE FUCHSIA
Portulaca grandiflora ROSE MOSS
Potentilla nepalensis CINQUEFOIL
Pueraria lobata KUDZU VINE
Rudbeckia hirta GLORIOSA DAISY
Sagina subulata PEARLWORT
Santolina Chamaecyparissus LAVENDER COTTON
Sedum species STONECROP
Sempervivum species HOUSELEEK
Stachys byzantina LAMB'S EARS
Talinum paniculatum JEWELS OF OPAR
Tithonia rotundifolia MEXICAN SUNFLOWER
Venidium fastuosum MONARCH OF THE VELDT, CAPE DAISY
Washingtonia robusta MEXICAN FAN PALM
Xanthisma texanum STAR OF TEXAS
Yucca species ADAM'S NEEDLE, SPANISH BAYONET

PLANTS THAT LIKE MOIST CONDITIONS

Bergenia cordifolia HEART LEAF BERGENIA
Cyclamen species CYCLAMEN
Galtonia candicans SUMMER HYACINTH
Gentiana species GENTIAN
Gerbera Jamesonii hybrids TRANSVAAL DAISY
Geum species AVENS
Gossypium hirsutum ORNAMENTAL COTTON
Helenium species SNEEZEWEED
Heliopsis helianthoides SUNFLOWER HELIOPSIS
Helleborus niger CHRISTMAS ROSE
Heuchera sanguinea CORAL BELLS
Hibiscus species MALLOW
Hippeastrum hybrids AMARYLLIS
Ilex species HOLLY
Impatiens species BALSAM, IMPATIENS
Iris Kaempferi JAPANESE IRIS
Laburnum anagyroides GOLDEN CHAIN
Lobelia species LOBELIA
Matthiola species STOCK
Mimulus species MONKEY FLOWER
Myosotis species FORGET-ME-NOT
Nicotiana alata FLOWERING TOBACCO
Ranunculus asiaticus PERSIAN RANUNCULUS, PERSIAN BUTTERCUP
Silene vulgaris subsp. **maritima** SEA CAMPION
Torenia Fournieri WISHBONE FLOWER
Trillium ovatum WAKE ROBIN
Trollius europaeus GLOBEFLOWER
Viola species VIOLA, VIOLET, PANSY

VINING PLANTS FOR SCREENS AND TRELLISES

Anredera cordifolia   MADIERA VINE, MIGNONETTE VINE
Antigonon leptopus   CORALVINE
Bougainvillea hybrids   PAPER FLOWER
Campsis radicans   TRUMPET VINE, TRUMPET CREEPER
Clematis virginiana   VIRGIN'S BOWER
Clitoria Ternata   BUTTERFLY PEA
Cobaea scandens   CUP AND SAUCER VINE
Cucurbita Pepo var. **ovifera**   YELLOW FLOWERED GOURDS
Diplocyclos palmatus   MARBLE VINE
Gloriosa species   GLORIOSA LILY
Humulus species   HOPS
Ipomoea species   MORNING GLORY et al
Jasminum humile   JASMINE
Lagenaria siceraria   WHITE FLOWERED GOURDS
Lathyrus latifolius   PERENNIAL PEA
Luffa aegyptiaca   DISHRAG GOURD
Merremia tuberosa   WOODROSE
Mina lobata   FLAG OF SPAIN
Passiflora species   PASSION FLOWER, PURPLE GRANADILLA
Pueraria lobata   KUDZU VINE
Thunbergia species   BLACK-EYED SUSAN VINE
Wisteria sinensis   CHINESE WISTERIA

ORNAMENTAL GRASSES

Agrostis nebulosa   CLOUD GRASS
Avena sterilis   ANIMATED OATS
Briza maxima   QUAKING GRASS
Coix Lacryma-Jobi   JOB'S TEARS
Cortaderia Selloana   PAMPAS GRASS
Hordeum jubatum   SQUIRREL TAIL GRASS
Lagurus ovatus   HARE'S TAIL GRASS
Pennisetum setaceum   FOUNTAIN GRASS
Rhynchelytrum repens   RUBY GRASS, NATAL GRASS
Setaria macrochaeta   PLAINS BRISTLE GRASS
Stipa pennata   FEATHER GRASS

PLANTS FOR DRIED FLOWERS AND FRUIT

Achillea species   YARROW
Allium species   FLOWERING ONION
Ammobium alatum 'Grandiflora' WINGED EVERLASTING
Anaphalis margaritacea   PEARLY EVERLASTING
Asclepias tuberosa   BUTTERFLY WEED
Belamcanda species   BLACKBERRY LILY
Catananche caerulea   CUPID'S DART
Celosia cristata   COCKSCOMB
Cirsium japonicum   THISTLE
Cucurbita Pepo var. **ovifera**   YELLOW FLOWERED GOURD
Daucus Carota var. **Carota**   QUEEN ANNE'S LACE
Echinops exaltatus   GLOBE THISTLE
Emilia javanica   PAINT BRUSH
Eryngium species   SEA HOLLY
Gomphrena species   GLOBE AMARANTH
Gypsophila species   BABY'S BREATH
Helichrysum bracteatum   STRAWFLOWER
Helipterum species   EVERLASTING, STRAWFLOWER
Lagenaria siceraria   WHITE FLOWERED GOURDS
Limonium species   STATICE, SEA LAVENDER
Lunaria annua   MONEY PLANT
Merremia tuberosa   WOODROSE
Molucella laevis   BELLS-OF-IRELAND
Nigella damascena   LOVE-IN-A-MIST
Physalis Alkekengi   CHINESE LANTERN
Proboscidea louisianica   UNICORN PLANT
Xeranthemum annuum   IMMORTELLE

PLANTS THAT MAY BE TREATED AS "TENDER" BULBS

Achimenes hybrids   MAGIC FLOWER, NUT ORCHID, WIDOW'S TEARS
Agapanthus africanus   LILY OF THE NILE
Anemone coronaria   POPPY ANEMONE
Begonia species   TUBEROUS BEGONIAS
Canna X generalis   CANNA
Clivia Belgian hybrids   KAFFIR LILY
Cyclamen persicum   FLORISTS' CYCLAMEN
Dahlia hybrids   DAHLIA
Eucomis bicolor   PINEAPPLE LILY
Freesia X hybrida   FREESIA
Galtonia candicans   SUMMER HYACINTH
Gladiolus X hortulanus   GLADIOLUS
Gloriosa species   GLORIOSA LILY
Hedychium coccineum   BUTTERFLY LILY
Hippeastrum hybrids   AMARYLLIS
Incarvillea Delavayi   HARDY GLOXINIA

Ranunculus asiaticus   PERSIAN RANUNCULUS, PERSIAN BUTTERCUP
Sinningia species   SINNINGIA
Smithiantha zebrina   NAEGELIA, TEMPLE BELLS
Streptocarpus species   CAPE PRIMROSE
Tigridia Pavonia   TIGER FLOWER
Zantedeschia species   CALLA LILY

GLOSSARY OF HORTICULTURAL TERMS

ACID: Having a pH below 7.0, opposed to alkaline.

ACRE: Area of land containing 43,560 sq. ft.

ADVENTITIOUS BUDS: Those produced abnormally as on the stem or root instead of leaf axils.

AERIAL ROOT: One growing out from the stem above ground level.

ALKALINE: Having pH above 7.0. The higher the pH number the more alkaline.

ALTERNATE: With single leaf or other structure at each node.

ANGIOSPERMS: Plants having their seeds enclosed in an ovary.

ANNUAL: A plant completing its full life cycle within 1 year. Perpetuated by seeding.

ANTHER: Pollen-bearing part of the stamen.

APOMICTIC: A hybrid which reproduces true to type from seed, which develops without fertilization.

AREOLE: A wooly tuft found on Cacti.

ARIL: An appendage growing out from the hilum of a seed, covering the seed partially or wholly.

ASEXUAL: By means other than by union of gametes.

AUXIN: Plant hormone influencing and regulating plant growth

AWN: A bristle-like appendage.

AXIL: The point on the stem immediately above the junction of stem and petiole.

AXIS: A stem of a plant upon which leaves or flowers are borne.

BASAL LEAVES: Those at the base of a plant.

BICOLOR: Two distinct colors in a flower.

BIENNIAL: Plants completing their growth cycle over a period of two years.

BIPINNATE: When the divisions of a pinnate leaf are again pinnately divided.

BISEXUAL: Having both stamens and pistils.

BLADE: The expanded part of the leaf.

BLANCHING: The exclusion of light to yield a white or light green plant part.

BLOSSOM: The flower.

BOLTING: Going to seed. Premature formation of a seed stalk.

BRACTS: Modified leaves that surround a flower or flower cluster.

BROADCASTING: Spreading fertilizer or seed uniformly over a garden area.

BUD: A dormant or undeveloped, branch, leaf, or flower, usually enclosed by protective scales.

BULB: A modified bud with fleshy scales, usually grown underground.

BUSH: A low, several to many-stemmed shrub without the distinct trunk.

CALLUS: Hard protuberance. The new tissue that covers an injury.

CALYX: The outer perianth of the flower; the collective term for sepals. The outer circle of floral segments.

CAMBIUM: The layer of delicate, rapidly-dividing living cells that form wood internally and bark externally.

CAMPANULATE: Bell-shaped.

CANKER: Plant diseases usually causing lesions on the bark of woody plants.

CAPSULE: Seed vessel.

CATKIN: A deciduous spike of unisexual flowers.

CHLOROPHYLL: The green coloring matter in plants.

CHLOROSIS: Lack of green coloring in a leaf due to nutritional factors and disease.

CLASS: General breakdown of a plant. All similar kinds placed in a class (Darwin Tulip).

CLONE: A group of plants produced vegetatively from a single original plant. They fail to come true from seed as races and strains do.

CLOVE: Small bulbs at the base of the main bulb, such as garlic.

COLD FRAME: A bottomless box usually with a window-like lid used to protect plants from weather or used to germinate cold-requiring seeds.

COMPOST: Decomposed vegetable debris, broken down by bacteria into a form of humus that feeds plants and improves soil structure.

CONIFER: Cone-bearing tree or shrub.

CORDATE: Heart-shaped (usually the base of a leaf).

CORM: The enlarged fleshy base of a stem, bulblike, but solid (Gladiolas) usually covered with a tissue-like covering (tunic). Most are annuals, producing a new corm on top of the old corm. Food storage is in the center.

COROLLA: The inner circle of floral segments consisting of the petals.

CORONA: Crown. Part of the flower extending between the corolla and the stamen or that part standing on the corolla. (Cup of a daffodil).

CORYMB: A flat topped or convex flowering cluster with outer flowers opening first.

COTYLEDON: Embryonic leaf.

CROSS: Hybrid of any description.

CROWN: The area from which the stem arises. The region or union between roots and above ground portions of the plant.

CULTIVAR: Man made rather than naturally formed hybrid.

CUT BACK: To prune.

CUTTING: A severed part of a plant used in propagation.

DECIDUOUS: Falling, not persistant. Shedding (usually refers to leaves).

DECUMBENT: Reclining or lying on the ground but with stems ascending or erect.

DETERMINATE: Growth stopped by development of terminal flower buds. Self-topping.

DICOTYLEDONS: Plants having two cotyledons.

DIGITATE: Radiating like the fingers of the hand.

DIOECIOUS: Plants bearing male flowers on one plant and female flowers on another.

DISBUDDING: Practice of removing some of the flower buds of certain types of plants (Chrysanthemums) to utilize plant energy in one or more buds to increase the size of the resulting flower.

DISC: 1. A fleshy development of the receptacle of a flower around or at the base of the ovary. 2. The tightly packed center of a flower head of the Compositae (daisy) family. 3. The center part of the lip of an orchid flower.

DIVISION: Separation of plant roots or cutting the entire plant to make several plants.

DORMANT: At rest. Not in growth.

DOUBLE: Plants having more than a double row of petals.

EMBRYO: The rudimentary plantlet within a seed.

ENDOSPERM: The nutritive tissue for the embryo, located in some seeds.

ENTIRE: Even margined (as leaves), without toothing or division.

EPIPHYTE: A plant often growing on another plant but deriving no nourishment from its host or growing medium.

ESPALIER: A woody plant, tree or shrub trained by pruning to two-dimensional form often against a wall or trellis.

EVERBLOOMING: Plants that bloom continually throughout the entire growing season.

EVERGREEN: Foliage remaining on the plant in its green condition throughout the year.

EVERLASTING: Plants with flowers or foliage which retain their color when dried.

EYE: The marked center of a flower. A bud on a tuber (potato). A single bud cutting.

F_1 (First filial): First generation of a cross.

FAMILY: A group of related genera. Name usually ends in "aceae". Plants of the same family are linked by similarities of flower, fruit and seed.

FASTIGATE: With close and erect branches.

FEMALE FLOWER: Having pistil but no stamens.

FILAMENT: Stalk of a stamen.

FLACCID: Weak, not rigid. Limp.

FLORET: An individual flower in a dense inflorescence.

FLOWER: The sexually reproductive part of a plant.

FORCING: The use of heat and light to induce early growth or flowering.

FROND: Leaf of a fern.

FRUIT: The seed-bearing part of a plant (Ripened ovary).

FUNNEL FORM: Said of a corolla with a tube gradually rising upward (Morning Glory).

GAMETE: The vehicle by which hereditary material is passed from parent to offspring.

GENUS: A group of related species whose flowers, fruit and seed have a similar structure although the leaves may be different.

GERMINATION: Sprouting of seed.

GLABROUS: Without hairs. Smooth.

GLAUCOUS: Covered with a bloom, bluish-white or grayish-white.

GRAFT: A branch or bud inserted into another plant with the intention that it would grow there.

GREEN MANURING: Incorporating a cover crop such as grain or clover into the soil to improve structure and fertility.

HABIT: The plant's mode of growth.

HARDENING OFF: Process of gradually acclimatizing plants or seedlings to new temperature and humidity conditions.

HARDINESS: The degree to which plants can tolerate cold temperatures.

HEEL CUTTING: A cutting on which a small slice of older wood is retained at the base of the cutting to maximize rooting.

HERB: Any plant which is not woody at least above ground. Also a plant grown for its parts as flavor, seasoning, or odor.

HERBACEOUS: Having no persistant woody parts above ground.

HERBICIDE: A chemical for control of weeds or undesired plant life.

HILUM: The small mark on the seed showing where it was attached to the ovary wall.

HIP: The fruit of the rose.

HOT BED: A structure similar to a cold frame but supplied with heat.

HUMUS: Decayed animal and vegetable matter. Organic matter.

HYBRID: A plant resulting from a cross between parents that are unlike. It may occur naturally or artificially.

HYDROPHYTE: Water plants.

HYDROPONIC: Growing plants in some medium other than soil; typically gravel and nutrient solutions.

IMPERFECT FLOWER: Having either stamens or pistils but not both.

INCISED: Cut sharply in the margin.

INDETERMINATE: Growth continuing indefinitely when leaf buds are formed at the tip of growth.

INDIGENOUS: Original to the country. Native.

INFLORESCENCE: The flower cluster.

INSECTICIDE: A material used to kill or control insects.

INTERNODE: The space or portion of stem between the two nodes.

INTERPLANTING: The method to utilize the garden area by planting late crops alongside early crops (such as beans among lettuce, etc.).

LATERAL: Buds along the stem as opposed to terminal or end buds.

LATEX: Milky juice of some plants such as milkweed.

LAYERING: Propagating a plant by covering a portion of the stem with soil or other rooting medium to force roots on the covered portion.

LEACHING: A loss of water soluble plant nutrients by the movement of water through the soil.

LEAFLET: An individual blade of a compound leaf.

LEADER: The primary or terminal shoot of a plant.

LEAF MOLD: Partially decomposed leaves.

LINEAR: Long and narrow with nearly parallel edges.

LOAM: Soil of equal parts of silt and sand and less than 20% clay.

LONGEVITY: Length of time seeds stay alive.

MALE FLOWER: Having stamens but no pistil.

MEDIUM: Potting soil.

MIDRIB: The central vein or rib of the leaf.

MONOCOTYLEDON: Plants having 1 cotyledon such as lilies and grasses.

MULCH: Any protective covering for soil such as straw, wood chips, hay, plastic, etc. used to control weed growth, cut down on evaporation, improve soil structure, etc.

MULE: An infertile hybrid.

MUTATION: A sudden genetic change resulting in an atypical plant or "sport".

NODE: The place on the stem which normally bears a leaf or leaves.

NPK: Symbols used for the "Big 3" nutrients needed by plants for growth; nitrogen, phosphorus, and potassium.

NUT: One seeded, hard and bony fruit.

NUTRIENT: One of the 16 chemical elements needed by plants to complete life cycle.

ODD PINNATE: Pinnate with a single leaflet at the apex.

ORGANIC MATTER: Plant and animal material in various stages of decomposition.

OVARY: That part of the pistil containing future seeds (ovules).

PALMATE: Shaped like the hand with segments radiating from a single point like fingers.

PANICLE: A loose, much-branched flower cluster.

PARTED: Divided nearly but not quite to the base.

PATHOGEN: A disease-causing organism.

PEAT MOSS: Particially decomposed plant parts mainly from sedges and mosses, usually found in bogs.

PEDUNCLE: The stem of a flower or flower cluster.

PERENNIAL: Plants living in the garden three or more years.

PERFECT FLOWER: Having both pistils and stamens—(bi-sexual).

PESTICIDE: Material used to control pests.

PETAL: One of the inner floral segments, usually other than green.

PETIOLE: The "stem" of a leaf.

pH: A measure of acidity or alkalinity, especially in soil, expressed numerically from 0-14 with 7 as neutral.

PHOTOPERIOD: The number of hours of light needed daily for proper plant maturity.

PHOTOSYNTHESIS: The manufacturing of carbohydrates within green leaves by energy derived from light and utilizing oxygen, carbon dioxide and water.

PINCH: To remove growing tip of stem to induce branching.

PINNATE: Feather-like formation of leaflets placed on either side of a midrib of a compound leaf.

PIP: Small seed of fleshy fruit (apple).

PISTIL: Female reproductive organ of flower consisting of ovary, style and stigma.

PIT: Single central seed of a fruit such as peach or cherry.

PITH: Inner part of a twig. Pulpy rather than woody.

POD: Dry fruit.

POLLEN: The male reproductive element typically carried from the stamen to the pistil by the wind or insects.

POLLINATION: The transferring of pollen.

POT BOUND: The condition of a potted plant when the roots become thickly matted because of lack of room to grow.

PROCUMBENT: Trailing.

PUBESCENT: Covered with hairs.

RACE: A permanent variety or group of individuals whose distinguishing characteristics are constant and reproduce true or to type from seed.

RACEME: A simple inflorescense of stalked flowers on a more or less elongated axis.

RAY: A marginal strap-like floret of a daisy flower head.

RECEPTACLE: The end of a stem in which parts of a flower are borne.

RECURVED: Curved backward or downward.

REFLEXED: Abruptly turned downward.

REST PERIOD: Normal period in a plant's life where it halts its growth.

RHIZOME: A horizontally extended, usually underground, stem often enlarged by food storage, usually creeping, and from which shoots and roots sprout.

RIB: A primary or prominent vein in a leaf.

ROOT: The part of the plant that absorbs most of the water and nutrients from the soil or air.

ROOTBOUND: See Pot Bound.

ROOTSTOCK: Underground stem or rhizome.

ROSETTE: A cluster of leaves or other organs in a compact circular arrangement.

ROTATION (crop):   Planting different crops on the same ground at different times to balance the drain on nutrients and to control plant diseases.

RUNNER: A slender, prostrate branch rooting at the end or at a joint; stolon.

SCARIFICATION: Scratching of the seed coat to facilitate germination.

SEED: Ripened ovule.

SELECTION: A special form of a plant chosen for certain characteristics.

SELF FERTILE: The pollen of the flowers of a single plant will fertilize the pistils of the flowers of that same plant.

SELF STERILE: The pollen of the flowers of a single plant will not fertilize the pistils of the flowers of that same plant.

SEPAL: A segment of the calyx, usually green.

SHRUB: A woody plant branched from the base.

SIDEDRESSING: The application of fertilizer during plant growth and worked into the soil alongside the plant.

SPADIX: A spike with a fleshy axis.

SPATHE: A bract enclosing an inflorescence, usually a spadix. (Anthurium).

SPECIES: A group of closely related plants which exhibit the characteristics distinguishing them from all other units within a genus; still not differing from one another beyond the limit of a recognizable pattern or variations.

SPIKE: A simple inflorescense with flowers sessile or nearly so on a common axis.

SPINE: A sharp pointed woody outgrowth from the stem.

SPORE: A simple reproductive body, such as ferns produce.

SPORT: A shoot usually arising from a single bud, different in character from the typical growth of the plant that produced it. A vegetative mutation.

STAMEN: The male organ of a flower consisting of a filament and pollen-bearing anther at its head.

STANDARD: 1. A plant standing upright with a single stalk. 2. The uppermost large petal of some flowers such as sweet peas.

STEM: The axis of a plant arising from its root bearing flowers or leaves.

STERILE: Not fertile.

STIGMA: The part of the pistil that receives the pollen (the organ at the tip of the style).

STIPULE: The appendage at the base of the petiole.

STOCK: The stem or plant portion into which a graft is inserted.

STOLON: Spreading stem above ground—runner. Often produces new plants at its tip.

STOMA (pl. Stomata) or Stomate: A breathing pore in the epidermis (outer skin) of a leaf.

STRAIN: A particularly fine selection from a seed grown variety.

STRATIFICATION: A process used to overcome dormancy of a seed. Usually a cold treatment in the refrigerator or freezer.

STYLE: A stalk between the ovary and the stigma.

SUBSHRUB: A small shrub which may have herbaceous stems.

SUCCESSIVE SOWING: Two or more sowings of the same crop in one season to lengthen the harvest.

SUCCULENT: Fleshy.

SUCKER: A shoot arising from the roots or beneath the ground's surface (corn). Also side shoots developing from the main stem as in tomatoes.

SYSTEMIC: The action of a chemical through the plant and absorbed by leaves or roots, and traveling throughout the plant's system.

TAPROOT: Exaggerated central root.

TERMINAL: A bud or shoot at the end or top of stem.

THINNING: The removal of surplus plants to allow room for sufficient development of the remaining plants.

THROAT: Where the limb of the corolla joins the corolla tube.

TOMENTOSE: Densely, woolly.

TRANSPIRATION: The evaporation of water through a plant leaf, especially through the leaf-breathing pores (stomata).

TRANSPLANT: Young plant started from seed. To move from one location to another.

TREE: A woody plant with one main stem at least 12-15' in height.

TRUSS: A compact flower cluster at the top of a stem.

TUBER: A thickened portion of an underground stem or branch provided with eyes (buds) on the sides, from which new plants are formed. Tubers are usually more round in shape than rhizomes and store food.

TURGID: Swollen as a result of internal water pressure.

UMBEL: An inflorescence (often flat topped) in which the individual flower stems project from a common point like the ribs of an umbrella. (Queen Anne's Lace).

VARIEGATED: Having marks, stripes or blotches of some color other than the basic one.

VARIETY: A group within a species with distinct characters that are not important enough to warrant it being classified as a separate species. A plant occurring naturally.

VEINS: Small ribs or branches of the framework of leaves.

VIABILITY: The ability of seeds to germinate.

VINE: A plant which trails over the ground or climbs by twining or attaching certain appendages to its support.

WETTING AGENT (Spreader): A material causing liquid to spread more uniformly over a leaf's surface.

WHORL: The arrangement of three or more leaves, flowers or other parts in a circle around the axis (stem) or common point.

CROSS REFERENCE INDEX

If you don't know the botanical name of the plant, but know the common name, simply look it up in this listing. Remember that Chapter V encompasses ornamental plants while Chapter VI covers vegetables and herbs. Also included in this index are commonly misused botanical names, plus those that are listed with other genera.

345

346

347

349

351

352

A COMBINATION VEGETABLE-FLOWER GARDEN
20 feet x 30 feet

Mr. F. W. Thode, Landscape Designer and Horticulturist, has designed a combination flower, herb and vegetable garden, the components of which are listed below.

No.	Plant	Amount
	VEGETABLES	
1	POLE BEANS	2 oz.
2	TOMATO	30 seeds
3	SWEET PEPPER	25 seeds
4	EGGPLANT	30 seeds
5	CABBAGE	1/16 oz.
6	BUSH BEANS	2 oz.
7	BEETS	¼ oz.
8	CARROTS	⅛ oz.
9	LETTUCE	1/16 oz.
10	BROCCOLI	1/16 oz.
11	SQUASH	25 seeds
12	SWEET CORN	2 oz.
13	CUCUMBER	30 seeds
	HERBS	
14	BASIL (OCIMUM BASILICUM)	Pkt.
15	CHIVES (ALLIUM SCH.)	Pkt.
16	DILL BOUQUET	Pkt.
17	ENGLISH THYME (THYMUS VULGARIS)	Pkt.
	FLOWERS	
18	MARIGOLD	50 seeds
19	AGERATUM	Pkt.
20	PETUNIA	100 seeds
21	ALYSSUM	Pkt.
22	PERIWINKLE, VINCA ROSEA	Pkt.
23	DIANTHUS	30 seeds
24	CELOSIA	Pkt.
25	ZINNIA	25 seeds

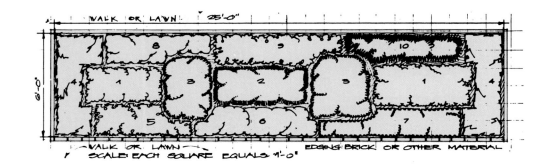

AN ISLAND BED FOR VEGETABLE & FLOWERS

The drawing above shows an island bed for a lawn or formal garden. Designed by Mr. F. W. Thode, it is both useful and ornamental. Components are listed below.

VEGETABLES & FLOWERS

No.	Plant	Amount
1	TOMATO	50 seeds
2	SWEET PEPPER	25 seeds
3	SWEET CORN	2 oz.
4	MARIGOLD	50 seeds
5	LETTUCE	1/16 oz.
6	PARSLEY	1/8 oz.
7	ZINNIA	100 seeds
8	DIANTHUS	60 seeds
9	PETUNIA	150 seeds
10	SNAPDRAGON	100 seeds

ALL VEGETABLES

No.	Plant	Amount
1	TOMATO	50 seeds
2	SQUASH	25 seeds
3	SWEET CORN	2 oz.
4	BUSH BEAN	2 oz.
5	CARROTS	1/16 oz.
6	LETTUCE	1/16 oz.
7	SWISS CHARD	1/4 oz.
8	BEETS	1/4 oz.
9	LETTUCE	1/16 oz.
10	RADISH	1/8 oz.

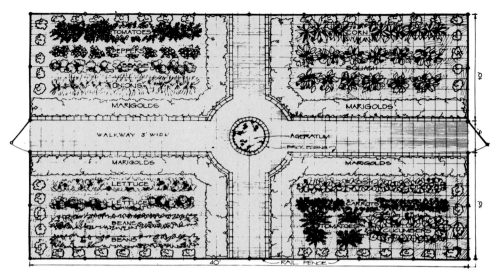

FLOWER AND VEGETABLE GARDEN

"Vegetables Make Beautiful Flowers" might well have been the theme of Park Seed Company's ornamental vegetable garden, which was planted in the spring of 1974 with popular vegetable varieties and also included plantings of Marigold, Zinnia and Ageratum. Visitors to Park's annual Field Day in July were fascinated with the loveliness of the vegetables as well as the flowers and expressed amazement at how much could be accomplished in a small space. Combining the practical with the esthetic is a good way to increase the enjoyment of home gardening and add beauty to the environment at the same time. The possibilities of plant combinations are unlimited and provide a challenge to the creative gardener.

No.	Plant	Amount
1	CARROT	⅛ oz.
2	MARIGOLD	250 seeds
3	LETTUCE	1/16 oz.
4	CORN	½ lb.
5	CUCUMBER	30 seeds
6	ZINNIA	(2 Pkts.)
7	BUSH BEAN	¼ lb.
8	AGERATUM	(I Pkt.)
9	SQUASH	20 seeds
10	SQUASH	20 seeds
11	RADISH	⅛ oz.
12	TOMATO	50 seeds
13	TOMATO	50 seeds
14	PEPPER	25 seeds
15	PEPPER	1/16 oz.
16	CABBAGE	1/16 oz.
17	WHITE ONION	½ oz.
18	ONION	1/32 oz.

MATERIALS NEEDED FOR FLOWER & VEGETABLE GARDEN

40 in. high Split Rail Fence: 3 rails; 120 feet total length; 2-3 ft. Gates; 14 Posts.
Approximately 250 bricks to line walkway.   Walkway: Gravel or Concrete.

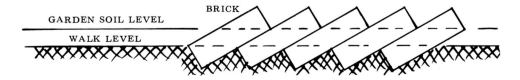

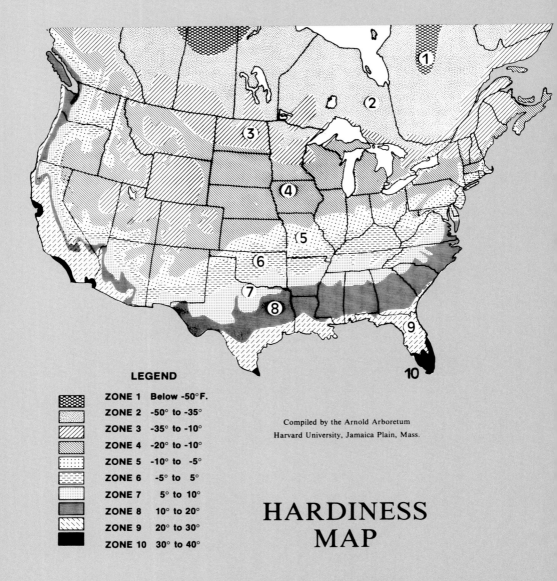

LEGEND

	ZONE 1	Below -50°F.
	ZONE 2	-50° to -35°
	ZONE 3	-35° to -10°
	ZONE 4	-20° to -10°
	ZONE 5	-10° to -5°
	ZONE 6	-5° to 5°
	ZONE 7	5° to 10°
	ZONE 8	10° to 20°
	ZONE 9	20° to 30°
	ZONE 10	30° to 40°

Compiled by the Arnold Arboretum
Harvard University, Jamaica Plain, Mass.

HARDINESS MAP

The above hardiness map was developed by the Arnold Arboretum, Harvard University, Jamaica Plain, Mass., and is reproduced through their courtesy. The hardiness zones 1-10 are based on the average annual minimum temperatures for each zone and divide the United States and Canada into areas where specific plants perform best as to winter hardiness. Many factors, such as altitude, degree of exposure to wind, modifying effect of bodies of water, soil types and the like can create variations of as much as two zones within a geographical area, but adhering to your specific zone will generally give you the best results. Often, however, inhabitants of the southernmost portion of one zone can safely use plants for the next, more northerly zone.

PRONOUNCING INDEX

The pronunciation of botanical names may be a problem to many of you (even those with training in Latin, since the Latin of horticulture is pronounced differently than that of Caesar). For this reason, we offer the following pronunciation guide.

Throughout, single vowels are pronounced short as follows.

a	as in an
e	as in Edward
i	as in in
o	as in bog
u	as in bun
g	is pronounced hard as in game.

ABELOMOSCHUS	A-bell-oh-mos'- kus
ABUTILON	Ah-boot'-i-lon
ACANTHUS	A-kan'-thus
ACHILLEA	Ak-ill-lee'-ah
ACHIMENES	Ah-kim'-in-eez
ACONITUM	A-kon-eye'-tum
ADIANTUM	Ad-ee-an'-tum
AESCHYNANTHUS	Esh-ee-nan'-thus
AGAPANTHUS	Ag-a-pan'-thus
AGAPETES	Ag-a-peet'-eez
AGARICUS	A-gar'-i-kus
AGERATUM	A-jer-ah'-tum
AGROSTIS	A-groohs'-tis
ALBIZIA	Al-bee'-zee-ah
ALCEA	Al-see'-ah
ALLIUM	Al'-lee-um
ALOE	Al'-low-ee
ALSTROMERIA	Al-strow-mare'-ee-ah
ALYSSUM	A-lise'-um
AMARANTHUS	A-ma-ran'-thus
AMMOBIUM	Am-mow'-bee-um
ANAPHALIS	A-naf-fa'-lis
ANCHUSA	An-ku'-sah
ANEMONE	A-nem'-oh-nee
ANETHUM	A-nee'-thum
ANGELICA	An-jel'-i-kah
ANREDERA	An-ray'-da-ra
ANTHEMIS	An'-thee-mus
ANTHRISCUS	An-thris'-kus
ANTHURIUM	An-thu'-re-um
ANTIGONON	An-tig'-oh-non
APHANOSTEPHUS	Af-an-oh-stee'-fus
APIUM	A'-pee-um
AQUILEGIA	Ak-wi-lee'-jee-ah
ARABIS	Ar'-a-bis
ARACHIS	Ar-ak'-is
ARCTOTIS	Ark-toe'-tis
ARENARIA	A-rah-nare'-ee-ah

ARMERIA	Ar-meer'-ee-ah
ARNICA	Ar'-nik-ah
ASARINA	Ass-a-ree'-nah
ASCLEPIAS	Ass-klee'-pe-as
ASPARAGUS	A-spar'-a-gus
ASPHODELINE	As-fo-de-lee'-nee
ASPLENIUM	Ass-plee'-nee-um
ASTER	Ass'-ter
ASTILBE	As-still'-bee
AUBRIETA	Aw-bree'-tah
AVENA	A-veen'-ah
BAPTISIA	Bap-teez'-ee-ah
BEGONIA	Be-gon'-ee-ah
BELAMCANDA	Bell-am-can'-dah
BELLIS	Bell'-iss
BERGENIA	Bur-geen'-ee-ah
BETA	Bay'-tah
BOUGAINVILLEA	Bu-gan-vill'-ee-ah
BRACHYCOME	Bra-kik'-o-mee
BRASSICA	Brass'-i-kah
BRIZIA	Breez'-ee-ah
BROWALLIA	Bro-wal'-ee-ah
BUDDLEIA	Bud'-lee-ah
CAESALPINIA	Sees-al-peen'-ee-ah
CALCEOLARIA	Kal-see-o-lare'-ee-ah
CALENDULA	Ka-len'-du-lah
CALLISTEPHUS	Kal-li-stee'-fuss
CALLUNA	Ka-loon'-ah
CAMELLIA	Ka-meel'-ee-ah
CAMPANULA	Kam-pan'-u-lah
CAMPSIS	Kamp'-sis
CANNA	Kan'-nah
CAPPARIS	Kap-par'-is
CAPSICUM	Kap'-sik-um
CARTHAMUS	Kar-tham'-us
CARUM	Ka'-rum
CATANANCHE	Kat-a-nan'-kee
CASSIA	Kass'-ee-ah
CATHARANTHUS	Kath-a-ran'-thus
CELOSIA	Se-los'-ee-a
CENTAUREA	Sen-taw'-ree-ah
CENTRATHERUM	Sen-tra'-the-rum
CERASTIUM	Se-ras'-tee-um
CERCIS	Sur'-sis
CHENOPODIUM	Ke-noe-poe'-dee-um
CHEIRANTHUS	Kae-ran'-thus
CHRYSANTHEMUM	Kri-san'-the-mum
CICER	Seeje'-ser
CICHORIUM	Se-kor'-ee-um
CIRSIUM	Sur'-see-um
CITRULLUS	Si-trul'-us
CLADANTHUS	Kal-dan'-thus
CLARKIA	Clark'-ee-ah
CLEMATIS	Klem'-a-tis
CLEOME	Klee-o'-me
CLITORIA	Kli-tor'-ee-ah
CLIVIA	Kleye'-vee-ah
COBAEA	Ko'-bay'-ah
CODIAEUM	Ko-dee-ee'-um
COFFEA	Koff'-ee-ah

COIX	Ko'-iks
COLEUS	Ko'-lee-us
COREOPSIS	Ko-ree-op'-sis
CORIANDRUM	Kor-ee-an'-drum
CORNUS	Kor'-nus
CORONILLA	Kor-o-nil'-ah
CORTADERIA	Kort-a-deer'-ee-ah
CORYDALIS	Kory-dal'-is
CORYNOCARPUS	Kory-no-kar'-pus
COSMOS	Kos'-mos
CREPIS	Kray'-pis
CROSSANDRA	Kro-san'-drah
CUCUMIS	Kew'-kew-mis
CUCURBITA	Ku-ker'-bi-tah
CUMINUM	Kew'-min-um
CUPHEA	Ku'-fee-ah
CUPRESSUS	Ku-press'-us
CYCLAMEN	Sik'-la-men
CYMBALARIA	Sim-ba-lare'-ee-ah
CYNOGLOSSUM	Seye-no-glos'-sum
CYPERUS	Seye'-peh-rus
CYPHOMANDRA	Seye-fo-man'-drah
CYTISSUS	Seye'-tis-sus
DAUCUS	Dow'-kus
DELPHINIUM	Del-fin'-ee-um
DIANTHUS	Deye-an'-thus
DICENTRA	Deye-sen'-trah
DICHONDRA	Deye-kon'-drah
DICTAMNUS	Dik-tam'-nus
DIGITALIS	Dij-i-tal'-is
DIMORPHOTHECA	Di-morf-o-the'-kah
DIPLOCYCLOS	Dip-lo-ceye'-klos
DIZYGOTHECA	Diz-zee-go-the'-kah
DOMBEYA	Dom-bee'-yah
DORONICUM	Do-ron'-i-kum
DRYAS	Dry'-ass
ECHEVERIA	Ek-a-var'-ee-ah
ECHINACEA	Ek-i-nace'-ee-ah
ECHINOPS	Ek'-in-ops
ECHIUM	Ek'-ee-um
ELEAGNUS	El-ee-ag'-nus
EMILIA	E-meel'-ee-ah
ENSETE	En-seet'-ee
EPISCIA	E-pees'-ee-ah
ERANTHUS	E-ran'-thus
EREMURUS	Er-a-mur'-us
ERIGERON	E-rig'-e-ron
ERINUS	E-rine'-us
ERUCA	E'-ru-kah
ERYNGIUM	E-rin'-je-um
ERYTHRINA	Eree-thrine'-ah
ERYTHRONIUM	Eree-throne'-e-um
ESCHSCHOLZIA	Es-shole'-ze-ah
EUCALYPTUS	You-ka-lip'-tiss
EUCNIDE	Youk-nee'-dee
EUCOMIS	You-kome'-is
EUPHORBIA	You-for'-bee-ah
EXACUM	Ex-ak'-um
FATSIA	Fat'-see-ah
FELICIA	Fe-lee'-she-ah

FICUS	Feye'-kus
FOENICULUM	Foe-nik'-you-lum
FRAGARIA	Fra-gare'-ee-ah
FRANKLINIA	Frank-lin'-ee-ah
FREESIA	Free'-zee-ah
FUCHSIA	Few'-sha (or Fuk'-see-a)
GAILLARDIA	Ga-lar'-dee-ah
GALTONIA	Gall-toe'-nee-ah
GARDENIA	Gar-deen'-ee-ah
GAZANIA	Ga-zane'-ee-ah
GENTIANA	Jen-tee-an'-ah
GERANIUM	Je-rane'-ee-um
GERBERA	Jer'-be-rah
GEUM	Gee'-um
GINKGO	Gin'-koh
GLADIOLUS	Glad-ee-oh'-lus
GLOBULARIA	Glow-byou-lare'-ee-ah
GLORIOSA	Glor-ee-oh'-sah
GLOXINIA	Gloks'-in-ee-ah
GLYCINE	Gleye-see'-nee
GOMPHRENA	Gom-free'-nah
GOSSYPIUM	Gos-sip'-e-um
GREVILLEA	Gra-vill'-ee-ah
GYPSOPHILA	Jip-sof'-i-lah
HARPEPHYLLUM	Harp-a-feye'-lum
HEDYCHIUM	He-dik'-ee-um
HELENIUM	He-leen'-ee-um
HELIANTHEMUM	Heel-ee-an'-the-mum
HELIANTHUS	Heel-ee-an'-thus
HELICHRYSUM	Hell-i-kris'-um
HELIOPSIS	Heel-ee-op'-sis
HELIPTERUM	Hee-lip'-ter-um
HELLEBORUS	Hell-le-bore'-us
HEMEROCALLIS	Hem-er-o-kal'-lis
HERNERIA	Her-nare'-ee-ah
HESPERIS	Hes'-per-us
HEUCHERA	Hew'-ka-rah
HIBISCUS	Hi-bis'-kus
HIPPEASTRUM	Hip-ee-ass'-trum
HORDEUM	Hor'-dee-um
HOSTA	Hos'-tah
HOYA	Hoy'-ah
HUMULUS	Hew'-mew-lus
HUNNEMANNIA	Hun-na-man'-nee-ah
HYPERICUM	Heye-per'-i-kum
HYPOESTES	Heye-po-ess'-teez
HYSSOPUS	Heye-so'-pus
IBERIS	Eye-beer'-is
ILEX	Eye'-lex
IMPATIENS	Im-pay'-shens
INCARVILLEA	In-kar-vill'-ee-ah
IPOMOEA	Ip-oh-mee'-ah
IPOMOPSIS	Ip-oh-mop'-sis
IRIS	Eye'-ris
JACARANDA	Jak-a-ran'-dah
JASIONE	Jas-ee-oh'-nee
JASMINUM	Jas'-mi-num
JUSTICIA	Jus'-ti-ka
KALANCHOE	Kal-an-koe'-ee
KALMIA	Kal'-mee-ah

KNIPHOFIA	Nip-hoe-fee-ah
KOCHIA	Koe'-kee-ah
LABURNUM	La-bur'-num
LAGENARIA	La-ja-nare'-ee-ah
LAGURUS	La-gu'-rus
LANTANA	Lan-ta'-nah
LATHYRUS	Lath'-i-rus
LACTUCA	Lak-took'-ah
LAVATERA	Lav-a-tee'-ra
LAVENDULA	La-ven-doo'-la
LAYIA	Lay'-ee-ah
LEONTOPODIUM	Lee-on-toe-poe'-dee-um
LEPIDIUM	Le-pee'-dee-um
LEVISTICUM	Le-vis'-ti-kum
LEWISIA	Loo-iss'-ee-ah
LIATRIS	Lee-at'-ris
LILIUM	Lil'-ee-um
LIMONIUM	Li-mown'-ee-um
LINARIA	Li-nare'-ee-ah
LINUM	Leye'-num
LIRIOPE	Li-reye'-oh-pee
LITHOPS	Lith'-ops
LIVISTONA	Liv-iss-toe'-nah
LOBELIA	Loe-bee'-lee-ah
LOBULARIA	Loe-bue-lare'-ee-ah
LONAS	Loe-nas'
LUFFA	Lu'-fah
LUNARIA	Lu-nare'-ee-ah
LUPINUS	Lu-peye'-nus
LYCHNIS	Lik'-nis
LYCOPERSICON	Leye-ko-per'-si-kon
LYTHRUM	Lith'-rum
MACHAERANTHERA	Mak-eye-ran'-tha-rah
MAGNOLIA	Mag-nole'-ee-ah
MALVA	Mal'-vah
MARRUBIUM	Ma-roo'-bee-um
MATRICARIA	Mat-rik-kay'-re-ah
MATTHIOLA	Ma-thee-oh'-la
MECONOPSIS	Me-ko-nop'-sis
MELISSA	Me-lis'-sah
MENTHA	Men'-thah
MENTZELIA	Ment-zee'-lee-a
MERREMIA	Mer-ree'-mee-a
MERYTA	Me-ree'-tah
MESEMBRYANTHEMUM	Mez-em-bree-an'-tha-mum
MIMOSA	Mi-moe'-sah
MIMULUS	Mim'-you-lus
MINA	Mee'-nah
MIRABILIS	Mi-rab'-i-lis
MOLUCCELLA	Mo-loo-sell'-a
MONARDA	Moe-nar'-dah
MONSTERA	Mon-ste'-rah
MYOSOTIS	My-oh-sow'-tis
NASTURTIUM	Nas-tur'-shum
NEMESIA	Ne-mee'-see-a
NEMOPHILA	Ne-mof'-i-lah
NEPENTHES	Nee-pen'-theez
NEPETA	Nep'-e-tah
NEPHROLEPSIS	Ne-fro-lip'-sis
NERTERA	Neer-teer'-ah

NICANDRA	Neye-kan'-drah
NICOTIANA	Ni-ko-she-an'-ah
NIEREMBERGIA	Nee-ram-ber'-jee-ah
NIGELLA	Neye-jel'-ah
NYMPHAEA	Nim-fay'-ah
OCIMIUM	Oh-see'-mum
OENOTHERA	Ee-no'-thee-rah
	(or Ee-noe-thee'-rah)
ORIGANUM	Oh-ree-ga'-num
OXYPETALUM	Ox-ee-pet'-a-lum
PAEONIA	Pay-oh'-nee-ah
PAPAVER	Pa-pa'-ver
PASSIFLORA	Pas-si-flo'-rah
PASTINACA	Pas-ti-nah'-kah
PELARGONIUM	Pe-lar-goe'-nee-um
PENNISETUM	Pen-ni-see'-tum
PENSTEMON	Pen'-ste-mon
PENTAS	Pen'-tas
PEPEROMIA	Pe-per-oh'-mee-ah
PERILLA	Pe-ril'-ah
PETROSELINIUM	Pet-row-se-line'-um
PETUNIA	Pe-toon'-ee-ah
PHASEOLUS	Faze-ee-oh'-lus
PHILODENDRON	Fil-oh-den'-dron
PHLOX	Floks
PHYGELIUS	Feye-jee'-lee-us
PHYSALIS	Feye-zal'-lis
PHYSOSTEGIA	Feye-zo-stee'-gee-ah
PICEA	Peye'-see-ah
PILEA	Peye'-lee-ah
PIMPINELLA	Pim'-pin-ell-lah
PINUS	Peye'-nus
PISUM	Pee'-sum
PITTOSPORUM	Pit-toe-spore'-um
PLATYCODON	Plat-ee-ko'-don
PLUMBAGO	Plum-bay'-goe
POLEMONIUM	Pol-ee-moe'-nee-um
POLYGONIUM	Pol-ee-goe'-num
PORTULACA	Por-tu-lak'-ah
POTENTILLA	Poe-ten-til'-ah
POTERIUM	Poh-ter'-ee-um
PRIMULA	Pri'-mu-lah
PROBOSCIDEA	Proe-boe-see'-dee-ah
PSEUDOPANAX	Soo-doe-pan'-ax
PTERIS	Te'-ris
PUERARIA	Poo-e-rare'-ee-ah
PUNICA	Poo'-ni-kah
RANUNCULUS	Ra-nun'-ki-lis
RAPHANUS	Ra-fan'-us
REHMANNIA	Ray-man'-nee-ah
RESEDA	Re-see'-dah
RHODODENDRON	Roe-doe-den'-dron
RHYNCHELYTRUM	Rine-ke-leye'-trum
RICINUS	Ri-seye'-nus
ROMNEYA	Rom'-nee-ah
ROSA	Roe'-sah
ROSMARINUS	Rose-mar-eye'-nus
RUDBECKIA	Rud-bek'-ee-ah
RUTA	Roo'-tah
SAGINA	Sa-jeye'-na
SAINTPAULIA	Saynt-paw'-lee-ah

SALPIGLOSSIS	Sal-pee-glos'-sis
SALVIA	Sal'-vee-ah
SANTOLINA	San-toe-leye'-nah
SANVITALIA	San-vi-tal'-ee-ah
SAPONARIA	Sa-poe-nare'-ee-ah
SATUREJA	Sat-you-raj'-ah
SAXIFRAGA	Saks-i-fra'-gah
SCABIOSA	Ska-bee-oh'-sah
SCHEFFLERA	Shef-lare'-ah
SCHIZANTHUS	Ski-zan'-thus
SEDUM	See'-dum
SEMPERVIVUM	Sem-per-veye'-vum
SENECIO	Se-nee'-shee-oh
SESAMUM	Ses'-a-mum
SETARIA	Se-tare'-ee-ah
SILENE	Seye-lee'-nee
SINNINGIA	Sin-nin'-jee-ah
SMITHIANA	Smith-ee-an'-ah
SOLANUM	Sow-lay'-num
SOPHORA	Sow-fore'-ah
SORGHUM	Sore'-gum
SPINACIA	Spi-nay'-shee-ah
STACHYS	Stay'-kis
STEPHANOTIS	Ste-fan-oh'-tis
STIPA	Steye'-pah
STOKESIA	Stow-kee'-zhee-ah
STRELITZIA	Stra-litz'-ee-ah
STREPTOCARPUS	Strep-toe-car'-pus
TAGETES	Ta-gee'-teez
TALINUM	Ta-leye'-num
TAXUS	Taks'-us
TETRANEMA	Tet-ra-nee'-mah
TEUCRIUM	Too'-kree-um
THALLICTRUM	Thal-lik'-trum
THERMOPSIS	Ther-mop'-sis
THUNBERGIA	Thun-ber'-jee-ah
THYMUS	Theye'-mus
TIGRIDIA	Teye-grid'-ee-ah
TITHONIA	Teye-thow'-nee-ah
TORENIA	Tow-ree'-nee-ah
TRACHYMENE	Tra-ki-mee'-nee
TRADESCANTIA	Tra-des-kan'-tee-ah
TRIFOLIUM	Treye-fo'-lee-um
TRILLIUM	Tril'-lee-um
TROLLIUS	Troe'-lee-us
TROPAEOLUM	Troe-pee-oh'-lum
VALERIANA	Val-lare-ee-an'-ah
VENIDIUM	Ve-nid'-ee-um
VERBASCUM	Ver-bass'-kum
VERBENA	Ver-bee'-nah
VERBESINA	Ver-be-see'-nah
VERONICA	Ve-ron'-i-kah
VIBURNUM	Veye-bur'-num
VIGNA	Vig'-nah
VIOLA	Veye-oh'-lah
WASHINGTONIA	Wash-ing-tone'-ee-ah
WISTERIA	Wi-stee'-ree-ah
WORSLEYA	War'-zlee-ah
XANTHISMA	Zan-this'-mah
XERANTHEMUM	Zer-an'-the-mum
YUCCA	Yuk'-a

ZANTEDESCHIA   Zan-ta-des'-kee-ah
ZEA   Zee'-ah
ZINNIA   Zin'-ee-ah